THE POLITICS OF PREGNANCY

EDITED BY
ANNETTE LAWSON
AND DEBORAH L. RHODE

THE POLITICS OF PREGNANCY

ADOLESCENT SEXUALITY

AND PUBLIC POLICY

YALE UNIVERSITY PRESS   NEW HAVEN & LONDON

Set in Palatino type by The Composing Room of Michigan, Inc. Printed in the United States of America by Edwards Brothers, Inc., Ann Arbor, Michigan.

Library of Congress Cataloging-in-Publication Data

The Politics of pregnancy : adolescent sexuality and public policy /
    edited by Annette Lawson and Deborah L. Rhode.
    p.   cm.
    Includes bibliographical references and index.
    ISBN 0-300-05717-2 (alk. paper)
    1. Teenage pregnancy—Government policy—United States. 2. Teenage pregnancy—Government policy—Great Britain. 3. Teenage pregnancy—United States—Prevention. 4. Teenage pregnancy—Great Britain—Prevention. I. Rhode, Deborah L. II. Lawson, Annette, 1936– .
HQ759.4.P64 1993
306.7'0835—dc20   92-38539
                                                   CIP

A catalogue record for this book is available from the British Library.

The paper in this book meets the guidelines for permanence and durability of the Committee on Production Guidelines for Book Longevity of the Council on Library Resources.

10   9   8   7   6   5   4   3   2   1

For Our Mothers

CONTENTS

ACKNOWLEDGMENTS

This book grows out of a conference sponsored by the Institute for Research on Women and Gender at Stanford University in April 1989. The conference was made possible by support from the Russell Sage Foundation, the Charles Stewart Mott Foundation, the Joe and Emily Lowe Foundation, the Beatrice M. Bain Research Group, and the March of Dimes Foundation. The editors worked together throughout this project, especially on its planning. Annette Lawson had the major responsibility for organizing the conference while Deborah Rhode ensured that this book was the result. We are particularly grateful to Dee Gustavson of the Institute for Research on Women and Gender, Joane Krause of Stanford Law School, and our editors, John Covell and Susan Laity, at Yale University Press for all their support and assistance. We are also indebted to David Lawson for his continued support and to Ralph Cavanagh in more ways than we can ever adequately acknowledge.

DEBORAH L. RHODE
ANNETTE LAWSON

INTRODUCTION

In many cultures, over many centuries, teenage pregnancy and childbirth have been a normal reproductive pattern. Over the past several decades, however, that pattern has increasingly been presented as a social problem. Particularly in the United States, which has the highest rates of adolescent pregnancy and childbirth among Western industrialized nations, the issue has prompted growing concern, but no coherent policy. Much of the problem arises from lack of consensus about what the problem actually is. Is the primary issue morality, fertility, or poverty? What makes early childbearing problematic? For whom? Under what circumstances? Should public policy focus largely on pregnancy prevention? Alternatively, should the goal be expanding adolescents' capacity for reproductive choice and reducing the disadvantages that some choices entail? The politically volatile nature of those questions became apparent during the 1992 American presidential campaign, when candidates squared off on whether, if their 12- or 13-year-old daughter became pregnant, she would "take the child to term."[1]

This book seeks to provide a better understanding of such questions by situating them in broader cultural contexts. To that end, scholars and policy analysts from diverse backgrounds in psychology, sociology, history,

1

philosophy, economics, medicine, and law address issues of common concern. By including commentators from both the United States and Great Britain, the volume also illumines the different patterns of teenage pregnancy in countries sharing many social and legal traditions. Through interchange cutting across conventional disciplinary and cultural boundaries, this volume seeks to deepen our understanding of adolescent fertility and the policy initiatives it demands.

A crucial first step is to recast the "problem" of teenage pregnancy and childbirth by locating them within historical, social, and political contexts. Accordingly, this volume begins with several chapters that focus on the factual and normative premises underlying current debates.

Part of the difficulty in addressing teenage pregnancy as a "problem" arises from the terms of public discourse. Under popular convention, *adolescent* and *teenage* are generally used interchangeably to encompass the period from about 13 to 19 years of age. As many authors in this volume note, however, adolescence is a relatively recent and culturally specific concept. Its characteristics as a distinct developmental phase remain subject to debate, and its use in connection with reproductive issues can be highly misleading. Pregnancy and childbirth present different concerns for 13-year-olds than for 19-year-olds, and some of those concerns vary across class, race, and ethnicity. Thus, although commentators throughout this volume generally speak of adolescence in its conventional chronological sense, they also emphasize its cultural particularity and draw distinctions where appropriate among different age, income, racial, and ethnic groups.

Such distinctions and their absence in most popular debate are explored in Part I of this book. Among the general public, the problem of adolescent pregnancy appears self-evident, given recent demographic trends. In the United States, an estimated 45 percent of all female teenagers have premarital sex, an increase of 15 percent over the past decade. Most are not consistent contraceptive users. As a result, about 40 percent of all female adolescents become pregnant at least once before age 20, and about four-fifths of these pregnancies are unintended. Twenty percent of female adolescents bear a child, about half of these mothers are unmarried, and less than 5 percent give the baby up for adoption. In families headed by 15- to 21-year-old females, more than four-fifths of children are poor; where the head of household is a young male, the proportion of poor children is about a third.[2]

Although lack of adequate statistics for the United Kingdom makes precise cross-cultural comparisons impossible, rates of teenage pregnancy there appear substantially lower. Available estimates indicate that from 112,000 to 119,000 adolescent pregnancies occur annually and about 3 percent of female teenagers give birth. What triggers the greatest concern may be not so much the aggregate levels of pregnancy as the sharp increase in nonmarital births. By the late 1980s, about three-quarters of adolescent mothers in the United Kingdom were unmarried.[3]

From a historical and cross-cultural perspective, however, what makes these trends problematic is less clear. Susan Harari, Maris Vinovskis, Diana M. Pearce, Sally Macintyre, and Sarah Cunningham-Burley explore a number of popular misconceptions about the adolescent pregnancy "crisis." Contrary to much alarmist rhetoric, neither the United States nor the United Kingdom is experiencing a sudden epidemic of "children having children."[4] The frequency of teenage childbirth has varied considerably over time and culture, and current levels are by no means unprecedented. Nor are they increasing significantly. In the quarter century between 1960 and 1985, adolescents' sexual activity and rates of pregnancy rose, but their rates of childbearing declined, largely as a result of greater access to abortion. Although the American teenage fertility rate began to rise slightly in the late 1980s, it still remains substantially lower than that of preceding decades.[5] So, too, although pregnancies among very young teenagers have risen, they account for only a small percentage of total adolescent births. In both the United States and the United Kingdom, about two-thirds of those births are to 18- and 19-year-olds, who are not commonly labeled children.[6]

What explains the sense of crisis in America and the more muted concerns in the United Kingdom is less the rate of births to teenage women than the socioeconomic context in which those births occur and the cultural ideology they challenge. As Annette Lawson notes later in this volume, adolescent pregnancy violates traditional assumptions about the boundaries of youth and female propriety. It also asserts teenagers' sexual independence at a time when they cannot readily achieve financial independence.[7]

In the United States, identifying adolescent pregnancy with specific racial, ethnic, and income groups accounts for further concerns. Rates of adolescent premarital sexual activity are substantially higher among blacks than among Hispanics or whites, particularly when measured among teenagers under 18. Black and Hispanic teenagers are also less likely than whites either to use contraception consistently or to have abortions. As a consequence, the rate of adolescent childbearing among blacks is almost two-and-a-half times higher than among whites, and among Hispanic teenagers, it is about twice as high as among whites. By the time they turn

18, about 7 percent of all whites, 14 percent of all Hispanics, and 26 percent of all black women have given birth. Substantial variations in marriage rates are also apparent: about 90 percent of blacks, 52 percent of Hispanics, and 45 percent of white adolescent mothers are single at the time of childbirth.[8] Teenagers from economically disadvantaged backgrounds have significantly higher rates of pregnancy, and early parenthood is associated with a range of poverty-related problems.[9]

Underlying what Angela McRobbie labels subdued moral panic[10] is a convergence of related trends: increased levels of sexual activity, especially outside of marital relationships; more unplanned pregnancies, resulting in more abortions; higher rates of nonmarital childbirths and single parenting, particularly among nonwhites; and greater numbers of young female-headed families living in poverty, dependent on welfare, and subject to all the disadvantages accompanying that status.[11]

Different constituencies attach different importance to these trends, and public debate is often confusing and confused about which of them constitute "the problem." As Macintyre and Cunningham-Burley note, many analyses conflate unplanned, unwanted, and unwed pregnancies and fail to acknowledge the broader norms they reflect.[12] The increase in all of these patterns—sexual activity, abortions, nonmarital childbirths, single parenting, and female poverty—is apparent to varying degrees among older as well as younger, white as well as nonwhite, populations. And in many cultures, at least some of these trends are relatively unproblematic. For example, high levels of adolescent sexual involvement and nonmarital childbirth provoke little controversy in Sweden or in many developing countries, and the frequency of abortion causes little public concern in others.[13] In the United Kingdom, where overall rates of teenage fertility are lower than in the United States but the proportion of nonmarital childbirths is higher, there is no consensus on whether adolescent pregnancy is in fact a serious social problem.[14]

Nor is there agreement in either nation over what exactly makes it problematic. Among conservatives, particularly in the United States, the issue has assumed broad symbolic importance; adolescent pregnancy signifies a threat to traditional moral values and family structures. As theorists like Joseph Gusfield, Murray Edelman, and Constance Nathanson note, rational policy analysis is generally difficult in contexts of symbolic politics, where individuals' sense of status, security, and way of life is at issue.[15] Teenage pregnancy is no exception. Among many constituencies, the objective is less to respond to adolescent needs than to affirm adult authority and conventional family norms.[16]

What complicates the issue still further are ambiguities in how the needs of teenagers should be assessed. Conventional analysis generally associates teenage pregnancy with a variety of adverse consequences, including disrupted education, reduced employment opportunities, and an increased likelihood of poverty for young mothers, together with greater health, psychological, cognitive, and educational problems for their children.[17] Yet according to some researchers, including Glynis Breakwell, Diana Pearce, Ann Phoenix, Sally Macintyre, Deborah Rhode, and Sarah Cunningham-Burley in this volume, the adverse consequences of adolescent pregnancy have been overstated. As we note, older teenagers are physically much better suited for childbearing than older women, and in some communities these teenagers are also better integrated into family support structures that assume caretaking responsibilities.[18] Parenting at any age often involves significant economic sacrifice, particularly in cultures with inadequate provision for family leave, childcare, and part-time work. Not all the disadvantages for adolescents' children are inherent in their birth status; many appear related to inadequacies in pre- and postnatal care and subsequent economic deprivation.[19]

Nor are all of the disadvantages associated with teenage fertility as pervasive or permanent as is sometimes supposed. One of the few long-term studies suggests that the vast majority of adolescent mothers are eventually able to complete their education, secure full-time employment, and avoid welfare dependency.[20] Two-thirds of their children have completed high school or are close to doing so and three-quarters of them have not become teenage parents.[21]

Such qualifications suggest reasons to reformulate the adolescent pregnancy "problem" but not to discount its significance. Some claims about the health risks to children and the availability of caregiving networks have provoked considerable dispute within the research community.[22] Chapters by Claire Brindis, Deborah Rhode, and Margaret C. Simms in Part IV revisit questions about the effects of adolescent pregnancy and their variations across age, class, race, and ethnicity. As these contributors all emphasize, the achievements of many adolescent mothers and their children should not deflect attention from the hardships they confront or from the substantial number who experience enduring difficulties.

On one point the commentators in this book generally agree. Many adverse consequences typically associated with adolescent childbirth are also partial causes; educational failure, lack of vocational opportunities, and low self-esteem contribute both to the likelihood of early pregnancy and to the disadvantages that follow from it.[23] Existing research provides no adequate basis for disentangling the effects of teenage childbearing from those of class, race, and ethnicity.[24] It is by no means clear how many of the adolescents experiencing the greatest difficulty would have fared better had they deferred motherhood.[25] Nor do we know how many of the problems for their children are directly attributable to inadequate parenting rather than to socioeconomic status.[26]

Moreover, contrary to popular rhetoric, adolescent pregnancy is by no means predominantly a "minority problem." In the United States, white teenagers account for about 68 percent of all adolescent births and 52 percent of births to unmarried mothers. Only 16 percent of adolescent mothers are unmarried black or Hispanic teens under age 18.[27] Although many minority groups are overrepresented in the populations at greatest risk, certain demographic trends are converging. Most significant, more whites are following the pattern of early nonmarital childbirth that was once largely limited to minority communities. In 1955, only 6 percent of white teenage childbearing occurred outside of marriage, compared with 41 percent among blacks; three decades later, the figures were approximately 42 percent for whites and 90 percent for blacks. According to some commentators, the same socioeconomic forces that are making marriage less attractive for blacks are likely to have similar effects among other low-income groups.[28]

Finally, racial and ethnic patterns vary considerably over time, class, and locale and reflect a complex interaction of cultural norms and structural constraints. Aggregate comparisons mask important variations; third-generation Cubans and recent Mexican-American immigrants have different family patterns, as do blacks from low-income urban ghettos and those from integrated middle-class suburbs. A representative illustration involves Hispanic marital rates: about 74 percent of adolescent Puerto Rican mothers remain single, compared with 37 percent of Central and South American mothers.[29] Similar variations exist across and within subgroups of Asian, Native American, and other minority communities.[30] Such differences counsel against homogenizing the experience of women of color or ignoring the other socioeconomic forces that affect it.

Phoenix's work on the United Kingdom similarly underscores the need for analyses that avoid simplistic racial or ethnic explanations for fertility patterns. The limited data available do not reveal an overrepresentation of minority groups among adolescent British mothers. A number of factors may help explain the divergence between patterns in the United States and those in the United Kingdom. In Britain much of the minority population consists of relatively recent emigrés who live in integrated areas and who have high rates of intermarriage with whites.[31] In the United States, the disproportionate rates of adolescent pregnancy among some minority groups are tied to a greater legacy of segregation and socioeconomic disadvantage.

Not only has popular analysis misdescribed the problem, it has also misjudged the prescription. Public debate generally vacillates between denying and exaggerating teenagers' responsibility for the hardship they confront. As Pearce notes, the common characterization of "children bearing children" achieves rhetorical power at the cost of disempowering and infantilizing its subjects.[32] Conversely, social policies built on the assumption that any teenager can "just say no" ignore much of the problem that they purport to address. Chapters in Parts I and II underscore the cultural constraints on individual decision making. Saying no in a society that links masculinity with virility and femininity with sexual attractiveness carries a cost. For many adolescents from disadvantaged backgrounds, childbirth is one of the few avenues available to satisfy needs to love and be loved.[33] Factors that encourage early childbirth and amplify its disadvantages reflect societal failures and demand societal responses.

Limitations in the way the adolescent pregnancy problem is conceptualized make for limitations in the policies addressing it. As subsequent discussion makes clear, the moralistic tenor of public debate has both obstructed programs enabling adolescents to make informed choice and constrained the choices available.

The chapters in Part II focus on those choices. Working from different disciplinary perspectives, all of the commentators share a common premise: individuals' reproductive decisions occur within a complex interaction of socioeconomic, ideological, and family influences, which can vary considerably across class, racial, ethnic, and cultural boundaries. Glynis Breakwell, Nancy Adler, and Jeanne Tschann explore some of these variations, as well as certain common patterns that help explain decision making on procreative issues. Their empirical studies, together with the ethnographies of Linda Burton and Carol Stack and the theoretical analyses of Annette Lawson and Sara Ruddick, suggest that adolescent choices are selectively rational in a sense that prevailing commentary often fails to acknowledge.

Three stages of a teenager's decision-making process are relevant: first, whether to engage in sexual activity; next, whether to use contraception; and finally, whether to bear a child. As to the first stage, Sara Ruddick's and Carole Joffe's chapters underscore how much of the conventional discourse on adolescent sexuality is a discourse of fear and admonition. That emphasis has also dominated American public policy; federal support has favored strategies focusing on abstinence, and few public schools or local governments offer adequate programs on sexual expression and birth control alternatives.[34] This orientation fails to address many individuals' dominant motivations, including needs for intimacy, independence, and peer approval. Such desires help explain the common pattern that Lawson and other commentators explore: adolescents engaging in sex that they do not find pleasurable.[35]

Altering this pattern will require multiple strategies that include, but are not limited to, empowering teenagers to "just say no." To make that choice plausible, we must expand other opportunities for meeting adolescents' needs. We must also acknowledge the positive aspects of sexual expression and help create the conditions under which it can occur. Better sex education for males as well as for females is part of the answer. However, achieving the ideal described in this volume will require fundamental changes in gender relations and social structures. Women of all ages should be able to control their own reproductive lives and to make choices that are informed rather than driven by the concerns of others.[36] To realize that vision, we must break the cultural linking of masculinity with sexual dominance and femininity with sexual passivity and subordination.

We must also make adequate birth control programs accessible to adolescents, and alter the cultural norms that inhibit their use. Empirical studies make clear that a significant number of teenagers underestimate the risks of unprotected sexual intercourse and overestimate the risks of various birth control methods.[37] For other adolescents, appearing unprepared for sex is a way of accommodating our culture's continuing double message and double standard concerning female morality. Women are expected to be sexually alluring but not too sexually available. By letting intercourse "just happen," female adolescents seek to avoid being stigmatized as either prudish or promiscuous. Such a strategy also absolves teenagers of having to obtain contraceptives and overcome the resistance of a male partner to their use.[38] Given these concerns, adolescents' failure to employ birth control is not as irrational as is commonly supposed. It reflects certain real costs that sexually active teenagers continue to face in America and to a lesser but still significant extent in Great Britain. Changing pregnancy patterns will require broader changes in gender norms.

Decisions to bear a child reflect a similar mix of individual needs and societal influences. Public debate too often invokes reductive dichotomies between wanted and unwanted pregnancies or confuses unintended with undesired childbirth.[39] In fact, adolescent attitudes toward motherhood range across a spectrum and are responsive to societal pressures, norms, and opportunities. Many teens are influenced less by affirmative desires for a child than by family and peer pressures; motherhood becomes a way to punish parents, to please grandparents or male partners, or to gain status.[40] Linda Burton and Carol Stack's ethnographies of low-income black communities illustrate how individual reproductive choices are subject to intergenerational caregiving patterns. Later chapters indicate how those patterns are, in turn, shaped by broader socioeconomic structures.

So too, as Lawson, Adler, and Tschann remind us, motivations to bear a child are both conscious and preconscious and frequently respond to deepseated needs for independence, identity, and love. Such needs are not easily deferred.[41] Nor are sufficient other means to satisfy them available for many adolescents, particularly those from disadvantaged backgrounds. Research on pregnancies among low-income youths suggests that many mothers were not motivated to have a child but were insufficiently motivated to avoid it: the economic opportunities sacrificed through early parenting did not appear sufficiently great to justify deferring childbirth.[42] Changing that opportunity structure will require fundamental social changes along the lines suggested in this book's final sections.

Until the last decade, fathers rarely figured in research or public policies on adolescent pregnancy, and only now is that omission being rectified. In part, the absence of men in analysis of "the problem" reflected the absence of men in the lives of their young families. As Gina Adams, Karen Pittman, and Raymond O'Brien note, data have been difficult to collect, for most teenage mothers do not formally identify the father of their child, and two-thirds do not include the father's age on the birth certificate. Most of these men are not living with their children, and a significant number are unaware of, or unwilling to admit, paternity.[43]

This pattern is emblematic of deeper gender norms. Although males bear half of the biological responsibility for pregnancy, they have increasingly avoided comparable social responsibility. For the most part, young men have not been expected to "just say no." Over the last quarter century, pressures to marry a pregnant partner have substantially weakened. What accounts for this trend and what, if anything, should be done to counteract it are the focus of chapters in Part III and a recurring theme of the policy analysis in Part IV.

As with other issues involving adolescent pregnancy, a basic problem lies in formulating the problem. Is it the declining frequency of marriage, the lack of economic support and psychological attachment by biological fathers, or the lack of any father figure for the child? To what extent should social policy seek to compel or encourage paternal involvement? And to what extent should it seek to make such involvement less critical to the child's welfare?

These issues arise in the context of a paradoxical shift in gender norms.

As the boundaries between traditional male and female roles increasingly blur, men are assuming both more and less family responsibility. The result is what Frank Furstenberg has previously described as the two faces of fatherhood: a larger percentage of men is involved to a larger extent in childrearing and domestic tasks, but a larger percentage is also utterly uninvolved.[44]

Such changes have become most apparent among adolescents and young adults. As noted earlier, in the United States about 60 percent of teenage mothers remain unmarried. Of young unmarried men (ages 18–23) who acknowledge being fathers, less than a fifth report living with any of their children.[45] According to the limited national data available, about two-thirds of these fathers provide some financial assistance to their children in the first year after birth, but most payments are small, irregular, and decline quickly. Similarly, about half of all children born to single adolescent mothers have some contact with their biological father a year after birth, but this involvement is usually intermittent and unsustained.[46]

Similar patterns emerge in Frank Furstenberg and Kathleen Mullan Harris's study of black adolescent mothers and their families in Baltimore. That study, which provides one of the only longitudinal profiles currently available, finds relatively little paternal involvement within four or five years of birth. By the children's mid-adolescence, less than a fifth of fathers were still living with their families; only about 10 percent of the never-married fathers and a third of the divorced fathers were providing any support. Overall, only 13 percent of the Baltimore teenagers reported significant attachment with a nonresidential biological father and 69 percent had no such attachment with any father figure.[47] In general, the study concludes that children benefit from close paternal relationships but that most of the relationships children have with their fathers are neither continuous nor close. Moreover, anything short of a close bond fails measurably to improve a child's life prospects. Although children in stable marital units do significantly better on measures of depression, criminal involvement, and school performance, only a minority of teenage mothers who marry during adolescence remain in such units.[48]

What accounts for the low levels of paternal involvement and what might be done about them are questions demanding further research and program evaluation. A central issue on which commentators disagree is to what extent the increase in female-headed households is attributable to a decrease in marriageable males, particularly in low-income minority communities.[49] However, American data leave no doubt that recent declines in education and employment opportunities together with increases in violence, drug use, suicide, and incarceration among young black males have had some impact on marriage and the capacity for child support.[50] Contrary to popular assumptions, these structural factors rather than norms condoning paternal irresponsibility are most clearly associated with behavior characteristic of low-income nonwhite communities. Many young fathers attempt to provide some parental support even as socioeconomic forces erode its possibility.[51] Yet in both the United States and United Kingdom relatively few adolescent pregnancy and parenting initiatives have included men or have focused on the systemic deprivation that men often confront.[52]

Altering these patterns will require policy initiatives both for poverty populations in general and for young fathers in particular. Many of the education, employment, counseling, drug treatment, and birth control programs discussed in Part IV should involve both sexes. In addition, as Adams, Pittman, and O'Brien indicate, we need to improve processes for establishing paternity and enforcing child-support obligations.[53] For fathers who lack financial resources, we should do more to encourage other forms of childrearing assistance. Promoting greater contraceptive and parental responsibility among men is crucial to insuring equality for women.[54] But where such responsibility is lacking, it is equally critical to reduce the disadvantages for women and children that result.

In most Western industrialized nations, taboos against early sexual activity and parenting are in decline, but public policies have not caught up.[55] As Rhode's later chapter argues, too much blame has been placed at the individual level, on teenagers who "want too much too soon" in sexual relationships. Inadequate attention has focused on the societal level, on the institutions that offer "too little too late"—too little birth control and prenatal assistance, too little reason to complete school, and too few opportunities for childcare and meaningful employment.[56]

In the final section of this book, Claire Brindis, Carole Joffe, Deborah Rhode, and Margaret Simms explore the societal initiatives that adolescent pregnancy demands. Building on themes developed throughout this volume, we propose strategies along two dimensions. One is to increase adolescents' access to birth control; the other is to alter the social conditions that simultaneously promote and punish early childbearing.

An irony of current American norms is that birth-control information and assistance are least accessible to the groups that need them most. About half of all sexually active teenagers lack adequate reproductive health services, and even fewer have access to sex-education programs that focus on pregnancy prevention.[57] Efforts to develop such programs have foundered because of restrictive school board policies, limitations on abortion services, and inadequate governmental support. As Joffe notes, it has often been impossible to design initiatives that neither "scare the parents nor bore the kids."[58] Much existing instruction focuses only on the biology of reproduction and fails to address other critical needs, such as enhancing self-esteem and decision-making skills.

Policies that require parental involvement for adolescents seeking contraception and abortion have been similarly ill-advised. Such requirements have increased unwanted pregnancy and childbearing among those least able to cope with the consequences: teenagers who are young, unsophisticated, and poor.[59] Contrary to the claims of conservatives, most studies find that restricting access to contraception discourages contraception, not sex.[60] Although increased parent-child communication regarding reproductive issues is desirable, virtually no experts believe that mandatory consent policies effectively serve that objective.[61] As cross-cultural research makes clear, countries with more accessible birth control information and services also have lower rates of adolescent childbirth.[62] If the goal is for teenagers to behave more responsibly in reproductive matters, there must be fewer costs in doing so.

More alternatives must also be available for adolescents who are ill-equipped for early parenthood. Many teenagers are unlikely to "just say no" to early sex or childbirth unless they have more opportunities for saying yes to something else. Better vocational, educational, and counseling programs are crucial both to increase adolescents' aspirations and to make those aspirations plausible.

For teenagers who choose childbirth, we must reduce the disadvantages that this choice often entails. Inadequacies in employment, health, childcare, substance abuse, and related welfare programs underpin the problems that adolescent pregnancy is often thought to generate. In communities with substantial drug and alcohol problems, the lack of treatment facilities for pregnant women has had particularly tragic results and has exposed a generation of children to permanent disabilities.[63] To reverse these trends, we must spend more, and more wisely, on a wide range of antipoverty programs. Such programs need better coordination and greater sensitivity to the diversity of experience across class, race, ethnicity, age, and gender.[64] Significant progress will require assistance not only to adolescent parents but also to the community and kinship networks on which those parents depend.

Much of the problem concerning adolescent pregnancy is that "talk is cheap and welfare programs are not."[65] But in the long run, society pays a greater price by failing to address the fundamental causes and consequences of teenage sexual activity. From even the most self-interested perspective, it makes sense to invest now in the generation that will support us later.

That investment needs to include further research on adolescent pregnancy and appropriate policy responses. We need more systematic information about the forces that construct and constrain reproductive patterns. What accounts for variations across different racial, ethnic, and socioeconomic groups? What strategies are most likely to encourage contraception and to assist adolescent parents? Which forms of school, media, and community outreach are most successful? What distinguishes those who cope well with early pregnancy or childbirth and what societal interventions could enable others to cope better? Adequately addressing these questions will require increased continuity in program support and evaluation. More stable, sustained funding must be available for strategies demonstrating the greatest success, and more longitudinal research is necessary to identify them.

Yet, although we have much to learn about what works best for sexually active adolescents, we already know more than enough about what does not work to build a better policy agenda. Our fundamental objective should be to strengthen the connection between principle and practice, between our rhetorical commitment to reproductive freedom and the resource priorities that this commitment demands.

Notes

1. For demographic data see Elise Jones et al., *Teenage Pregnancy in Industrialized Countries* (New Haven: Yale University Press, 1986), pp. 23, 37; Cheryl Hayes, ed., *Risking the Future: Report of the Panel on Adolescent Pregnancy and Childbirth of the National Research Council, Final Report* (Washington, D.C.: National Academy Press, 1987), pp. 1.2, 2.20–2.30. The U.S. birth rate for teens under 17 is higher than that of any developed country, and its rate for those between 15 and 19 is the highest outside Eastern Europe. Stanley K. Henshaw, Asta M. Kenney, Debra Somberg, and Jennifer Van Vort, *Teenage Pregnancy in the United States: The Scope of the Problem and State Responses* (New York: Alan Guttmacher Institute, 1989).

The campaign statement occurred after Vice President Dan Quayle indicated that he would support an adult daughter's decision to have an abortion despite his belief that abortion should be illegal. His wife subsequently made clear that if their 13-year-old daughter became pregnant now, she would have the child, and the vice president agreed. Kevin Sack, "Quayle Insists Abortion Remarks Don't Signal Change in His View," *New York Times*, 24 July 1992, p. A-1 (quoting Marilyn Quayle).

2. See Children's Defense Fund, *Teenage Pregnancy: An Advocates' Guide to the Numbers* (Washington, D.C.: Children's Defense Fund, Jan. 1988); Stanley K. Henshaw and Jennifer Van Vort, "Teenage Abortion, Birth, and Pregnancy Statis-

tics: An Update," *Family Planning Perspectives* 21 (1989): 85; sources cited in Deborah L. Rhode, "Adolescent Pregnancy and Public Policy" (chap. 15).

3. Sally Macintyre and Sarah Cunningham-Burley, "Teenage Pregnancy as a Social Problem: A Perspective from the United Kingdom" (chap. 3); Ann Phoenix, "The Social Construction of Teenage Motherhood: A Black and White Issue?" (chap. 4).

4. Compare Dorothy I. Height, "What Must Be Done about Children Having Children," *Ebony,* March 1985, p. 76, with Hayes, *Risking the Future,* and Leon Dash, *When Children Want Children: The Urban Crisis of Teenage Childbearing* (New York: William Morrow, 1989); see Maris A. Vinovskis, *An "Epidemic" of Adolescent Pregnancy? Some Historical and Policy Perspectives* (New York: Oxford University Press, 1988), pp. 22–30; Susan E. Harari and Maris A. Vinovskis, "Adolescent Sexuality, Pregnancy and Childbearing in the Past" (chap. 1), Macintyre and Cunningham-Burley, "Teenage Pregnancy as a Social Problem."

5. See sources cited in n. 2; Vinovskis, *"Epidemic,"* p. 25; National Center for Health Statistics, *Advanced Report on Final Natality Statistics, 1988* (15 Aug. 1990).

6. See Phoenix, "Social Construction"; Children's Defense Fund, *Teenage Pregnancy,* p. 11. See generally Diana M. Pearce, " 'Children Having Children': Teenage Pregnancy and Public Policy from the Woman's Perspective" (chap. 2).

7. Annette Lawson, "Multiple Fractures: The Cultural Construction of Teenage Sexuality and Pregnancy" (chap. 5).

8. U.S. Congress. *Hispanic Teenagers: A Reproductive Profile in Demography of Adolescent Pregnancy in the U.S.: Joint Hearing before the Subcomm. on Census and Population and the Subcomm. on Health and Development* (Report of the Guttmacher Institute). 99th Cong., 1985. Serial no. 99-5; Henshaw and Van Vort, "Teenage Abortion, Birth and Pregnancy Statistics"; Children's Defense Fund, *Teenage Pregnancy,* pp. 20–26. For slightly different statistics, see Norma Y. Lopez, *Hispanic Teenage Pregnancy: Overview and Implications* (Washington, D.C.: Policy Analysis Center, Office of Research, Advocacy, and Legislation, National Council of La Raza, 1987). Error rates in some of these estimates may be unusually high because 95 percent of Hispanics who identify themselves with a racial group identify themselves as white. In some survey data, therefore, Hispanics are counted twice, once under white and once under Hispanic. Children's Defense Fund, *Teenage Pregnancy,* p. 20.

9. See Hayes, *Risking the Future;* Frank Furstenberg, Jr., Jeanne Brooks-Gunn, and S. Philip Morgan, *Adolescent Mothers in Later Life* (Cambridge: Cambridge University Press, 1987); Children's Defense Fund, *Teenage Pregnancy;* Claire Brindis, "Antecedents and Consequences: The Need for Diverse Strategies in Adolescent Pregnancy Prevention" (chap. 13); Rhode, "Adolescent Pregnancy."

10. Angela McRobbie, quoted by Ann Phoenix, "Social Construction." See also Constance L. Nathanson, *Dangerous Passage: The Social Control of Sexuality in Women's Adolescence* (Philadelphia: Temple University Press, 1992), pp. 14–16 (discussing moral panic that adolescent pregnancy arouses. Nathanson notes that such reactions are particularly likely when normative violations are coupled with challenges to the norms themselves).

11. See sources cited in nn. 1 and 2; Brindis, "Antecedents and Consequences."

12. Macintyre and Cunningham-Burley, "Teenage Pregnancy as a Social Problem."

13. Jones et al., *Teenage Pregnancy in Industrialized Countries*, pp. 191, 219; Elise Jones et al., "Teenage Pregnancy in Developed Countries: Determinants and Policy Implications," *Family Planning Perspectives* 17 (1985): 53; and Britta Hoem, "Early Phases of Family Formation in Contemporary Sweden," in Margaret K. Rosenheim and Mark F. Testa, eds., *Early Parenthood and the Transition to Adulthood* (New Brunswick, N.J.: Rutgers University Press, forthcoming).

14. Compare Phoenix, "Social Construction" (characterizing British public response to adolescent pregnancy as subdued moral panic), with Glynis M. Breakwell, "Psychological and Social Characteristics of Teenagers Who Have Children" (chap. 8) (suggesting that adolescent pregnancy is not a major social issue in Britain).

15. Joseph Gusfield, "Moral Passage: The Symbolic Process in Public Designations of Deviance," *Social Problems* 15 (1967): 175; Murray Edelman, *The Symbolic Uses of Politics* (Urbana: University of Illinois Press, 1964); Nathanson, *Dangerous Passage*, pp. 14–16.

16. See Lawson, "Multiple Fractures"; Rhode, "Adolescent Pregnancy"; Carole Joffe, "Sexual Politics and the Teenage Pregnancy Prevention Worker in the United States" (chap. 14).

17. See sources cited in n. 9.

18. In addition to the contributions in this volume, see Arline T. Geronimus, "On Teenage Childbearing and Neonatal Mortality in the United States," *Population and Development Review* 13 (June 1987): 245; Mary G. Edwards, "Teenage Childbearing: Redefining the Problem for Public Policy." Paper presented at the American Political Science Association, 30 August 1990; Catherine Kohler Riessman and Constance A. Nathanson, "The Management of Reproduction: Social Construction of Risk and Responsibility," in Linda H. Aiken and David Mechanic, *Applications of Social Science to Clinical Medicine and Health Policy* (New Brunswick, N.J.: Rutgers University Press, 1986); Mark F. Testa, "Racial Variation in the Early Life Course of Adolescent Welfare Mothers," in Rosenheim and Testa, *Early Parenthood*.

19. See sources cited in n. 18.

20. Furstenberg, Brooks-Gunn, and Morgan, *Adolescent Mothers*.

21. Frank F. Furstenberg, Mary Elizabeth Hughes, and Jeanne Brooks-Gunn, "The Next Generation: Children of Teenage Mothers Grow Up," in Rosenheim and Testa, *Early Parenthood*.

22. Karen Pittman, "A Rebuttal of Two Controversial Teen Pregnancy Studies: Special Report" (Washington, D.C.: Children's Defense Fund, May 1990) (criticizing Geronimus's study for considering only neonatal mortality while excluding risks to older infants and for relying on dated studies on caregiving networks); see also research discussed in Rhode, "Adolescent Pregnancy."

23. Nancy E. Adler and Jeanne M. Tschann, "Conscious and Preconscious Motivation for Pregnancy among Female Adolescents" (chap. 7); Brindis, "Antecedents and Consequences"; see also Dawn M. Upchurch and James McCarthy, "The

Timing of a First Birth and High School Completion," *American Sociological Review* 55 (1990): 224.

24. For discussion of causal ambiguities, see Frank F. Furstenberg, Jr., and Jeanne Brooks-Gunn, "Teenage Childbearing; Causes, Consequences and Remedies," in Aiken and Mechanic, *Applications of Social Science*, p. 316.

25. See Macintyre and Cunningham-Burley, "Teenage Pregnancy as a Social Problem"; Phoenix, "Social Construction"; Furstenberg, Brooks-Gunn, and Morgan, *Adolescent Mothers*, pp. 396–97. For data suggesting that blacks gain few economic advantages from deferring motherhood, see Elaine McCrate, "Labor Market Segmentation and Relative Black/White Teenage Birth Rates," *Review of Black Political Economy* (1990): 37; Shelly Lundberg and Robert D. Plotneck, "Teenage Childbearing and Adult Wages." Discussion Paper 90-24 (Washington, D.C.: Institute for Economic Resources, 1989); Arline T. Geronimus and Sanders Korenman, "The Socioeconomic Consequences of Teen Childbearing Reconsidered." Research Report 90-190 (Ann Arbor: University of Michigan Population Studies Center, Sept. 1990); For data suggesting advantages of delaying childbirth see Steven A. Holmes, "Teenage Study Hints Gain for Those Having Abortion," *New York Times*, 25 January 1990, p. A-13.

26. Furstenberg, Hughes, and Brooks-Gunn, "The Next Generation"; Anne C. Peterson and Lisa J. Crockett, "Adolescent Sexuality, Pregnancy and Childbearing; Developmental Perspectives," in Rosenheim and Testa, *Early Parenthood*; Irwin Garfinkle and Sara McLanahan, *Single Mothers and Their Children: A New American Dilemma* (Washington, D.C.: Urban Institute, 1986).

27. Children's Defense Fund, *Teenage Pregnancy*, p. 20.

28. Children's Defense Fund, *Teenage Pregnancy*, pp. 26–30; Frank F. Furstenberg, Jr., "Racial Differences in Teenage Sexuality, Pregnancy, and Adolescent Childbearing," in David P. Willis, ed., *Health Policies and Black Americans* (New Brunswick, N.J.: Transaction, 1989), pp. 381–403.

29. Children's Defense Fund, *Teenage Pregnancy*, p. 23; U.S. Congress, *Hispanic Teenagers*; Lopez, *Hispanic Teenage Pregnancy*.

30. For discussion of differences within the Asian-American population (e.g., between those of Japanese, Chinese, Vietnamese, Thai, Cambodian, and Indonesian background), see Claire Brindis and Rita J. Jeremy, *Adolescent Pregnancy and Parenting in California: A Strategic Plan for Action* (San Francisco: Center for Population and Reproductive Health Policy, University of California, 1988). For discussion of Native American groups, see, e.g., Rayna Green, "Native American Women: A Review Essay," *Signs* 6 (1980): 248; Beverly Horn, "Cultural Beliefs and Teenage Pregnancy," *Nurse Practitioner* 8 (1983): 35; and Charles W. Slemenda, "Sociocultural Factors Affecting Acceptance of Family Planning Services by Navajo Women," *Human Organization* 37 (1978): 190.

31. Phoenix, "Social Construction."

32. Pearce, "'Children Having Children.'"

33. See Adler and Tschann, "Motivation"; Sara Ruddick, "Procreative Choice for Adolescent Women" (chap. 6).

34. See Ruddick, "Procreative Choice"; Joffe, "Sexual Politics." See also Brindis, "Antecedents and Consequences"; Rhode, "Adolescent Pregnancy."

35. Lawson, "Multiple Fractures." See also Dash, *When Children Want Children*, pp. 125, 265.

36. Ruddick, "Procreative Choice"; Linda M. Burton and Carol B. Stack, "Conscripting Kin: Reflections on Family, Generation, and Culture" (chap. 9).

37. Kristin A. Moore, Margaret C. Simms, and Charles L. Betsey, *Choice and Circumstance: Racial Differences in Adolescent Sexuality and Fertility* (New Brunswick, N.J.: Transaction, 1986), pp. 33–35, 44–45; Catherine S. Chilman, *Adolescent Sexuality in a Changing American Society: Social and Psychological Perspectives for the Human Services Professions*, 2d ed. (New York: John Wiley & Sons, 1983), pp. 110–25; Kristin Luker, *Taking Chances: Abortion and the Decision Not to Contracept* (Berkeley: University of California Press, 1975); Dash, *When Children Want Children*, pp. 68, 115, 127, 136.

38. Lawson, "Multiple Fractures"; Jones et al., *Teenage Pregnancy in Industrialized Countries*, p. 63; Brindis and Jeremy, *Adolescent Pregnancy and Parenting in California*, pp. 32–41.

39. Lorraine V. Klerman and James F. Jekel, "Unwanted Pregnancy," in M. Bracken, ed., *Perinatal Epidemeology* (New York, Oxford University Press, 1984): 283–91.

40. Burton and Stack, "Conscripting Kin"; Carole Joffe, *Regulation of Sexuality* (Philadelphia: Temple University Press, 1986), pp. 157–88; Dash, *When Children Want Children*, pp. 12–13, 121–25, 216, 230, 265; Elijah Anderson, "Sex Codes and Family Life among Poor Inner City Youths," *Annals of the American Academy of Political and Social Science* 501 (1989): 59.

41. Adler and Tschann, "Motivation"; Lawson, "Multiple Fractures."

42. Denise F. Polit and Janet R. Kahn, "Early Subsequent Pregnancy among Economically Disadvantaged Mothers," *American Journal of Public Health* 26 (1986); 167, 170–77; sources cited in n. 25.

43. Gina Adams, Karen Pittman, and Raymond O'Brien, "Adolescent and Young Adult Fathers: Problems and Solutions" (chap. 11).

44. Frank F. Furstenberg, Jr., "Good Dads–Bad Dads: Two Faces of Fatherhood," in Andrew Cherlin, ed., *The Changing American Family and Public Policy* (Washington, D.C.: Urban Institute, 1988).

45. Adams, Pittman, and O'Brien, "Adolescent and Young Adult Fathers"; Children's Defense Fund, *Adolescent and Young Adult Fathers: Problems and Solutions* (Washington, D.C.: Children's Defense Fund, May 1988).

46. See sources cited in n. 45.

47. Frank F. Furstenberg, Jr., and Kathleen Mullan Harris, "When Fathers Matter/Why Fathers Matter: The Impact of Paternal Involvement on the Offspring of Adolescent Mothers" (chap. 10).

48. *Ibid.*

49. For accounts stressing declines in the marriage pool and their underlying causes, see William Julius Wilson, *The Truly Disadvantaged* (Chicago: University of

Chicago Press, 1987): William Julius Wilson and Kathryn M. Neckerman, "Poverty and Family Structure: The Widening Gap between Evidence and Public Policy Issues," in Sheldon H. Danzig and Daniel H. Weinberg, eds., *Fighting Poverty: What Works and What Doesn't* (Cambridge: Harvard University Press, 1986), p. 232; Tom Joe, "The Other Side of Black Female-Headed Families: The Status of Adult Black Men," *Family Planning Perspectives* 19 (1984): 74; Sally J. Andrade, "Family Planning Practices of Mexican Americans," in Margaret B. Melville, ed., *Twice a Minority: Mexican American Women* (St. Louis: C. V. Mosby Co., 1980), p. 17. For accounts that critically review these explanations for the rise in female-headed households, see Margaret C. Simms, "Adolescent Pregnancy among Blacks in the United States: Why Is It a Policy Issue?" (chap. 12); Maris Vinovskis, "Teenage Pregnancy and the Underclass," *Public Interest* 93 (1988): 87; R. I. Lerman, "Economics of the Family: Employment Opportunities of Young Men and Family Formation," *American Economic Review* (May 1989): 79 (challenging the importance of unemployment in accounting for marital patterns).

50. See sources cited in n. 41; Jewell Taylor Gibbs, "The Social Costs of Teenage Pregnancy and Parenting in the Black Community," in Rosenheim and Testa, *Early Parenthood.*

51. For discussion of the disjuncture between norms supporting parental responsibility and the capacity of low-income fathers to provide assistance, see Mercer L. Sullivan, *The Male Role in Teenage Pregnancy and Parenting, New Directions for Public Policy* (New York: Vera Institute of Justice, 1990); Mercer L. Sullivan, "Absent Fathers in the Inner City," *Annals of the American Academy of Political and Social Science* 501 (January 1989): 48. But see also Anderson, "Sex Codes." See generally Mark Testa, Nan Marie Astone, Marilyn Krogh, and Kathryn M. Neckerman, "Employment and Marriage among Inner-City Fathers," *Annals of the American Academy of Political and Social Science* 501 (1989): 79. However, as is clear from other studies of child support provided by divorced and unmarried fathers, capacity to pay does not accurately predict willingness to pay. See David L. Chambers, *Making Fathers Pay: The Enforcement of Child Support* (Chicago: University of Chicago Press, 1977), pp. 107–21; Deborah L. Rhode and Martha Minow, "Reforming the Questions, Questioning the Reforms: Feminist Perspectives on Divorce Reform," in Herma Hill Kay and Stephen Sugarman, eds., *Divorce Reform at the Crossroads* (New Haven: Yale University Press, 1990).

52. Furstenberg and Harris, "When Fathers Matter"; Children's Defense Fund, *Adolescent and Young Adult Fathers,* p. 21; Children's Defense Fund: *Teenage Pregnancy,* pp. 28–31; Children's Defense Fund, *Where the Boys Are: Teenage Pregnancy Prevention Strategies* (Washington, D.C.: Children's Defense Fund, 1988).

53. Adams, Pittman, and O'Brien, "Adolescent and Young Adult Fathers."

54. Deborah L. Rhode, *Justice and Gender* (Cambridge: Harvard University Press, 1989), p. 219.

55. See Jones et al., *Teenage Pregnancy in Industrialized Countries,* p. 230; Rhode, "Adolescent Pregnancy and Public Policy"; Joffe, "Sexual Politics."

56. Rhode, "Adolescent Pregnancy," quoting Sharon Thompson, "Search for

Tomorrow: On Feminism and the Reconstruction of Teen Romance," in Carole Vance, ed., *Pleasure and Danger* (Boston: Routledge and Kegan Paul, 1984).

57. Congressional Caucus for Women's Issues, *Update*, 30 October 1989, p. 1. See also Brindis and Jeremy, *Adolescent Pregnancy and Parenting in California*, pp. 45–48; Hayes, *Risking the Future*, pp. 17–18; Henshaw, Kenney, Somberg, and Van Vort, *Teenage Pregnancy*, p. 56.

58. Joffe, "Sexual Politics"; see also Joffe, *Regulation of Sexuality.*

59. See sources cited in Rhode, "Adolescent Pregnancy and Public Policy"; American Civil Liberties Union, Reproductive Freedom Project, *Parental Notice Laws* (New York: American Civil Liberties Union Foundation, 1986); Virginia G. Cartoof and Lorraine Klerman, "Parental Consent for Abortion: Impact of the Massachusetts Law," *American Journal of Public Health* 26 (1986): 597; Hodgson v. Minnesota, 648 F. Supp. 756, 763–69 (C.D. Minn.) rev'd, 497 U.S. 417 (1990).

60. Rhode, "Adolescent Pregnancy"; Brigid Rentaul, "Cognitus Interruptus: The Courts and Minor's Access to Contraceptives," *Yale Law and Policy Review* 5 (1986): 212; Hayes, *Risking the Future*, 6.6, 7.7; and sources cited in n. 59.

61. See sources cited in n. 59; Robert H. Mnookin, "*Bellotti v. Baird*: A Hard Case," in Robert H. Mnookin, *In the Interests of Children* (New York, W. H. Freeman, 1975); Susan F. Newcomer and Richard Udry, "Parent-Child Communication and Adolescent Sexual Behavior," *Family Planning Perspectives* 17 (1985): 169.

62. Jones et al., *Teenage Pregnancy in Industrialized Countries*, pp. 232–33.

63. Dan R. Griffith, "New Study of Cocaine-Exposed Infants Underscores Need for Treatment Programs and Education," *Perinatal Addiction Research and Education Update* (March 1989): 3; Molly McNulty, "Combating Pregnancy Discrimination in Access to Substance Abuse Treatment for Low-Income Women," *Clearinghouse Review* 23 (May 1989): 21; "Substance Abuse Treatment for Women: Crisis in Access," *Health Advocate* 160 (Spring 1989): 9; Sheila Ronkin, Jack FitzSimmons, Ronald Wapner, and Loretta Finnegan, "Protecting Mother and Fetus From Narcotic Abuse," *Contemporary Ob./Gyn.*, March 1988, p. 178; Susan Diesenhouse, "Drug Treatment Is Scarcer Than Ever for Women," *New York Times*, 7 January 1990, p. E-15.

64. Brindis, "Antecedents and Consequences"; Simms, "Adolescent Pregnancy among Blacks"; Wilson and Neckerman, "Poverty and Family Structure"; David Ellwood, "Conclusion," in David Ellwood and Phoebe H. Cottinghan, eds., *Welfare Policy for the 1990s* (Cambridge: Harvard University Press, 1989).

65. Rhode, *Justice and Gender*, p. 131.

PART ONE *THE CULTURAL CONSTRUCTION OF TEENAGE PREGNANCY*

SUSAN E. HARARI
MARIS A. VINOVSKIS

1 *ADOLESCENT SEXUALITY, PREGNANCY, AND CHILDBEARING IN THE PAST*

Contemporary social scientists and the general American public view adolescence as an important developmental period during which children undergo the physical, emotional, and social growth that prepares them for adulthood. Adolescence is also seen as a potentially difficult journey, one on which an individual's sole responsibility is to change from a fragile youth to a strong and well-rounded adult. As a result of these beliefs, modern American teenagers pass through a historically unusual period of dependency. They typically live at home, attend school, and fail to contribute to the family income.

Because of the perceived fragility and structurally age-specific nature of contemporary adolescence, most parents, educators, politicians, and social welfare agencies see pregnancy as a disaster. Recent research, however, has found that teenage childbearing, even when out of wedlock, may not be as damaging to the young mother as previously thought. Yet popular belief holds that by carrying a child to term, and especially by raising the child herself, a young mother automatically condemns both of them to a life of poverty.

Social scientists have been active in questioning many of these assumptions, but have done so in a historical vacuum. As historians, we are drawn to a little-investigated part of this issue: namely, how teenage pregnancy has been perceived in other periods of American history. Lacking this perspective, researchers often assume that strict repressive sexual codes successfully curbed teenage sexual activity in the past or, conversely, that youthful marriage was so widespread that few teenage girls had the opportunity to bear children outside of marriage. But teenage sexuality, pregnancy, and childbearing caused significant problems in the seventeenth, eighteenth, and nineteenth centuries, and only by exploring the historical record can we understand why they have become major domestic priorities today.

Teenage pregnancy and childbearing in and of themselves were not a particularly burning social issue in the past. Contemporary America harbors an age-conscious and age-segregated society. This was not true of the seventeenth, eighteenth, and nineteenth centuries. Before the late nineteenth century, Americans did not attend age-segregated schools and had no specific age for retirement. Society judged people on the basis of their assets and abilities, not on the basis of age.[1] Before the twentieth century, parents did not allow their teenage sons and daughters a long period of dependency.[2] A teenager in colonial New England had been financially useful to his or her family since childhood. Girls and boys frequently left home at age 13 or 14 in order to attend school or learn household skills or trades.[3]

By the middle of the nineteenth century economic and social changes prompted the acceptance of adolescence as an important phase in the life course. Formal schooling became more important and more common, and the family became smaller, which enabled parents to devote more time and energy to child development.[4] Societal acceptance of psychological theories on the importance of this period of growth also furthered the development of a contemporary notion of adolescence.[5] Correspondingly, in the late nineteenth century an out-of-wedlock birth became a more tragic event for both a girl and her family.

Illegitimacy was of considerably more concern to society in earlier periods of American history than teenage pregnancy itself. Religion played a central role in American lives in the seventeenth, eighteenth, and nineteenth centuries, and sexual activity and births outside of marriage were considered sinful. Early Americans found sexual experimentation by young never-marrieds less problematic than adultery, however, especially if the ensuing birth was legitimate. Pregnant girls chose between social ostracization and marriage, the latter of which almost completely restored their standing within the community. Because the vast majority of women in America during these years did eventually marry and raise families, women who became pregnant as teenagers did not face a much different life from that of their peers who married later. Out-of-wedlock children, however, posed financial problems for the community. Before the development of the welfare state, state-run orphanages, and foster care systems, out-of-wedlock children and their mothers became financial burdens to their families and the community—regardless of the age of the mother. So pregnant teenagers faced strong pressure to marry, thus relieving the community of their future support.

Little work has been done on the problem of teenage sexuality, pregnancy, and childbearing in America's past, although the topic has recently attracted research and comment. Studies on family life have provided some groundwork, but because the research has not focused specifically on teenagers and premarital pregnancy, most of the information on them is sketchy. It also tends to follow the geographic and class confines set by the field of family history. We know quite a bit about family life in New England, for example, but until the 1970s, we knew little about family life in the Southern colonies. Historians have not yet explored the attitudes toward teenage pregnancy held by African Americans, ethnic immigrants, Native Americans, or even different classes. We say this not to excuse any deficiencies in this chapter but instead to remind the reader of how many opportunities exist for further research in a potentially rich field.

Colonial and Antebellum America's Response to Teenage Pregnancy

Little evidence exists to show that teenage sexuality and childbearing were singled out as major social problems before the mid-1970s.[6] Two simple explanations can be suggested for this lack of concern. The age at menarche for women may have been higher during earlier periods of American history than it is now; therefore, teenage girls may not have been at risk of an unintended pregnancy. Furthermore, women may have married earlier, which would have had a similar effect.

The Puritans did not consider a marriage valid unless both partners had reached sexual maturity and could consummate it. In fact the Puritans deemed inability to consummate a marriage a valid reason for annulment.[7] Thus the age at menarche was the youngest age at which a girl could marry; there were few prepubescent brides in the New England colonies.[8]

Unfortunately, we do not have firm data regarding the age at menarche in colonial America, although we can set the age at about 15 for the late nineteenth century.[9] The onset of menarche appears to be closely linked to environmental conditions such as diet, health, and socioeconomic status.

Thus, we can assume that colonial women began menses at about the same age, for they resembled their nineteenth-century counterparts in stature and diet.[10] The fact that the average height of enlistees in the United States army remained fairly constant from 1789 to 1894 reinforces the supposition that little dietary change occurred during this period, height usually being a good indicator of an individual's nutritional history.[11] Then as now, however, the onset of menarche does not necessarily signify the ability to conceive. Adolescents typically experience a period of subfecundity that reduces fertility considerably.[12] Therefore even if adolescent girls in early America experienced the onset of menarche at age 15 or 16, sexually active teenagers would probably not have conceived at these ages.[13]

What conclusions can be drawn from this data? Colonial and nineteenth-century Americans probably were not faced with the problem of pregnancies to very young girls (under the age of 15). Today, we find sexual activity and subsequent pregnancy in young teenagers disturbing; Puritans apparently did not have to face this issue. Based on the available evidence, however, colonial girls could have conceived premaritally. The Puritan lack of concern at the age of the teenagers cannot be explained by simple biological differences.

Early historians of the American family believed that girls married very young, often before age 16.[14] If we assume that teenagers married soon after puberty in colonial and nineteenth-century America, then we would not expect to find them producing out-of-wedlock children in need of public financial support.[15] Recent scholarship, however, has convincingly argued that few colonial women in New England married or had children during their teens.[16] In the seventeenth and eighteenth centuries American women tended to marry in their early 20s, while men married in their late 20s. The age at first marriage rose slightly in the nineteenth century; in Massachusetts the age at first marriage was about 24 for women and 26 for men from 1845 to 1860.[17]

If a relatively late age at menarche and relatively early age at marriage did not protect these girls from teenage pregnancy then perhaps they were protected by a strong moral code that discouraged premarital sexual activity. Certainly the Puritans have a reputation for strict and repressive attitudes toward sex, and we generally think of Victorian Americans as having conservative views. But new historical evidence shows that the Puritans were much less hostile toward human sexuality than once believed. The Puritans regarded sex as a welcome and essential part of marriage, although they stressed self-control and denial for unmarried couples.[18] Strong sanctions against premarital sex prevailed only from about 1630 to

1660.[19] After 1660 engaged couples increasingly indulged in sexual activity during the period of their engagement.[20]

As we might guess, this increase in premarital sex led to an increase in premaritally conceived first births. In the early seventeenth century less than 10 percent of the first births studied by Smith and Hindus were conceived out of wedlock.[21] But by the second half of the eighteenth century, the rate of premarital conceptions rose to almost 30 percent of first births. This increase in premarital pregnancy paralleled a steady, visible erosion of church and civil opposition to premarital sexual activity. Across New England the number of civil prosecutions for fornication declined, as did parents' ability to persuade their children to marry partners of the parents' choosing.[22] Without opposition from the church, civil authorities, and the community, sexual intimacy became a normal part of most courtships. It should be noted, however, that premarital sex was confined mainly to couples already planning to get married or formally engaged. The idea of a casual date that included sexual intercourse would have been foreign to the Puritans.[23]

We know less about premarital births and sexuality in the other American colonies, but some work has been done on the Chesapeake region.[24] Unlike the Puritan families that came to New England, most white immigrants to the South were unmarried, indentured servants, with men vastly outnumbering women. The men were usually young: more than half were between the ages of 18 and 22, while the women were somewhat older. The majority of women were between 18 and 25, with half between the ages of 20 and 22. Out-of-wedlock births were relatively high, with about one-fifth of the female servants in Charles County claiming to have borne an illegitimate child.[25] The first generation of immigrant servant women arriving in the Chesapeake married in their mid-twenties, following the completion of their indentures. In contrast, their daughters, the first native-born generation, married very young, sometimes before their 16th birthdays, and almost always before age 21. Bridal pregnancy was not uncommon in these native-born brides; about 20 percent of the brides in one Chesapeake county gave birth within eight-and-one-half months of marriage.[26] With time, the second generation came to resemble their New England counterparts, with premarital intercourse confined largely to engaged couples.

The early nineteenth century ushered in a substantial decrease in premaritally conceived births throughout the United States, and by the Civil War society no longer tolerated intercourse as a normal part of courtship. The advent of the Second Great Awakening in the 1780s, which rapidly spread throughout the nation in the early nineteenth century, most likely caused this change in behavior. Reformers associated with the evangelical religious movement viewed any premarital sexual activity as sinful.[27] Medical writings also accused premarital sexual activity of squandering youthful strength and vitality.[28] This belief endured well into the twentieth century: Alfred Kinsey pointed out in 1948 that "millions of youths have been told that in order to 'be prepared' one must conserve one's vitality by avoiding any wastage of vital fluids in boyhood." This information had, Kinsey reported, appeared in every Boy Scout manual published between 1911 and 1945.[29] Prohibitions against premarital sex may also have been strengthened by renewed emphasis on the importance of purity and innocence in young women. According to literary sources of the day, a "fallen woman" might render herself unfit for marriage, risking her reputation and perhaps even her sanity.[30]

In spite of the social sanctions that colonial and nineteenth-century Americans set up to handle illicit sexual activity, a fair number of young, unmarried women did experience out-of-wedlock pregnancies. Were teenagers singled out as a group who, by virtue of their age, needed special attention or assistance? Rarely, because the notion of adolescence as a separate and distinct phase of the life course was not to appear in the United States until the late nineteenth and early twentieth century.[31] When early Americans did express concerns about immoral behavior publicly (of premarital sexual activity or intemperance, for example), they directed their complaints to the general populace rather than singling out adolescents.

The easiest social solution to an out-of-wedlock pregnancy has always been a quick marriage. To early Americans, teenage pregnancy and early childbearing in the context of an economically viable marriage was not a problem, because neither partner suffered any real setback. Girls and boys were both receiving common-school educations by the mid-nineteenth century, but most students finished their schooling by age 15 or 16, so pregnancy would not have interrupted their education.[32] An early marriage did not disrupt a woman's long-term career plans, because few women were able to think about the possibility of any career outside that of full-time wife and mother.[33] Few couples divorced, so teenage pregnancy was not associated with a higher rate of marital dissolution, either.[34] Given the harsh punishments for bearing a bastard child and the limited rights of such children as they grew to adulthood, marriage was in the best interest of both the mother and her unborn child.[35] Although parents and community leaders discouraged premarital sexual activity and adolescent marriage and childbearing, these became disasters only if the young couple could not support themselves and their child.

Teenage pregnancy did not strike early Americans as problematic unless the couple was unwed, and even then society had fashioned solutions with which it was satisfied. A quick marriage saved the young woman's reputation, insured financial support for her child, and relieved the community of any future support. Furthermore, the problems that we associate today with early marriages (high incidence of divorce, interruption of the girl's education and maturation process, an end to her opportunities for a meaningful career, and an unstable home for the baby) were either not deemed meaningful or paled in comparison to other bleak alternatives. In the years following the Civil War changes in the role of women, the definition of youth, and the acceptability of premarital sexual activity would combine to make early marriage a less desirable solution.

Teenage Pregnancy in the Modern Age

By the late nineteenth century, premarital pregnancies became a more daunting social problem—particularly if they did not end in marriage. Rather than a slight embarrassment, premarital pregnancy became a traumatic and shameful event that ruined a girl's chance of marriage or respectability and torpedoed family aspirations of upward social mobility.[36] This change came as a result of expanded roles for women, an evolving concept of adolescence, and concerns over the prevailing double standard in sexual morality.

For middle-class teenagers, especially for native-born girls in urban areas, adolescence became a lengthy period of financial dependence, in which education rather than labor in some family enterprise was the main occupation. In the eighteenth century, women's formal education had been limited and haphazard. On the eve of the signing of the Declaration of Independence, 80 percent of adult men could sign their names compared to 40 to 45 percent of women. In comparison, the 1850 census found that 80 percent of all white women in America over the age of 20 were literate.[37]

What most differentiated girls of the late nineteenth century from their mothers was their growing access to secondary education in coeducational public high schools. By the 1920s, some high school experience (although not necessarily high school graduation) had become standard for whites of all classes and for urban blacks.[38] High school experience exposed a young woman to a world of peers that supplanted her family as the major influence in her life. Ironically, while general family life was becoming more private and withdrawn, teenagers were becoming much more subject to a culture wholly alien to their parents. This youth culture would become so seemingly powerful in the twentieth century that many would come to see it as a threat to both family and community standards.

In the late nineteenth century social reformers set up homes for unwed mothers as an alternative to the forced marriages that had previously been the most common solution to unwed pregnancy. Unlike earlier public maternity wards, these homes sought to combine compassion with moral uplift. A local Women's Christian Temperance Union chapter founded one such home, the Anchorage, in Elmira, New York. The girls coming to the Anchorage ranged in age from 13 to 21 and came from a variety of social classes. To the reform-minded women who established the refuge, the girls who came to them were victims of a double standard of morality. The blame for illegitimate pregnancies was society's, for it allowed and even encouraged premarital sexual activity for men. The ultimate solution to this disparity, they felt, was the creation of a single standard of conduct for both sexes. The reformers did not pursue marriage as a solution to the girls' pregnancies, although they did try to obtain some kind of compensation from the male seducers to cover medical and living expenses. Instead, the Anchorage program encouraged its clients to forget the whole unfortunate episode. Few women kept their children, although the older a girl, the more likely she was to do so. Matrons tried to convince young mothers that keeping their children would only hinder their own lives and those of the children. After a prolonged stay at the Anchorage (often as long as twenty months, in order to effect moral rehabilitation) many girls found their way into domestic service.[39]

During the same period Charles Crittenton, a New York merchant, began to establish a network of homes for unwed mothers that bore the name of his deceased daughter Florence. The first Crittenton Mission, founded in 1883 in downtown New York, focused mainly on reforming young prostitutes. Crittenton and his supporters soon concluded that their efforts would be better served if they could catch girls before they drifted into a life of professional prostitution. Eventually the Crittenton Homes evolved into a loose association of maternity homes that housed pregnant girls and unwed mothers and their children.

Unlike the Anchorage, the Crittenton Homes insisted on keeping the mother together with her child. In fact, in order to join the Crittenton network, applicant groups had to agree that everything possible would be done to avoid separation. Little information exists to explain this crucial difference. Age does not seem to be a factor, as both the Crittenton Homes and the Anchorage took in very young girls. Unfortunately, little is known about the class origins of the girls who made use of these institutions. If wealthy or middle class girls (who would have had a more stable financial situation) had used the Crittenton Homes, this might have explained the Mission's goal of keeping mother and child together. But this seems unlikely, for Crittenton girls were encouraged to pursue domestic service after their stays ended.

Frankly evangelical in origins, the Crittenton Homes became more scientific and professional in the early twentieth century. The girls had originally been described as "object[s] of compassion, to be received into the atmosphere of love and helpfulness . . . during the time of [their] greatest trial." The Mission supplied kindness and honest employment once the mother was ready to leave; the approach was casual, and the staff was often volunteer or, if paid, lacking professional training. By the 1930s, the girl was seen as a "social unit, whose poor adjustment to her surroundings may have begun long before she came within the Home's range of vision, and may be resumed in an aggravated form after she leaves this Home unless she gets continuing assistance." In addition, by the 1930s, not only a girl's environment, but also her age contributed to her downfall: "The low average age of the inmates of the Florence Crittenton Homes emphasizes the fact that before her first offense the unfortunate girl is simply a growing adolescent human being, with little knowledge of herself, or the world, unusually susceptible to the evil that may surround her."[40] This passage demonstrates that teenage out-of-wedlock pregnancies had become a special concern of the Crittenton Home network by the 1930s, supporting the argument that a belief in adolescence as a fragile period of human development had begun to evolve sometime in the late nineteenth and early twentieth centuries.

Sex reemerged as part of courtship proceedings in the early twentieth century, as the nineteenth-century moral standards and religiosity that had curbed premarital intimacy eroded. In addition, social workers and psychologists now encouraged parents to allow children more freedom from interference and free time to spend with their peers. They also instructed parents to be emotionally expressive toward their children. This new "compassionate family" was small and placed increased importance on love and companionship between spouses and between parents and their children.[41] Resumption of premarital intercourse did not lead to a correspondingly high number of premarital pregnancies, perhaps because of increased familiarity with birth-control techniques and a better understanding of human physiology.

Material gathered by Alfred Kinsey and his colleagues in the 1940s and 1950s provides much of the evidence supporting a claim that adolescent sexual activity increased in the early part of the twentieth century.[42] Many valid criticisms can be made of Kinsey's work: his sample was predominantly white and middle-class, his approach was that of a zoologist rather than a sociologist, and the answers his subjects gave were based on their memories of events. Few teenagers were included in the study, and most of the information described as detailing adolescent experience came from adults remembering events in their youth. Still, the Kinsey research is important because it is the first large-scale investigation of American sexual mores and habits and the only rigorous, scientific data available on its period.[43]

Of primary interest here are the comparisons Kinsey made between the sexual behavior of women born before 1900 and those born after. All these data showed substantial increases in the levels of premarital petting and intercourse. By age 35, for example, 80 percent of women born before 1900 had participated in some premarital petting, compared with 91 percent of those born after 1900 and 99 percent of those born between 1910 and 1929. The younger generations began petting at an earlier age; of women born before 1900, half were 18 before their first petting experience, but in the youngest generation interviewed, half of the girls had petted before age 16. Kinsey also noted the absence of socialized roles for the mother, the family, the church, or the school to play in helping girls prepare for sexual relations. Instead, petting itself gave girls their "first real understanding of heterosexual experience."[44]

Kinsey found that patterns in premarital intercourse followed those of premarital petting. Among women born before 1900, half as many had had premarital intercourse as had women born in any later decade. Among those who remained unmarried by age 25, for example, 14 percent of the older generation had had premarital sex compared to 36 percent of those born between 1900 and 1910. As with petting, most of this increase had occurred among women born between 1900 and 1910.[45]

Despite the increase in premarital sex, Kinsey's findings indicate that the circumstances surrounding sexual activity had not changed substantially since the colonial era. Although nearly 50 percent of the women in his sample had experienced premarital coitus, they could hardly be described as wildly promiscuous. Most women had first experienced coitus in the year preceding marriage, often with their fiancés. Also, except among women who married early, premarital sex was rarely engaged in during early adolescence. Kinsey concluded that early premarital coitus tended to lead to early marriage and that the possibility of a forthcoming marriage tended to soften attitudes toward sex.[46]

Kinsey found that 3 percent of the women in the total sample, irrespective of age at marriage, had first experienced coitus by age 15, 20 percent between the ages of 16 and 20, and 35 percent between the ages of 21 and 25, but we do not know the marital status of these women at the time of first intercourse.[47] Women with less education were more likely to have had their first sexual encounter at a young age; whereas 18 percent of the women with a grade school education had first experienced coitus by age 15, only 1 percent in the college sample had. The findings on class status were similar, explaining the phenomenon. Girls raised in working-class families were more likely to have premarital intercourse as adolescents than girls in middle- and upper-class families because they were more likely to marry at an earlier age, and premarital sex was typically part of courtship.[48]

Kinsey explained the increase in premarital sexual activity as the inevitable outcome of a new, "more deliberate" approach to sexual relations in the post-war era. The works of Havelock Ellis and Sigmund Freud were widely read, leading to freer discussions about human sexuality. It should also be pointed out that nineteenth-century moral reformers had lobbied for expansion of sex education and more openness about human sexuality; they believed frank information would demystify sexuality, making girls less naive about its consequences. Kinsey believed that World War I itself had contributed to the increase in premarital sex, because so many young men had come into contact with the "Central European sexual pattern," which differed from the American, and because of the class mix resulting from a draft army. A disparate list of other causes included increased knowledge of birth-control techniques, the increasingly urban nature of American life, and the widespread decline in prostitution.[49]

Based on his findings, Kinsey argued for dismantling outdated moral conventions, but his view was not popular. In discussing *Sexual Behavior in the Human Male*, Mrs. Esther Emerson Sweeney, director of the American Social Hygiene Association, admonished Dr. Kinsey for his suggestion that moral standards should be weakened simply because of the number of infractions. Murder and thievery were not condoned, she noted, simply because they were on the increase. The American people, she argued, "should not be equally ready to brush aside and tolerate moral lapses as inconsequential." She suggested that schools and churches should provide more structured guidance in moral development.[50]

By the 1920s, school was the main arena for dating, and dating was the main entry into sexual relations. Before 1900, encounters between middle-class girls and boys had been limited to chaperoned parties or home visits, both of which could be closely monitored by adults.[51] Dating represented a significant change, because dates depended on peers for control rather than parents. And, thanks to the invention of the automobile and the movie theater, couples now had somewhere private to go.[52]

The new system had its own strict and patrolled conventions. John Modell argues that teenage middle-class girls designed the system of dating and had the most to gain from it. Dating broke down many of the conventional boundaries between male and female behavior. Girls could have sexual experiences, smoke, drink, and dance. Because of these new freedoms, and given the fact that the goal for a young woman was still a conventional marriage, some rules were necessary to protect her from ruining her reputation. A sexually active girl could have a great many dates, so cliques and gossip served to set the upper limits for acceptable behavior. Petting was allowed, but girls always had to be the restraining factor in sexual situations. Girls who engaged in premarital coitus and advertised their actions were denigrated, even if they had been motivated by love.[53]

Although little research has been done on adolescent pregnancies during the 1930s, we do know that the birth rates of women aged 15–19 reached their lowest point in this century during the Depression.[54] In fact, marriage and childbearing for all age groups declined in this period. The Depression did not reduce the percentage of marriages that legitimized births; social convention continued to outweigh the more prudent economic course of delaying marriage until better times.[55] But it did have a negative effect on young people and their courtship habits. Families often chose to economize in areas crucial to the adolescent dating system: pocket money, automobiles, and new clothes.

The twentieth century can be seen as an era characterized by a declining rate of teenage births, smaller families, later marriages, and a climbing divorce rate. But during World War II and the 1950s, the country temporarily changed course.[56] Rates of birth to adolescents shot up dramatically, reaching a peak of 97.3 births per thousand women aged 15–19 in 1957.

One explanation for this increase may have been the development of the dating institution of "going steady." Modell claims going steady is of more recent vintage than dating; consequently, the parents of 1950s teenagers had probably not gone steady during their own high school years. Just how many students did have a steady is unclear. The author of one of the many guides to teenage behavior published in the 1950s admitted that every high school had some steady dating but claimed that two-thirds of teenagers never fastened on to one person.[57] Another author thought that most students had gone steady at some time or another.[58]

Although going steady was usually described in negative terms, the manuals openly discussed why it was so attractive for young people. For both boys and girls, having a steady meant an end to dating uncertainties. Being someone's steady conveyed a certain amount of prestige among one's peers. For girls, having a steady boyfriend meant a date for every important occasion and allowed them to take more initiative in planning dates without seeming fresh. But boys benefited the most from steady dating, for as both Modell and the manuals acknowledge, having a steady girl friend meant regular access to sex.[59]

But any positive virtues of the steady system were more than outweighed by the negatives, according to these manuals. Long lists of what was wrong with going steady skirted the main issue: going steady led to physical intimacy. The manuals supplied other reasons to avoid steady dating as well, the most important of which was that teenagers would be giving up opportunities to meet new people and have a variety of experiences. One goal of dating was to learn more about the opposite sex in preparation for marriage and, obviously, a girl or boy who dated only one person learned less. Going steady could lead to an ill-considered early marriage, entered into before a teenager really knew what he or she wanted in a marriage partner.[60] Although the authors did not provide hard evidence that going steady inevitably led to premarital pregnancy, they had reason on their side. "It is unrealistic," wrote Ann Landers, "to assume that healthy, red-blooded high school kids can be together, day in and day out, month after month—sometimes year after year—and keep their physical urges under perfect control."[61]

Before the development of dependable, simple contraception, premarital intercourse could not be easily separated from premarital pregnancy. The manual authors spoke of pregnancy as the ultimate, unavoidable consequence of intercourse. Landers condemned the "knucklehead who tells me if I really want to befriend teen-agers, I should give them some helpful hints on how to avoid pregnancy instead of being so doggone puritanical and unrealistic. . . . There is no 100 percent foolproof, surefire way to avoid pregnancy."[62] As with petting, responsibility for avoiding intercourse lay with girls, so most precautions were directed at them. Girls who avoided pregnancy but engaged in intercourse still risked "loss of standing among their associates."[63] Considerable emphasis was also placed on saving one's virginity for a future husband: "No casual love-making, no transitory excitement of seeming to be sophisticated and daring is worth the surrender of faith, love, and truth you owe your husband."[64] Premarital intercourse was described as physically unsatisfying for girls because boys looking to lose their virginity made poor sex partners, being anxious and awkward.[65] And, eventually, premarital intercourse could negatively affect marital relations. Having suffered through hurried and unsatisfying lovemaking before marriage, a young woman might come to dread sexual intercourse. All the manuals suggested that girls engaging in premarital sex could expect to experience strong feelings of guilt.

In the 1950s it was thought that even engaged couples would do well to avoid premarital intercourse. Here again the manuals argued that entering marriage as a virgin was a wonderful thing, for both men and women: "The bride and groom who have never shared sexual intercourse with anyone else bring a very special dowry."[66] On the practical side, engagement no longer led automatically to marriage. Instead, engagement functioned ideally as a trial period during which the couple could decide whether they were suited to one another. Justin and Mary Landis concluded that because one-third to one-half of engagements did not end in marriage, couples would do well to avoid intercourse. Some might feel compelled to marry, no matter how ill-suited they turned out to be, because of their physical intimacy.[67] After a broken engagement, the girl would be left wondering if her next fiancé would abandon her once he learned of her previous "experience."[68]

The manuals described the early marriage forced by an unplanned pregnancy as one with little chance for success.[69] A girl planning to marry might not see much use for a high school diploma, but eventually she would regret her decision to drop out of school.[70] All the authors wrote that early marriage destroyed the fun and carefree way of life that every teen deserved. Finally, while the occasional early marriage could be "brilliant" most teenagers were probably too immature to know what they wanted in a spouse.[71] "A girl may be very much in love when she is in high school. But she may also know that she wants in the future to have the security of marriage to a man who has had enough training to support adequately the children they may have. She may also have abilities herself that she would like to develop before she undertakes the steady responsibilities of homemaking and motherhood. If she takes time now to think of all she wants from life both now and in the future, she may hesitate to marry very quickly while she is still in her teens."[72]

Usually marriage presented a better solution to the problem of premarital pregnancy than the girl's other options: abortion, adoption, or raising a child out of wedlock. Ann Landers commented briefly on the dangers of illegal abortion and the heartache of out-of-wedlock births. Another author wrote: "The girl who bears her fatherless child carries him in sorrow," because keeping the child meant social ostracism and putting it up for adoption risked feelings of guilt and loss.[73] Writing honestly and openly, Maxine Davis described the abortion process at its best (expensive and difficult to obtain) and at its worst (dangerous and frightening), hoping to sway any teenage girl who still contemplated a premarital tryst.

Today we regard the 1950s as a more innocent time. The nostalgia craze for that decade has given us images of 3-D movies, sock-hops, poodle skirts, and a cleaner, more sentimental brand of rock and roll. Compared to the drug use, violence, and sexual revolution of the 1960s, the 1950s seem safe. To the parents of adolescents in the years following World War II, however, the youth culture seducing their children was alarming and potentially dangerous. Middle-class parents equated youth culture with lower-class values, which they feared would infect their children. Symptomatic of this frightening set of customs were zoot suits, blue jeans, crime comic books, and, more seriously, casual sex and violence.[74]

Although movies in the 1930s and 1940s often dealt with youth (for example, the Andy Hardy series), these films were intended for a broader audience and usually reinforced the traditional values of American family life. The rise of television and the collapse of the old studio system in the 1950s altered the movie industry. Films increasingly targeted the teenage audience and highlighted the generational conflict between adolescents and their parents.[75] Films also began to test the limits of the Hollywood film code by treating the issue of adolescent pregnancy. The original screenplay for the 1959 film *Blue Denim* featured an abortion as the solution to an unwanted pregnancy. The film board rejected this scenario and MGM tried to make the film more acceptable by offering to end the story with either an adoption or a miscarriage. When 20th-Century Fox acquired the rights to *Blue Denim*, the studio suggested allowing the unmarried girl to keep her baby and postponing discussion of marriage until she and her boyfriend were old enough to make a mature decision. The final version of the film, however, featured a marriage.[76]

Times had changed by the time *The Young Lovers*, starring Peter Fonda as a struggling college student, was made a few years later. In this film, the two lovers are California freshmen. Fonda deserts his girlfriend when he discovers her pregnancy and she chooses to visit an abortionist on her own. Unable to go through with the abortion, she drops out of college and prepares to leave for the east coast with her mother to have the baby. Will she keep the child, put it up for adoption, or marry Fonda? The ending provided is ambiguous. Fonda's friend in the film provides an interesting parallel: drafted to serve in the armed forces, he declines his girlfriend's offer of herself, her virginity, claiming he would rather wait until they can be married. While the lovers in *Blue Denim* necessarily chose marriage, the ending of *The Young Lovers*, just four years later, is much less conclusive.

Still, both films condemn premarital sex regardless of whether it is plagued by an unintended pregnancy.

An analysis of teenage sexuality in American movies from 1930 to 1980 found that after the 1950s more sexual activity was depicted and with younger teenagers.[77] Because most of these films focus on male characters, they ignore the problems girls face in coping with their emerging sexuality. Rather than showing parents as sympathetic and helpful, movies in the past three decades have emphasized the negative aspects of the relationship between parents and their offspring.

By the 1960s teenage pregnancy had become an interesting topic to many researchers and as a result, far more information is readily available on it. In the 1960s the rate of out-of-wedlock births continued to increase, as did the number of teenagers engaged in premarital coitus. But the rate of teenage pregnancy began to decline from the high levels it had reached in 1957. Given this decline, why did concern about teenage pregnancy grow as the phenomenon itself became less prevalent?

As we have seen, teenage premarital pregnancy appeared less problematic in 1957 because marriage was regarded as an adequate solution. Husbands could provide financial support, so teenage pregnancy did not carry the stigma of illegitimacy and welfare dependency. But increases in the number of women eligible for Aid to Families with Dependent Children (AFDC), changes in their marital status, and amendments to AFDC would change this in the 1960s. In 1950 Congress amended the Aid to Dependent Children program, which had only supported underage children, to provide benefits to the custodial parent of dependent children, renaming it Aid to Families with Dependent Children, in order to encourage poor mothers to stay home to care for their children. Throughout the 1960s, welfare costs continued to rise as separated, divorced, and single mothers began to outnumber widows. As part of the War on Poverty, Congress passed bills establishing Medicaid in 1965 and expanding housing assistance and the food stamp program. In addition, states began to increase cash welfare benefits and to accept more applicants for welfare programs.[78] By the 1970s, the proportion and number of adolescent births had increased dramatically and so had the taxpayers' bill for welfare benefits available to unwed mothers.

The decision of many young unwed mothers to keep their children further increased the welfare burden. During the 1970s, rates of nonmarital childbearing rose steadily, while rates of marital childbearing among adolescents declined. Although blacks have always been more likely to give birth outside of marriage, the change in the behavior of white adolescents also alarmed those concerned about the costs of AFDC: nonmarital birth rates to white girls rose by 74 percent between 1970 and 1984.[79]

Opportunities and expectations outside of marriage for young women had also improved since the 1950s. Policymakers could no longer assume that a majority of women would marry and become homemakers and mothers; many women pursued full-time employment, higher education, or demanding careers.[80] As the divorce rate rose, even women who did marry had to face the possibility that they might eventually have to support themselves and their children.[81] Careers required a high school diploma at the least, and usually a college education as well. Given these new circumstances, dropping out of high school to bear and raise a child put a teenage girl at a serious disadvantage.

Another factor behind the increased concern over adolescent pregnancy in the 1970s was the legalization of abortion in 1973. In 1971, teenagers between the ages of 15 and 19 obtained 150,000 legal abortions. In 1973 the number almost doubled, to 280,000. An estimated 40 percent of all pregnancies to girls between 15 and 19 now end in abortion and among girls under 15, abortions began to outnumber births as early as 1974.[82] Much of the congressional concern and support for adolescent parenting programs (especially the Adolescent Family Life program, proposed by Senator Jeremiah Denton, R-AL) came from "pro-life" forces who saw these programs as an acceptable alternative to abortion.

The role of public interest groups in fanning the flame of public concern over adolescent pregnancy cannot be overstated. The Alan Guttmacher Institute (the former research arm of Planned Parenthood) played a key role in popularizing the phrase "an epidemic of adolescent pregnancy" by its use in a highly influential pamphlet entitled *11 Million Teenagers: What Can Be Done About the Epidemic of Adolescent Pregnancies in the United States*.[83] Eunice Shriver and the Joseph P. Kennedy, Jr., Foundation also lobbied heavily on behalf of teenagers, but they focused their attention on care programs for pregnant adolescents and young mothers rather than on family planning clinics for sexually active teenagers.[84]

The founders of the Charles Crittenton Missions would be alarmed by today's widespread acceptance of out-of-wedlock births. Although still cause for embarrassment or shame in some sectors of society, the illegitimate births of rich or famous women are openly celebrated. If we compare the reception of out-of-wedlock births to Jerry Hall or Jessica Lange to the pregnancy of Ingrid Bergman in the 1940s, we can see that public attitudes toward the mother have indeed softened considerably. Wrote one commentator on the Crittenton legacy: "Once remove the stigma from unmarried motherhood and the necessity for such 'rescue work' would, of course, quite vanish away. The problem would become one purely of morals and religion, with no social implications at all. . . . Such a state of affairs will hardly come about in the United States in our lifetime, if ever. Whatever the theorists may decide, the masses of the people will continue to look askance for a long, long while to come at the mother without a marriage ring."[85]

If almost everyone today agrees that adolescent pregnancy is a major, national problem, there is no consensus on the definition of the problem, who is responsible for dealing with it, or what is the appropriate solution.[86] Many Americans, particularly those who regard themselves as political liberals, regret the high rate of early sexual activity among teenagers but accept it and focus their attention on providing federally funded family planning programs to prevent unintended pregnancies. Others believe that at least some adolescent childbearing will occur no matter how much we promote contraceptives for sexually active teenagers and therefore support comprehensive care programs to alleviate the negative consequences of early parenthood. Finally, a significant and politically influential conservative minority sees the recent rise in teenage premarital sexual activity as the real problem and advocate programs to encourage sexual abstinence among unmarried teenagers. For this group, family planning programs for teenagers are part of the problem rather than the solution. They believe that much, if not most, of the recent increases in teenage sexual activity can be explained by the legitimacy it has been accorded by public funding of family planning clinics.

Unfortunately, the political debate over the definition of the problem of teenage pregnancy often ignores the needs and responsibilities of some of the key parties involved. The well-being of the adolescent mother's child, for example, may be worse served in the long run than we have realized, for it is being ignored in most comprehensive care programs, which focus on the short-term needs of the young mother.[87] Similarly, the financial and emotional responsibilities of the father to his child have generally been neglected by policymakers.[88]

Although teenage sexuality, pregnancy, and early childbearing have always existed, they have rarely been singled out as particular problems necessitating special state or federal programs. In the seventeenth, eighteenth, and nineteenth centuries, most problems associated with teenagers were treated as part of broader social issues not specific to any age group. A combination of social, demographic, and political factors in the 1970s and 1980s, however, led to the conclusion that an unprecedented epidemic of teenage pregnancy existed, warranting concerted federal action.

Unfortunately, most analysts and policymakers who deal with these issues today are unaware of their historical origins or context. In part this results from lack of solid historical work on this subject. For example, we know little about the fathers of out-of-wedlock children, today or in the past. African American women today make up a disproportionate number of unwed mothers and yet little is known about teenage mothers during slavery or after Emancipation. Similarly, the development of institutions to handle the problems of out-of-wedlock pregnancy would provide an interesting focus for investigation. Throughout the twentieth century, professional social workers and psychologists replaced moral crusaders and volunteers in homes for unwed mothers; how did this shift in personnel affect the service provided? Popular culture and its relation to attitudes toward teenage pregnancy would also make a worthwhile research topic. And of course the emergence of teenage pregnancy as a major domestic problem today still awaits more detailed analysis.

We will not find simple or easy answers for the problems associated with teenage pregnancy. To address the needs of pregnant teenagers, their partners, and their children, we need to acknowledge that the current problems associated with teenage sexuality, pregnancy, and childbearing are neither simple nor self-evident, but are shaped by our historical and social experiences and perceptions. A historical approach can, however, provide us with a broader framework useful in understanding the complex interactions between adolescent maturation and the changing social context. Information about teenage pregnancy and societal reactions in the past should not be used mechanically for guiding current policies, but it can sensitize us to the importance of appreciating the impact of economic and cultural changes on the lives of teenagers and provide us with a broader range of policy options for trying to guide our children through adolescence.

Notes

1. David Angus, Jeffrey Mirel, and Maris A. Vinovskis, "Historical Development of Age-Stratification in Schooling," *Teacher's College Record* 90 (1988): 211–36; Howard P. Chudacoff, *How Old Are You? Age Consciousness in American Culture* (Princeton: Princeton University Press, 1989).

2. Gerald F. Moran, "Adolescence in Colonial America," in Richard M. Lerner, Anne C. Petersen, and Jeanne Brooks-Gunn, eds., *Encyclopedia of Adolescence* (New York: Garland, 1991), 1:157–71; Susan M. Juster and Maris A. Vinovskis, "Adoles-

cence in Nineteenth-Century America," in Lerner et al., *Encyclopedia of Adolescence*, 2:698–707.

3. John Demos, *A Little Commonwealth: Family Life in Plymouth Colony* (New York: Oxford University Press, 1970); Steven Mintz and Susan Kellogg, *Domestic Revolutions: A Social History of American Family Life* (New York: Free Press, 1988); Moran, "Adolescence in Colonial America."

4. Maris A. Vinovskis, "Family and Schooling in Colonial and Nineteenth-Century America," *Journal of Family History* 12 (1987): 19–37.

5. Juster and Vinovskis, "Adolescence in Nineteenth-Century America."

6. Maris A. Vinovskis, "Adolescent Sexuality and Childbearing in Early America," in Jane B. Lancaster and Beatrix A. Hamburg, eds., *School-Age Pregnancy and Parenthood: Biosocial Dimensions* (New York: Aldine, 1986), pp. 303–22.

7. Peter Laslett, "Age at Menarche in Europe since the Eighteenth Century," *Journal of Interdisciplinary History* 2 (1971): 221–36.

8. Maris A. Vinovskis, *An "Epidemic" of Adolescent Pregnancy? Some Historical and Policy Perspectives* (New York: Oxford University Press, 1988).

9. Grace Wyshak and Rose E. Frisch, "Evidence for a Secular Trend in Age of Menarche," *New England Journal of Medicine* 306 (1982): 245–306.

10. Robert Fogel, "Nutrition and the Decline in Mortality since 1700: Some Additional Preliminary Findings," National Bureau of Economic Research Working Paper Series, no. 1802 (1986); Rose E. Frisch and Janet W. McArthur, "Menstrual Cycles: Fatness as a Determinant of Minimum Weight Necessary for Their Maintenance or Onset," *Science* 435 (1974); 949–51; Alice H. Jones, *Wealth of a Nation To Be: The American Colonies on the Eve of the Revolution* (New York: Columbia University Press, 1980).

11. Lee Soltow and Edward Stevens, *The Rise of Literacy and the Common School in the United States: A Socioeconomic Analysis to 1870* (Chicago: University of Chicago Press, 1981).

12. Prem P. Talwar, "Adolescent Sterility in an Indian Population," *Human Biology* 37 (1965): 256–61; James Trussell and Richard Steckel, "The Age of Slaves at Menarche and Their First Birth," *Journal of Interdisciplinary History* 8 (1978): 477–505.

13. Vinovskis, "Epidemic."

14. Alice M. Earle, *Colonial Dames and Goodwives* (Boston: MacMillan, 1895); Arthur Calhoun, *A Social History of the American Family.* 3 vols. (New York: Barnes and Noble, 1960).

15. Josephina J. Card and Laureis L. Wise, "Teenage Mothers and Teenage Fathers: The Impact of Early Childbearing on the Parents' Personal and Professional Lives," *Family Planning Perspectives* 10 (1978): 199–295; Frank F. Furstenberg, Jr., *Unplanned Parenthood: The Social Consequences of Teenage Childbearing* (New York: Free Press, 1976); Kristin A. Moore and Linda J. Waite, "Early Childbearing and Educational Attainment," *Family Planning Perspectives* 9 (1977): 220–25.

16. Demos, *A Little Commonwealth;* Philip J. Greven, Jr., *Four Generations: Population, Land, and Family in Colonial Andover, Massachusetts* (Ithaca, N.Y.: Cornell University Press, 1970); Kenneth A. Lockridge, *A New England Town, The First Hundred Years: Dedham, Massachusetts* (New York: Norton, 1970).

17. Maris A. Vinovskis, *Fertility in Massachusetts from the Revolution to the Civil War* (New York: Academic Press, 1981).

18. Edmund S. Morgan, *The Puritan Family: Religion and Domestic Relations in Seventeenth-Century New England* (New York: Harper and Row, 1966); Roger Thompson, *Sex in Middlesex: Popular Mores in a Massachusetts County, 1649–1699* (Amherst: University of Massachusetts Press, 1986).

19. Thompson, *Sex in Middlesex.*

20. Daniel Scott Smith and Michael S. Hindus, "Premarital Pregnancy in America, 1640–1971: An Overview and Interpretation," *Journal of Interdisciplinary History* 5 (1975): 537–70; Patricia J. Tracy, *Jonathan Edwards, Pastor: Religion and Society in Eighteenth-Century Northampton* (New York: Hill and Wang, 1979).

21. Smith and Hindus, "Premarital Pregnancy in America."

22. Smith and Hindus, "Premarital Pregnancy in America"; Daniel Scott Smith, "Parental Power and Marriage Patterns: An Analysis of Historical Trends in Hingham, Massachusetts," *Journal of Marriage and the Family* 35 (1973): 406–18.

23. Vinovskis, *"Epidemic."*

24. Susan Harari and Maris A. Vinovskis, "Rediscovering the Family in the Past," in Kurt Kreppner and Richard M. Lerner, eds., *Family Systems and Life-Span Development* (Hillsdale, N.J.: Lawrence Erlbaum, 1989), pp. 381–94.

25. Lois G. Carr and Lorena S. Walsh, "The Planter's Wife: The Experience of White Women in Seventeenth-Century Maryland," in Michael Gordon, ed., *The American Family in Social-Historical Perspective*. 3rd ed. (New York: St. Martin's Press, 1983), pp. 321–46.

26. *Ibid.*

27. Susan Juster, "Disorderly Women: The Feminization of Sin in New England, 1770–1830." Paper presented at the annual meeting of the Social Science History Association, Chicago, 1988.

28. Vern L. Bullogh, *The Subordinate Sex: A History of Attitudes Toward Women* (Urbana: University of Illinois Press, 1973); *Physiology of Marriage* (Boston: John P. Jewett, 1856).

29. Alfred Kinsey, Wardell B. Pomeroy, and Clyde E. Martin, *Sexual Behavior in the Human Male* (Philadelphia: W. B. Saunders, 1948).

30. Ellen K. Rothman, *Hands and Hearts: A History of Courtship in America* (New York: Basic Books, 1984).

31. John Demos and Virginia Demos, "Adolescence in Historical Perspective," *Journal of Marriage and the Family* 31 (1969): 632–38; Susan Juster and Maris A. Vinovskis, "Changing Perspectives on the American Family in the Past," *Annual Review of Sociology* 13 (1987): 193–216; Juster and Vinovskis, "Adolescence in Nineteenth-Century America."

32. Lawrence A. Cremin, *American Education: The National Experience, 1783–1876* (New York: Harper and Row, 1980); Carl F. Kaestle and Maris A. Vinovskis, *Education and Social Change in Nineteenth-Century Massachusetts* (Cambridge: Cambridge University Press, 1980).

33. Carl N. Degler, *At Odds: Women and the Family in America from the Revolution to the Present* (New York: Oxford University Press, 1980); Karen A. Mason, Maris A.

Vinovskis, and Tamara K. Hareven, "Women's Work and the Life Course in Essex County, Massachusetts, 1880," in Tamara K. Hareven, ed., *Transitions: The Family and the Life Course in Historical Perspective* (New York: Academic Press, 1978), pp. 187–216.

34. Robert L. Griswold, *Family and Divorce in California, 1850–1900: Victorian Illusions and Everyday Realities* (Albany: State University of New York, 1982).

35. Michael Grossberg, *Governing the Hearth: Law and Family in Nineteenth-Century America* (Chapel Hill: University of North Carolina Press, 1985).

36. Joan J. Brumberg, " 'Ruined' Girls: Changing Community Responses to Illegitimacy in Upstate New York, 1890–1920," *Journal of Social History* 18 (1985): 363–74.

37. Degler, *At Odds*, 308.

38. John Modell, *Into One's Own: From Youth to Adulthood in the United States, 1920–1975* (Berkeley: University of California Press, 1989), p. 78.

39. Brumberg, " 'Ruined' Girls."

40. All quotes in this paragraph from Otto Wilson, *Fifty Years of Work With Girls, 1893–1933: The Story of the Florence Crittenton Homes* (Alexandria, Va.: Florence Crittenton Mission, 1933), p. 71.

41. Mintz and Kellogg, *Domestic Revolutions*, p. 108.

42. Kinsey et al., *Sexual Behavior in the Male*; Alfred C. Kinsey, Wardell B. Pomeroy, Clyde E. Martin, and Paul H. Gebhard, *Sexual Behavior in the Human Female* (Philadelphia: W. B. Saunders, 1953).

43. Wardell B. Pomeroy, *Dr. Kinsey and the Institute for Sex Research* (New York: Harper and Row, 1972); Paul Robinson, *The Modernization of Sex: Havelock Ellis, Alfred Kinsey, William Masters and Virginia Masters* (New York: Harper and Row, 1976).

44. Kinsey et al., *Sexual Behavior in the Female*, pp. 242–64.

45. *Ibid.*, p. 298.

46. *Ibid.*, p. 287.

47. *Ibid.*, p. 288.

48. *Ibid.*, pp. 295–97.

49. *Ibid.*, pp. 299–300.

50. *New York Times*, 21 October 1950, p. 14.

51. Rothman, *Hands and Hearts*.

52. Beth L. Bailey, *From Front Porch to Back Seat: Courtship in Twentieth-Century America* (Baltimore: Johns Hopkins University Press, 1988); Modell, *Into One's Own*, pp. 86–90.

53. Modell, *Into One's Own*, pp. 96–99.

54. Vinovskis, "Epidemic," p. 26.

55. Modell, *Into One's Own*, p. 135.

56. Andrew J. Cherlin, *Marriage, Divorce, and Remarriage* (Cambridge: Harvard University Press, 1981).

57. Justin C. Landis and Mary G. Landis, *Personal Adjustment, Marriage, and Family Living* (New York: Prentice-Hall, 1955), p. 66.

58. Maxine Davis, *Sex and the Adolescent* (New York: Pocket Books, 1958), p. 125.

59. Modell, *Into One's Own*, p. 237; Ann Landers, *Ann Landers Talks to Teenagers about Sex* (New York: Prentice-Hall, 1963), pp. 22–23.

60. Landis and Landis, *Personal Adjustment*, p. 69.

61. Ann Landers, *Landers Talks to Teenagers*, p. 31.

62. *Ibid.*, p. 47.

63. Landis and Landis, *Personal Adjustment*, p. 79.

64. E. A. Haupt, *The* Seventeen *Book of Young Living* (New York: Popular Library, 1957), p. 148.

65. Landers, *Landers Talks to Teenagers*, p. 45.

66. Davis, *Sex and the Adolescent*, p. 145.

67. Landis and Landis, *Personal Adjustment*, p. 155.

68. Landers, *Landers Talks to Teenagers*, p. 43.

69. Landis and Landis, *Personal Adjustment*, p. 78.

70. *Ibid.*, p. 133.

71. Haupt, Seventeen *Book of Young Living*, p. 189.

72. Landis and Landis, *Personal Adjustment*, p. 134.

73. Davis, *Sex and the Adolescent*, p. 157.

74. James Gilbert, *A Cycle of Outrage: America's Reaction to the Juvenile Delinquent in the 1950s* (New York: Oxford University Press, 1986).

75. Thomas Doherty, *Teenagers and Teenpics: The Juvenilization of American Movies in the 1950s* (Boston: Unwin Hyman, 1988).

76. Gilbert, *Cycle of Outrage*, pp. 190–91.

77. David M. Considine, "The Depiction of Adolescent Sexuality in Motion Pictures, 1930–1980." Ph.D. diss., University of Wisconsin, 1981.

78. Irwin Garfinkel and Sara S. McLanahan, *Single Mothers and Their Children: A New American Dilemma* (Washington, D.C.: Urban Institute Press, 1986).

79. Cheryl Hayes, ed., *Risking the Future: Adolescent Sexuality, Pregnancy, and Childbearing* (Washington, D.C.: National Academy Press, 1987), 1:65.

80. Rochelle Gatlin, *American Women since 1945* (Jackson: University of Mississippi Press, 1987); Mintz and Kellogg, *Domestic Revolutions*.

81. Lenore J. Weitzman, *The Divorce Revolution: The Unexpected Social and Economic Consequences for Women and Children in America* (New York: Free Press, 1985).

82. Hayes, *Risking the Future*, 58.

83. Alan Guttmacher Institute, *11 Million Teenagers: What Can Be Done about the Epidemic of Adolescent Pregnancies in the United States* (New York: Planned Parenthood Federation of America, 1976).

84. Vinovskis, *"Epidemic."*

85. Wilson, *Fifty Years of Work with Girls*, p. 14.

86. Maris A. Vinovskis, "Historical Perspectives on Adolescent Pregnancy," in Margaret Rosenheim and Mark Testa, eds., *Teenage Parenting, Policies of the 1990s*.

87. Frank F. Furstenberg, Jr., Jeanne Brooks-Gunn, and Lindsay Chase-Lansdale, "Teenaged Pregnancy and Childbearing," *American Psychologist* 44 (1989): 313–20.

88. Lindsay Chase-Lansdale and Maris A. Vinovskis, "Should Adolescent Mothers Be Discouraged from Marrying?" *Public Interest* 87 (1987): 23–37.

DIANA M. PEARCE

2 "CHILDREN HAVING CHILDREN": TEENAGE PREGNANCY AND PUBLIC POLICY FROM THE WOMAN'S PERSPECTIVE

They have no ability to make rational adult decisions, or appropriate choices. . . . The children have absolutely no idea. They cannot make a decision about whether to buy jeans or milk for their babies. They basically lack decision-making skills.
—Donna Bryant, Executive Director, Urban Affairs Corporation

"Children having children" is a phrase that has been key to making teenage pregnancy a major national concern.[1] It is a powerful phrase, as are its corresponding images, such as those of the Children's Defense Fund posters on teen pregnancy. For example, one poster features a very young, very pregnant girl, with the caption, "She learned to multiply before she could divide." But it achieves its power at the cost of depicting teenage mothers as child victims, even as failures, even though the portrayal is almost always sympathetic.

"Children having children" is a phrase that—whether intended or not—excludes perspectives that view pregnant and parenting teens as adults and can preclude the kinds of solutions that affirm and empower young women to control their own lives and overcome barriers they face.

This chapter considers how viewing teen pregnancy from the perspective of "children having children" affects public debates and public policies

46

about teenage pregnancy. Sometimes this perspective is made explicit, while at other times it is buried in moral, medical, or other arguments. Nevertheless, public debates and policy often cast an issue in strong relief, revealing not only the public's beliefs about "the facts" but also its moral construction of the problem. In the case of teenage pregnancy the issues raised are many, including sexual freedom, single parenting, welfare dependence, and the underclass.[2]

Causes of Teenage Pregnancy

In the strictly physiological sense, "children having children" is an oxymoron. In fact, in our own national history and in much of the world today, marriage and childbirth for teenage women are the norm. Thus the definition of teenagers who become pregnant as children reflects a cultural construction of the ending of childhood that is considerably later than the actual physical transition.

Becoming pregnant as a teen/child is in fact the result of two sets of related but separate actions: becoming sexually active and not practicing (effective) contraception. It is striking to note that teen pregnancy programs that derive from the perspective of "children having children" almost always focus on the first behavior—becoming sexually active at "too early" an age—to the virtual exclusion of an emphasis on the second behavior, being sexually responsible. Of course, emphasizing preventing teenage pregnancy by limiting teen sex clearly reflects the notion that teens are children and as children should not be engaging in behavior that is defined as adult. On the other hand, emphasizing responsible sexual practices accepts teens as adults—at least in the area of sexual behavior—and seeks in fact to reinforce responsible adult sexual behavior and choices.

The debate over school-based clinics for teens illustrates these contrasting views of teens as either children inappropriately engaging in (adult) sexual behavior, or adults behaving as adults sexually, but irresponsibly. The overriding concern of public policymakers, one on which proposals for such clinics often rise and fall, is whether the presence of a clinic near or in a high school encourages—some would say even entices—increased numbers of teenagers to become sexually active. For example, even though a *Washington Post* article discusses at length several studies that show that school-based clinics lower pregnancy rates, prevent repeat pregnancies, lower perinatal deaths, reduce the post-partum drop-out rate, as well as address other teenage health issues (drug and alcohol abuse, diabetes, and so forth) in the school, the article is headlined "Counselling by School Clinics Said to Aid Sexual Restraint."[3] As a result, although school-based clinics are apparently more effective in preventing teenage pregnancy than other types of prevention programs, fear of encouraging sex among children derails them: the survey of states made by the House of Representatives' Select Committee on Children, Youth, and Families in 1986 found that six states had proposed legislation during the previous year to create school-based clinics, but it had not passed in any of them.[4]

Indeed, for some legislators, the real issue is teens becoming sexually active, not teen pregnancy. In the Select Committee survey, the Minority report expressed dismay that the reduction in teen births had been achieved by increased abortions rather than through a reduction in sexual activity among adolescents, and that little attention had been accorded in the main report on how to "prevent teens from becoming sexually active."[5]

Laws and policies mandating parental notification and permission to obtain health services, birth-control information, and contraceptives as well as abortions are also indicators of a view that the real problem behind adolescent pregnancy is that children are inappropriately engaging in adult sexual behavior, and that adult control, especially parental authority, over teenagers should be central to any adolescent pregnancy prevention program.

Although rarely mentioned, the impact of "children having children" campaigns on teens themselves—whether they are sexually active, already pregnant, or parenting—is at best confusing and at worst off-putting, although they are the very people the programs seek to reach. If, as many researchers have demonstrated, early sexual activity and "premature" parenthood are the result of teens asserting or confirming their adulthood, being told they are children is, at a minimum, alienating.

In addition, the "children having children" perspective may be perceived as ethnic or class oppression; that is, it may be seen as white and/or middle-class program staff seeking to impose standards of behavior that are alien and inappropriate to the cultures of the teens themselves. Particularly for young poor and/or minority women, many adolescent pregnancy prevention programs do not affirm the positive impulse underlying early sexuality and motherhood: the desire to achieve or gain recognized adult status. Thus, for many teen parents, their families, and their communities, casting teenage parenthood as an immature act of a child that has mostly negative consequences is seen as at best naive and at worst evidence of deep misperceptions of their lives. "Children having children" campaigns miss the point that in the context of the available choices, particularly for minority, poor, and rural youth, becoming a teen parent *is* a rational, often acceptable (to the teen's immediate community or family), adult choice. Indeed, in some communities teenage motherhood is both normative and traditional: for example, since the early twentieth century, it has been the pattern for almost 40 percent of black women in the United States to become mothers before they turn 20 years old.[6]

Finally, it should be noted that teenage pregnancy prevention strategies are differentiated by gender. To the extent that males are included at all, which is minimal at best, they are targeted with messages that assume that they are sexually active and focus on "responsible" behavior, thus implicitly accepting their adult status. One poster states, for example, that "All brothers should not be fathers." In contrast, both the depiction of females and the messages sent them often combine an emphasis on failure ("flunking" a pregnancy test) with suggestions that teenage females are more concerned with childish issues: for example, one poster says, "Try explaining this pimple" (referring to the bellybutton on a very pregnant stomach), and another compares having a child to being "grounded" for eighteen years. Lack of acceptance of sexual activity in teenage females results in a message, though covert, emphasizing postponement, "just say no," and similar approaches that are simply not used for male teens; it also means that there is no parallel poster with the statement, "Not all sisters should be mothers." Even liberals sometimes seem uncertain whether a strategy of encouraging sexual responsibility in sexually active young *women* is desirable, reflecting an ambivalence about the choices made by young women that is rarely expressed for male teenagers. In short, the double standard is still with us. Moreover, it means that "children having children" is implicitly more about the inappropriateness of young women's than young men's behavior.

Welfare Policies toward Teenage Parents

Although all teenage parents are affected by the view that they are "children having children," poor parents, specifically teen mothers on welfare, are particularly affected. Three welfare policies reflecting this perspective were implemented during the 1980s for teenage parents; these changes have restricted the income support, choice of living arrangements, and schooling and employment options for poor teenage mothers. Let us examine each of these in turn.

The first policy classifies the minor parent who is living with her or his parents as a child. Up until 1984, it was possible for a minor parent to be eligible for income support through Aid to Families with Dependent Children (AFDC, or welfare), regardless of whether she lived with her parent(s). That is, only her and her child's income would be counted toward eligibility. The changes in federal law passed in 1984 instituted "grandparent deeming," which mandates that all of the household's resources be counted as available to support the child for whom AFDC eligibility is being sought. This change makes the minor parent as well as the grandchild the responsibility of the grandparents, thus treating the minor parent as a dependent child, and the grandparents as the only responsible adults. This has led to resentment on the part of the grandparents, who do not feel that they should be held responsible for their daughter's child.[7] It has also decreased the number of teenage parents with access to services and income support: in some cases, although the single parent and child qualify separately, they do not qualify when the whole household is considered, even though it may be quite poor.[8] Some poor teen parents are thus forced to choose between what welfare provides (income and services, including health care through Medicaid) and what living with their families offers (emotional support, help with child care, and the like). Many cannot have both as it now stands.

The second policy change was instituted to limit the number of single parents, especially teenage parents, who set up separate households, by requiring teen parents to live with their own parents. The policy came about in part because influential research by Ellwood and Bane had determined that although availability of welfare does not encourage *formation* of single-parent families, welfare does *facilitate* setting up a separate household by minor parents once a single-parent family has been formed.[9] Since for many years policymakers have widely assumed that the tendency of women who go on welfare as teenagers to become relatively long-term welfare recipients is due to, or at least significantly encouraged by, the formation of separate households, they therefore sought to limit the number of separate households set up by teenage mothers on welfare. This concern with long-term welfare dependency, coupled with a continuing view of adolescent parents as inappropriately engaging in adult behavior, led to the provision in the Family Support Act of 1988 (FSA: the federal welfare reform act) that allows states to require minor parents to live with their parent(s) in order to receive AFDC. Though most minor parents do live with their parents, the change has meant that the burden of proof is generally now on the minor parent to demonstrate why she should *not* live with her parent(s). It should not be assumed that all minor parents are going to assert their rights to challenge this requirement even when they should. In fact, it is likely that in cases of abuse, or overcrowding and stress, in the grandparents' household, this rule's effect will not be in the best interest of teenage mothers or their parents.

The combination of this provision with the earlier mandate of "grandparent deeming" has made it difficult for poor teenage parents to assume the roles and responsibilities of adult heads of household, for they get little or no public support for doing so. Poor teen parents who turn to welfare find that the choice to become a parent is both condemned by the larger society and privatized as the problem of the grandparents involved. In the eyes of AFDC today, the teenage parent is viewed as the responsibility of *her* parents—she is still their "child"—both economically and in terms of making judgments about her future.

A third policy, included in the FSA, puts new emphasis on education and training meant to lead to rapid employment for most welfare recipients. But although it exempts most mothers of children of less than 3 years old (which states can lower to less than 1 year), teenage mothers are treated more harshly: they can be required to participate in educational activities immediately after their child's birth.

Under the FSA, each state must require welfare recipients who are teen mothers, and who have not finished high school, to return to school full time, regardless of the age of their youngest child. In addition, if it is determined that 18- and 19-year-old parents are failing to make "good progress" in school or that education is "inappropriate" in individual cases, the state may require these teenage mothers to participate in whatever other work and training programs the state deems appropriate, again, regardless of the age of their children.

Even more than welfare recipients generally, this treatment virtually denies teenage parents any rights to determine what they and their children need, thus reinforcing their "child" status. Moreover, it devalues the teens' parenting and ability to decide what is best for themselves and their young children: by implication, *any* childcare is better than the teen parents' own parenting. Finally, by mandating that all poor teenage parents on welfare must return to school, the policy ignores the problems of educational institutions and assumes that a high school education, as it is now constituted, is the answer for all teenage parents.

All three of these provisions reflect a view that teenage parents are "children having children" and therefore need to be treated as children: children live with their parents, children do not make their own decisions, even about their own lives, and children belong in school. As children, they are incapable by definition of taking on the adult role of "parents": therefore, anyone else, such as a grandparent or childcare worker, is acceptable, perhaps even preferable, as a parent substitute or co-parent.

It should be noted, finally, that in this area, as with the poster campaigns and in other policies, there is a difference by gender. Although the FSA does escalate the efforts of the government to collect child support from absent parents (nearly always fathers) and has a voluntary demonstration project targeted on teen fathers (which provides temporary employment, to increase their child support), both of the FSA provisions treat the teen fathers as adults. In contrast, the harsh treatment of poor parents who turn to welfare falls overwhelmingly on teenage mothers. While teenage mothers are given little choice but to live with their parents and return to school (if they wish to receive income support, health care through Medicaid, food stamps, and other benefits), no one has suggested that nonsupporting teen fathers be forced to return to school or go to work so that they can pay child support.

Teenage Pregnancy and Welfare Dependency

Teenage pregnancy is often seen as at the heart of the larger problem of long-term welfare dependency. What is problematic about welfare dependency, particularly *long-term* dependency, is not that women are dependent, for women are supposed to be dependent on men—first their fathers and then their husbands—but that they are *not* supposed to be dependent on public income support.[10]

In fact, of course, the real issue behind the relation between teenage pregnancy and welfare dependency is single parenting—in other words, mothers living and surviving economically without men. The problem is usually seen to be the lack of fathers or male role models as both cause and consequence of teenage pregnancy.[11] Although the public policy concern is ostensibly the fiscal burden of supporting single-parent families for relatively long periods of time, it is the specter of single-parent families existing without need of men living in the households that provides the emotional steam behind this issue.[12] Teen parents, both because many come from single-parent homes and because many have never married, particularly evoke this fear. As one teenage mother stated on Bill Moyers's television show on teen pregnancy when asked whether she needed help from a man in raising her child, "Not really. I don't have a father. My father wasn't in the home. So, you know, it really—male figures are not substantially important in the family."[13]

Likewise, public policy solutions reflect ambiguity about what is the real problem and therefore the real solution. Thus, the Family Support Act, in addition to the specific provisions described above that treat teen mothers as children, also has provisions which mandate that states target welfare recipients who first became mothers when they were teenagers, because of their higher risk of becoming long-term welfare recipients. Of course, these FSA mandates giving priority in job training and education programs to women who are or were teenage mothers essentially treat them as adults. At the same time, however, because the programs themselves are underfunded, and thus cannot provide meaningful education and training or adequate support services, they cannot lead to real independence and economic self-sufficiency for most participants. Thus, this one instance of acknowledging adult status to teenage mothers remains in most cases a hollow gesture. Worse, in times of recession and state budget cuts, they become a means of harassment and continued poverty for teenage mothers and their children, as they are forced through short-term programs and into low-wage, dead-end jobs. In sum, the none-too-clear message to the teenager embodied in welfare programs and policies is: "You are a child, even if you become a parent, so you should live with your parents and/or go back to school. You should not be dependent upon welfare, especially for a long time, nor should you expect that welfare-related education or training programs will help you become *really* economically self-sufficient, and/or economically independent of men."

Teenage Pregnancy and the Underclass

Current policy formulations incorporating the "children having children" perspective regard teenage pregnancy as problematic, both because of what it indicates (inappropriately early sexual activeness) and what it leads to (single parenting and/or long-term welfare dependency). Much of the current debate on the root causes of poverty, however, see teen pregnancy as merely a symptom of the dynamics of modern poverty, specifically urban black poverty, summarized as the underclass phenomenon.

Underclass theory does not directly conceptualize teenage pregnancy as "children having children," but it does so indirectly in two ways. First, the underclass theory poses a one-way causal mechanism in which economic and social forces affect the actions of black men, who then act in underclass ways, including getting teenage women pregnant, making women the child-like victims. Women are not central actors, the subjects, but the acted upon, the objects, the dependent children. In addition, by lumping teenage pregnancy together with such phenomena as street crime and the drug trade as underclass behaviors, teenage pregnancy is indirectly cast as not only morally bad but as inappropriately adult behavior being exhibited by those too young to be sexually active and/or parents.

At the center of the underclass concept is the young black male: an unemployed, unmarried, drifting high school dropout, who is engaged in the underground economy at best or street crime and drugs at worst. Beyond that, the underclass theory evokes vague notions of a group of people who share these characteristics over time, pass them on from generation to generation, and are concentrated in ghettoes, largely isolated from the surrounding community.

The best-known recent formulation of the underclass theory is that of William J. Wilson.[14] According to Wilson the fundamental dynamic of the underclass phenomenon, driving all other trends including teenage pregnancy, is the increasing marginalization of the black male: his high rates of unemployment make him an undesirable candidate for marriage, his crimes result in incarceration and make him unavailable, and as the frequent victim of crime and violence, his numbers are reduced. In contrast, teen pregnancy is only an *indicator* of the underclass. In short, teenage pregnancy, along with high proportions of women-maintained households and high rates of welfare dependency, are epiphenomena.

Because underclass theories view teenage pregnancy, at least among poor, urban, black teens, as caused by what is happening in the lives of the fathers—especially in the economic-employment realm—such conceptions make teenage mothers passive and, implicitly, like dependent children. The lack of marriage or marital instability is attributed entirely to the economic position of black men.[15] The underclass concept does not accept that black women, like all women, may choose not to marry or to leave a man for reasons other than his economic or employment status; these other reasons may include domestic violence and abuse, or black women's ability to be economically independent.

Ironically, Wilson and other underclass theorists believe that increased single parenting among *white* women is due to their increased ability to achieve economic independence from men, even though black women have historically led—been ahead of—white women, both in labor force participation rates, and rates of single parenting. It is also ironic in that it gives agency to white but not black women. Underclass theory denies that black women, including young women who become pregnant, are independent actors in their own right. In short, underclass theory relegates teen mothers to the status of children.

Underclass theory also makes teenage pregnancy a behavior of "children having children" through a double set of syllogisms which couple male and female behaviors as equivalent indicators of the underclass, and deem behavior that violates presumably society-wide norms of responsible adult behavior as childish. First, a clear assumption of underclass theory is that female underclass behaviors—including teenage pregnancy and rates of women-maintained households and welfare use—are closely related to male underclass behaviors, such as street crime, drug use, and unemployment geographically, socially, and sexually. This assumption is deeply embedded in much underclass research, so that indicators of male and female underclass behaviors are used together and interchangeably to pinpoint the underclass.[16] At one level, this is simply moral logic: street crime and teenage pregnancy are both undesirable, "bad," and therefore, by definition, underclass behaviors. Equally important are the empirical limitations: male underclass behaviors, such as crime and drug use, are difficult to measure (should self-reports or police reports be used to determine rates and incidence?), statistically rarer, and difficult to pinpoint geographically (should the location be the address of the crime, of the criminal, or of the victim?). Out-of-wedlock births or welfare use, by contrast, are a matter of public record, geographically more easily designated, and more common.

Even more problematic than the geographical linking of male and female underclass behaviors is the social-sexual linking, the presumption, in other words, that the males engaging in underclass behaviors are the fathers of the children born to teenage mothers. The sheer numbers, of course, make that impossible—many more black women become mothers as teenagers (approximately 40 percent) than there are underclass men: potential fathers who engage in street crime and drugs as a way of life. Anecdotal evidence (unfortunately, there is little research that addresses the issue) suggests that a significant proportion of the children born to unmarried teenage mothers have fathers who are not only *not* teens, and often much older, but are stable, employed, and sometimes married to other women.

The public policy implications of underclass theories are not yet clear. But the prospects are not positive, particularly for those concerned about teenage pregnancy. If teen pregnancy and, by extension, welfare dependency and the increase in women-maintained families are seen as primarily the result of economic marginalization of black men, it will be difficult to focus public policy attention on the need for programs that give young mothers access to nontraditional job training and that emphasize developing their capacity to create alternative life plans, become economically independent, raise their self-esteem, and the like. Underclass theories can also be used to deemphasize structural factors that limit opportunities, deflecting attention from strategies that address the continuing barriers of race as well as gender.

Elements of a Feminist Public Policy Agenda on Teenage Pregnancy

Rather than outline a programmatic approach to teenage pregnancy, I think the first step is to envision how abandoning the "children having children" perspective would change the ways in which policymakers address teen pregnancy issues.

First, such a change in perspective would mean the affirmation of young women who have chosen to be sexually active, an implicit acknowledgment of their status as adults in this sphere. That would, in turn, mean an adult-oriented emphasis on making available the means to make free choices about their sexual activities and the consequences of such actions. Contraception, abortion, and prenatal care would be available regardless of income, race, and residence, and without requiring permission from parents or parent substitutes. Abortion rights in particular should be more actively extended to those precluded from exercising them because of lack of money.

Second, the policy would mean that those young women who choose to have children would be supported in that choice; rather than castigating and isolating them—which seems to have little effect anyway—the goal would be to enhance the chances that they will become both good parents and productive citizens. Programs for pregnant and parenting teens and those at risk would seek to empower young women to make their own choices about their futures and to support those choices, through the availability of educational programs, support services, and health care suited to their particular needs.

Third, it would mean that welfare programs, rather than taking away choices and controlling teens' lives, would instead support the choices of parenting teens regarding education, employment, parenting, and living arrangements (with their parents, with other young parents or adults, or on their own). Not only would welfare enable teen mothers to take control of their own lives, it would also no longer decide a priori what was best for all teen mothers.

Fourth, this policy would mean respect and support for community and cultural institutions, particularly in minority communities that can and do provide support for teenage mothers. It would mean the development of programs to support and strengthen the kin networks and extended family relationships that have been shown to provide needed support to teenage mothers.[17] Conversely, it would mean a decreased emphasis on marriage and the isolated nuclear family as the only viable family form or locus for parenting.

Finally, it would mean that all programs wou'd explicitly seek to make teenage women proud to be women, utilizing methods such as support groups and grass-roots neighborhood-based organizations (such as tenant organizations) that have been important in developing the self-esteem for women of all ages and economic conditions.

In sum, abandoning the "children having children" perspective would mean providing young women with the opportunity to make a real, free choice whether to become pregnant or to bear a child. Having a child is a positive act—but the consequences that follow in American society are disproportionately negative for many teens. Thus, in order to make the choice a really free one, we must make efforts to reduce the negative consequences, both economic and emotional, borne by teenage mothers and their children.

Of course, ultimately, abandoning "children having children" means valuing women of *all* ages and valuing the work that *all* mothers do. In public policy terms, this means broadbased programs that reduce women's poverty and support them in their roles as parent and family caregiver: universal childcare, pay equity, desegregation of occupations, equal access to health care for children as well as adults, decent income support (welfare and child allowances), enforced child support, and so forth. The agenda is a long one, but there is a real connection between the way we conceptualize teenage pregnancy in public policy and public policies toward employed women, single parents, and teenage sexuality. Discarding the phrase "children having children" is thus the first step not only toward helping young teenage mothers have better lives but also toward opening up the opportunities for all women to lead fuller lives, no matter how far they depart from the prescribed norms of marriage and motherhood.

Notes

1. See, e.g., Children's Defense Fund, *Preventing Children Having Children.* Clearinghouse Paper No. 1 (Washington, D.C.: Children's Defense Fund, 1985); Dorothy I. Height, "What Must Be Done about Children Having Children," *Ebony,* March 1985, 76–84.

2. Kristin Luker, "The Social Construction of Teenage Pregnancy." Unpublished paper.

3. Center for Population Options, "Survey Shows School-Based Clinics Do Not Cause Promiscuity" (Washington, D.C.: Center for Population Options, 6 March 1987); "Counselling by School Clinics Said to Aid Sexual Restraint," *Washington Post,* 16 March 1987 (citing CPO and Johns Hopkins studies).

4. U.S. Congress. House. Select Committee on Children, Youth and Families, "Teen Pregnancy: What is Being Done? A State-by-State Look" (Washington, D.C.: U.S. GPO, 1986).

5. House. Select Committee, "Teen Pregnancy," p. 378.

6. Height, "What Must Be Done," p. 78.

7. House. Select Committee, "Teen Pregnancy," pp. 70–73.

8. *Ibid.*

9. David Ellwood and Mary Jo Bane, "The Impact of AFDC on Family Structure and Living Arrangements." Report to the U.S. Department of Health and Human

Services (Washington, D.C.: U.S. Department of Health and Human Services, 1984). It should be noted that this research was done on data from the 1970s and does not reflect the dramatic increase in housing costs in the 1980s, which has made the issue of separate households moot for most welfare-recipient families, especially teenage parents.

10. Deborah Zinn, *A Socio-historical Analysis of the Concept of Dependency, 1930–1980.* Ph.D. diss., University of Michigan, 1986.

11. See William Julius Wilson, *The Truly Disadvantaged: The Inner City, the Underclass, and Public Policy* (Chicago: University of Chicago Press, 1987); also, Elijah Anderson, "Sex Codes and Family Life among Inner-city Youths," *Annals of the American Academy of Political and Social Sciences* 501 (January 1989): 59–78.

12. See Rose Weitz, "What Price Independence? Social Reactions to Lesbians, Spinsters, Widows, and Nuns," in Jo Freeman, ed., *Women: A Feminist Perspective,* 3rd ed. (Palo Alto, Calif.: Mayfield, 1984), for a discussion of the similar historical and cross-cultural reactions to women who became "too" independent of men, individually or collectively.

13. CBS Reports, "The Vanishing Family: Crisis in Black America," 18 February 1986.

14. Wilson, *Truly Disadvantaged.*

15. Wilson, *Truly Disadvantaged.*

16. Wilson, *Truly Disadvantaged;* Erol Ricketts and Isabel V. Sawhill, "Defining and Measuring the Underclass," *Journal of Policy Analysis and Management* 7, 2 (1988): 316–25. Note that the latter, however, does not use teen pregnancy or motherhood as an underclass indicator, but the authors do use as indicators the proportion of single mothers of all ages and the proportion of them on welfare as indicators of underclassness of a neighborhood/census tract.

17. Carol Stack, *All Our Kin: Strategies for Survival in a Black Community* (New York: Harper and Row, 1974).

SALLY MACINTYRE
SARAH CUNNINGHAM-BURLEY

3 TEENAGE PREGNANCY AS A SOCIAL PROBLEM: A PERSPECTIVE FROM THE UNITED KINGDOM

Trends in Teenage Pregnancy in the United Kingdom

Recent trends in teenage pregnancy in the United Kingdom largely resemble those discernible at older ages. We think it important to emphasize this, because the slippage between concepts described below can lead people to forget that many women over 20 have unplanned or unwanted pregnancies and may be unmarried or unsupported. It is also worth pointing out that no one expresses much concern about older mothers—for example those having children when they are over 35 or 40—even though they may face obstetric and social hazards and may often be unsupported, and even though the rates of pregnancy among these age groups are increasing.

In the United Kingdom the birth rate for 15- to 19-year-olds peaked in 1971 (at 50.6 per thousand births) and has been declining since (to 30.9 per thousand births in 1987). This decline has mirrored the decline shown in fertility rates for all ages taken together (from 83.2 in 1971 to 62.0 in 1987). Fertility rates for women age 35 and over have, however, risen since 1977. The fertility rates for teenagers in England and Wales are projected to remain stable into the next century, while those for 30- to 39-year-olds are expected to increase.[1]

The number of live births to teenagers has been decreasing within marriage and increasing outside marriage. In England and Wales the number of live births within marriage to women under 20 fell from 61,100 in 1971 to 15,600 in 1987; the numbers occurring outside marriage increased from 21,600 to 60,400 over the same period. Again, this pattern is not peculiar to teenagers but is noticeable at all ages: taking all ages together, the numbers occurring within marriage fell from 717,500 to 523,100, and the numbers occurring outside marriage increased from 65,700 to 158,400 between 1971 and 1987. The trend toward births outside formal marriage is marked, continuing at all ages, and in no way unique to teenagers.[2] The outcome of teenage pregnancies has changed over the last decade. Between 1975 and 1985 the proportion of pregnancies in women under 20 that ended in abortion increased from 26 percent to 33 percent, those which ended in illegitimate births registered only by the mother rose from 13 percent to 17 percent, illegitimate births registered by both parents rose from 8 percent to 24 percent, and births within marriage fell from 31 percent to 15 percent. Although the proportion of teenage pregnancies ending in abortion has increased more than it has for older women, the *numbers* of abortions to women under 20 have not been increasing faster than the numbers for other ages. The total number of pregnancies in women under 20 rose from 112,000 to 119,000 over the 1980s.[3]

Again it must be stressed that these trends are not unique to teenagers; between 1976 and 1986, total pregnancies at all ages rose from 672,000 to 819,000. The proportion ending in illegitimate births registered by both parents rose from 4 percent to 13 percent, and the proportion of births within marriage fell from 72 percent to 58 percent.[4] Particularly striking at all ages is the increasing proportion of births occurring outside marriage (though not necessarily to single parents; many of these unmarried parents may jointly register the birth and be cohabiting). Although the proportion of illegitimate live births as a proportion of all births has been increasing (from 8 percent in 1971 to 21 percent in 1986), so have the percentages of illegitimate live births registered in joint names (from 45 percent in 1971 to 66 percent in 1986).[5]

In sum, then, fertility rates and numbers of births are declining among teenagers in the United Kingdom; of teenage pregnancies, more are now likely to result in abortions or in births to unmarried parents. These trends are not specific to this age group, but in broad outline mirror what is happening to all ages (other than the 35 and over age group, among whom fertility rates are rising). A simple comparison of teenage pregnancies over time would reveal increasing numbers of abortions and illegitimate births and could lead to the conclusion that teen pregnancy is more problematic than a decade ago; placing the trends alongside those for all ages should help us avoid "teen-specific" expressions of concern, explanatory models, and suggested solutions.

Similar trends are evident in the United States. The number of births to women under 20 has fallen from 656,000 in 1970 to 480,000 in 1984. The rate per thousand women aged 10–14 remained similar (1.2 in 1970 and in 1984) and the rate per thousand women aged 15–19 dropped from 68.3 to 50.9 over this period.[6]

The teenage fertility rate is considerably higher in the United States than in other industrialized countries (although it is lower than that in many developing countries). In 1984 or 1985 the lowest rates were recorded in Japan (4.1 live births per thousand women ages 15–19) and northern European countries such as the Netherlands (6.8) and West Germany (8.6). Canada and Australia had rates of 23.2 and 26.5, respectively. Constituent countries of the United Kingdom had relatively high rates (Northern Ireland 28.7, England and Wales 29.5, Scotland 30.9). The rate for the United States, at 52.0, was the highest recorded by a considerable margin (22.0 per thousand more live births than the next highest rate).[7]

Clearie and his colleagues point out that a decline in the teenage birth rate, an increase in the abortion ratio, and the increasing proportion of illegitimate births are trends common to sixteen industrialized nations that were studied in the early 1980s.[8] Explanations for these trends therefore need to be sought at a broader level than in historical, cultural, or political features of individual countries.

Teenage Pregnancy as a Social Problem

Two problems are commonly found in the literature on teenage pregnancy. First, authors frequently simply *assume* that teenage pregnancy is a problem. Second, commentators often conflate aspects of teenage pregnancy that are analytically and empirically distinct—such as chronological age, marital status, and the planned or wanted nature of the pregnancy.

Until recently most commentators have not appeared to see any need to justify their concern with adolescent pregnancy. This failure to specify why we should be worried often proves particularly irritating because it leads to a lack of precision about the nature of the perceived problem of adolescent pregnancy. It is often simply take for granted that conceptions (or births or abortions) occurring in the teenage years are problematic. For whom they are problematic, and in what ways, are topics that are too infrequently discussed. But unless we are clear in our definition of the problem, how can we analyze its features or propose solutions to it?

Is the problem one of poverty, physical or psychological immaturity, role-confusion ("schoolgirl-mothers"), not being married, too early sexual activity, threatening the institution of the nuclear family (with its scripts for age-appropriate behavior), failure to complete education or training, making demands on welfare, precipitating early, fragile marriages, homelessness, or inadequate parenting skills? All these and more are implied and sometimes stated to be concomitants of teenage pregnancy. More often, however, they are bundled up together as a gestalt of "the problem."

Sometimes the problem seems to be defined as the frequency of teenage pregnancy—that the rate of teenage pregnancy is increasing, for example, or that it is higher than in other comparable countries. Denise Polit and Janet Kahn, two American authors, introduce their work thus:

> Teenage sexuality, pregnancy and parenthood have become topics of intense national debate in the United States. Although solutions to the problem are subject to considerable controversy, there is no doubt that a problem exists; the "fact" has been documented in terms of an increase in the rate of premarital intercourse among American adolescents; a higher rate of early childbearing in the U.S. than in other industrialized countries; and a range of negative consequences associated with teenage parenthood including high rates of prematurity and other health risks to the infant, and high rates of divorce, educational deficits, and economic hardship for the mother.[9]

That high rates of teenage pregnancy are in themselves seen as problematic is a highly culture-bound perception. Many countries in the developing world have much higher rates of teenage pregnancy than the United States but do not regard this as a problem; in these countries teenage pregnancy is the norm, both statistically and morally.[10]

British authors who conducted a survey of teenage pregnancy in Britain in the early 1980s noted in their report that fertility rates among teenage women had fallen from 50 to 31 per thousand between 1970 and 1980, and that the abortion rate had doubled from 9 to 18 per thousand over the same period. They then asked, "So why was a study of this kind thought to be necessary when teenage motherhood was no longer a growing phenomenon?[11] Their reply was twofold: early motherhood poses increased risks to both mother and child, and early parenthood has adverse effects on the future life chances of the young parents. That they felt the need to justify their survey in the light of a decreasing incidence of teenage pregnancy is interesting, for it suggests that had the incidence been rising, no such explanation might have been felt necessary. Other authors have stated simply that teenage pregnancy is a matter for concern, as here: "With the magnitude of teenage pregnancy and its accompanying disadvantages to adolescents, their children, and society, researchers increasingly are seeking answers to complicated questions about unmarried mothers. Whether unwed motherhood is viewed as a social evil, unfortunate accident, an irresponsible act, or the right of an individual, an important first step toward intervention is to determine its cause."[12] (Note here not only the assumption of a problem, but the slippage from the concept of adolescent pregnancy to that of unwed mothers.)

Because adolescent pregnancy is seen as a problem and those who engage in it as deviant socially, if not morally,[13] it is thought to be in need of explanation and there is a large literature trying to explain teenage pregnancy. One of our favorite conclusions in this field is: "*Probably* one of the most immediate causes of adolescent births is intercourse itself" (emphasis ours).[14] The tendency to try to account for deviant reproductive behavior, such as single women becoming pregnant or married women remaining childless while taking for granted the motives and antecedents of "orthodox" reproductive behavior has been noted before.[15] Ignorance about contraception, psychopathology, desire to prove adulthood, lack of family restraint, cultural patterns, desire to obtain welfare benefits, immorality, getting out of school—a host of reasons are given for childbirth in women under 20, while "maternal instinct" is thought to suffice for those over 20. Because explanations for "deviant" reproduction are separated from understanding of "normal" reproduction, most such explanations are weak, decontextualized, and naive.

What does require explanation is why teenage pregnancy is periodically viewed as such a social problem. The empirical magnitude of a problem need bear no relation to the amount of public outcry it evokes.[16] It is interesting that Simms and Smith's survey of teenage mothers and their partners was conducted when the fertility rate for teenagers in the United Kingdom was "the lowest since 1955."[17] Vinovskis has demonstrated that the concern in the United States that culminated in the Adolescent Health Services and Pregnancy Prevention Act of 1978 came at a time when both the rate and numbers of teenage pregnancies were declining (the rate had fallen by 44.8 percent during the previous twenty-five years).[18] Furstenberg and colleagues give an interesting account of the emergence of teenage childbearing as a social problem in the United States,[19] and Vinovskis's historical perspective provides a valuable corrective to descriptions of the "epidemic" of teenage pregnancy.[20] We think it important, especially in a volume of this sort, to raise the question of why teenage pregnancy is viewed with such concern in the contemporary United States, and why this concern has varied historically.

In the United Kingdom the view that adolescent pregnancy is detrimental to mother and baby has come under increasing challenge, with a number of commentators pointing to the confounding effects of lack of prenatal care, poor social and economic circumstances, and marital status on the apparent relation between youth and a variety of adverse outcomes.[21] Studies in the United Kingdom in the 1980s confirm that in many cases the assumed adverse outcomes either to do not occur or are explicable in terms of other correlates of adolescent pregnancy. For example, a Glasgow study reports that "pregnancy in the teenage girl is no more hazardous than pregnancy in older women and . . . the majority will enjoy a complication-free pregnancy. Despite the poor social background of our parents [the subjects], anaemia was the only significantly increased complication."[22] It was also found that the teenagers who remained single had higher rates of premature labor and perinatal mortality compared to those who were married, however, and that the unmarried teenagers were particularly at risk. In an analysis of Aberdeen data, it has similarly been shown that age was not a predictor of perinatal outcome when other variables such as social class, marital status, parity (number of previous pregnancies or children), and smoking were taken into account.[23] Wolkind and Kruk, comparing random samples of women experiencing first pregnancies in their teens and over 20, found that despite the greater likelihood of teens coming from a deprived background and experiencing material disadvantage, the teenage mothers and their children did as well as the older women and their children on a number of short-term and long-term measures. The mothers and children were followed up for seven years after the birth: "Almost equal numbers of teenagers and older women were, at the end of the study, living in two parent families. The children born to the mothers of the two groups did not differ significantly in any aspect of health, development and behaviour. Areas examined included birthweight, Apgar score, admission to hospital, episodes of illness and the prevalence of a wide variety of physical and behavioural symptoms shown in both home, and at 82 months, school."[24] We may now be in a phase of academic concern about the issue of teenage pregnancy in the United Kingdom that involves rejection of previous received wisdom about the damage and dangers of teenage pregnancy.[25]

Similar trends may be found in the United States. As Phipps-Yonas concluded from a review of the literature:

> There is consistent evidence from a number of studies that the typical expectant teenager is biologically ready for pregnancy and childbirth. She and her infant are not at risk medically, provided that she

received good prenatal care and nutrition—a big "if," since these conditions are often not met. Other summary statements are more difficult to make. While it is well established that many teenage mothers face futures marked by instability and failure, it is not clear that their subsequent problems are consequences of their early child-bearing; they may simply represent correlates, later components of patterns set down long before the pregnancies occurred.[26]

Because of the perception that teenage pregnancy is a problem, how-ever, investigators or their readers may focus on the evidence of difficulties and ignore evidence of lack of them. Frank Furstenberg and Kathleen Mullan Harris's analysis comparing the children of teen mothers in Bal-timore to their counterparts studied by the National Survey of Children (NSC), a representative survey of youth between the ages of 17 and 22, suggests that this perception may be exaggerated: "At least among blacks, teenage childbearing appears to have only a modest effect in determining the life chances of youths in their late teens. . . . The patterns of educa-tional attainment and early fertility among children of teen mothers in the Baltimore study and the NSC were almost identical. . . . Other measures of emotional well-being yielded comparable results. When compared to the children of later childbearers, the offspring of adolescent mothers did not do as well on a wide range of outcomes, but this differential in perfor-mance was not very large."[27] Other work by Furstenberg and colleagues reached similar conclusions.[28] Yet such important findings have not de-monstrably affected public perceptions; it is almost as though teenage pregnancy *must* be a problem.

We do not wish to deny that a pregnancy—and its outcome—may well be problematic for many teenagers. But we want to stress that it may be equally problematic for women of other ages. Because most studies of teenage pregnancy compare teenagers who become pregnant with teen-agers who do not rather than comparing teenagers who become pregnant with older women who become pregnant, this elementary point may be missed and all sorts of evils attributed to teenage pregnancies that are extrinsic to "teenageness."

Let us consider the hypothetical example of a woman of 16 and another of 26. Of the first it is often said that her motives for having a child are suspect because she seeks an object to love and to return her love, that she desires to achieve adult status, or that she wants to gain independence from her parents. But a 26-year-old might have identical motives, which in her case are taken to be normal and possibly admirable. These psychologi-cal motives are thus highly socially and age dependent, being considered pathological at one age and normal at another (indeed the 26-year-old who does *not* want a child to love and be loved by may be considered disturbed). The argument that 26-year-olds are more realistic about what it means to have a baby is often unsubstantiated. Indeed, we have found that teenagers may be more realistic about what to expect with motherhood than older women, both because they may more recently have had younger siblings in the house and because they may come from larger families.[29]

Relatedly, it is often assumed that a 16-year-old will be a lone and unsupported mother whereas a 26-year-old will be partnered and emotionally supported. Two points can be made about this, one short term and one long term. First, in Britain at least, the sort of woman who typically has a baby at 16 is more likely to be living with or near her family, gaining social support and practical services from them. The loneliest women, and those least well integrated into helpful networks, are often the geographically mobile middle-class women who do not have their first babies until their late 20s.[30] Second, children of lone mothers may not remain in a lone-mother family for very long. Among children registered solely by their mothers in the period 1978–81, nearly 40 percent were living in a married-couple family (or cohabiting couple describing themselves as married) by the time of the 1981 census.[31] Of children born in the early 1970s, 83 percent of those born to lone mothers were living in two-parent families by the age of 16, compared with 79 percent of children born to two-parent families.[32]

In the United States much of the concern about teenage motherhood is centered around educational and economic issues, early motherhood being seen as disruptive to education and financially ruinous. Although it is true that older women are more likely to have completed their education and be established in their occupations, having children can be highly disruptive of women's careers and costly (in terms of both direct and opportunity losses) at all ages. The argument that if only they forbore from having babies while in their teens women would succeed in the educational and occupational markets and therefore not live in poverty rings hollow in many industrialized societies, in which opportunities for emotionally and financially rewarding jobs for women are severely restricted.

The obverse of saying that the problems of teenage pregnancy are not specific to the teen years is that the pleasures of pregnancy and parenthood are not unique to older age groups; yet the literature on teenage pregnancy seems only to focus on the pains rather than the pleasures of early parenthood. Parents themselves often express the view that early childbearing is good for both parent and child: "It's good for the child to have you young while they are young."[33]

The Confusion of Concepts of Teenage Pregnancy

There is a pervasive tendency for people writing about teenage pregnancy to confuse four distinct (though sometimes empirically overlapping) concepts: pregnancy to women below the age of, say, 20; unplanned pregnancies; unwanted pregnancies; and pregnancies to unmarried or unsupported women. The slippage between the concepts of pregnancy in young women, unplanned or unwanted pregnancies, and pregnancies to unmarried or unsupported women is unhelpful but ubiquitous. In Colin Francome's article the summary mentions only the concept *teenage pregnancy*, but the first line of the text is: "The concern about *unwanted pregnancy* in recent years has been expressed in comments from parents, sex educators, the government and religious leaders" (emphasis ours).[34] Only indirect and oblique mention is made in the text of the fact that he is talking about young people. In a statement in a World Health Organization publication about pregnancy occurring "unexpectedly to a frightened teenager who anticipates serious social disapproval when her condition becomes known,"[35] the authors do not appear to think it necessary to specify that they are referring to an *unmarried* woman; we are supposed to assume it. In an article on the effect on adolescent sexual behavior of the availability of contraceptives at a local family planning clinic, Ruth Kornfield never states whether she (or the community she is studying) is concerned only with unmarried teenagers being sexually active and obtaining contraceptives, although it appears that this is probably the case; adolescent sexuality seems to be so thoroughly associated with premarital sexuality that marriage is never mentioned.[36] These examples could be multiplied many times; our intention is not to pillory particular authors but to point to the fact that defining the problem of teenage pregnancy is hindered by the continual confusion of different issues: youth, single status, and unplanned or unwanted pregnancies.

Drawing on data from a qualitative interview study of fifty-two women in Glasgow, Scotland, aged 16–25 who were pregnant with their first child, we can illustrate some of these issues. The study itself is part of a larger investigation of the relation between marital status and pregnancy outcome. The women were interviewed twice during their pregnancy and again after the birth about their health and way of life, social and material circumstances, and experience of pregnancy. All the pregnancies ended with live births. We can thus make some comparisons between the teenagers in this group and the older women. We shall focus here specifically on age and marital status, age and planned vs. unplanned pregnancies, and age and support.

Fifteen teenagers aged 16–19 were interviewed, and thirty-seven women aged 20–25. As would be expected from national data, not all the teenagers were single. Two were married when they became pregnant, and three married after they became pregnant but before the baby was born. (One of these had married, then separated.) Two of those who had conceived premaritally and one of the married women lived with their partner with their families of origin. The remaining ten were single, but the nature of their relationships with the fathers varied. One was cohabiting with the father. Five were in a stable relationship with the father, seeing him on most days, and the father was involved in plans for the future of the child and the mother. All these women felt that it was not the best time to move in with or marry the father: they wanted to wait and see how affairs turned out. Four of these were living with their families of origin and one with a friend, while waiting to be housed by the local authority in her own flat. Of the remaining four single teenagers, three maintained a relationship with the father but were less certain of a future together. Out of our fifteen teenagers, then, only one no longer saw the father of their child. She was not, however, totally unsupported: she lived with her sister and saw her large family frequently.

Of the thirty-seven women aged 20–25, a larger proportion were married at the time they conceived, as we would expect. Seventeen were married, of whom sixteen lived with their husbands only. A further four women married after they had become pregnant. Three of these initially lived with their husbands with their family of origin, and then moved into accommodation with their husbands only. One was living with her partner and subsequently married him. Of the sixteen single women in this age group, three (one of whom was divorced) were cohabiting, all three living in separate households. Three were single with no relationship with the father of the child; two of these lived with their families of origin and one in a hostel. As with the teenagers, few were unsupported by a partner or family. Another woman still saw the father but was unsure whether the relationship would continue. The remaining seven single women (one of whom was divorced) had a stable relationship with the father. Four of these were living with their family of origin and one with her grandparents, with whom she had always lived. Two had their own accommodations, although both of them spent a lot of time with their own and their partner's families.

The relation between age and marital status is thus more complicated than some of the literature assumes. Although a higher proportion of teenagers were single, many of these had stable relationships with the father. Indeed, one positive element of changing mores is that few of these expressed any felt pressure to marry. A nineteen-year-old woman, cohabiting with her boyfriend, said: "Oh well, we did at the beginning think about getting married before the baby was born, and I said well it's up to yourself (her boyfriend), I'm not bothered because I was always quite fond of him anyhow, and I fell pregnant and we were really happy about it, and I don't think you need to get married, really I don't."[37]

Young women may therefore be less likely to remain in a poor relationship because of pregnancy. Unmarried parenting is increasingly becoming the cultural norm among some sectors of the population. An eighteen-year-old woman who was engaged described how common young and unmarried parenthood was in her social group and how the news of her pregnancy evoked pleasure rather than censure: "I felt like at first I was like that—'oh no'—you know I felt I was really quite young and everything and I thought—'oh no—there's a lot of responsibility' but (my boyfriend) Alan was like that—'oh that's great!' and my pal was like that—'oh that's great, and everything, I'm going to be an aunty.' I find now like, my boyfriend, his brother got married a couple of weeks ago and his wife's pregnant as well, and there's two of his best pals, their girlfriends are pregnant at the same time." As we have pointed out, it is often assumed that pregnancies among teenagers but not among older women are unplanned and unwanted. The rising abortion rate among older women casts doubt on this assumption, as do our own interview data.

Most of the pregnancies among both the teenagers and the older women were described as unplanned. Of the teenagers, twelve said that their pregnancies were unplanned, and three of them got married after they became pregnant. A further three teenagers, two married, one cohabiting, described their pregnancies as planned.

Twelve of the women aged 20–25 said that their pregnancies were planned. Ten were married, two cohabiting. Five other pregnancies, four to women who were married and one to a woman who was cohabiting, could be described as semi-planned, to wit:

> SCB (SARAH CUNNINGHAM-BURLEY): Were you planning on having a family then?
>
> R (RESPONDENT): Well we were and we weren't.
>
> HUSBAND: Let's put it this way. We weren't taking any precautions, and if a family came we would be delighted, if it didn't we wouldn't be too concerned.

The remaining twenty pregnancies were described as unplanned, although the processes involved varied from habitually not contracepting, failure of contraception, or taking a chance. Three married women described their pregnancies as unplanned, as did the four who conceived premaritally and the thirteen single women. A 22-year-old woman said:

    R: I've got the cap.

  SCB: So you got pregnant using that?

    R: No, just being lazy, but we're quite happy now. I would have waited about another year I think. I would like to have been in a bigger house and then started a family, but it's happened this way and we'll get by.

It is important to note, however, that the unplanned pregnancies were seldom described as unwanted. A 20-year-old woman described her feelings thus: "It's not really affected me, I mean, I'm really really pleased that I'm pregnant." And a 21-year-old single woman described her family's feelings: "It'll be something, something new in the house, new life in the house."

How did social support, material circumstances, and life chances differ between the two groups? All fifteen teenagers interviewed described themselves as having a lot of support from family and friends. Indeed, many were living with their family of origin. Against this positive backdrop of closeness must be placed the material disadvantages that many of these young women and their families experienced, however. All of the teenagers had left school at the minimum leaving age, and nine said that they had no qualifications. Twelve were currently unemployed, and of the three who were working only one was planning to return to work after the baby was born.

Of the older women, twenty-nine described themselves as receiving a lot of support, especially from family, even though fewer of them lived with their families of origin. Six had little support: two because their families were not in the country, and the others because they either had little family or did not get on well with them. A further two described themselves as providing support for older parents. Most of the married women were living in their own homes, although they still saw their families on a regular basis. Many of the single women, however, still lived with their families of origin, thus receiving daily support and contact. More of the older group were advantaged in terms of material and educational resources: they were more likely to own their own houses, be employed, and have a higher level of education. Twenty-nine had left school at the minimum leaving age, of whom twelve had no qualifications. Thirteen were unemployed, and of those at work, most intended to return, at least part time, after their maternity leave.

Our data do not support the argument that teenage pregnancy per se results in poverty and disadvantage. The patterns of disadvantage were set before pregnancy, and the worst effects of pregnancy were mitigated by supportive family structures. The problems facing pregnant adolescents are real. But they are as likely to be a cause as a result of pregnancy. Until we can focus on them, we cannot give meaningful help to pregnant teenagers and their children.

Notes

1. Office of Population Censuses and Surveys (OPCS), *Population Trends* 54 (London: HMSO, Winter 1988).

2. OPCS, *Population Trends* 54.

3. Central Statistical Office (CSO), *Social Trends* 18 (1988) (London: HMSO, 1989).

4. CSO, *Social Trends* 19 (1989) (London: HMSO, 1989).

5. CSO, *Social Trends* 18.

6. U.S. Bureau of the Census, *Statistical Abstract of the United States 1987*. 107th ed. (Washington, D.C.: Department of Commerce, 1986), table 24.

7. United Nations Department of International Economic and Social Affairs, *U.N. Demographic Year Book* (New York: United Nations, 1988).

8. Andrew F. Clearie, Lucy Ann Hollingsworth, Marla Q. Jameson, and Murray L. Vincent, "International Trends in Teenage Pregnancy: An Overview of 16 Countries," *Biology and Society* 2 (1985): 23–30.

9. Denise Polit and Janet Kahn, "Early Subsequent Pregnancy among Economically Disadvantaged Teenage Mothers," *American Journal of Public Health* 76, 2 (February 1986): 167.

10. *U.N. Demographic Yearbook*, table 82.

11. Madeline Simms and Christopher Smith, *Teenage Mothers and Their Partners: A Survey in England and Wales*. Department of Health and Social Security Research Report, No. 15 (London: HMSO, 1986), p. 1.

12. Marie Patten, "Self Concept and Self Esteem: Factors in Adolescent Pregnancy," *Adolescence* 16 (Winter 1981): 775.

13. William Ray Arney and Bernard J. Bergen, "Power and Visibility: The Invention of Teenage Pregnancy," *Social Science and Medicine* 18, 1 (1984): 11–19.

14. Patten, "Self Concept and Self Esteem."

15. Sally Macintyre, *Single and Pregnant* (London: Croom Helm, 1977); Sally Macintyre, "Who Wants Babies? The Social Construction of Instincts," in Diana Barker and Sheila Allen, eds, *Sexual Divisions and Society* (London: Tavistock, 1976).

16. Herbert Blumer, "Social Problems as Collective Behaviour," *Social Problems* 18, 3 (1971): 298–306; R. C. Fuller and R. R. Myers, "The Natural History of a Social Problem," *American Sociological Review* 6 (1941): 321–28.

17. Simms and Smith, *Teenage Mothers and Their Partners*.

18. Maris Vinovskis, *An "Epidemic" of Adolescent Pregnancy? Some Historical and Policy Perspectives* (New York: Oxford University Press, 1988), p. 25.

19. Frank Furstenberg, Jr., Jeanne Brooks-Gunn and S. Philip Morgan, *Adolescent Mothers in Later Life* (Cambridge: Cambridge University Press, 1987).

20. Vinovskis, *"Epidemic."*

21. Sarah Cunningham-Burley, "The Epidemiology of Teenage Pregnancy." Paper presented at the Royal College of Physicians' conference on adolescent medicine, London, 17–18 March 1987; Susan Williams, John Forbes, Gillian McIlwaine, and Kathryn Rosenberg, "Poverty and Teenage Pregnancy," *British Medical Journal* 294 (January 1987): 20–21.

22. G. K. Osbourne, R. C. L. Howat and M. M. Jordan, "The Obstetric Outcome of Teenage Pregnancy," *British Journal of Obstetrics and Gynaecology* 88 (1981): 215–21.

23. Sarah Cunningham-Burley, Russell Ecob and Michael Samphier, "Marital Status and Pregnancy Outcome: A Multi-variate Analysis of Aberdeen Data." Paper presented at the annual meeting of the British Sociological Association, Medical Sociology Group, Scottish Section, Edinburgh, September 1988.

24. S. N. Wolkind and S. Kruk, "Teenage Pregnancy and Motherhood," *Journal of the Royal Society of Medicine* 78 (February 1985): 112–16.

25. W. Thomas Boyce, Catherine Schaefer, and Chris Uitti, "Permanence and Change: Psychosocial Factors in the Outcome of Adolescent Pregnancy," *Social Science and Medicine* 21, 11 (1985): 1279–87; B. Zuckerman, J. J. Alpert, E. Dooling, R. Hingson, H. Kayne, S. Morelock, and E. Oppenheimer, "Neonatal Outcome: Is Adolescent Pregnancy a Risk Factor?" *Pediatrics* 71 (1983): 489–93.

26. Susan Phipps-Yonas, "Teenage Pregnancy and Motherhood: A Review of the Literature," *American Journal of Orthopsychiatry* 50, 3 (July 1980): 419–20.

27. Frank Furstenberg, Jr., and Kathleen Mullan Harris, "When Fathers Matter/Why Fathers Matter: The Impact of Paternal Involvement on the Offspring of Adolescent Mothers" (chap. 10).

28. Frank F. Furstenberg, Jr., Jeanne Brooks-Gunn, and S. Philip Morgan, "Adolescent Mothers and Their Children in Later Life," *Family Planning Perspectives* 19, 4 (July/August 1987): 142–51; Furstenberg, Brooks-Gunn, and Morgan, *Adolescent Mothers.*

29. Sally Macintyre, *Expectations and Experiences of First Pregnancy.* Institute of Medical Sociology Occasional Paper, no. 5 (Aberdeen: University of Aberdeen, 1981).

30. Macintyre, *Expectations and Experiences of First Pregnancy.*

31. Audrey Brown, "Family Circumstances of Young Children," *Population Trends* 43 (1986): 18–23.

32. Lynda Clarke, "Children's Changing Circumstances: Recent Trends and Future Prospects." Paper presented at the British Society for Population Studies conference, "Population, Family, and Welfare Provision: Changing Structure and Choice," Birmingham, 6–8 September 1989.

33. Macintyre, *Expectations and Experiences of First Pregnancy.*

34. Colin Francome, "Unwanted Pregnancies amongst Teenagers," *Journal of Biosocial Science* 15 (1983): 139.

35. World Health Organization, *Young People's Health: A Challenge to Society.* Technical Report Series, no. 731 (Geneva: World Health Organization, 1986), p. 26.

36. Ruth Kornfield, "Who's to Blame: Adolescent Sexual Activity," *Journal of Adolescence* 8 (1985): 17–31.

37. All quotations from this study are from Sarah Cunningham-Burley, "Marital Status, Social Circumstance, and Health Behaviour: Preliminary Evidence from a Sociological Investigation of a Group of Primiparous Women." MRC Medical Sociology Unit Working Paper, no. 11. Glasgow, 1988.

ANN PHOENIX

4 THE SOCIAL CONSTRUCTION OF TEENAGE MOTHERHOOD: A BLACK AND WHITE ISSUE?

The United States and Britain share an overwhelmingly negative social construction of teenage motherhood. In both countries media reports and academic literature on women who give birth in their teenage years focus on problems associated with teenage motherhood. The two societies also share negative social constructions of their racial minorities. Academics, blacks and others, in both societies have devoted a great deal of time and energy to demonstrating how academic studies and the media are imbued with negative images of people of color.[1]

The issue of teenage motherhood provides an example of the intersection of the negative constructions of teenage mothers with those of people of color. Although teenage motherhood is stigmatized generally both in the United States and Britain, concern about black teenage mothers is expressed more frequently and is often more heightened than that about their white peers. But is motherhood necessarily as problematic as much academic and popular literature would suggest just because it occurs in the teenage years? And does a focus on race in teenage motherhood assist our understanding of the causes and consequences of motherhood early in life? This chapter addresses these issues.

Issues of Race in Britain and the United States

In a 1989 newspaper article Angela McRobbie describes British attitudes to teenage motherhood as constituting a "subdued moral panic."[2] U.S. attitudes to early motherhood may be similarly described as moral panic, although less subdued. The scale and pattern of teenage motherhood differs in the two countries, however.

In the United States and in Britain (as in many other industrialized countries) birth rates to women under 20 have fallen over the last two decades. Pregnancy and motherhood in teenage women is much more common in the United States than it is in Britain. Currently about 3 percent of British teenage women give birth each year, compared with 5 percent of teenage women in the United States. There is also a disparity in the proportion of teenage pregnancies that are resolved through legal abortion. A third of the British pregnancies are resolved by abortion, while more than two-fifths of those to U.S. teenage women are. Widely publicized research sponsored by the Alan Guttmacher Institute demonstrates that the United States differs vastly from other industrialized countries in trends and incidence of early motherhood. British trends are similar to Canadian, and fall between those of the rest of Europe and those of the United States.[3]

Rates of single parenthood have increased in both Britain and the United States over the last twenty years. The British rise has, however, been more dramatic, so that British rates of single parenthood in women under 20 are now only slightly less than those in Sweden (where legal marriage is uncommon in any age group). Just over half the births to teenage women in the United States are to single women, while more than three-quarters of those to teenage women in Britain are. The two countries share a roughly similar age distribution of teenage mothers. Most of those who become mothers in their teenage years are between 18 and 19 years old (about two-thirds in Britain and about three times the number of younger teenagers in the United States).[4]

The contexts in which these differences in trends and incidence of early motherhood occur are, not surprisingly, somewhat different. Both British and U.S. 16-year-olds with few qualifications are likely to face enormous difficulties in finding employment, particularly well-paid employment with career prospects. In Britain, however, it is not unusual for young people to leave school at 16 years of age, having taken their General Certificates of School Education. In the United States 16-year-olds who leave school are referred to as dropouts and lack the qualifications necessary for many jobs. As a result British mothers under 20 are likely to be seen as less problematic than are those from the United States.

The United States and Britain share a similar problem orientation to their black populations. In spite of laws prohibiting discrimination on racial or other grounds, such discrimination is common in both societies and serves to maintain black-white power differentials. In both societies black people are generally less likely than white to obtain educational qualifications, more likely to experience unemployment and to live in poverty. The ways in which the two societies approach the issue of race are, however, not uniform. One obvious example of their two approaches lies in how they collect national statistics on race and ethnicity. In the United States national and local social statistics are routinely broken down by race. Thus it is, for example, an easy matter to calculate the percentage of births to black women under 20 both vis à vis women under 20 in general and black women as a group.

In Britain statistics equivalent to those routinely collected in the United States do not exist. Currently the most complete record of black people's status in Britain is still the 1982 Policy Studies Institute representative survey of black people in Britain.[5] There are regular national surveys such as the General Household Survey and the Labour Force Survey that record race of respondent. But recording color and ethnicity for official statistics is such a hotly disputed issue in Britain that only recently did the government Office of Population Censuses and Surveys actually ask questions concerning respondents' color or national origins rather than simply recording interviewers' assessments. Indeed, the decision to include the ethnic question in the 1991 national census was taken only in November 1989 by the Secretary of State for Health. The 1981 census did not include it. A test census including a question on color and country of origin held in the north-London borough of Haringey in 1979 was subject to a local campaign, "Say No to Racist Census." The resulting low response rate led to the question being shelved, and continued reliance was placed on the unsatisfactory "birthplace of parents" as a proxy for "race." A question on race was included in the 1989 test census and informed the Secretary of State's decision about whether its inclusion would jeopardize completion rates for the 1991 census. Barker reported that the test census achieved regional response rates which ranged from a too-low 42 percent to a satisfactory 93 percent.[6] In November 1989, however, Kenneth Clarke, Secretary of State for Health, reported to the House of Commons that over all only 1 percent of respondents had refused to cooperate with the test census specifically because of the race question. Few black people had commented on the question spontaneously, but one in five had voiced objections when prompted. On that basis he had decided that inclusion of the race question would not jeopardize completion rates on the 1991 national census but would yield valuable information in the fight against racial discrimination and for equal opportunity.[7]

What accounts for the differences between the United States, where recording race seems to be accepted by black and other minority ethnic groups, and Britain, where it is more politically controversial? A major reason lies in the most recent histories of black populations in Britain and in the United States. The majority of black British people were either themselves migrants to Britain or have parents or grandparents who were. Thus, although over 90 percent of people under 20 of Caribbean origin are British-born, their Caribbean heritage is relatively recent. This would be insignificant if some British politicians and white British people had not made it clear that the black British presence is undesirable—they feel that there are too many black people resident in Britain. A famous example of this attitude was Margaret Thatcher's 1979 election speech suggestion that British people are being swamped by an alien culture. On the other hand, having been resident in the United States since the days of slavery, the majority of the African American population is longer established than many groups of white Americans. Blacks are therefore not subject to threats of repatriation. It is extremely unlikely that any black British people could ever really be repatriated, but political realities are irrelevant to the perception of a threat.

Despite the paucity of national statistics on the black British population, sufficient information is available to permit some comparisons between the United Kingdom and the United States. First, the terminology of color has aroused controversy in both countries, but the controversies have differed. The word *black*, for example, has somewhat different meanings in the United States than it has in Britain. In Britain *black* was originally imported from the United States by people of African and African Caribbean origin and used (as in the United States) to apply only to themselves. It has since been extended by many people of African and Asian descent to include people whose origins lie in southeast Asia. This usage has been disputed by people of all colors, however, and has recently been dropped by the Quasi Autonomous Non-Governmental Organisation, the Commission for Racial Equality. Nonetheless, *black* continues to be used by some for people of all colors. The expression *people of color*, found in the United States, has not entered general use in Britain. The nearest equivalent, *ethnic minority*, is also not universally popular.

The black British population is smaller than the black population of the United States. Roughly 5 percent of the British population is black (people of Asian, African Caribbean, and African descent combined), compared with the United States, where about 12 percent of the population is African

American. There are approximately twice as many people of Asian as of African Caribbean descent, and relatively few whose most recent origins are directly African. As in the United States, black people are not evenly distributed throughout Britain but are concentrated in the capital, other major cities, and metropolitan areas. Britain's black population has never been subject to segregation in the way that blacks in the United States have. In the late 1960s and early 1970s, however, some education authorities did institute short-lived busing policies to ensure that schools did not have large proportions of West Indian children.

The populations of African Caribbean origin in Britain and in the United States are perceived in different ways in their respective countries. Whether there is any basis in fact, blacks who come from the Caribbean (who constitute a tiny percentage of U.S. blacks) are believed to be more industrious, successful members of U.S. society than the longer-established African American population. By way of contrast, most people of African Caribbean origin in Britain gain few educational qualifications, do not enter high status professions, and are stereotyped as indigent and unintelligent.

A major difference between Britain and the United States lies in rates of intermarriage between blacks and whites. Intermarriage is rare in the United States but is relatively common in Britain among blacks of African Caribbean origin. Data gathered for the British Labour Force Survey indicate that there has been a large increase in intermarriage. Roughly one-third of British people of African Caribbean origin under 30 apparently now marry or cohabit with white British people (those who have children together but are not coresident have not been recorded). The pattern of these unions has changed during the 1980s. Intermarriage between blacks and whites in Britain used to be limited almost exclusively to black men and white women. For people under 30, however, there are roughly equal numbers of black men and black women of African Caribbean origin in mixed marriages or cohabitations. Rates of intermarriage between people of Southeast Asian origin and white Britishers are much lower (about 5 percent for those under 30).

The relatively high rates of intermarriage between black people of African Caribbean origin and white British people results partly from the fact that having attended the same schools and lived in the same neighborhoods young people of similar social class have acquired shared cultural practices. In separate studies, Roger Hewitt and Simon Jones, for example, found that there are groups of young white people who talk like black Londoners, engage in cultural practices that have been developed by and are more common among young black people, and are keen to be accepted into black youth cultures.[8] This is one demonstration of the dynamic nature of cultural forms.

There are no national statistics on the incidence of teenage motherhood among young black women in Britain. Some local studies suggest that there is a higher incidence of early motherhood among West Indian women and that West Indian women are more likely than white women to remain single when they give birth in their teenage years.[9] Yet there is little systematic evidence of this. A representative national survey of mothers in their teenage years found that 4 percent were West Indian and 5 percent, Asian.[10] This may not constitute an overrepresentation of young black women in the under 20 age group, however, for in some areas young blacks constitute a higher proportion of their age group than do older people. Until national figures are available, it is impossible to determine this. More than three-quarters of women who give birth in their teenage years are now single, moreover, so it is unlikely that black British women of African Caribbean origin have a much higher rate of single motherhood than their white peers.

Do Teenage Mothers Constitute a Social Problem?

For many people the terms *teenage, adolescent,* and *young mother* (especially in combination) are associated with a range of social problems. In comparison with older mothers, women who become mothers in their teenage years have been reported to have a high rate of unplanned pregnancies, to suffer from complications during pregnancy, to be depressed after birth, to gain few educational qualifications, and to be reliant on state provision of housing and money. Their children have similarly been found to achieve less than children born to older mothers and to be more likely to suffer accidental and nonaccidental injuries.[11]

Yet the widespread assumption that teenage motherhood is necessarily associated with a gloomy catalogue of ills is increasingly being challenged in two important ways. First, negative outcomes are not as common as is generally believed. Only a minority of teenage mothers and their children are in fact reported to suffer such poor outcomes. A generally negative reaction to motherhood at a young age is, therefore, increasingly recognized as inappropriate. King and Fullard's study of 14- to 19-year-old mothers in the United States, for example, led the authors to decide that "the most important conclusion for the present study is that sweeping condemnations of teenage mothers are no longer appropriate."[12] In their report they suggest that individual differences between women who give birth in their teenage years need to be taken into account since many women fare well. True, Simms and Smith, in their national study of British teenage mothers and their partners, found that 11 percent of those they interviewed when their children were a year old reported that they were sorry they became mothers when they did.[13] Obviously, it is far from ideal that a tenth of the women Simms and Smith interviewed regretted becoming mothers, but this finding needs to be put into context. First, the majority of Simms and Smith's sample were satisfied at becoming mothers when they had. Second, some older women also fare badly in motherhood[14] or find motherhood, either in the first months or when children are older, difficult to cope with.[15]

With regard to how the children born to teenage women do, many studies that claim deleterious effects for early motherhood find that developmental test scores of children born to mothers under 20 fall within the normal standardized range of scores. In comparison with the average scores of children born to older mothers, however, children of teenage mothers have a lower average score.[16] In a large-scale British national study, Butler and his colleagues found significant differences between the test scores of children at 5 years of age born to mothers under 20 and those born to mothers over 20. The largest differences, however, were between children whose mothers were under 18 and those whose mothers were over 30. Differences either disappeared or were vastly reduced if 18- and 19-year-old mothers (who constitute the majority of mothers under 20) were compared with older mothers. When analyses of covariance were performed on the data, socioeconomic as well as a range of other factors accounted for more variance in children's test and behavior scores than maternal age did.[17] These findings indicate that a division claimed between teenage mothers and older mothers is relatively spurious. Women 18 and 19 years old have more in common with 20- and 21-year-olds than they do with 16-year-olds. And the youngest teenagers (and hence teenagers who are least likely to become mothers) are most likely to be dissatisfied with motherhood, and their children are most likely to show poor development. In addition socioeconomic factors are a critical influence on how mothers of any age group fare. It seems, therefore, that negative aspects of becoming a mother early in life have been overstated.[18] Indeed, there is evidence that the late teenage years are biologically well-suited to childbearing.[19]

That teenage motherhood necessarily leads to poor outcomes has been challenged in another way. Some researchers now argue that the negative factors associated with early childbearing may not be consequences of motherhood in the teenage years but may instead provide the context within which motherhood becomes acceptable or desirable.[20] Arline T.

Geronimus used a combination of sociological, ethnographic, and bio-medical data on teenage motherhood to argue that the continued assumption that there are "true age effects" in young motherhood leads researchers to "run the risk of missing more important determinants of neonatal mortality." By considering the whole reproductive age span rather than simply the teenage years, Geronimus found that there are greater differences between black and white neonatal mortality rates where the mothers are between 24 and 29 years old than at any other time in the reproductive age span. Geronimus argues that the explanation for black teenagers of 17 or more (who are more likely than white teenagers to become mothers) having better neonatal mortality rates than black first-time mothers in their middle 20s is that teenagers have had less exposure to the negative effects caused by living in poverty and with the socio-economic consequences of racial discrimination than have older black women. Thus, a social policy approach that assumes true age effects could advocate deferring black teenage childbirth and hence potentially increase rather than reduce disparities between black and white neonatal mortality rates.[21] Similarly, dropping out of school may not be caused by early motherhood but may be more likely to predate than to follow conception in teenage women.[22]

Some researchers are now critical of the evidence on which worrying conclusions like those described above have been based. Michael Lamb and Albert Ester point out: "Although this has become an increasingly popular area of research, our knowledge of adolescent parenting is still surprisingly limited. Among the problems accounting for this are methodological inadequacies."[23] And Dimity Carlson and colleagues note: "More recent studies which control for factors such as SES [socioeconomic status], nutrition, maternal age, race (white/black), and prenatal care reveal good obstetric and paediatric outcomes among adolescent mothers."[24]

Once an issue (like teenage motherhood) has been defined as problematic, that definition gains its own momentum. Thus, negative findings concerning a minority of individuals are overgeneralized to include the whole group, and individuals within the group are considered only in relation to their problem status. The cause of the problem is couched in individualistic terms which result in victims being blamed for causing the perceived problem.[25] Not surprisingly, therefore, researchers in the area of teenage motherhood (who in terms of social class, color, and gender tend to be distant from their respondents) generally start from the assumption that motherhood in the teenage years is problematic and highlight negative findings.

Why Is Teenage Motherhood Defined as Problematic?

The discussion above suggests that the negative social construction of teenage motherhood cannot simply be attributed to its effects on young mothers and their children. Instead, three other interrelated issues can be identified. In the first place, teenage pregnancy and motherhood force public recognition of heterosexual activity that many people find uncomfortable. "The subject of teenage pregnancy seems to raise almost every politically explosive social issue facing the American public: the battle over abortion rights: contraceptives and the ticklish question of whether adolescents should have access to them. . . . Indeed, even the basic issue of adolescent sexuality is a subject that makes many Americans squirm."[26]

It is indeed true that a higher proportion of pregnancies is terminated in the under 20 age group than in any other age group (nearly a half in the United States and nearly a third in Britain). Partly as a result of the availability of legal abortion, motherhood is now less common for women under 20 than it was in the late 1950s in the United States and the late 1960s in Britain. This picture may, however, change in the United States, where recent Supreme Court decisions have made it harder for poor women to obtain abortions.

In both Britain and the United States there have been dramatic increases in the proportion of teenage women who give birth while they are single. In the United States more than half are single, and the figure is even higher in Britain (where four-fifths of mothers under 20 are now single). Teenage mothers do not, therefore, conform to dominant reproductive ideologies that insist on marriage preceding conception.

Virtually all societies differentiate childhood and adulthood. In Western societies adolescence is now conceptualized as a developmental period of transition between the two. Adolescence is not well defined, however, and it is difficult to be certain when maturity has been reached. There is, after all, limited correspondence between the ages of biological and social maturity. Furthermore, legal recognition of social maturity is piecemeal: rights and responsibilities are attained at different ages.

The boundaries between childhood and adulthood have become less well defined over the course of the twentieth century. Longer compulsory education and increasing participation in further education have kept more teenagers dependent for longer periods. Similarly, with high rates of youth unemployment fewer young men from low socioeconomic groups are able to signal their transition to adult status by obtaining their first paycheck. For young women, marriage was the status marker equivalent to young men's first paycheck. But over the last twenty years rates of marriage to teenage women have declined. In Britain in 1971 31 percent of all first marriages were to teenage women but by 1986 just under 14 percent were. The signifiers of adult status are thus harder to achieve than they once were, and adolescence is an ambiguous period.

If the status of adolescents is ambiguous, the status of adolescent mothers is even more so. The very juxtaposition of these two words is almost contradictory. While *adolescence* represents a period of preparation for adulthood, pregnancy and motherhood are considered the preserve of adult women.[27] Women who become pregnant in their teenage years are thus perceived to have taken on an adult role during a period in life when they are not socially constructed as adults.

Emotional concern for "children having children" is exacerbated by the belief that motherhood may disrupt the psychological work of adolescence, a period often conceptualized as a time of storm and stress, marked by conflicts with authority figures, when identity comes sharply into focus. Having to attend to the needs of an infant arguably hinders the focus on a mother's emergent self.[28] Yet adolescence is not uniform or necessarily stormy,[29] and little is known about whether the psychological development that occurs in adolescence is qualitatively different from the psychological development that takes place during other periods of life.

Furthermore, although many writers on teenage motherhood assume that adolescence and the teenage years are coterminus, the fact that the majority of women who give birth before they are under 20 are actually 18 or 19 years of age makes it debatable whether, in fact, most are really *adolescent* in the way that society defines the term.

It is well established that a tendency toward teenage motherhood is not evenly distributed throughout society. On the whole, teenage mothers tend to come from larger than average families of low socioeconomic status. They are more likely than older mothers to have parents who are separated.[30] Their children's fathers generally come from similarly poor backgrounds. The relatively high rates of welfare dependence together with poor educational achievements and employment prospects have led some researchers to suggest that those women who can least afford to are most likely to have children.[31] Because *good parents* are socially constructed as people who make independent economic provision for their children, those who depend on welfare payments cannot fit in with society's definition of adequate parenting.

Simply deferring motherhood would not necessarily improve most women's material circumstances, however.[32] In the London study done at the Thomas Coram Research Unit only one-fifth of the 16- to 19-year-old first-time mothers interviewed had taken one "O" level or its equivalent (national exams that, like the General Certificate of School Education that recently replaced them, were generally taken at 16 years of age in Britain). Many had experienced periods of unemployment before they became pregnant and their children's fathers also experienced a high rate of unemployment. Their parents suffered higher than average rates of unemployment as well. For many women, therefore, there was no reason to believe that either deferring motherhood or marrying would necessarily lead to an improvement in their economic circumstances. Partly because of this, some women felt no reason to defer motherhood beyond the teenage years.[33]

Current debates on the feminization of poverty have focused on the fact that most households with children dependent on welfare are female-headed.[34] Despite increases in rates of births to single women, most such households are created through divorce.[35] Although concerns are expressed that mothers under 20 are swelling the numbers of truly disadvantaged, older women form the majority of single mothers living in poverty. And in both Britain and the United States single parents (who are predominantly mothers) are more likely than other parents to live in poverty.[36] It thus seems that not age per se but socioeconomic circumstances are problematic for women who become mothers early in life. Furthermore, teenage motherhood does not cause poverty, for women who give birth before they are 20 years of age are generally already poor.

Even if deferring motherhood would not *necessarily* improve women's material conditions, it could be argued that childbearing early in life should best be avoided if it depressed the economic chances of *some* women and their children. From their seventeen-year follow-up of teenage mothers Furstenberg and colleagues echo Card's conclusions[37] that early motherhood has some long-term negative consequences: "Although the adolescent mothers in this study fared much better in later life (in terms of jobs, welfare, and subsequent childbearing) than many observers would have predicted, they unquestionably remained at a disadvantage compared to women who postponed childbearing."[38] From a public policy standpoint this would be an important finding were it indeed the case. It is difficult, however, to be certain that this conclusion is as definite as Furstenberg and colleagues claim. At their seventeen-year follow-up of teenage mothers and their children, Furstenberg's group was unable to reinterview the matched comparison group they had recruited in 1976 and, instead, had to use information from four national large-scale data sets in order to estimate how their sample from Baltimore compared with its black age peers throughout the United States who did not become teenage mothers. The absence of a directly comparable group of black women who deferred motherhood makes it difficult to estimate true age effects.

Other research findings contradict Furstenberg and his colleagues' strong claim. Geronimus and Korenman[39] used multivariate analyses to explore the relation between early motherhood and women's socio-economic status. A methodological innovation in these analyses was the inclusion of a comparison of sisters who had given birth at different ages. Geronimus and Korenman found that in comparison with their sisters who gave birth in their teens, the additional schooling experienced by women who gave birth after their teens had little positive impact on improving their family income. Their findings are confirmed in work by McCrate,[40] who used econometric analyses of the National Longitudinal Survey of Youth. McCrate defines teenage mothers as women of 17 years or under, on the grounds that these are the ages at which school is supposed to be young people's major preoccupation. She uses a human-capital approach to argue that black women who become mothers in their teenage years accurately anticipate discrimination in the employment market. As a result, because discrimination suppresses black women's opportunities in the employment market, young black women have less incentive to avoid teenage births than young white women. Births to teenagers are not as costly for blacks as for whites. Some support for McCrate's ideas that educational qualifications do not by themselves give a precise indication of future labor market experience is provided by Sullivan's ethnographic work. Sullivan reports that lack of qualifications had little impact on young white men's access to relatively well-paid employment.[41]

In considering Furstenberg and his colleagues' conclusions, we must also ask whether relatively crude indices for comparison (such as class, color, and age) sufficiently discriminate among the factors that lead some women to become mothers early in life. A major problem is that matching samples on race, class, and age does not necessarily ensure their similarity in other important ways. People of the same class, race, and age differ, for example, in their attitudes to and experience of education. And because educational attainment either before or after birth is a major influence on whether women who become mothers before they are 20 will eventually become self-supporting, those differences are important. In addition, social class in itself is a difficult concept to operationalize: it is difficult to know how to control for socioeconomic status in studies of mothers under 20.[42]

The correlates of social class have been shown to differ for black and white people. In Britain black people tend to be better-educated than whites within the same occupational groupings. Black people are also more likely to be unemployed, however, than white people with similar educational qualifications.[43] A similar situation exists in the United States.[44] The existence of racial discrimination thus serves to ensure that race and social class are, to a large extent, linked.

The issue of the interrelationship between teenage mothers, female-headed households, and poverty is likely to continue exercising those involved in this field. It is, however, an issue that requires more complex analysis than it has frequently been given.

Black Mothers and White Mothers

I have discussed ways in which British and U.S. societies consider both teenage motherhood and black people problematic. It is not surprising, therefore, that black mothers under 20 have been subjected to more negative attention than have white mothers under 20. This is particularly the case when they are single (and in the United States it is clear that most black teenage mothers are). Black mothers under 20 thus provide an example of the intersection of three negative social constructions (black people, teenage mothers, and female-headed households). Similar arguments can be applied to women from other minority groups (for example Hispanic women), who are also considered to pose problems with regard to early motherhood. I shall use black women as an example here, however.

Many of the problems associated with black people are considered to result from the pathology of black families. "The point implied in much of the literature is that a lot of the culturally 'abnormal' behaviour of minority groups can be traced back to supposed family deficiencies. Additionally, the problematic black family background is often implicated in explanations for unrest, decay and violence in the inner cities."[45]

Public concern about single black teenage mothers in the United States developed in a context in which black family structures had already been defined as problematic by some writers: "The intellectual history of this problem [lone black mothers under 20] begins not with teenage pregnancy, which only became a public concern around 1970, but with worries about black family structure that began in the 1960s with the Moynihan Report (1965)."[46]

In societies in which black family structures are considered to be responsible for producing inner-city problems of poverty and crime, associating blackness with another stigmatized group (teenage mothers) produces moral panic. Single, black mothers under 20 are feared to be producing problematic children and to be draining the state's resources while so doing.

Although eugenic beliefs and policies are not now officially sanctioned, most Western societies wish to influence the quantity and quality of children produced in them.[47] In societies such as Britain and the United States, which are permeated by racial discrimination and racist ideologies against blacks and other minority groups, fears about race and reproduction serve to focus more public attention on devalued black mothers than on similar white mothers and make of them a potent political issue. Thus, although black mothers and children are frequently omitted from research studies when "normal families" are being examined, there are many studies that focus exclusively or predominantly on black, lone, and/or teenage mothers.[48]

Martha Ward interviewed professionals working in the field of adolescent pregnancy in Louisiana. She suggests that black and white professionals use different models to inform their interests in and concerns about 'adolescent pregnancy.'

> Many leading black professionals state their views that population policy, certain economic policies, and programs for adolescent pregnancy are, in fact, a "hidden white agenda." In private interviews, the fears of genocide are openly discussed. . . . At the regular conferences and task force meetings held on the subject, white leaders will go to elaborate lengths to dissuade their black colleagues that genocide is not the population policy of either the U.S. government or the state of Louisiana. . . .
>
> The white social-structural model is built on the ideal of "the quality of urban life." At the conservative end of the spectrum, the concrete concerns are crime, the cycle of poverty, or the availability of trained and willing workers. . . . The liberal end of the spectrum will emphasize the rates of infant mortality . . . , good prenatal care and the now voluminous documentation about the relationships of age at first pregnancy, family size, educational achievement, career development and social mobility.[49]

Ward suggests that both black and white proponents of "this socio-structural model" consider that early motherhood is caused by a variety of social ills. It is perhaps to be expected that black professionals would additionally be concerned about the possible eugenic underpinnings of state interest in black motherhood in women under 20. There have been instances of sterilization abuse on black women in the United States, and interest in black teenage mothers occurs in a society where racial discrimination is common.[50]

The concentration on black women in much of the work being done on mothers under 20 could be considered simply benign—an example of scientists attempting to understand social problems in order to help alleviate them. Recent work influenced by the French philosopher of science, Michel Foucault, however, suggests another interpretation:

> The sciences claim to describe a population in order that they can better be governed. The rise of sciences therefore is not simply about academic disciplines, but, as we shall see, it is about the development of specific practices through which families, mothers, children, might be "known" in order better to regulate them. . . . However, as in all struggles for power, this knowledge is constructed out of an uneasy compromise. . . . Regulation is not neutral, but is about a knowledge which suppresses and silences other knowledges in producing its own vision. What always has to be regulated is the threat of uprising, the bid for freedom of the oppressed.[51]

Many writers and researchers on teenage pregnancy in general and black teenage pregnancy in particular are explicit about their aim of reducing conceptions and births to women under 20. Researchers' aims of regulating these births are often clearly inspired by good intentions for improving the chances of young women from lower socioeconomic groups and/or the black population. Nonetheless, the focus on black family forms as responsible for black people's problems within British and U.S. society focuses attention on black cultural forms and deflects it from other explanations. The ways in which racial discrimination intersects with social and economic factors, therefore, receive less attention than they otherwise might and less than they deserve.

In the United States early childbearing is more common among black and Hispanic women than it is among whites. Young black women are more likely to be single when they give birth than are other young women.[52] There has, as a result, been a tendency to view early motherhood as a problem of minority groups, particularly blacks, and to present qualitatively different explanations for the incidence of teenage motherhood in minority than in white women. Sociocultural explanations have generally been advanced for the incidence of pregnancy in young black women and psychological ones for the occurrence of early pregnancy in white women.[53] Despite the absence of national statistics researchers have noticed a similar tendency in Britain.[54]

In both Britain and the United States, then, early motherhood has been viewed as a black problem,[55] in spite of the fact that this popular image cannot be substantiated by the available data: "The increasing incidence of unplanned adolescent pregnancy in America has been largely portrayed by the media, often with sensationalism, as a problem unique to the black population."[56] "Pregnancy in adolescents is not just a technical or demographic issue. It has cultural and practical dimensions. Nationally, unmarried black teenagers are five times more likely to give birth than white teenagers. . . . This has long-term societal consequences of incalculable dimensions: and black leaders are increasingly concerned."[57] "Without dismissing the seriousness of the problem within the black community, the findings of this report also help refute the popular myth that teenage pregnancy and childbearing are primarily or exclusively 'black' problems."[58]

As a result of the pervasive social construction of early motherhood as a black problem, it is often assumed that black and white young women become mothers for different reasons and that higher rates of early, single motherhood in black than in white women can be explained simply as a black cultural pattern. Such assumptions have served to obscure rather than aid understanding trends of early motherhood. It is worth highlighting two ways in which this is the case.

Rates of single motherhood in young white women have vastly increased in the United States, so that although young black women still have a much higher rate of single motherhood than young white women the difference in the rates has been reduced. "Blacks may simply have been the pacesetters for the population at large."[59] Furthermore, white teenage women in the United States now have a higher rate of births than women in the same age groups in most other industrialized countries, regardless of whether (as in Britain) those countries have sizable black populations.[60] Early childbearing in single women can no longer, therefore, be considered a black cultural issue.

Rates of single motherhood in black teenage women have not always been high. In the 1950s it was exceptional for black mothers under 20 to be single when they gave birth.[61] But marriage among black teenagers in the United States has virtually disappeared.[62] In 1960 nearly a third of all 18- and 19-year-old black women in the United States were married, compared with less than 3 percent in 1984, when 89 percent of births to black teenagers were to single women.[63] There have thus been parallel changes in childbearing patterns for white and black teenagers. High rates of early childbearing in black women cannot satisfactorily be explained simply by reference to cultural differences in factors such as attitude and family functioning or group relationships.[64]

For these reasons it is important to establish rather than to assume differences between black and white women under 20, and if that can be done, to explain them. Certainly, differences exist between black and white mothers under 20, and those differences are important. Data from the United States consistently show that young black women are more likely than their white peers to engage in sexual activity early, to become pregnant, and to have children while remaining single.[65] Those differences are well documented. It is less clear how they can be explained. Some writers have looked at attitudinal factors while others have concentrated on socioeconomic differences. Attitudinal factors are clearly important to an understanding of motherhood in women under 20. Yet the fact that black people in U.S. (as well as British) society are more likely than whites to experience poverty must also be taken into account. Davis, for example, attempted to isolate the effects of race on adolescent pregnancy and infant mortality. He concluded that: "The key to this entire process is the relationship between poverty, teenage pregnancy and LBW [low birth weight]. Race is important only because it affects poverty. . . . In general, and relative to its direct effects on infant mortality, the strongest effect of race seems to be by way of poverty, not teenage pregnancies."[66]

It is common for black as well as white writers to express concern that black single teenage childbearing is likely to be generally deleterious to black people.[67] Yet it is generally acknowledged that marriage rates in young black women have diminished as unemployment in young black males has increased. Wilson suggests that contrary to some reports that the provision of welfare payments encourages single parenting, "among blacks, increasing male joblessness is related to the rising proportions of families headed by women" as well as to a shortage of marriageable males.[68] Staples suggests that commitment to marriage has not diminished among young black people but that structural constraints prevent them from marrying.[69]

Wilson thinks that a separate factor explains the increase in white female-headed households; namely women's increasing financial independence.[70] Yet there seems no clear reason for postulating different explanations for black and white single motherhood. Most white women who become mothers in their teens, for example, are unlikely to be financially independent and in Britain there has been a large increase in single parenthood among all mothers under 20. There may thus be fewer differences between black and white teenage mothers than between black and white mothers in other age groups.

The undoubted differences in structural position between black and white people may give the impression that their behavior necessarily has different etiology, but the automatic presumption of different influences may impede our understanding of the common factors underpinning apparently different behavior. Furstenberg provides a clear example of how black teenage women and their white peers may have the same motivations for marrying or staying single but be impelled in different directions by cultural factors. "For whites, marriage operates as a major recovery route, offering an alternative or, at least, an important supplement to their own earning ability. Low education and restricted job opportunities, therefore, are not quite as costly as they are for black young mothers. On the other hand, the advantages of delaying parenthood are not so great for blacks as well. . . . The cruel fact is that for blacks delaying childbearing has a relatively low payoff. They are damned if they do and damned if they don't."[71]

Furstenberg and colleagues' seventeen-year longitudinal follow-up of black mothers who had been 17 years old when they had their first child similarly found that marriage did not increase most young black women's economic advantage. "We also must report that marriage per se contributes little to a woman's economic chances. . . . Only those who married early and remained married escaped economic disadvantage, and as we saw earlier, many of the early marriages quickly dissolved." In fact "only 26% of the sample were in a first marriage; just 16% had remained married to the father of the study child."[72]

A longitudinal study of British mothers aged 16–19 (79 interviewed in-depth and 102 on demographic factors in late pregnancy) conducted at the Thomas Coram Research Unit lends support to the notion that economic considerations influence young couples' decisions to marry. Women were asked about their attitudes to men and marriage in general and for themselves in particular. None of those who were married when they conceived gave economic reasons for contracting marriage. It was, however, clear that the male partners of the fifth (22 percent) of women who married before pregnancy were employed in jobs which were well paid in comparison with those of other women's male partners.[73] Because mothers under 20 generally have male partners who are poorly qualified and unskilled, increasing rates of unemployment among young, unskilled males may largely account for the dramatic increases in the proportion of young women who are single rather than married when they give birth.[74]

Invoking cultural differences to explain differences in patterns of behavior sometimes leads to simplistic theorizing of culture as a concept. Yet because cultural practices are dynamic, dependent on the societies in which they occur, it is possible for people who were once culturally distinct to share features of their cultural practices. As noted, recent British work demonstrates that some white British young people, for example, take on black youth cultural forms.[75] In Britain a simple bipolar distinction is increasingly likely to fail to reflect the complexity of race in British society, for an increasing number of young people are of mixed parentage and researchers now argue that children of mixed parentage see themselves not as black or white, but as distinctively mixed.[76]

Sullivan provides a useful way of conceptualizing culture so that a focus on cultural differences does not ignore the circumstances in which people live.[77] Sullivan conducted an ethnographic study of three groups of young men living in Brooklyn who fathered children with teenage women; poor blacks, poor Hispanics, and poor whites. He found no differences among the young men in reported early sexual activity but marked differences among them in attitudes to abortion, marriage, and fathering. Hispanics most disapproved of abortion; blacks were ambivalent, and whites most likely to approve. Whites and Hispanics were more likely to marry after conception than blacks, but unmarried blacks were more likely than any of the other two groups to have continuing contact with their children and to provide direct childcare when with them. These responses to fathering children occurred amid favorable economic circumstances. Half the black young men stayed longer in full-time education than either of the other groups, and they found clerical or service-sector jobs with better prospects for upward mobility than their Hispanic peers. But they received less money than their less-qualified white peers. For the white youths decent jobs and housing were available through social network contacts, so that those who married were able to support their families and obtain housing without having equal educational qualifications.

A study like Sullivan's is important in pointing out the inextricable linking of "structural economic factors, culture, and social ecology in shaping processes of family and household formation." The distinctive range of responses to early pregnancy in each of the three ethnic groups was affected by the resources that were available within their communities. Poor access to decent jobs, for example, was an important influence on responses in the two minority communities. Thus, cultural values were not "unchanging, primordial entities but rather . . . collective responses of people with distinctive group histories to different and changing structural positions in society."[78] Equally important, there were similarities as well as differences among individuals in different neighborhoods. Blocked opportunities caused by poor experiences of the labor market or drug dependence occurred in all the neighborhoods, but on different scales. Men with these experiences did not tend to marry the mothers of their children.

The argument here is that although there are likely to be important cultural influences on black and white teenage mothers and their partners, cultural differences need to be demonstrated rather than assumed. Sullivan's small-scale study provides indications of cultural differences and commonalities between blacks, Hispanics, and whites because he uses detailed ethnography, which lends itself to the examination of cultural practices. Commonalities in the social constructions and experiences of blacks and whites clearly exist but hitherto have been given little recognition. An example of similarities in the social constructions is provided by a British study of young women moving from the labor market to un/employment. Griffin found that teachers held similar views of working-class white and black young women. "Teachers tended to attribute the problems of working class students to their supposedly 'deviant' families rather than to material conditions such as unemployment or poverty. . . . Catholic families were particularly likely to be seen as problems. 'They shouldn't have so many children if they can't afford it,' as Ms Ryman told me. . . . White teachers also referred to black students' family lives as a potential source of 'problems.' "[79]

Just as there are similarities among different racial groups, so there are differences within groups. Black people do not constitute an essential, unitary category any more than white people, women, or different social classes.[80] Yet comparisons of blacks and whites frequently treat race as unitary and as a proxy for cultural differences, constructing whites as the norm from which blacks deviate.[81]

Notes

1. Centre for Contemporary Cultural Studies, *The Empire Strikes Back* (London: Hutchinson, 1982); Paul Gilroy, *There Ain't No Black in the Union Jack* (London: Hutchinson, 1988); Maria de la luz Rez and John Halcon, "Racism in Academia: The Old Wolf Revisited," *Harvard Educational Review* 58, 3 (1988): 299–314; Diane Scott-Jones and Sharon Nelson-Le Gall, "Defining Black Families: Past and Present," in Edward Seidman and Julian Rappaport, eds., *Redefining Social Problems* (London: Plenum Press, 1986).

2. Angela McRobbie, "Motherhood, a teenage job?" *The Guardian*, 5 September 1989.

3. Elise Jones, Jacqueline Darroch Forrest, Noreen Goldman, Stanley Henshaw, Richard Lincoln, Jeannie I. Rosoff, Charles F. Westoff, and Deirdre Wulf, *Teenage Pregnancy in Industrialized Countries* (New Haven: Yale University Press, 1986).

4. Jones et al., *Teenage Pregnancy in Industrialized Countries*.

5. Colin Brown, *Black and White in Britain: The Third PSI Survey* (London: PSI, 1984).

6. Paul Barker, "The ethnic question," *The Independent*, 7 November 1989.

7. David Brindle, "Race Question in Census," *The Guardian*, 14 November 1989.

8. Roger Hewitt, *White Talk, Black Talk* (Cambridge: Cambridge University Press, 1987); Simon Jones, *Black Culture, White Youth: The Reggae Tradition from JA to UK* (London: Macmillan, 1988).

9. Carolynne Skinner, *The Elusive Mr. Right* (London: Carolina Publications, 1986).

10. Madeleine Simms and Christopher Smith, *Teenage Mothers and Their Partners*. Department of Health and Social Security Research Report, no. 15 (London: HMSO, 1986).

11. Simms and Smith, *Teenage Mothers and Their Partners*; Judith Bury, *Teenage Pregnancy in Britain* (London: Birth Control Trust, 1984); Catherine Chilman, "Social and Psychological Research concerning Adolescent Childbearing: 1970–1980," *Journal of Marriage and the Family* 42 (1980): 793–805; Catherine Chilman, "Some Psychosocial Aspects of Adolescent Sexual and Contraceptive Behaviors in a Changing American Society," in Jane B. Lancaster and Beatrice A. Hamburg, Eds., *School Age Pregnancy and Parenthood: Biosocial Dimensions* (New York: Aldine de Gruyter, 1986); Frank Furstenberg, Jr., Jeanne Brooks-Gunn, and S. Philip Morgan, *Adolescent Mothers in Later Life* (Cambridge: Cambridge University Press, 1987); Jane Wadsworth, Brent Taylor, Albert Osborn, and Neville Butler, "Teenage Mothering: Child Development at Five Years," *Journal of Child Psychology and Psychiatry* 25 (1984): 305–13.

12. Timothy King and William Fullard, "Teenage Mothers and Their Infants: New Findings on the Home Environment," *Journal of Adolescence* 5 (1982): 345.

13. Simms and Smith, *Teenage Mothers and Their Partners*.

14. See Sally Macintyre and Sarah Cunningham-Burley, "Teenage Pregnancy as a Social Problem: A Perspective from the United Kingdom" (chap. 3).

15. Mary Georgina Boulton, *On Being a Mother* (London: Tavistock, 1983); Ann Oakley, *Becoming a Mother* (Harmondsworth: Penguin, 1980).

16. For a U.S. example, see Dimity Carlson, Richard La Barba, Joseph Sclafani, and Clint Bowers, "Cognitive and Motor Development in Infants of Adolescent Mothers: A Longitudinal Analysis," *International Journal of Behavioral Development* 9 (1986): 1–14.

17. Wadsworth et al., "Teenage Mothering."

18. Carlson et al., "Cognitive and Motor Development," Frank Furstenberg, Jr., "Race Differences in Teenage Sexuality, Pregnancy, and Adolescent Childbearing," *Milbank Quarterly* 65 (1987): 381–403.

19. Naomi Morris, "Editorial: The Biological Advantages and Social Disadvantages of Teenage Pregnancy," *American Journal of Public Health* 71 (1981): 796.

20. Arline T. Geronimus, "On Teenage Childbearing and Neonatal Mortality in the United States," *Population and Development Review* 13 (1987): 245–78; Arline T. Geronimus and Sanders Korenman, "The Socioeconomic Consequences of Teen Childbearing Reconsidered." Research Report 90-190 (Ann Arbor: University of Michigan Population Studies Center, 1990); Catherine Kohler Riessman and Constance Nathanson, "The Management of Reproduction: Social Construction of Risk

and Responsibility," in L. Aiken and D. Mechanic, eds., *Applications of Social Science to Clinical Medicine and Health Policy* (New Brunswick, N.J.: Rutgers University Press, 1986); Constance Willard Williams, *Black Teenage Mothers: Pregnancy and Child Rearing from Their Perspective* (Lexington, Mass.: Lexington Books, 1990).

21. Geronimus, "On Teenage Childbearing"; quote, p. 253.

22. See Claire Brindis, "Antecedents and Consequences: The Need for Diverse Strategies in Adolescent Pregnancy Prevention" (chap. 13) and Deborah L. Rhode, "Adolescent Pregnancy and Public Policy" (chap. 15).

23. Michael Lamb and Albert Elster, "Parental Behavior of Adolescent Mothers and Fathers," in Albert Elster and Michael Lamb, eds., *Adolescent Fatherhood* (Hillsdale, N.J.: Lawrence Erlbaum, 1986).

24. Carlson et al., "Cognitive and Motor Development."

25. E. Seidman and J. Rappaport, "Framing the Issues," in E. Seidman and J. Rappaport, eds., *Redefining Social Problems* (London: Plenum Press, 1986).

26. Claire Wallis, "Children Having Children," *Time*, 9 December 1985, p. 30.

27. Anne Murcott, "The Social Construction of Teenage Pregnancy: A Problem in the Ideologies of Childhood and Reproduction," *Sociology of Health and Illness* 2 (1980): 1–19.

28. Esther Schaler Bucholz and Barbara Gol, "More than Playing House: A Developmental Perspective on the Strengths in Teenage Motherhood," *American Journal of Orthopsychiatry* 56 (1986): 347–59.

29. Phil Cohen, *Rethinking the Youth Question*. Working paper 3 (London: Post-Sixteen Education Centre, University of London, 1986); John Coleman, *Adolescence* (London: Routledge and Kegan Paul, 1976); Chris Griffin, *Typical Girls: Young Women from School to the Job Market* (London: Routledge and Kegan Paul, 1985).

30. Simms and Smith, *Teenage Mothers and Their Partners*.

31. Frank Bolton, *The Pregnant Adolescent* (Beverly Hills: Sage, 1980); Karen Pittman, *Adolescent Pregnancy: Whose Problem Is It?* (Washington, D.C.: Children's Defense Fund Adolescent Pregnancy Prevention Clearinghouse, 1986); Simms and Smith, *Teenage Mothers and Their Partners*.

32. Bury, *Teenage Pregnancy*; Jones et al., *Teenage Pregnancy in Industrialized Countries*.

33. Ann Phoenix, *Young Mothers?* (Cambridge: Polity Press, 1991).

34. Nancy Fraser, "Women, Welfare and the Politics of Need Interpretation," *Thesis Eleven* 17 (1987): 88–106; S. Shaver, "Comment on Fraser," *Thesis Eleven* 17 (1987): 107–10; Jane Millar, "Lone Parents Cross Culturally." Paper presented at a Department of Health and Social Security research seminar, London, 24 May 1988.

35. Millar, "Lone Parents."

36. William Julius Wilson, *The Truly Disadvantaged: The Inner City, the Underclass and Public Policy* (Chicago: University of Chicago Press, 1987); National Council for One Parent Families, *Informational Manual* (London: NCOPF, 1990).

37. Josefina Card, "Long-term Consequences for Children of Teenage Parents," *Demography* 18 (1981): 137–56.

38. Furstenberg et al., *Adolescent Mothers,* p. 133.

39. Geronimus and Korenman, "Socioeconomic Consequences of Teen Childbearing."

40. Elaine McCrate, "Discrimination, Returns to Education, and Teenage Childbearing." Paper presented at the conference on "Discrimination Policies and Research in the Post-Reagan Era," Middlebury, Vt., 6–8 April 1989.

41. Mercer L. Sullivan, "Absent Fathers in the Inner City," *Annals of the American Academy of Political and Social Science* 501 (1989): 48–58.

42. Neville Butler, Bernard Ineichen, Brent Taylor, and Jane Wadsworth, *Teenage Mothering.* Report to the Department of Health and Social Security (Bristol: University of Bristol, 1981).

43. Brown, *Black and White in Britain;* Barbara Tizard, Peter Blatchford, Jessica Burke, Clare Farquhar, and Ian Plewis, *Young Children at School and at Home in the Inner City* (London: Lawrence Erlbaum, 1988).

44. Marian Edelman and Karen Johnson Pittman, "Adolescent Pregnancy: Black and White," *Journal of Community Health* 11 (1986): 63–69.

45. Arthur Brittan and Mary Maynard, *Sexism, Racism and Oppression* (Oxford: Basil Blackwell, 1984), p. 134.

46. Williams, *Black Teenage Mothers,* p. 1.

47. Ann Phoenix, "Black Women and the Maternity Services," in J. Garcia, R. Kilpatrick, and M. Richards, eds., *The Politics of Maternity Care: Services for Childbearing Women in Twentieth-Century Britain* (Oxford: Clarendon Press, 1990).

48. Ann Phoenix, "Theories of Gender and Black Families," in G. Weiner and M. Arnot, eds., *Gender under Scrutiny: New Inquiries in Education* (London: Hutchinson, 1987).

49. Martha Ward, "The Politics of Adolescent Pregnancy: Turf and Teens in Louisiana," in W. Penn Handwerker, ed., *Births and Power: Social Change and the Politics of Reproduction* (San Francisco: Boulder Press, 1989), pp. 151, 152.

50. Angela Davis, *Women, Race and Class* (London: Women's Press, 1981).

51. Valerie Walkerdine and Helen Lucey, *Democracy in the Kitchen: Regulating Mothers and Socialising Daughters* (London: Virago, 1989), p. 34.

52. Jones et al., *Teenage Pregnancy in Industrialized Countries.*

53. S. Phipps-Yonas, "Teenage Pregnancy and Motherhood: A Review of the Literature," *American Journal of Orthopsychiatry* 50 (1980): 403–31.

54. Ann Phoenix, "Narrow Definitions of Culture: The Case of Early Motherhood," in S. Westwood and P. Bhachu, eds., *Enterprising Women: Ethnicity, Economy and Gender Relations* (London: Routledge, 1988).

55. Furstenberg et al., *Adolescent Mothers.*

56. Jones et al., *Teenage Pregnancy in Industrialized Countries,* p. 6.

57. Wilson, *Truly Disadvantaged,* p. 10.

58. Furstenberg et al., *Adolescent Mothers,* pp. 220–21.

59. Furstenberg et al., *Adolescent Mothers,* p. 5; See also Frank Furstenberg, Jr., S. Philip Morgan, Kristin Moore, and James Peterson, "Race Differences in the Timing of Adolescent Intercourse." *American Sociological Review* 52 (1987): 511–18.

60. Sullivan, "Absent Fathers."

61. Richard Davis, "Adolescent Pregnancy and Infant Mortality: Isolating the Effects of Race," *Adolescence* 23 (1988): 899–908.

62. Lois Benjamin, "The New Caste: Toward an Alternative Framework for Understanding Adolescent Pregnancy," *Practice* 5 (1987): 98–109; Joyce Ladner, "The Impact of Teenage Pregnancy on the Black Family," in H. Piper McAdoo, ed., *Black Families*. 2d ed. (London: Sage, 1988); Wilson, *Truly Disadvantaged*.

63. Richard Davis, "Teenage Pregnancy: A Theoretical Analysis of a Social Problem," *Adolescence* 24 (1989): 19–28; Edelman and Pittman, "Adolescent Pregnancy," pp. 63–69.

64. Wilson, *Truly Disadvantaged*.

65. Robert Staples, "An Overview of Race and Marital Status," in McAdoo, *Black Families*.

66. Davis, "Teenage Pregnancy," p. 906.

67. Ladner, *Teenage Pregnancy*.

68. Wilson, *Truly Disadvantaged*, p. 83.

69. Staples, "Overview of Race and Marital Status."

70. Wilson, *Truly Disadvantaged*.

71. Furstenberg, "Race Differences," pp. 396–97.

72. Furstenberg et al., *Adolescent Mothers*, pp. 67, 31.

73. Phoenix, *Young Mothers?*

74. Simms and Smith, *Teenage Mothers and Their Partners*.

75. Hewitt, *White Talk, Black Talk*; Jones, *Black Culture, White Youth*.

76. Anne Wilson, *Mixed Race Children* (London: Batsford, 1987).

77. Sullivan, "Absent Fathers."

78. *Ibid.*, p. 57.

79. Griffin, *Typical Girls*, p. 46.

80. See for example, Carol Stack, *All Our Kin: Strategies for Survival in a Black Community* (New York: Harper and Row, 1974); Linda M. Burton and Carol B. Stack "Conscripting Kin: Reflections on Family, Generation, and Culture" (chap. 9).

81. Scott-Jones and Nelson-Le Gall, "Defining Black Families."

PART TWO ADOLESCENT CHOICES

ANNETTE LAWSON

5 *MULTIPLE FRACTURES:*
THE CULTURAL CONSTRUCTION
OF TEENAGE SEXUALITY
AND PREGNANCY

"No man has ever touched me."
"I wasn't there."

These feelings were expressed by two young women in Bristol, England, in 1989.[1] The first was expecting her second child, her eldest being 17 months; the second had a baby of a few months. This chapter is an attempt at understanding these striking words—so at odds, it would seem, with the facts of concrete experience. Both girls were 15 and, as is compulsory at this age, still in full-time education. As "schoolgirl mothers," taking their babies with them, they both attended daily a special unit devoted to their educational needs. No longer schoolgirls like other 15-year-olds, their primary identification was now mother and mother-to-be. They spoke in the informal, comfortable setting of a room in the unit, chatting for more than an hour with other similarly placed teenagers under the guidance of their teacher in a "lesson," or session, on personal and social relationships. They sought to explain their experience of sex and of becoming pregnant.[2]

Perhaps they spoke in this manner as a means of avoiding confrontation about contraception or a homily on the subject of responsibility. But when asked about their feelings for the children they now cared for, they made no excuses. "She's lovely. The best thing in the world. I wouldn't never give her up." Nor were they afraid to express conservative views about abortion. "It's wrong," "It's murder." And about adoption: "It's not natural."

These young women displayed little conflict about their role as mothers and comfortably rejected those who in turn would reject becoming a mother or refuse to rear a child to whom they had given birth. In relation to the business of sex, of beginning the process however, their feelings were far from clearcut.

Disturbed by these remarks of the young mothers in Bristol, I have focused in this chapter primarily on younger teenage women—those under 17, for it is in this age group that the "problem" of teenage pregnancy may be highlighted.[3] While relatively few teenagers who become mothers are in this younger age group (only about 17 percent of live births to teenagers were to women under 17 in England and Wales in 1986[4] and a similar picture pertains in the United States), I shall nonetheless focus mainly on the young women who choose to bear and keep their child— that is, very young mothers.

I acknowledge that for the older teenage woman, specifically those of 18 and 19, the problems of expressing themselves sexually, becoming pregnant, and bearing children may be less acute, occurring when they may have completed the equivalent of high school and may have a stronger grasp on the reality of their chances for employment. Children of older teenagers may also receive stronger support from their fathers, kinship networks, and the state. The 18- or 19-year-old may not be mature and may also be poor, but the law places her in a much less contradictory position between childhood and adulthood, and she is not required to pursue full-time education. Especially is this true in the United Kingdom, where most young people still legitimately leave school at 16 or 17 years of age.

This is not to say the conditions for childbearing and rearing are healthy or good for the older teenager, but there is no clear evidence that they differ significantly from those pertaining to older women of similar ethnic, racial, or class backgrounds. There is, one might say, no good time for a woman to have a baby in modern America or Britain, for the conditions that have provided support for mothers and babies are changing—not always for the better.

Multiple Fractures

To the objective listener, the words of the two young women quoted above are decidedly unscientific. It makes no sense and is indeed nonsense for a young woman holding a child in her arms to whom she has given birth to claim that "no man has ever touched" her and for the other, whose swelling belly informs the observer better than any words, that she "wasn't there." They speak about sexual intercourse in "unscientific" ways. They "knew" the facts and had been exposed to them quite thoroughly in school, but they expressed their experience in nonscientific terms.

This wholesale rejection of what seems self-evidently to have happened can be understood within a framework similar to that employed by Emily Martin in her work on the experiences of women in Baltimore.[5] Analysis of her interview with a range of women drawn from black, white, and various class positions revealed important class variations in the acceptance or rejection of the common medico-scientific explanation given for menstruation as "failed reproduction." Martin argues that working-class women's rejection of this scientific explanation arises from the fact they have less to gain from productive labor in society.[6] Separating an internal experiential self from bodily "facts" can in this way be understood as a form of alienation: a peculiarly apt metaphor given that, following sex, a productive activity—producing a child—may result.

Although alienation generally implies dysfunction, a process that denies wholeness and integrity to the person laboring to produce goods or services, the denial and the splitting of the self expressed with such astonishing clarity by these two young women need not be understood as damaging. Rather, the capacity to separate and divide the self into parts can be protective and functional, as Richard Sennett and Jonathan Cobb, describing working-class men believe: "Dividing the self defends against the pain a person would otherwise feel, if he had to submit the whole of himself to a society which makes his position a vulnerable and anxiety-laden one."[7]

Teenagers are generally in such "a vulnerable and anxiety-laden" position, and most show some kind of rebellion as they seek not to submit the *whole* of themselves to the dictates of the wider (white) society: injunctions to stay in school, say no to drugs, drink, and sex, study hard, play sports, assist with the family chores, be responsible but without serious obligations, and be attractive. Simultaneously, they must participate in the group culture of peers at school and in the neighborhood, especially with respect to appearance, musical taste, and sexual behavior. Adolescents must, in a word, be responsive to the prescriptions of their age group, which are often in conflict with those of authorities, to whom they are also responsible. Division of the self in the face of such conflicting demands might indeed defend against pain.

Denial of the scientific facts of sex permits a fragmentation of the self, in this case of the body from the psyche—the mind or soul or selfhood where a teenager experiences her emotions. Certainly both young women quoted above had been "there" and were "touched," but these things happened to their bodies, not to their *selves*. On this level of meaning, although they may have felt the tactile sensations of intercourse, they did not feel active participation or pleasure. Their emotions were not touched, their deepest feelings absent. Hence, no man had "ever touched" one, and the other "wasn't there."

In addition, the younger teenage woman regularly reports her pregnancy as an event that happened *to* her: she does not say that she had any control over her sexual encounter and its possible or probable outcome.[8] Various researchers suggest a lack of knowledge, or of understanding, lies behind such feeling, while others consider a lack of discussion relating information to the adolescent's sexual needs to be central.[9] Given the kinds of sexual harassment and power plays common in the school playground,[10] it should not surprise us that as she develops her social (gender) identity,[11] a young teenage woman is less likely to experience herself as an active agent with a body that belongs to her, inseparable from herself, fundamental to her very existence, than is a young man of similar age. The "I" or the self is (or for our two girls, was) absent from the body.

Denial of scientific facts also permits a young woman denial of responsibility for participation in the act that leads to pregnancy. Yet this route is one not often preferred. Ann Phoenix quotes young mothers who worry about what *they* have done, but she makes clear that their reaction to pregnancy depends a good deal on their orientation to it beforehand. Many planned for babies or wanted them, others did not "mind."[12] Mixed reactions are common at any age when a woman becomes pregnant and, like women whose husbands betray them, those who are shocked by the discovery of pregnancy first blame themselves and then think about contributing factors.[13]

Women are also ready to shoulder responsibility for the man's feelings and needs. One young mother said, "You get them all worked up and it's got to go somewhere, hasn't it?" With words like these, the young woman accepts the blame for his feelings and finds a reason to let him "have it off" in her. In a primitive way, the female becomes little better than the sex object from which her older sisters have been trying to escape for some decades: a thing the male desires and a receptacle for his satisfaction. Here, the body is not merely experienced as separate from an internal self but is itself further subdivided into parts. The vagina is a bit of the body that a man uses and perhaps even defiles—but, again, it does not represent the mother herself. She is fragmented.

It almost appears as if she is only a receptacle for male emissions—bodily waste products—that then are transformed within her body into the child she eventually so treasures. Perhaps the mother can even feel that she actively creates the child rather than accepting it as something that, magically, without her participation, happens to her. The child, it seems, allows her a wholeness and a sense of self that sex certainly does not. Paradoxically, she can be heard not as denying science in this fragmentation of her body into parts but as following scientific example, for this is often how medicine treats bodies, describing parts and dealing with symptoms independent of the whole. Particularly is this true of gynecology and obstetrics.[14] Only recently has holistic medicine begun to achieve a more acceptable place in practice.

By definition, as she becomes a mother, the teenager fails to fulfill her allotted role at school and, having been failed by the broader structures within which she moves,[15] she finds a way to become valuable to at least one other—her baby. This does not mean she literally fails to graduate nor that she will not return to school but rather that she is demonstrably in conflict with authoritative expectations. As we will see below, she is out of time.

Yet as a parent, she gains social power, entering a new world, albeit one that is difficult for her to negotiate and hard to survive in.[16] And in relation to her own baby, someone even more vulnerable than she, she also wields great power.

In the sections that follow, I examine both the structure and culture of the adolescent's world, revealing a series of contradictions or fractures with which she must contend. She acts at each level both in sympathy with and alienated from her environment. In addition, the teenage mother, by breaking the chronologies of the hegemonic culture, pollutes the category *child* and become a deviant *adult*.[17] One strategy for dealing with her contradictory position is to erect a series of protective boundaries, deny concrete experiences and creatively formulate her own meanings.

The Changing Family

Substantial demographic upheavals are occurring throughout the Western world. Fertility remains barely at and generally below replacement levels, marriage is being delayed or, perhaps, rejected, while many are choosing to live together and bear their children out of wedlock; people are living longer, divorce continues at a high level, and remarriage is common. It is important to stress, however, that the vast majority of individuals do marry at some point in their lives and that most children spend most of their childhood with two parents, even though increasing numbers also experience periods with just one parent, almost always the mother.[18] At the same time the massive increase in the numbers of women, especially married women, who work outside the home for money has changed childcare practices and affects fertility rates. The choices made by teenagers and their feelings about their sexual behavior and childbearing contribute to and have to be set in the context of these broad family changes. Indeed, teenagers, far from being out of step and alienated from their social worlds, actually follow trends similar to those of their elders.

For the United States, general European trends need to be broken down by racial and ethnic background of the mother as well, because in America such rates vary substantially. Overall figures show fewer births for all women: in 1972 there were 61.7 births per thousand women between ages 15 and 19, compared with 51.3 per thousand in 1985. Even for those very young—under 15—the rate fell slightly, from 5.8 per thousand in 1972 to 5.5 in 1985. This change masks the fact that between 1977 and 1985 the rate fell by only one percentage point for whites but by ten percentage points for black women aged 15 to 19.[19]

Marriage is certainly no longer the safe harbor of Christopher Lasch's well-known title.[20] In the United States in 1988, 43 percent of men and 30 percent of women had not married by the age of 30, compared with 19 percent and 11 percent, respectively, in 1970.[21] In 1960 the median age at first marriage in America was just over 20 for women and just under 23 for men; in 1983 it was just under 23 for women and just over 25 for men. At every age proportionately fewer black than white and Hispanic women were married in 1983 than in 1970.[22] Between 1960 and 1984 the percentage of black women aged 15–19 who were ever married dropped from 16.2 to 1.6, and for black males, from 3.4 to 1.8. Put together the birth and marriage rates and this translates into a major increase in young black mothers unsupported by male partners.[23] Evidently, although white and black patterns of out-of-wedlock births in the United States are now converging, there is a considerable discrepancy still, with babies being born disproportionately to unmarried black women.[24]

Around one-quarter of all births in both the United Kingdom and the United States are now to single women. About one-third of these in America and about one-quarter in the United Kingdom are to mothers under 20 years of age. Nearly 60 percent of the teenage mothers who gave birth in 1985 in the United States were unmarried—a substantial change from 1970, when fewer than one-third of teenage mothers were unmarried—and few of the younger teenage mothers married. In other words, shotgun weddings are largely a thing of the past. Like their older sisters, teenagers are not accepting marriage as a solution to their pregnancies, whether planned and wanted or unplanned and/or unwanted.

Although this is insufficient in itself to explain the decline in the marriage rate, it is becoming normal for substantial numbers of young people to spend at least some time cohabiting.[25] But teenagers are less likely than older women to be in a long-term committed relationship or to be sharing an address.[26] In the United States most of the young mothers who were unmarried, according to the Children's Defense Fund, were not supported by any man.[27] By contrast, Simms and Smith found that most young mothers in the United Kingdom were at least in touch with the fathers of their babies. Half of the single men did not live with their partners and babies but almost all had seen their baby at least once and often several times in the week preceding the interview and were delighted to be fathers, believing the experience had changed them for the better, into responsible people.[28] It seems that for those teenage mothers who do have a relationship with the father at the time of their child's birth, the relationship can be, as it also may be for older women, an important source of both emotional and material support.

In addition both parents generally now work. In the United Kingdom, most of this work among married women is part-time, at least until the children begin full-time education.[29] Lone mothers in both societies, lacking good childcare facilities, are able to work less than their married or cohabiting peers. In America, about 40 percent of *single* mothers with preschoolers are not employed outside the home—7 percent of *all* mothers with preschoolers.[30] For the teenager who may well have dropped out of school, not being able to work further alienates her from her peers, although she may remain embedded in her local community and in close touch with family and kin.

Nonetheless, changing family structures mean further splitting for young mothers of loyalty to various households and communities and a new set of models in their own generation markedly at variance with those of parents and grandparents. Yet there are some *continuing* family and community patterns—including early childbearing—that also create a split. This division lies between the demands of a wider culture to conform to particular chronologies and of their own families to follow a different timetable. Although scholars dispute the regularity of the pattern of early childbearing and its significance,[31] many teenage parents grew up in families split by separation and divorce, and a substantial proportion (not the majority) are themselves children of teenage mothers.

Among white working-class families in Britain for example, Simms and

Smith found nearly one-third of teenage mothers had mothers who had also had babies as teenagers. The fathers, too, often came from families with a tradition of early childbearing.[32] Indeed, one of the two young women quoted earlier was the child of a teenage (married) mother and the other's parents had divorced; she had no contact with her father. In some working-class communities in Britain, this pattern has been common, and similar patterns have been observed in the United States. Burton and Stack, in chapter 9 of this volume, describe black family patterns in which early childbearing without marriage represents the norm.

In such families, the custom is often that the teenage mothers do not take full charge of the baby for they have other tasks allotted; rather, that is the grandmother's expected role. This is well illustrated by the black American of 30 or so who tells her pregnant 13-year-old, "I want this baby. . . . I need to raise a child. That's my job now. My mama did it. It's my turn now." She had been mothered in her own infancy by her grandmother, and her daughter had been mothered by hers; now she wants to be "mother."[33] Similarly, in Bristol, a grandmother whose 15-year-old daughter was pregnant exclaimed, "It's so lovely. Just what I want—a grandchild. It'll make my life worth while again."[34] In her family the father (husband to the grandmother) had disappeared five years before the interview and both older daughters had borne babies as teenagers.

If at first sight such sentiments appear deeply at variance with hegemonic ideals and to limit life chances for the young mothers (as well as the grandmothers), we should reflect on the fact that such women also express shared cultural ideals for self-fulfillment. Legitimate channels for engaging in those ideals are often limited to them, however, so that other strategies must be developed, sometimes with greater connection to their own and their families' past experience. The way these mothers and daughters share in the cultural ideal of meeting their own needs and finding a sense of value is through making and caring for babies. For the older woman a grandchild represents a rediscovery of self. For the younger ones, a discovery. Of course, not all or even the majority of grandmothers-to-be greet the news of their daughters' pregnancy with delight or even with equanimity, but in Britain the testimony of 20 percent of unmarried and about 40 percent of married teenage mothers gives evidence of parental pleasure from both mothers and fathers.[35]

Similarly, the increase in single parenthood does not necessarily imply that dreams of intimate and long-term relationships have been abandoned. Rather, the solidity of the institution of marriage that used to frame such relationships has lost stability, and many people no longer (and some never did) put their trust in it.

Sometimes material conditions and trust in institutions and their regulatory functions are congruent with the goals of individuals—their hopes and fears—and at other times they are not.[36] In the years following World War II a consensus existed about the importance of social institutions, and individuals trusted the overall goals of their governments as welfare, educational, and health systems were established, demonstrating concern for security and social progress. But during the past decades, particularly in the United States and the United Kingdom, welfare services have been cut back, and despite the rhetoric of self-help and enterprise, for many it has become increasingly hard to obtain health care, housing, and a decent standard of living. In such circumstances trust in social institutions rationally deteriorates. We might most appropriately pose the question "Why would people still trust marriage and wish to engage in it?" as "Why not?" Shared normative values are less evident—the "collective conscience" is fragmented. Individuals must work out anew for each situation their own values.[37]

In sexuality, reproductive practice, and family formation, especially, there is little consensus on what behaviors constitute deviance. For example, pregnancy may be deviant from one perspective, abortion from another; sexual experimentation acceptable for males but not for females; fathering a desirable goal for low-status young black men with poor employment and educational alternatives but mothering a disgrace for middle-class young white women. Moreover, Marsiglio and Scanzoni, reviewing theoretical perspectives on pregnant and parenting black adolescents in America, suggest that not only blacks have been moving away from conventional normative patterns but whites as well, because "they too find them unworkable." This "unworkability" is owing not simply to deprivation but also to the growth of individualism; that is, individual adults pursue less the goals and values of their parents and more the ones calculated to be in their own best interests and to meet their own desires.[38] For the teenager, these are more closely formulated in relation to parents' values, but their own peer groups take on increasing importance in value formation.

So far as material conditions are concerned, most literature, both in America and Britain, indicates the poverty, educational failure, and low achievement of the pregnant teenager. They have been failed by their schools and, perhaps, by their families. Many chapters in the present volume alone attest to these findings (see Macintyre and Cunningham-Burley, Phoenix, Brindis, Simms, and Rhode), and they need no further rehearsal. Although social security in the United Kingdom and welfare in the United States is paid to pregnant young women, their trust in either institution is unlikely to run deep, especially when housing provision—often the most vital need—is the least well accommodated.[39]

There is little congruence now, it would seem, in the goals of the individual, material conditions, trust in institutions and their regulatory functions. The young person is not exempt from the fracturing of the societal framework. Yet, within that framework, beliefs are often widely shared.

Mythologies

Most teenagers share with their elders a dream of finding the right and lasting partner. They maintain this dream even while having become "sexually active" younger and with a greater number of partners than in earlier times.[40] Furthermore, like their elders, and although they have often not achieved it, they think cohabitation before marriage is a good idea.[41]

Perhaps because these goals are not in conflict with those of their elders, most teenagers readily reveal their dreams. They find nothing shameful about them. Jane Kritzman, researching sexuality among adolescents in high schools in New York City, found that despite some differences of emphasis, males and females, black and white, middle- and working-class youngsters readily expressed yearnings for romance and for heterosexual, intimate relationships "where you can be real friends."[42] They wished for a relationship that was whole and rounded, not fragmented into sex and talk as if the two were unconnected. The longing is for a lover who will be caring at every level—"someone you can really talk to." Young men, especially Hispanics, were particularly romantic.[43]

This Myth of Romantic Marriage—the ideal of finding a lifelong partner for an erotic and nurturing relationship[44]—provides a script that has already been written yet lies open to creative rewriting: a script to be lived and dramatically enacted. It belongs not only to the pubertal youngster or the teenager but to all ages and classes. It is expressed everywhere in the society, for to love and be loved in an erotic and intimate relationship has become a moral goal—*the* moral goal for millions, especially among women.[45] One is required (the message is powerfully conveyed by the media, especially on television and especially in the soaps) to become "mature," and maturity includes the capacity to love and be committed to one other person in a long-term relationship. In the United Kingdom in the early 1990s, for example, an Australian soap called "Neighbors" achieved the status of a cult. In it, teenagers, in common with their elders, struggle to make lasting but erotic relationships and attempt to deal with fidelity and the problems of commitment to others, including their children. One

teenager has a baby and experiences the conflict between practical difficulties and her relational desires.

Meanwhile, there is another mythology that for many forms a part of
the Myth of Romantic Marriage rather than competing with it. In this
version, if the dreamer makes the kind of erotic and loving relationship
that she seeks, she will simultaneously find self-fulfillment. Yet other sto-
rylines warn that self-fulfillment cannot be achieved within marriage,
without paid work, and even, in one version, with children. The development of self is sometimes understood as "self-ish"—lacking space for the
child. I have termed this narrative of self actualization, the Myth of Me. For
the teenager, how or whether to develop self-potential is unclear, because
the youngster is in the process of developing a sense of identity strong
enough (as Ruddick in this volume points out) to make rational choices in
her own self-interest. Nonetheless, who she will be and what she will be is
deeply integrated into the adolescent's vision of the future and impacts
what she does in the present and how she copes with constraints to her
development.

Chronology and Gender Scripts

The adolescent pursues her dreams within a number of material and
cultural constraints. Indeed, the "problem" of adolescent pregnancy is
comprehensible only when set within a broad, socially-constructed chronology. Despite variation among different ethnic and class groups as to
both acceptability and timing, the overwhelming hegemonic ideal orders
events much as follows: childhood and education, work and sexual experimentation (recent shifts permit both females and males to engage in this
but still show more ambivalence about females), marriage and children.
This chronology, generally speaking, requires that education be completed
(at least to high school level) before entering a committed relationship
(married or not) and that if premarital sex occurs, it do so within such a
relationship. Only later should childbearing be contemplated, preferably
when there is the money to support and the shelter to house the new
family. The state and other agencies of control attempt to delay the onset of
sexual activity, especially for girls, preferably until a committed relationship is formed and at least until late adolescence.

The female adolescent lives in a society that has lengthened the dependent, educational period of her life even as the age of menarche has become earlier.[46] The phrase "children having children," addressed in chapter 2 of this volume by Diana Pearce, arouses powerful feelings precisely
because it reflects this paradox. The very young mother is deviant by virtue

of her obvious rebellion against the proper chronology of events as she flaunts her out-of-time acts. Mary Douglas has suggested that it is when there are such grave contradictions or obvious paradoxes that "exaggerated avoidances develop around sexual relations."[47]

America is particularly inflicted with exaggerated avoidances that prevent adequate contraceptive education and practical help. Carole Joffe's devastating examination in chapter 14 of this volume of the taboos against mentioning a condom in American schools—this at a time of an AIDS epidemic—is shocking to a European audience, and the United Kingdom lags well behind the facilitating environment of countries such as Sweden, where adolescent fertility is the lowest in the world.[48]

Within this environment, American scholars describe sexual expressiveness during preadolescence (if measured by the onset of puberty) as largely a matter of play, but the same behaviors—hugging, kissing, holding hands, games of looking and touching—become infused with more serious intent and a sense of danger after puberty.[49] According to psychodynamic understanding of development, the genitalia become the newly or rediscovered foci of pleasure and anxiety. In one 1985 sample of American youngsters aged 13–18, 72 percent admitted to erotic fantasy, although, in another study, girls admitted to this less frequently than boys.[50] The gender difference grows less as the youngsters develop through adolescence: while 80 percent of boys aged 13–15 and 77 percent aged 16–18 said they often thought about sex, this was true of 54 percent and 60 percent, respectively, of girls.

During the 1970s adolescents in America reported feeling somewhat pressured by the changes in sexual permissiveness and hence of demands on them: 20 percent of both boys and girls in the 1970s compared with 10 percent in the 1960s thought they were "way behind" sexually.[51] This sample was also quite confident about its sexuality overall, but girls—even slightly older girls—took longer than did boys to become secure and were less certain of their attractiveness to boys. There were also substantial gender differences in the experience of sexual pleasure. The two young mothers quoted earlier would have been among the 40 percent of girls who did not enjoy sexual experiences, compared with the mere 14 percent of boys in the younger age group.

Although intercourse itself is normally kept profoundly private, much of the activity that leads to it—the preparation of the self as it were—is shared, among adolescents especially, with close peer group members. There are scripts for performance, modes of dress, habits of speech, patterns of dance, and likes and dislikes (particularly of music) that must be acquired for membership into a particular group. Although successful sexual relationships might lead to abandonment of the group (particularly for young men), activities within it are also often geared to sexual success. These dramas include gender and sexual scripts that often contain contradictory commands: to experiment sexually, especially if you are a male, for example, but to be responsible and caring. Commitment is expected, but to be too serious too young is unwise. Girls in particular suffer the taunts and conflicts of male peers both if they do pursue sexual expressiveness and, when choosing to reject the advances of particular boys in school, if they do not. In either case girls rapidly gain a name for themselves of "slag" (slut) or "whore."[52] The place for intimacy and feeling in adolescent gender scripts is not clear.[53]

Our two young women reflect some of these contradictions. The adolescent must control her desires but seek to satisfy them; keep her bodily boundaries intact, yet become a mature person capable of adult expressions of love; avoid damaging labels but meet her own needs and those of her lover as she perceives them. Indeed, in saying she was not there, our teenager insists on her own inviolable space within her body, a space that cannot be touched even by penetration. She also distances herself from the responsibility for her own participation, responsibility that might lead to undesirable labeling and remove her from the group to which she most wishes to belong. With this statement she also, paradoxically, shares an attitude with the older generation who believe in the right to sexual privacy, evident in slogans such as "Mr. Bush, stay out of my bedroom!" "Don't tread on me!" and "Take your court out of my crotch!"—all flaunted as banners and bumper stickers in the battle to retain a woman's right to choose to terminate a pregnancy in America.

Similarly, the mother of the 17-month-old expecting her second baby who explained to her teacher that she would not dream of terminating her pregnancy because "abortion is wrong," and would not consider giving it up for adoption "because that's not natural," expresses ideas firmly held by her own single mother. Her attitudes, then, are both in line with and defy the moral order of conventional society. She seems to wish simultaneously to join it and rebel against it, but she can also be understood as taking, albeit somewhat early, a path that is clearly gender-specific and defined as appropriate, even fulfilling. She carries her baby to term and keeps it just when her dream of pursuing the Myth of Romantic Marriage is least likely to be realized, perhaps precisely because she has engaged in out-of-time adult sexual intercourse.

Adolescent fathers, too, have also engaged in out-of-time behaviors. But the young father is rarely blamed for having sex, in part because it is commonly assumed that he needs sex quite "naturally." Rather, females are blamed for rule breaking where sexual and emotional ties are concerned or even for behavior that is not identified as rule breaking. It may not count as breaching rules to have sex, for that depends on whose rules are being followed, those of Church, parents, school, or peers. Without pregnancy, the fact need not be known. By contrast, becoming pregnant normally requires considerable explanation and is widely seen as rule breaking. Young women blame themselves for their male partner's sexual feelings (simultaneously denying their own) and take responsibility for placating him. There is nothing reciprocal about their feelings, for the corollary does not hold. She does not hold him responsible for arousing her; he is not expected to take responsibility for pleasing her. Nor of protecting her from the possibility of pregnancy. Indeed, a young man whose opportunities for exhibiting his manhood and competence are limited may especially desire to proclaim the fact of his fathering. The interests of each may not coincide. The statements offered by the two young mothers at the outset of this chapter can also be understood as representing this gender split.

Teenagers generally act as if men are entitled to sex and lack responsibility for the fruits of sexual intercourse, an attitude given celluloid validity in Spike Lee's recent film *Do the Right Thing*.[54] Mookie (a young black man with a poorly paid job delivering pizzas) has fathered a baby with Tina, a teenage Hispanic woman. He comes and goes and occasionally gives her a little money. She tries hard for a different, more stable and supportive, relationship, and his sister asks him to accept his responsibilities, but Mookie seems to visit Tina only when he wants sex.

Within such communities, the young man and the young woman have been taught and are practicing divergent gender scripts. It may be that they share a dream or mythology, but in practice gender has overwhelmingly diverted the star parts. It is still the case that through early socialization and practical opportunity via both legitimate (education, employment, marriage) and illegitimate (criminal or rule-breaking activities) channels, females must take on responsibility and, hence, blame for emotional ties, for the success or failure of families (however constituted), and for ensuring the men "have had enough."[55] A woman can control (to some extent) her participation in sexual activity and may, as Tina does although the two young English mothers did not, take great pleasure in it. She will risk her material well-being but retain control over her baby.

In order to explain the kind of variation experienced by the young white mothers in Bristol and Tina, the young Hispanic in Brooklyn, a subcultural dimension is, however, necessary. Nancy Adler and Jeanne Tschann in chapter 7 of this volume show how black, Hispanic, and white youngsters in the United States vary in their desire (conscious or preconscious) for pregnancy, while Bernard Iniechen argues that although much is similar in the experience of black and white teenage mothers in England, the fundamental pronatalist attitudes of the black mothers in his sample were in marked contrast with the attitudes of the white mothers. "They valued children (or, more certainly, babies) for themselves, without having the resources to follow societal norms in respect of their children's upbringing." Rather different racial scripts follow from this. One young woman said: "You should have all the children there are inside you." By contrast the young white mothers were more fatalistic, seeming to believe that women are not permitted and are not able to write their own scripts. Like the two adolescents quoted at the beginning, they felt unable to control their most important life experiences.[56]

Carol Aneshensel and her colleagues turned similarly to cultural explanations to unravel ethnic differences in their sample. Hispanic (Mexican-American) young women (aged 13–19) from Los Angeles were more likely to have given birth, but no more likely to have been pregnant and were *less likely* to have had sexual intercourse than other white non-Hispanic teenagers from similar class backgrounds.[57] Aneshenesel and her colleagues explain that the values of the minority group itself rather than any particular characteristics of the teenagers or of their socioeconomic status must account for these differences.[58] For example, high pro-family values among Mexican-Americans discourage premarital intercourse, and there is careful control of teenagers' dating. But these values also discourage the use of contraceptives and abortion among those who do have sex early. The patterns of early marriage and high pregnancy rates among women who have ever married are especially marked among those born in Mexico compared with those born in the United States, and they are consistent with this reasoning.[59]

Ann Phoenix in chapter 4 of this volume and elsewhere, however, finds little to support such claims and has argued that the idea of *culture* employed in such studies is nebulous. *African Caribbean* in the British context covers the disparate cultures of many islands; most of the black teenagers becoming mothers in the 1980s were born in the United Kingdom and most have never even visited their parents' islands. Readers of transcripts of Phoenix's interviews with black and white teenage mothers could not tell them apart. Wherever they live in England, black, like white, teenagers are, she argues, the product of modern working-class youth culture, not of black Caribbean culture some thousands of miles distant.[60]

These opposing positions can be accommodated, however, by acknowledging multiple sources of influence, varying in importance at different times and for particular individuals and groups. For teenagers these have been mediated primarily through educational and family settings and processes. Some recent studies of educational outcomes, for example, suggest that similar parenting strategies, maternal variables (like age, personality, and patterns of work), and family processes have similar effects for black, Hispanic, and non-Hispanic white grade school students.[61]

Categorical Ambiguity

As each young person follows a script developed within worlds varying by class and culture but offering only a limited number of parts, she or he may arouse intense reactions. There is nothing inherently right or wrong, good or bad, about a young woman's pregnancy, but in Western society the young unmarried adolescent girl who becomes pregnant and decides to keep her baby offends important moral categories and breaches boundaries defined by age.[62] Her actions have been punished through material deprivation and social ostracism.[63] In India, by contrast, the 15-year-old bride who has *not* yet produced a child would cause tears and recrimination. It is not her age that defines her but her gender, marital status, and reproductive capacity.

"The body," writes Pat Caplan, is "a metaphor for society; there is a clear correlation between how people see their bodies and how they see their own society."[64] Caplan also points out that most often the woman's body occupies this special position, for women generally hold less power than men, whose domination of women requires them to maintain control over women's bodies. It would not be stretching the imagination too far to suggest that teenagers such as the two quoted at the beginning of this chapter see their own bodies as beyond their control, managed by others—especially those who desire and would possess them—and yet also promising power.

At the outset I suggested these two were not untypical in their avoidance strategy. Sharon Thompson's "trickster" adolescents are, however, rare. She had ten in her sample of four hundred. But they laugh, con, play the hard and nasty, turn the tables, and enjoy their bodies, flaunting their youth and sexuality and having babies while playing with many men who are not the father. This is, perhaps, a much more effective route of power but a difficult one to manage,[65] especially because from the perspective of the other, the teenager's body has a different meaning. She is innocent and yet dangerous, a child, yet an adult. Her body serves as a boundary that needs protection and also requires control. Both the trickster and the young women who were not "there" simply employ diverse strategies to deal with societal definitions.

When the young adolescent becomes pregnant she confronts Western society with a dilemma: is she still a child, representing dependent innocence, or an adult, representing independent maturity? When she is below marriageable age, her rule breaking cannot be mitigated or "rectified," especially in communities where abortion is never a *desirable* solution and often unacceptable.

Chronological age is thus a fundamental social category used in important ways to grant or withhold privileges. Adolescence (a category of rather recent history) has boundaries that are particularly unclear at the upper limits. It serves a useful function in permitting educational and other developmental processes to occur without too much pressure on the child to transform rapidly into the adult. But it is well understood to contain only people who are *in transition* from child to adult, neither one nor the other, dependent but not wholly so, becoming sexually adult without the adult's responsibilities or privileges of sexual expression. Adolescent *mothers* therefore exist as a challenge and obvious rebellion against the categories in which they *should* reside—albeit temporarily—for in this perspective they are children who are also mothers and, by this definition, adults.[66]

Certain rituals and certain changes in the law and in social security benefits illustrate these tensions well.

In England at the present time a girl under 16 is presumed to be unable to give her consent to sexual intercourse, and she is therefore not legally "entitled" to be pregnant. Such reasoning is carried through into regulations over welfare benefits. Here, the law does not differentiate between very young and older adolescents—between those, say, under 14 and those 14–16. Up to the 16th birthday, a person in England is required to be in full-time education, may not marry (even with the parents' consent), and is the responsibility of the parent or guardian. Currently, therefore, if a girl under 16 is pregnant and has decided to carry her baby to term, she may not receive the maternity allowance (a flat payment in early 1992 of about $75 meant to help mothers prepare for their babies).[67] Her mother may claim it on her behalf only if she is herself in receipt of income support including "child benefit," an allowance payable to all mothers regardless of income, for her pregnant daughter. Once the baby is born the grandmother has no legal responsibility for her grandchild. When the teenager decides to keep her baby, she becomes entitled, *as a mother*, to child benefit and to single-parent allowance and, although clearly a child in most respects, is now simultaneously an adult mother. The ideological paradox is made even more poignant by the size of the benefit, approximately $18 per week in 1990, which is scarcely adequate to keep a baby in diapers.

If she is lucky, the young mother may live in an area that provides not only tuition at home but a "schoolgirl mother's unit" of the kind attended by our two young Bristol mothers. Here she can take her baby, who will be looked after by qualified nursery nurses while she continues her education, which generally includes work on social and personal relationships. Even in these units, however, there is greater provision for the mothers than for the babies. In one, for example, there are places for sixteen young women and only eight babies. The staff must either bend the law to take in more than their space permits or try to cover the girl's needs by teaching her at home, where she lacks a peer group and is often lonely and depressed.

Like most of her peers, the adolescent mother in the United Kingdom then leaves school. Because she has now passed the age at which she *must* receive education, it is most unlikely that there will be any special program for her, and no daycare provision will be made for her baby. Even under present legislation, when all young people between 16 and 18 must either be in school or at work or on a youth-training scheme, there is virtually no provision for infant care. Unless, then, she has a relative, friend, or partner who can help her care for her child, her chances of continuing her education, receiving further training, or finding work are extremely limited.

Yet, while teenage mothers are realistic enough to express anger and frustration with "the system," and many say they were too young, few regret their early childbearing. It is not surprising that the most successful programs rely on a promise of self-determination and the capacity of the young to plan for life within sometimes harsh contexts that would keep them within tight boundaries.[68]

As the two young women in my example make clear, the circumstances of conception present the most severe problem from their perspective—much more than the facts of pregnancy or motherhood. Indeed, these two events are neither difficult to comprehend nor altogether unwelcome, despite hardship and an ambivalent societal response, for the ethical rules that govern their decisions are much clearer; hence the statements "I'm having this baby. Abortion is wrong" and "I'm keeping my baby. Adoption's not natural."

Increasingly, such responses to adolescent fertility begin to make sense: as alternative choices for satisfying lives diminish, so parenthood becomes perhaps the most rewarding activity available for both women and men. For the teenage mother, a knowledge of her own creativity and success, adult status, and a degree of independence is achieved; for the young father, a sense of his own potency. For both parents childbirth often brings new and positive self-perceptions as well as social power. Thus chronologies for action appear to be altered to meet personal-cultural needs as well as in response to structural failures.

Even the unscientific rhetoric of the very young mother can now be understood as a strong response to the efforts of older adults to intervene further with her desire and, perhaps, ability to manage her own body as well as her baby. Her response requires multiple fractures of her emotions and intellect, mind and body, self as child-adolescent and self as young woman, young woman and young person, sexual woman and mother, myth inheritor and myth builder.

Notes

1. From Frances Hudson, *Taking It Lying Down: Sexuality and Teenage Motherhood* (London: Macmillan, 1991). Very early pregnancy occurs quite commonly as a result of incest, rape, or abuse. It also is more likely in girls who have been subject to sexual abuse in the past. There is no evidence that this was true for either of these two young women.

2. Frances Hudson was the group leader. The mood was serious and reflective.

I make no specific claims as to the typicality of their insights except to say that many people working with teenagers, especially pregnant teenagers, find that such statements are not uncommon (personal communications from Frances Hudson, Bernard Iniechen, and Sue Sharpe, 1989–90). In the literature, too, statements like these are not hard to find. Even if they are produced in response to authoritative adults and perhaps fail to represent "real" feelings, the question of why the youngsters need to present their experience in such a way remains to be answered. By contrast, one group of African American teenagers accounted for themselves as "tricksters" in sex, romance, and pregnancy, taking delight in their power to disturb expectations—especially those of their lovers. See Sharon Thompson, "'Drastic Entertainments': Teenage Mothers' Signifying Narratives," in Faye Ginsburg and Anna Lowenhaupt Tring, eds., *Uncertain Terms: Negotiating Gender in American Culture* (Boston: Beacon Press, 1990), pp. 269–81.

Other examples of teenage young women talking about their experiences and feelings include: Ann Phoenix, *Young Mothers?* (Oxford: Basil Blackwell, 1991); Diana M. L. Birch, *Are You My Sister, Mummy?* (London: Youth Support, 1988); Sue Lees, *Losing Out: Sexuality and Adolescent Girls* (London: Hutchinson, 1986); Paula McGuire, *It Won't Happen To Me: Teenagers Talk About Pregnancy* (New York: Delta, 1983); Jacqueline Sarsby, *Romantic Love and Society,* (Harmondsworth: Penguin 1983); Sue Sharpe, *Falling For Love: Teenage Mothers Talk* (London: Virago, 1987); Carolyn Skinner, *Elusive Mr. Right: The Social and Personal Context of a Young Woman's Use of Contraception* (London: Carolina, 1986); Emma Clark, *Young Single Mothers Today: A*

Qualitative Study of Housing and Support Needs (London: National Council for One-Parent Families, 1989).

3. I elsewhere argue that provided the interests of the most vulnerable are protected, the sociologist properly pursues self-interest. See Annette Lawson, "Whose Side Are We On Now? Ethical Issues in Social Research and Medical Practice," *Social Science and Medicine* 32, 5 (1991): 591–99. It is also good Durkheimian sociological practice to focus on the margins and extremes where problems (the abnormal or pathological) may best be seen in order to illuminate the normal.

4. Office of Population Censuses and Surveys. Series on Fertility and Mortality, FMI 15 (London: HMSO, 1986).

5. Emily Martin, *The Woman in the Body* (Boston: Beacon Press, 1987).

6. Martin, *Woman in the Body*, p. 110.

7. Richard Sennett and Jonathan Cobb, *The Hidden Injuries of Class* (New York: Vintage, 1972), p. 19.

8. Lesley Holly, "Schoolgirl Mothers," in Lesley Holly, ed., *Girls and Sexuality* (Philadelphia: Open University Press, 1989), chap. 6.

9. Kristin Moore, Margaret Simms, and Charles Betsey, *Choice and Circumstance: Racial Differences in Adolescent Sexuality and Fertility* (Oxford: Transaction, 1986), pp. 31–45); Holly, "Schoolgirl Mothers," pp. 74–75.

10. Sue Lees, *Losing Out: Sexuality and Adolescent Girls* (Dover, N.H.: Hutchinson, 1986). Jacqui Halson, "The Sexual Harassment of Young Women," in Holly, *Girls and Sexuality*, chap. 10.

11. Dominic Abrams, "Gender Identity and Adolescence," in Suzanne Skevington and Deborah Baker, eds., *The Social Identity of Women* (London: Sage, 1989).

12. Phoenix, *Young Mothers?* chap. 3.

13. Annette Lawson, *Adultery: An Analysis of Love and Betrayal* (New York: Basic Books, 1988).

14. See Ann Oakley, *Becoming a Mother* (Oxford: Martin Robertson, 1979), and *Women Confined* (Oxford: Martin Robertson, 1980); and Pamela Eakin, ed., *The American Way of Birth* (Philadelphia: Temple University Press, 1986).

15. See Claire Brindis, "Antecedents and Consequences: The Need for Diverse Strategies in Adolescent Pregnancy Prevention" (chap. 13), Deborah L. Rhode, "Adolescent Pregnancy and Public Policy" (chap. 15), Sara Ruddick, "Procreative Choice for Adolescent Women" (chap. 6), and Margaret C. Simms, "Adolescent Pregnancy among Blacks in the United States: Why Is It a Policy Issue?" (chap. 12). Patrice Flax, accounting for one case, demonstrated the vulnerability of the teenager and the redefinition she undergoes as she has first one and then another child: moving out of school, where people are not much more grown up (as she feels) than babies themselves, taking on serious concerns—those of a mother—and losing touch with friends of her age who no longer share her passions. See "Donna, the 16-Year-Old Mother of Kenneth: A Case History with Policy Implications." Paper presented at the Stanford Institute for Women and Gender conference on adolescent pregnancy, Stanford, Calif., April 1989.

16. Bernard Iniechen, "Contraceptive Experience and Attitudes to Motherhood of Teenage Mothers," *Journal of Biosocial Science* 18 (1986): 387–94, especially p. 392; Carol P. MacCormack and Alizon Draper, "Social and Cognitive Aspects of Female Sexuality in Jamaica," in Pat Caplan, ed., *The Cultural Construction of Sexuality* (London: Tavistock, 1987), pp. 143–65, especially p. 143.

17. Anne Murcott, "The Social Construction of Teenage Pregnancy: A Problem in the Ideologies of Childhood and Reproduction," *Sociology of Health and Illness* 2, 1 (March 1980): 1–23.

18. Kathleen Kiernan and Malcolm Wicks, *Family Change and Future Policy* (London: Family Policy Studies Centre and the Joseph Rowntree Memorial Trust, 1990); Andrew Cherlin and Frank Furstenberg, Jr., eds., *Journal of Family Issues* 9, 3 (September 1988). Special issue on the European family.

19. Stanley K. Henshaw, Asta M. Kenney, Debra Somberg, and Jennifer Van Vort, *Teenage Pregnancy in the United States: The Scope of the Problem and State Responses*, (New York: Alan Guttmacher Institute, 1989), p. 12 and tables 3, 4, and 5.

20. Christopher Lasch, *Haven in a Heartless World* (New York: Basic Books, 1977).

21. U.S. Bureau of the Census, "Household and Marital Status." Population Profile, Special Studies, Series P-23, no. 159 (Washington, D.C.: Department of Commerce, 1989).

22. In 1984, 79 percent of Hispanic, 85 percent of white, but 97 percent of black young women ages 18–19 had never married. See Cheryl D. Hayes, ed., *Risking the Future: Adolescent Sexuality, Pregnancy and Childbearing* (Washington, D.C.: National Academy Press, 1987), p. 37. In addition, in 1984, 89 percent of live nonmarital births to adolescents aged 15–19 years were to blacks, 50.1 percent to Hispanics, and 41.5 percent to whites. See Hayes, *Risking the Future*, pp. 65–66.

23. Hayes, *Risking the Future*, pp. 77–78, and 36, citing the U.S. Bureau of the Census, "Marital Status and Living Arrangements." Current Population Reports, Series P-20, no. 389 (Washington, D.C.: Department of Commerce, March 1983).

24. The out-of-wedlock birth rate for white teenagers has tripled while there has been a 10 percent increase for black teenagers, but this still leaves a higher incidence of out-of-wedlock births to black teenage women. Kristin Moore, Margaret Simms, and Charles L. Betsey, *Choice and Circumstance: Racial Differences in Adolescent Sexuality and Fertility* (Oxford: Transaction, 1989), especially chap. 2; the National Center for Health Statistics, table 15.1, in Frank Furstenberg, Jr., Jeanne Brooks-Gunn, and S. Philip Morgan, *Adolescent Mothers in Later Life* (Cambridge: Cambridge University Press, 1987).

25. Among divorced people especially, fairly extensive periods may be spent sharing homes without marrying. See Kathleen Kiernan, "The British Family: Contemporary Trends and Issues," *Journal of Family Issues* 9, 3 (1988): 301–03; Linda Clarke, *Children's Changing Circumstances: Recent Trends and Future Prospects*. Research Paper 89-4, Centre for Population Studies (London: December 1989); Annette Lawson, "When Families Break Up," *Encyclopedia of Personal Relationships: Human Behavior* (New York: Marshal Cavendish, 1990), pp. 2206–11, and *Lifeplans* (Oxford: Andromeda Press, 1993).

26. About one-third of births to teenage women, nearly one-half of those to women aged 20–24, and close to two-thirds of those to older women in the United Kingdom in 1985 were to cohabiting couples (Kiernan, "The British Family").

27. Children's Defense Fund, *Teenage Pregnancy: An Advocates' Guide to the Numbers* (Washington, D.C.: Children's Defense Fund, January 1988); Karen Pittman quoted by Tamar Lewin, "Fewer Teen Mothers, But More Are Unmarried," *New York Times*, 20 March 1988, p. E-6.

28. Simms and Smith, *Teenage Mothers and Their Partners*, pp. 92–99.

29. Kiernan and Wicks, *Family Change*, p. 26.

30. This pattern of employment is not identical in Britain and America because the former now sustains about a 10 percent unemployment rate among married men, so although in both countries married women work part time while their children are young, working is more common and lasts for a more extended period in the United Kingdom than in the United States. Even in the United States, however, only when the figures for *all* mothers with preschoolers who work part or full time are added together do they amount to greater than half. In fact, one-third of mothers with preschoolers fit the traditional pattern of father as earner, mother at home. See Clarke, "Children's Changing Circumstances," p. 17, table 9; David Blankenhorn, "Ozzie and Harriet: Have Reports of Their Death Been Greatly Exaggerated?" *Family Affairs* 2, 2 (Summer/Fall 1989): 10.

31. It may be that the American and British patterns vary. See Frank Furstenberg, Jr., Jeanne Brooks-Gunn, and S. Philip Morgan, *Adolescent Mothers in Later Life* (Cambridge: Cambridge University Press, 1987), and Sarah McCue Horwitz, Lorraine V. Klerman, H. Sung Kuo, and James F. Jekel, "Intergenerational Transmission of School-age Parenthood," *Family Planning Perspectives* 23, 4 (1991): 168–73, who suggest the children of teenage mothers are not more likely than the children of older mothers to become teenage parents. See sources cited in Rhode, "Adolescent Pregnancy."

32. Simms and Smith, *Teenage Mothers and Their Partners*, p. 7. On average, 8 percent of teenage parents of the generation in this study were born to teenage mothers.

33. Linda M. Burton and Carol B. Stack, "Conscripting Kin: Reflections on Family, Generation, and Culture" (chap. 9).

34. Frances Hudson, personal communication, September 1989.

35. Simms and Smith, *Teenage Mothers and Their Partners*, pp. 15–16, shows that 19 percent of mothers and 15 percent of fathers were *initially* pleased about a single teenager's pregnancy; 43 percent of mothers and 41 percent of fathers were reported as pleased, and 26 percent of mothers and 30 percent of fathers were upset *overall*. There is marked variation also by social class and ethnicity: the higher the class, the greater the pleasure. Asian (Indian and Pakistani) parents were most pleased, followed by white and West Indian parents, respectively, but these figures are not separated by marital status of the mothers. See also Phoenix, *Young Mothers?* pp. 86–88.

36. Ron Lesthaeghe and Johan Surkyn, "Cultural Dynamics and Economic The-

ories of Fertility Change," *Population and Development Review* 14, 1 (March 1988): 40.

37. Robert Bellah, Richard Madsen, William Sullivan, Ann Swidler, and Steven Tipton, *Habits of the Heart* (Berkeley: University of California, 1985), suggests a deterioration in the overall consensus about moral values in America in modern times.

38. William Marsiglio and John H. Scanzoni, "Pregnant and Parenting Black Adolescents: Theoretical and Policy Perspectives." Paper presented at the annual meeting of the Society for the Study of Social Problems, Berkeley, Calif., August 1989. Forthcoming in Arlene R. Stiffman and Larry E. Davis, eds., *Advances in Adolescent Mental Health*. Vol. 5: *Ethnic Issues* (Greenwich, Conn.: JAI Press).

39. Simms and Smith, *Teenage Mothers and Their Partners*, pp. 60–67; Emma Clark, *Young Single Mothers Today: A Qualitative Study of Housing and Support Needs* (London: National Council for One-Parent Families, Summer 1989).

40. Joint Working Party on Pregnant Schoolgirls and Schoolgirl Mothers, *Pregnant at School* (London: National Council for One-Parent Families, September 1979); Sandra L. Hofferth, Joan R. Kahn, and Wendy Baldwin, "Premarital Sexual Activity among U.S. Teenaged Women over the Past Three Decades," *Family Planning Perspectives* 19, 2 (March 1987): 46–53; Lawson, *Adultery*, pp. 70–71.

41. Catharine Guy, *Asking About Marriage* (Rugby: National Marriage Guidance Council, 1983).

42. Jane Kritzman, "The Impact of Class on White Teenage Girls' Constructions of Sex and Love—A Group Approach." Paper presented at the Stanford Institute for Women and Gender conference on adolescent pregnancy, Stanford, Calif., April 1989. See similar conclusions reached by Patricia Miller and William Simon, "The Development of Sexuality in Adolescence," in Joseph Adelson, ed., *Handbook of Adolescent Psychology*, (New York: John Wiley and Sons, 1980); Sharon Thompson, "The Search for Tomorrow: On Feminism and the Reconstruction of Teen Romance," in Carol Vance, eds., *Pleasure and Danger* (London: Routledge and Kegan Paul, 1984).

43. Kritzman, "Impact of Class."

44. Lawson, *Adultery*, especially the prologue.

45. Ann Swidler, "Love and Work in American Culture," in Neil Smelser and Erik Erikson, eds., *Themes of Love and Work in Adulthood* (Cambridge: Harvard University Press, 1980), pp. 120–47; Bellah et al., *Habits of the Heart*; Lawson, *Adultery*, pp. 23–27.

46. "Whilst in the 1880s most girls did not reach menarche until after the age of sixteen, in 1983 in the United Kingdom there were 8.3 conceptions per 1,000 fifteen year olds," F. C. W. Wu, "The Biology of Puberty," in Peter Diggory et al., eds., *Natural Human Fertility* (London: Macmillan, 1986), pp. 89–101.

47. Mary Douglas, *Purity and Danger: An Analysis of Concepts of Pollution and Taboo* (Harmondsworth: Pelican, 1970), p. 147.

48. Britta Hoem and Jan. M. Hoem, "The Swedish Family," *Journal of Family Issues* 9, 3 (1988): 397–424. Also see Elise Jones, J. Darrock Forrest, N. Goldman,

S. K. Henshaw, R. Lincoln, J. I. Rosoff, C. F. Westoff, and D. Wulf, "Teenage Pregnancy in Developed Countries: Determinants and Policy Implications," *Family Planning Perspectives* 17 (1985): 53–63.

49. H. Katchadourian, "Sexuality," in S. S. Feldman and R. Elliott, eds., *At the Threshold: The Developing Adolescent* (Cambridge: Harvard University Press, 1990).

50. Robert Coles and Geoffrey Stokes, *Sex and the American Teenager* (New York: Harper and Row, 1985).

51. Daniel Offer, E. Ostrov, and K. Howard, *The Adolescent: A Psychological Self Portrait* (New York: Basic Books, 1981), pp. 62–63. These cohort differences are valuable for understanding the impact of historical time on the life course, which Glen Elder has mapped for children of the Depression. See *Children of the Great Depression* (Chicago: University of Chicago Press, 1974).

52. Lees, *Losing Out*.

53. For an exposition of the idea of gender and sexual scripts, see John Gagnon and William Simon, *Sexual Conduct: The Social Sources of Human Sexuality* (Chicago: Aldine, 1973); Judith Laws and Pepper Schwartz, *Sexual Scripts: The Social Construction of Female Sexuality* (Hinsdale, Ill: Dryden Press, 1977); Lawson, *Adultery*, especially chap. 2.

54. Alison Jaggar understands fathers to be agents of the standards of the wider society rather than equal helpmeets or, as she writes, "parental co-workers" with mothers. This might be applied to the feelings young women have of their sexual partners. See *Feminist Politics and Human Nature* (Sussex: Harvester, 1983).

55. Margaret Forster's most recent novel, *Have the Men Had Enough?* (London: Penguin, 1990), describes the life of an elderly working-class woman who as sister, daughter, wife, mother, and grandmother has always been concerned to ensure her men had enough. In old age, her daughter-in-law must care for her.

56. Bernard Iniechen, "Teenage Motherhood in Bristol: The Contrasting Experience of Afro-Caribbean and White Girls," *New Community* 12, 1 (1984–85): 52–58; quote, p. 56. The study included ninety-two "teenage" girls, of whom sixty-seven were white with white partners and eighteen were African Caribbean with African Caribbean partners. The remaining seven were either Asian or of mixed racial origin. All had been born or brought up in Bristol in the West of England. In the United States, W. Miller notes that most teenagers' babies are "wanted" as opposed to "intended": "Relationship between Intendedness of Conception and the Wantedness of Pregnancy," *Journal of Nervous and Mental Disease* 159 (1974): 396–406.

57. Carol Aneshensel, Eve Fielder, and Rosina Becerra, "Fertility and Fertility-Related Behavior among Mexican-American and Non-Hispanic White Female Adolescents," *Journal of Health and Social Behavior* 30 (March 1989): 56–76.

58. The "characteristics" hypothesis asserts that "fertility is affected not by minority status *per se* but by the social, economic and demographic characteristics associated with minority group membership." The "minority" hypothesis asserts that "minority status has an independent effect net of characteristics," Aneshensel et al., "Fertility and Fertility-Related Behavior," p. 58.

59. Aneshensel et al., "Fertility and Fertility-Related Behavior," p. 74.

60. Ann Phoenix, "Narrow Definitions of Culture: The Case of Early Motherhood," in S. Westwood and P. Bhachu, eds., *Enterprising Women: Ethnicity, Economy and Gender Relations* (London: Routledge, 1988).

61. Sanford Dornbusch, "The Sociology of Adolescence," *Annual Review of Sociology* 15 (1989): 233–59.

62. See Catharine Kohler Reissman and Constance A. Nathanson, "The Management of Reproduction: Social Construction and Risk and Responsibility," in Linda H. Aiken and David Mechanic, eds., *Applications of Social Science to Clinical Medicine and Health Policy* (New Brunswick, N.J.: Rutgers University Press, 1986), pp. 251–61: "Societal concern with adolescent sexuality has been aroused less by the practice itself than by the visibility of its consequences in the form of pregnancy and (particularly out-of-wedlock) birth," p. 254. Joseph Gusfield has observed that "neither 'problems,' nor their 'solutions' are inherent in particular objective conditions"; the designation of federal funds for adolescent pregnancy marked its debut as a public problem; p. 255.

63. As mental hospitals in Britain have closed, elderly women, "institutionalized" by their years "inside"—unable to adapt to the external world of daily decision making and responsibilities—have been released from back wards, where they were placed only because in their youth they had borne an illegitimate child. Exclusion from civil society was their reward.

64. Caplan, *Cultural Construction*, p. 14. Studies of Gypsies in California and France (Caplan, *Cultural Construction*, p. 15) and of Italians in southern Italy (Victoria Goddard, "Honour and Shame: The Control of Women's Sexuality and Group Identity in Naples," in Caplan, *Cultural Construction*, pp. 166–92) all point to the particular importance of the female body in this respect, especially for minority groups who need to defend their social boundaries against "foreign" or dominant cultures.

65. Thompson, "'Drastic Entertainments.'"

66. Anne Murcott, "Social Construction of Teenage Pregnancy."

67. Maternity allowance is, in any event, payable only when the mother has been in work and paying national insurance contributions for twenty-six weeks out of the fifty-two preceding the twenty-sixth week of her pregnancy. Thus, even if an older teenager is pregnant but still at school, she would not qualify for this allowance.

68. Janetta Yanez, "Life Planning: The Integration of Education/Employment and Family Planning in Adolescent Pregnancy." Paper presented at the Stanford Institute for Women and Gender conference on adolescent pregnancy, Stanford, Calif., April 1989.

SARA RUDDICK

6 PROCREATIVE CHOICE
FOR ADOLESCENT WOMEN

Certain feminist philosophers have been trying to develop a woman-respecting "ethics of care."[1] Such an ethics should surely listen to, learn from, and come to the aid of very young mothers who are still in need of—even as they are trying to engage in—caring activities. Toward this end, I have been trying to develop a concept of choice appropriate for but not limited to adolescent women. Yet, in spite of thinking about mothering and more generally about care for more than a decade, I have found it difficult to speak of very young mothers within the context or in the language of current U.S. discussions of "adolescent" pregnancy and mothering.[2] I therefore begin by clarifying the terms and politics of my thinking.

Disaster and Timeliness

In national debates the adolescent mother is a symbol of sexual and social disorder; her pregnancy and even more her decision to give birth are represented as causes as well as symptoms of intergenerational cycles of poverty and despair. Unlike drug addiction and AIDS, with which they are often associated,[3] neither giving birth nor mothering are intrinsically disastrous to the young women, men, and children affected by them. Yet repeatedly, even in the absence of addiction or disease, adolescent birth-giving and mothering are said to be a disaster for the nation or community in which they occur and for individual young women and their children.

In this scenario of catastrophe, it is nearly impossible to disentangle the burdens of adolescent birthgiving or mothering from the sufferings of many Americans who are impoverished, assaulted by racist practices, desperately isolated in rural settings, or, especially in cities, chronically subject to violent attack. *Parents,* whatever their age, need safe places to live, food, effective medical services, and caring centers to which they can entrust their children. Impoverished and assaulted *adolescents,* whatever their sexual or parental activities, urgently require quality education, job training, and access to employment. The particular struggles of very young mothers and their children may reveal but do not create radical injustice and racism. Adolescent mothering becomes a "disaster" because of economic and social policies and because of the illiteracy, disease, and despair they foster, not because of the sexual and procreative behavior of young women or men.

An adolescent woman's birthgiving and mothering, even though not intrinsically disastrous, might nonetheless be untimely. This alleged untimeliness has to do with adolescent development, a distinctive and formative process of biological, psychological, and intellectual growth that occurs between childhood and adulthood. The claim is that adolescent women are not yet sufficiently "developed" to mother well. To make matters worse, adolescent mothering interferes with a woman's already insufficient development.

"In many cases, the young mothers of these children are themselves hardly removed from childhood—their education is incomplete, their preparation for parenthood underdeveloped, and their own personal potential unfulfilled."[4] These developmental risks are not limited to young women living in poverty, though the consequences for them of untimeliness are typically more severe.

On my admittedly partial and amateur reading, I do not see a consensus among sympathetic sociologists and policymakers about the untimeliness of adolescent motherhood. People tend to agree that, at least in the contemporary United States, adolescent mothering (but not necessarily pregnancy) burdens young women and their children in ways that later mothering does not. The comparative disadvantages of earlier mothering seem to persist even when adolescent women are compared only with somewhat older women of the same class and ethnicity. But these comparative disadvantages seem to be exaggerated and are often of shorter duration than is anticipated by reports gathered shortly after the birth of the child.

And some sociologists argue that, given the assaultive conditions that African American, Hispanic, or other minority mothers suffer, whatever their age, adolescent women may actually enjoy comparative advantages over older, similarly circumstanced women. In particular, very young mothers may get benefits such as health care, educational support, and childcare that are not available to their older childbearing sisters.[5]

The diagnosis of *untimeliness* with regard to mothering also risks ethnocentricity and cultural arrogance. Across the world and down the centuries, very young women have borne and cared for children. The experience of "adolescence," although tied to biosexual maturity, varies by class, ethnicity, religious expectations, education, and a host of other cultural factors. Even the possibility of adolescence as it is understood in the psychological literature requires a period of "childhood" and at least some breathing or growing space between a particular culture's idea of childhood and the various adulthoods it offers. Where adolescence exists, it defines a process whose beginning and end vary individually as well as culturally.

Given this variability, it is not surprising that the literature (and lore) of adolescent mothering often attributes the persistent negative judgments on young mothers to a myopic or arrogant imposition of a middle-class norm which is also, historically, white and Anglo. To speak only of the United States, the families and cultures of Hispanic, African American, or other marginalized young women may not recognize "adolescence." For them, young mothering may be expected and even desirable. Moreover, diagnoses of untimeliness may well cloak a fear of adolescent sexuality and the independence of which it is a symbol and means.[6]

While I am aware of the dangers of imposing alien standards upon young mothers, I also distrust the view that adolescence is a privilege of economically advantaged classes and perhaps the lucky and talented tenth of oppressed or disadvantaged classes. I fear that a respect for diversity can legitimate the systematic and abusive neglect many young mothers suffer. For example, even in a culturally heterogeneous country like the United States, there are typical and predictable advantages to completing high school.[7] More subjectively, nothing in the literature I have read suggests that any group of young people is free of the complex experiences and deeply felt emotions of adolescence. On the contrary, the literature of adolescent pregnancy resounds with young women's conflicted desires to love and be loved, to be responsible to and for others, and yet to be "free."

As long as young women are not blamed for social disasters not of their making, it should be possible to develop concepts of procreative choice that respect distinctive cultural practices but also recognize typical disadvantages of untimely pregnancy. What counts as untimely varies with individual and social circumstances. It is hard to imagine conditions, at least in the United States, in which motherhood would be appropriate for a 13-year-old. But there is no reason to believe, in advance of knowing individual circumstances and cultural practices, that a 19-year-old mother will suffer distinct disadvantages solely because of age. (Although, to repeat, if she is isolated, assaulted by racism, or impoverished, she will suffer whatever her age.)

Judgments of untimeliness should be tentative. Their purpose is not primarily to diagnose and certainly not to blame but rather to prevent or alleviate unnecessary suffering for young women and their children. Everyone writes from a particular social and political location. Our words can and should be tested by their usefulness to those most actively struggling with adolescent sexuality and procreative choice. Only they can say whether the concepts we offer foster adolescent development and inspire hope in adolescents and their elders.

Reconceiving Choice

Important choices often appear in retrospect to be dramatic moments, vertical markers determining the track of a life. But the *capacity* to choose is a matter of character and admits of degrees. A choosing person is increasingly active, less passive; her desires and reasons are increasingly integrated; she is less self-deceived or ignorant, more knowing. In literature on early mothering, the capacity to choose appears as "self-efficacy" or "a sense of control," both characteristics that "promote success" in the lives of schoolage mothers.[8]

To become a choosing person is a lifelong, developmental task, with advances and setbacks but no final achievement or failure. A 5-year-old can be a more or less choosing person; an adolescent's unplanned and unwanted pregnancy may express the weakness of her capacity to choose but it provides her, simultaneously, with an occasion for developing realistic responsible agency. Barring disabling disease, it is always possible to strengthen or deplete the capacity to choose.

There are, however, occasions and conditions in which the possibility of becoming a choosing person is seriously threatened. People have to be trained and encouraged to use the tools for choice their culture provides that are appropriate to their age. From childhood on, they must have experiences of choosing, occasions when they feel that their actions issue from and attain responsible desires. Neglect, bigotry, abuse, inadequate education, or even repeated frustration can sabotage the desire for, even the conception of, responsible choice. Although the capacity to choose originates in earliest childhood and develops over a lifetime, cultures that include adolescence as a concept provide thereby poignant and risky occasions for strengthening the capacity to choose. Conversely, as children become adolescents and then adults, they find it increasingly difficult to recuperate from damaging neglect or abuse. Adolescents who are denied the tools of choice or the occasion to use them effectively may know only dimly the rewards and responsibilities of being a choosing person.

While adolescence is a testing and fertile time for developing the capacity to choose, the dominant, individualist conception of choice may appear to exclude adolescent women and adolescents of both sexes from low-income groups. In individualist cultures the capacity to choose is often identified with independence, the capacity to act or to stand alone. By contrast, women are said to be dependent upon relationships and all people with low incomes are considered dependent upon the resources of others.

The "ethics of care" mentioned earlier suggests an alternative conception of choice as inherently relational and dependent. Briefly, in an ethic of care self-identity, and hence identity as a choosing person, is created and expressed within relationships. An infant becoming a child acquires and names a self in and through her connections with others. Even the first ego, the bodily ego, is always already social, constituted in and constructed by relationships in which bodies are held, touched, spoken to, heard, hurt, and comforted. On this view, to be independent or to stand alone is to engage in a particular form of relationship. Any person chooses within and among real or fantasied, past or present, relationships.

From a relational perspective, different ages present distinctive challenges for choice. Adolescents are confronted in their relationships with what Carol Gilligan, following Albert Hirschman, calls "exit-voice dilemmas."[9] On the one hand, maturity and cultural expectations make it increasingly easy for adolescents to resolve conflicts within relationships by "exiting" (breaking) the relationship. At the same time, many adolescents are loyal to friends, families, and social groups, even when these loyalties seem to conflict with self-fulfillment. Moved by loyalty, these adolescents try to change a relationship so that they can, self-respectingly, stay within it, struggling to "span the discontinuity of puberty and renegotiate a series of social connections."[10] In Hirschman's language, rather than exiting they give "voice" to their desires and refusals.

Gilligan and her associates have suggested that young men may tend to prefer "the neatness of exit over the messiness and heartbreak of voice"; young women, by contrast, may evince a primary concern with maintaining attachment and connection.[11] Gilligan and her associates reached their conclusions primarily from studies of advantaged groups. But future studies may reveal that young women and men of assaulted or subordinated groups often exhibit especially strong loyalties, and among these adolescents, young women may prove to be especially likely to express (give voice to) the values of attachment. Janie Victoria Ward has written that "for Black females the orientation toward racial identity and pride begins early in life."[12] Michelle Fine and Nancie Zaine have described low-income African American and Hispanic female adolescents as "nested inside relationships of care, responsibility, and sometimes violence, their lives . . . woven with others. . . . Inside their lives, the needs of self and others are braided together."[13] For these young women, as for many of Gilligan's subjects, choice is not opposed to responsibility. Rather, conflicts of responsibility are occasions for developing and revealing the capacity to choose.

When the dominant culture opposes self-regard to responsibility for others and identifies choice with the independent self, young women may appear to be passive even as they make what are to them self-respecting and self-defining choices. In Fine and Zaine's words, "enacting responsibilities they do not consider inherently incompatible, female students are often forced to sacrifice their own educations and aspirations in the service of others."[14] Fine and Zaine pose a double challenge to adolescent young women and their elders: to imagine relationships that include a choosing self even as they include the other(s) with whom each person chooses connection. Young women often have to learn, in Carol Gilligan's words, to "include themselves in the circle of care"[15] while their elders, and in particular their teachers, must devise programs that are not incompatible with family or with sexual and procreative relationships. An adolescent choosing person needs to learn to resist compulsions to please, save face, or fit in; simultaneously this independence must be seen as making richer, mutually enabling, reciprocal dependencies possible. A young woman can recognize the dangers of feeling most her*self* when most sturdily connected; she may become entrapped in the web of her connections, bound to people who neglect or abuse her. But she can also appreciate that isolation and disconnection usually leave a person less able to resist domination or to engage in rewarding projects, more prey to uncorrected fantasy, ignorance, and the whims of others. In sum, elders and adolescents can avoid the appearance as well as the material enactment of a destructive division between "selfish" survival on the one hand and self-sacrificing love on the other.

Granted a relational conception of self, dependency appears to be socially as well as ontologically a human condition. Anyone chooses amid others within a world that is partly defined by the availability and distribution of technological, economic, and political resources. The capacity to choose is constituted in advance by access to the means through which choice is realized. In Aristotle's words, "Choice is [not] anything like a wish. . . . We may form a wish for some result which could never be achieved by our own efforts. . . . Nobody, however, *chooses* things like that. . . . Choice is evidently concerned with things which we regard as attainable. . . . When we choose, we choose something within our reach."[16] The capacity to choose is not a personal trait developed apart from the conditions in which exertion and effort are effective. The person who has access to education, job training, health care, and counseling is as much a creature of these enabling experiences as another person is of poverty, bigotry, and indifference. An affluent, trained, and employed mother in her late 20s is as dependent upon the resources available to her as is a poor, school age mother. The choices of both women are shaped by resources and social power; the conditions, not the condition, of dependency distinguish them.

Some conditions of dependency are humiliating and frustrating; they foster helplessness. Others—often misdescribed as independence—promote self-efficacy and self-esteem within a range of dependencies. Current styles of administering our insufficient welfare services, along with societal stigmatization of welfare dependence, often produce individual helplessness and shame. In public discourse, stigmatizing mothers on welfare obscures the dependencies of all mothers and their children as well as the desire of most people to perform services and acquire skills that others will reward.

Discourses of Desire and Refusal

The capacity to choose is a human good. For an adolescent woman, this good—or its absence—is grounded in and often expressed through sexual and procreative choice. That is, however various a girl's pleasures and projects, they depend upon and reveal her ability to create or reject sexual intimacies; to choose or refuse to give birth; and to undertake, postpone, or reject the work of mothering. Sexuality and procreativity are, even in the best societies, complex and mysteriously unpredictable. But in the contemporary United States the character of these activities and the connections between them are unnecessarily marked by superstition, fear, fantasy, and desires to dominate.

Let me demystify these activities by underlining quite banal facts. Sexuality, birthgiving, and mothering are separable activities and distinct in character. Sexual life begins in childhood and lasts beyond procreative capacities. It is interlaced with fear and longing, pivoting around pleasure so poignant that it demands repetition. For many heterosexual as well as lesbian women, conception is a rare event in an ongoing life of sexual fantasy and engagement that typically includes varieties of experimentation, pleasure, pain, intimacy, and abuse.

Birthgiving begins in but need not follow upon conception. To give birth is to engage in a temporally defined, intrinsically female project with a clear termination and goal. A successful birthgiver need not herself mother her infant nor is birthgiving necessary or sufficient for mothering well. Mothering is a kind of *work* defined by the demands of children for protection, nurturance, and training. Men as well as women are mothers to the extent that they engage in the work of mothering, to different degrees at different phases of their lives.

Although conceptually separable and distinct in character, procreative activities are socially and biologically connected in ways no choosing person can ignore. Although most sexual acts do not lead to conception, and although some conceptions occur through artificial insemination, birthgiving typically originates in heterosexual activity. All mothering, whether by women or men, depends upon some woman's birthgiving. Although not all birthgivers become mothers, a successful birthgiving project requires someone to mother an infant.

To present these separable and connected activities as grounds and potential expressions of choice requires a double-faceted discourse of desire and refusal.[17] A negative discourse, of refusal, recognizes the sexual violence visited upon women (and less often on men) and warns against the dangers of sexually transmitted diseases. This discourse stresses the social sacrifices, physical discipline, and pain required of birthgivers. It identifies the medical risks (if any) to very young birthgivers and their infants and rehearses the dangers to infants when birthgivers do not take appropriate care of themselves. This discourse highlights the burdens of mothering and the costs very young mothers pay in pleasures, employability, and education. The central concepts of this negative discourse are minatory or prohibitive, concepts that say "watch out," "stop," "don't." The defining aim of this negative discourse is to strengthen and legitimate women's "power to refuse."[18]

A positive discourse, of desire, recognizes the pleasures of sexuality and the rewards of sexual intimacy. It speaks of birthgivers' sense of achievement and the delight many birthgivers take in carrying, giving birth to, and marveling at an emerging, then newborn infant. It talks of

good moments in relationships with children and the relationships between adults that children foster and describes with respectful appreciation the demanding work of mothering. The central concepts of this positive discourse are enabling, concepts that say "act," "enjoy," "create," and
"nurture." Its defining aim is to legitimate and enrich women's capacity to
desire and enjoy.

Negative and positive are both integral to procreative choice. Yet in
discussions and readings about adolescent procreativity, I find amid a
discourse of fear and admonition scant evidence of enabling concepts.
Indeed, positive conceptions of mothering, birthgiving, and even sexuality are themselves interpreted negatively—as dangerously likely to lead
to sexual promiscuity, abortion, unhealthy birthgiving, or disastrous
mothering. Adolescent women often seem desperately in need of a discourse that enables and entitles them to refuse. They are badly served by
utopian celebrations of sexual liberty and sentimental accolades of birth
and mothering. Yet adolescents have at least some inkling, gleaned from
fantasy, observation, and experimentation, of the pleasures not only of
sexuality but also of birthgiving and mothering. Unless their intimations of
pleasure are addressed, they cannot find their experiences within official
stories or trust the officials who tell them. They become isolated, less able
to name the complexities of their feelings, and thus less capable of becoming choosing people. Hence the need for what Michelle Fine calls "the
missing discourse of desire."[19]

To suggest how a double discourse of desire and refusal could be taught
to adolescents, I posit here a sketch for an education for procreative choice.
Although I do not assume that classrooms will be sexually segregated, I am
concerned in this particular sketch with the education of girls and young
women. Men are equally deserving and in need of an education for procreative choice; they should not be excluded from the pleasures or excused
the responsibilities of procreativity. But much of what I read suggests that
in respect to pregnancy and childbirth young men and women typically
have distinct, sometimes incompatible, conflicts, dreams, and desires.[20] In
focusing on women I respect these differences and hope that others will
sketch a comparable education focused on men.

Educating for Choice

Sex education, even in a repressive climate, is increasingly acceptable. Researchers have shown that adolescents are more likely to seek out
and effectively use contraceptive devices when they have unashamedly

talked about sex with teachers and counselors.[21] More urgent, students need to learn how to guard against AIDS as well as against less lethal sexually transmitted diseases. Any honest detailing of the facts of sexuality and contraception improves upon ignorance and superstition. But if confined to biology and postponed until adolescence, sex education may not markedly affect adolescents' capacity for procreative choice. Sexuality begins in early childhood and from the beginning is embedded in real and fantasied relationships with people central to a child's life.

The sex education I imagine for adolescents starts early, just as does sexual life. By the time they reach adolescence, young women and men have explored their own bodies and often those of their friends. They have watched, heard, and sometimes been abused by sexual adults. Although physical maturity gives new urgency to the connections and violations to which sexual intimacy is liable, adolescent learning takes place against a background of experiences and fantasies.

In my sex education program students—that is, children—would be encouraged to speak of their sexual experiences: to write, paint, or dramatize what they have felt and observed. They would learn to identify and depict particular sexual acts as hurtful, repellent, or merely boring. In cooperation and sometimes with the direct aid of teachers and counselors, they would learn to defend themselves against intrusion or cruelty from peers or adults. Equally, they would learn to name without shame their curiosities and distinctive sources of sexual pleasure—homo-, hetero-, or autoerotic. They would, with the help of teachers, postpone judgments of their sexual pleasures except in the special case that they themselves not only dreamt of but acted out cruel or hurtful desires.

This sex education as I imagine it would foster memory and honest speech. Young people would be enabled to name and evaluate local sexual practices, for example preserving "virginity" by substituting anal for vaginal intercourse or refusing contraceptives as "unnatural," "unfeminine," or "emasculating."[22] They would remember and recognize homoerotic desires and explore the homophobia that seems to pervade the fantasies of adolescents in many classes and cultures and can provoke a fearful need to prove heterosexuality, sometimes through violence against the different other, often through causing or displaying a gender-confirming pregnancy.

Crucial to honesty and probably its consequence would be critical evaluation of the sexual division of work, power, and nurturing within the culture and at home. Although men increasingly share the work and responsibilities of mothering, women across class, race, and ethnicity bear an undue and unfair responsibility for childcare and child support. This sexual disparity crucially affects poor, marginalized, or very young women.[23]

In my sex education program, young women would scrutinize critically the meanings of masculinity and femininity in their particular culture and in dominant cultural myths. They would share their fantasies of security or romance as well as corollary fears of abandonment that confound adolescents' power to refuse unjust, hurtful relationships. They would explore the ways in which the alleged privileges of masculinity are acted out by women and men in different economic circumstances. Whatever their race, they would attend to the burdens and temptations of masculinity in societies that project evil intentions onto racially other bodies, especially those of adolescent males.

From an early age, children would learn the biological connection between birthgiving and heterosexual genital intercourse. They would explore the fantasies that link sexual desires with the desire to impregnate or give birth. Because they would consider birthgiving as a project with distinct responsibilities and pleasures quite unlike those of sexual intimacy, they would learn about various kinds of contraception as they learn about sex itself.

Later, as adolescents learn the demands and promises of birthgiving, girls and young women could reflect upon the circumstances in which they would choose to initiate and/or continue pregnancy.[24] Discourses of desire and refusal would reveal realistically the birth experiences in particular social groups. Those who had already given birth could speak in the same sentence of the pleasures and sufferings of pregnancy—of, for example, a sense of bodily creative power allied with a sense of sexual unattractiveness. They could speak accurately of the effects, positive and negative, of pregnancy and childbearing on lovers and families. In particular, they could connect fantasy with the daily demands of maternal work and discuss they ways in which they or the fathers of their children got, or failed to get, the material support that mothering requires and to which mothers and children are entitled. The aim of these stories would be to dispel ignorance and foster the knowledge that makes choice possible.

Birthgiving is a project with an end: the birth of an infant. Although some adolescents choose to release their infants for adoption, most decide to mother them.[25] Education for choice does not stop when mothering begins. As the *Women's Ways of Knowing* authors report and Jill McClean Taylor confirms, becoming a mother often contributes to intellectual development, even initiating an "epistemological revolution" in a woman's sense of herself as a knower and in her capacity to envision herself as active and able to respect her own needs.[26] Mothers of any age are changed by and change with their children, but adolescents, who come to mothering at various points in a transitional phase of development, seem especially likely to be intellectually changed by their work.

Speaking out in the midst of a literature of sadness and frustration, adolescent mothers themselves often express their pride in what they have learned from mothering. A 17-year-old reports: "At first, you know, I was real scared. I didn't want to have the baby. . . . But I like being a mom now. I can handle it. All my friends keep telling me, 'Janelle, you're in a closet.' But I'm not in no closet. And if I am, well they should leave me alone. It's fun in the closet now that I know what I'm doing and everything."[27] Similarly, in a high school social studies class a mother of a 2-year-old defends herself against the assumption that adolescent pregnancy is devastating to mother and child: "If I didn't get pregnant I would have continued on a downward path, going nowhere. They say teenage pregnancy is bad for you, but it was good for me. I know I can't mess around now, I got to worry about what's good for Tiffany and me."[28]

Although mothering can afford young women a conspicuous opportunity for purposive learning, maternal education cannot be left up to mother and child. Whatever their age or circumstances, first-time mothers need services, companionship, and counsel. The needs of adolescent impoverished first-time mothers are distinctive not in kind but in urgency. An impoverished adolescent still living at home, fearful of returning to school, and/or trying to keep a job may be desperate for a place to which she can bring her children and where she can talk with new and experienced mothers outside her family. Because they are young, and because they have often been damaged by poverty or bigotry, impoverished adolescent mothers are said to long for trustworthy adults who offer real skills in the context of "enabling, often healing, relationships." Because they are (at least in the contemporary United States) impoverished in an unjust and often uncaring society, young mothers usually have to learn ways to overcome despair and defeat, to become their own and their children's political advocates. For even new skills and new relationships will come to little "if there are not realistic opportunities for young people to become participating members of society."[29]

I do not have the space to elaborate my curricular fantasies of mothering education. But I am confident that it is possible to develop ways of teaching and learning that open up worlds for mothers rather than shutting them out. "Project Redirection" and "Listening Partners" (to cite only two examples familiar to me) worked with women who were impoverished and isolated, selecting for special attention mothers who were most deprived and at risk. Project Redirection, a service program directed to young low-income pregnant and parenting adolescents, reported that even the most alienated and "failing" young mothers enjoy learning about mothering. Their successes suggest that when a mother increases, and is affirmed in, her maternal abilities, she is better able to develop her self. She is more apt either to stay in or return to school, to thoughtfully choose the time of further birthgiving, and to develop skills and find employment.[30] More recently, Mary Belenky and her associates in the project Listening Partners have attested to young mothers' hunger for self-knowledge and dialogue: "The participants accepted the discussion of children and families as important, but yearned for the luxury of placing themselves at the focus of the dialogue. Like so many community agencies and institutions, we had rushed them to a 'safer' focus for discussion (e.g., toward their families); but the participants were ready to take on the hard task of looking at themselves."[31]

Not surprisingly, Belenky and her colleagues found that a woman's growing respect for the complexity of her own mental life was causally connected with her increasing ability to see in her child's behavior the expression of his or her complex, respectworthy spirit. The needs of mother and child are indeed "braided together."[32]

> Women who can imagine their own intellectual powers are more likely to imagine and draw out the thoughts of their own children. . . . Only a mother who has some understanding that she herself can think and originate ideas is likely to be interested in the ways her children are confronting and thinking through the problems they face. Such a mother is more apt to become a "mid-wife" teacher who uses connected procedures to draw out her child's thinking—asking good questions, receiving the child's stories, and participating in the give and take of mutual dialogue.[33]

It would be sentimental to minimize the difficulties adolescent mothers confront and the frequent frustration of elders who come to their aid.[34] But it is also clear that many young mothers can acquire, and foster in their children, the sense of control and self-efficacy that choosing persons enjoy. All mothers, however mature and schooled, all children, however fortunate, depend upon communities that care for their children; mothering is collective work. But the double-faceted vulnerability of very young women and their children is ineluctably poignant. It is my hope that we, the elders, can make alliances despite our racial, class, and religious divisions, in order to demand for the youngest mothers among us the resources of hope that mothering requires and to which all mothers and children are entitled.

Notes

An earlier version of this chapter appeared in the *Women's Studies Quarterly* 19, 1 and 2 (1991): 102–20. I am grateful to Jill McLean Taylor and an anonymous reader at Stanford for helpful suggestions and criticisms and to Carol Ascher for many kinds of information, support, and advice.

1. I have in mind especially Carol Gilligan, *In a Different Voice* (Cambridge: Harvard University Press, 1982), and Carol Gilligan, Jill McClean Taylor, and Janie Victoria Ward, eds., *Mapping the Moral Domain* (Cambridge: Harvard University Press, 1988); Nel Noddings, *Caring* and *Women and Evil* (Berkeley: University of California Press, 1984 and 1990); Mary Field Belenky, Blythe McVicker Clinchy, Nancy Rule Goldberger, Jill Mattuck Tarule, *Women's Ways of Knowing* (New York: Basic Books, 1986); Patricia Hill Collins, *Black Feminist Thought* (Boston: Unwin Hyman, 1990); and my own *Maternal Thinking: Toward a Politics of Peace* (Boston: Beacon Press, 1989).

2. There are many fine discussions of the social construction and politics of "adolescent pregnancy." See for example Rosalind Petchesky, *Abortion and Woman's Choice* (New York: Longman, 1984), especially chap. 6; and Carole Joffe, *The Regulation of Sexuality: Experiences of Family Planning Workers* (Philadelphia: Temple University Press, 1986); related chapters in this volume.

3. Even healthy adolescent pregnancy is associated in the literature with AIDS and drug addiction, and it is this unexamined association that I challenge. Drug addiction, AIDS, and birthgiving are sometimes enacted in one adolescent female person's body, but pregnant adolescent women may be normally healthy. Unlike adolescent pregnancy, both drug addiction and AIDS are intrinsically disastrous, although their prevalence and the suffering they cause are exacerbated by social policies of neglect. The education of choice that I imagine later would include addiction and AIDS prevention and treatment.

4. Committee on Policy for Racial Justice, *A Policy Framework for Racial Justice* (Washington, D.C.: Joint Center for Political Studies, 1983), p. 10, quoted in Margaret C. Simms, "Adolescent Pregnancy among Blacks in the United States: Why Is It a Policy Issue?" (chap. 12). The judgment of untimeliness is pervasive. See, for example, Elijah Anderson, "Sex Codes and Family Life among Poor Inner City Youths" *Annals of the American Academy* 501 (1989): 59–78: "These are kids—mainly 15, 16, 17 years old. Their bodies are mature but they are emotionally immature" (p. 76).

5. For example, Frank Furstenberg, Jr., Jeanne Brooks-Gunn, and S. Philip Morgan argue that the deleterious effects of adolescent pregnancy and mothering, though real, are exaggerated. See *Adolescent Mothers in Later Life* (Cambridge: Cambridge University Press, 1987). In the 1989 conference at Stanford, Furstenberg suggested that the comparative disadvantage to adolescent mothers will be greater when adolescents have access to abortion, for the more capable adolescents will choose to terminate their pregnancies. See also Sarah McCue Horwitz, Lorraine V. Klerman, H. Sung Kuo, and James F. Jekel, "School-Age Mothers: Predictors of Long-Term Educational and Economic Outcomes," *Pediatrics* 87, 6 (June 1991): 862–

88. Arline T. Geronimus seems to argue for the advantage of very early childbearing. See "On Teenage Childbearing and Neonatal Mortality in the United States," *Population and Development Review* 13, 2 (June 1987): 245–79. I am grateful to Jill McClean Taylor for discussing these issues with me and summarizing relevant literature.

6. Various people have suggested to me in conversation that in their own social groups, or in groups with which they are acquainted, mid-adolescent mothering is normal and either accepted or lamented depending on individual circumstances. Mothers, or families, may desire a particular daughter's early pregnancy. See Linda M. Burton and Carol B. Stack, "Conscripting Kin: Reflections on Family, Generation, and Culture" (chap. 9). See also Joyce Ladner, *Tomorrow's Tomorrow: The Black Woman* (New York: Doubleday, 1971). Pregnancies may be desired openly or secretly, consciously or unconsciously by the young women themselves. See for example Leon Dash, *When Children Want Children: The Urban Crisis of Teen Age Childbearing* (New York: William Morrow, 1989).

7. Of course, schools do seem alien to particular cultures, such as Amish, certain Native American groups, and sometimes to marginalized and subordinate groups. Notoriously, high school often fails young women. Nonetheless, dropping out has its penalties, especially when a pregnant drop-out is not given a second chance to finish her education.

8. See Sarah McCue Horwitz, Lorraine V. Klerman, H. Sung Kuo, and James F. Jekel, "Intergenerational Transmission of School-Age Parenthood," *Family Planning Perspectives* 23, 4 (July/August 1991): 168–73. Self-efficacy is an antidote to the "maternal depression" which is both a consequence and predictor of early mothering for a young woman and later her children. Correlatively, self-efficacy depends upon and confirms a minimal, flexible, reliant hopefulness.

9. Carol Gilligan, "Exit-Voice Dilemmas," in Gilligan, Taylor, and Ward, *Mapping the Moral Domain*, pp. 141–58.

10. *Ibid.*, p. 143.

11. Gilligan, quoting Hirschman, "Exit-Voice Dilemmas," p. 146. Toni Morrison has repeatedly explored conceptions of masculinity and men's exiting as reflected in her male characters. See especially Ajax in *Sula*, Milkman in *Song of Solomon*, and Paul D. in *Beloved*.

12. Janie Victoria Ward, "Racial Identity and Transformation," in Carol Gilligan, Nona Lyons, and Trudy J. Hammer, eds., *Making Connections* (Cambridge: Harvard University Press, 1990), p. 229.

13. Michelle Fine and Nancie Zaine, "Bein' Wrapped Too Tight: When Low-Income Women Drop Out of High School," *Women's Studies Quarterly* 19, 1 and 2 (Spring/Summer 1991): 85–86.

14. *Ibid.*, p. 86.

15. Gilligan, *In a Different Voice*, which also develops the construction of conflict in terms of "selfish" survival vs. sacrifice.

16. Aristotle, *Nicomachean Ethics*, from Book III, Chapters 2 and 3. Translated by J. A. K. Thomson (Harmondsworth: Penguin, 1953), pp. 83 and 87.

17. I take the term "discourse of desire" from Michelle Fine, "Sexuality, Schooling, and Adolescent Females: The Missing Discourse of Desire," *Harvard Educational Review* 58 (February 1988): 29–53. Fine distinguishes a discourse of "sexuality as violence" and a discourse of "sexuality as victimization," both of which I include in the negative discourse aimed to strengthen the power to refuse. Fine also distinguishes a discourse of "sexuality as individual morality" that I have not identified (but may perhaps speak in.)

18. The phrase "power to refuse" comes from Simone Weil. This notion and its corollary, the necessity of consent, is central to her work. For a useful explication of this and other aspects of Weil's work see Peter Winch, *Simone Weil: "The Just Balance"* (Cambridge: Cambridge University Press, 1989).

19. See Fine, "Sexuality, Schooling, and Adolescent Females."

20. Differences between women and men take different forms in different subcultures, and may be atypically pronounced among adolescents, especially with regard to sexuality, birthgiving, and parenting. On radical differences between young men and women's attitudes to birthgiving among inner city poor blacks see Anderson, "Sex Codes."

21. This finding is well documented. Furstenberg, Brooks-Gunn, and Morgan, *Adolescent Mothers*, confirms it, as does Fine in "Sexuality, Schooling, and Adolescent Females." For a persuasive argument see Elise Jones et al. *Teen Age Pregnancies in Industrialized Countries* (New Haven: Yale University Press, 1986). There is a simpler point. According to Elijah Anderson, among "black poor inner city adolescents," many young women "have only an abstract notion of where babies come from and generally know nothing about birth control until after they have had their first child, and sometimes not even then." "Sex Codes," p. 76.

22. For the practices of substituting anal for vaginal intercourse see Ana Maria Alonso and Maria Teresa Koreck, "Silences: 'Hispanics,' AIDS, and Sexual Practices," *Differences* 1, 1 (Winter 1989): 101–24. The view that contraception endangers masculinity or the natural feminine, is widely reported. See for example Dash, *When Children Want Children*. In evaluating sexual practices, the prevention of AIDS and of conception would be related to but distinguished from each other.

23. Questions about men's participation in mothering are often buried in disparaging language about "female-headed households" or the ideology of marriage. While children are said to benefit from the presence of good fathers, delinquent or abusive fathers are worse than no father at all. See Frank F. Furstenberg, Jr., and Kathleen Mullan Harris, "When Fathers Matter/Why Fathers Matter: The Impact of Paternal Involvement on the Offspring of Adolescent Mothers" (chap. 10). Nor does marriage make good on the promises that official anguish about unwed mothers imply. According to Fine and Zaine, "teen pregnancy *compounded by marriage* is more likely to result in divorce, domestic violence, a second child, and a disrupted education than pregnancy [and, presumably, birth and mothering] alone" ("Bein' Wrapped Too Tight," pp. 88, 89, emphasis mine). Nonetheless, many women seem to want and typically benefit from mutually respecting parenting partnerships, heterosexual or lesbian.

24. Optimally, a woman chooses to engage in the project of giving birth and then sets out to become pregnant. On my view, the best contraceptive would, like the IUD, require a choice to *initiate* birthgiving. The IUD, however, seems inappropriate psychologically and medically for adolescent women. I recognize that many adolescents and their families believe that the smallest embryo is already an infant. Although I find this view metaphysically incomprehensible and the social restrictions to which it gives rise cruel, socially unjust, and dangerous for women and children, I do not doubt many women's passionate commitment to this belief. Despite the fundamental divisions among us, I hope that parents, teachers, and counselors could find ways to work together to maximize the chosen character of any adolescent's birth project, including those whose beliefs preclude abortion. See Kristin Luker, *Abortion and the Politics of Motherhood* (Berkeley: University of California Press, 1984), and Faye D. Ginsburg, *Contested Lives: The Abortion Debate in an American Community* (Berkeley: University of California Press, 1989). Ginsburg's book especially hopes for dialogue between proponents and opponents of reproductive choice.

25. A birthgiver may have good and sufficient reason to entrust the mothering of an infant to whom she has given birth to other mothers. It is important here that the reasons be hers and that she have the time and resources to reflect and act upon them. While it is necessary to combat widespread exploitation of birthgivers, usually poor women, these abuses do not, on my view, make it impossible to develop adoption practices that respect birthgivers. For reasons of space, and because most adolescent birthgivers in the United States keep their children, I have not considered adoption here.

26. Belenky et al., *Women's Ways of Knowing*, p. 35, Jill McLean Taylor, "Development of Self, Moral Voice and the Meaning of Adolescent Motherhood: The Narratives of Fourteen Adolescent Mothers," Ph.D. diss., Harvard University, 1989. The mothers Belenky and McLean study are in schools or centers where they receive compassionate and skilled support.

27. Quoted in Elisabeth Marek, "The Lives of Teenage Mothers: Schoolbooks, Boyfriends and Babies," *Harper's,* April 1989, p. 58.

28. Reported in Michelle Fine, "Sexuality, Schooling, and Adolescent Females," p. 37.

29. Quotations are from Judith S. Musick, "The High Stakes Challenge of Programs for Adolescent Mothers," in P. B. Edelman and J. Ladner, eds., *Adolescence and Poverty: Challenges for the 1990s* (Lanhan, Md.: Center for National Policy Press, 1991), pp. 129, 131.

30. Denise Polit, Janet Kahn, and David Stevens, *Final Impacts from Project Redirection* (New York: Manpower Development Research Center, 1985). In this project young women seemed most apt to stay in and found most rewarding their classes on mothering. The young women in Project Redirection showed gains compared with peers who did not have such a program but these gains were only temporary, which suggests—and personal reports confirm—that young mothers need ongoing programs. One does not become a choosing person in a year.

31. Mary Field Belenky, Lynne A. Bond, and Jacqueline S. Weinstock, "From Silence to Voice: Developing the Ways of Knowing." Unpublished paper, University of Vermont. Listening Partners is an educational program addressed to isolated, impoverished rural Vermont women who are mothers of preschool-age children. Manuscript available from authors.

32. See note 13, above, and accompanying text.

33. Belenky et al., "From Silence to Voice." In the authors' words, parenting strategies reflect maternal epistemologies: mothers in the videotaped mother-child interactions with more complex epistemological perspectives used more cognitively engaging statements and questions with their children and endorsed more cognitively stimulating and non-authoritarian parent-child communication strategies—those that are more likely to draw children into active participation and problem solving.

34. Judith S. Musick speaks about the "frustration and bitter disappointment" of people working with adolescents at risk ("High Stakes Challenge"). In The Regulation of Sexuality Carole Joffe movingly documents the exasperation and discouragement of those who work in family planning clinics. Joffe says that young women, lovers, family, and elders of all sorts must do more talking and listening. It is also important to recognize publicly and to reward economically the ongoing, difficult, undersupported, and underacknowledged work of kin, counselors, and teachers who remain committed to impoverished young mothers in spite of frequent cause for despair.

NANCY E. ADLER
JEANNE M. TSCHANN

7 CONSCIOUS AND PRECONSCIOUS MOTIVATION FOR PREGNANCY AMONG FEMALE ADOLESCENTS

Most approaches to studying teenage pregnancy take as their starting point the assumption that pregnancy among teenagers is unintentional and unwanted. The variables they examine are those that explain why an adolescent who wants to avoid pregnancy might become pregnant, such as lack of accurate information, lack of access to contraceptives and other obstacles to using them, conflicts over sexual activity, and lack of communication or interpersonal skills needed to negotiate effective use of contraceptives.[1] These approaches reflect current social policies discouraging teenage premarital pregnancy.[2] But there are countervailing forces favoring pregnancy, particularly in some ethnic groups, and there may be greater motivation for pregnancy among teenagers than is generally acknowledged. Thus, in examining individual behavior it is important to consider the extent to which pregnancy may be "wanted" and to which it may reflect motivation at either the conscious or preconscious level.

Existence of Motivation for Pregnancy

Several studies suggest that conscious motivation may play a role in the occurrence of teenage pregnancy. In a nationwide survey of young

144

women, of those who failed to use contraception at least some of the time, 16 percent reported conscious motives for pregnancy: they said they were either trying to have a baby or would not mind if they became pregnant.[3] The expressed desire for pregnancy is higher among pregnant adolescents (about 25 percent) compared to nonpregnant adolescents, although after-the-fact rationalization may be occurring to some degree.[4]

Research examining motivational factors for pregnancy among teenagers has generally been based on small samples or case studies of young women who are already pregnant, lacking comparison groups of teenagers who have not become pregnant. However, findings of this research are suggestive of the variety of conscious and preconscious factors that may induce adolescents to become pregnant. Studies of pregnant teenagers have shown that they may be motivated by hopes of achieving adult status, prestige, or autonomy through pregnancy,[5] by a desire to demonstrate love or commitment to a partner,[6] and/or by the wish to replace a real or threatened loss of a significant person.[7] In addition, pressure from others for a baby may contribute to motivation for pregnancy at either a conscious or preconscious level. The adolescent may be aware that her boyfriend wants her to get pregnant, and pleasing him may be explicitly linked in her mind to not using birth control. In contrast, a teenager who tries to gain autonomy by providing a parent with a substitute object to nurture,[8] or who is affected by a "covert mandate" from her parents,[9] may not be aware of this source of motivation. (Burton and Stack discuss more explicit mandates in chapter 9 of this volume.)

Theoretical Models of Motivation for Pregnancy

Most of the early research on motivation for pregnancy was largely based on concepts derived from psychoanalytic theory, focusing on unconscious motives. These studies shared assumptions of a "maternal motivation" based on a psychological drive.[10]

In recent years, however, theories involving conscious choice behavior have been influential in shaping views of motivation in research on fertility[11] as well as in psychology as a whole. In particular, expectancy x value models have dominated motivational psychology.[12] There are a number of specific models that fall under this general category, but all stress beliefs and values held by the individual about the behavior in question, and they share the assumption that individuals act on the basis of their expectations regarding the consequences of taking a given action and the values they attach to those consequences.[13]

Expectancy x value models have been successfully used to explain and predict a wide range of behaviors, including reproductive behaviors. For example, Beach and his colleagues[14] used one variant of these models, subjective expected utility theory, in studying reproductive behaviors. According to this theory, behavior reflects the individual's assessment of the possible outcomes of the alternate courses of action open to him or her. The individual is most likely to choose that alternative for which he or she has the highest subjective evaluation of benefits versus costs. Researchers have used the theory to help individuals decide whether to have a child, and they have successfully predicted intended and actual behavior.

The model that has been used most frequently to examine reproductive decisions is the theory of reasoned action.[15] This model incorporates social normative expectations as well as beliefs and values. According to the model, the best predictor of a given behavior is intention to engage in the behavior. Intention is influenced by two factors. One is the individual's attitude toward taking the action, which reflects his or her evaluation of the likelihood that certain consequences will result from it, weighted by the values attached to those outcomes. The other is the person's view of social pressures to engage in or refrain from engaging in the behavior. This, in turn, reflects perceptions of what specific other people want him or her to do, weighted by the individual's motivation to do or not to do what the others wish. This model has been successfully applied to understanding and predicting a range of reproductive intentions and behavior, including the decision to have another child,[16] to continue or terminate a pregnancy,[17] and to use specific contraceptive methods.[18]

In a recently completed study, we applied the theory of reasoned action to adolescents making decisions about contraception and their subsequent use of contraceptives. The model was found to be useful in understanding and predicting adolescent behavior.[19] Further, results indicated that the adolescents' feelings about pregnancy predicted their subsequent use of contraceptives. Those adolescents who believed that other people important to them were strongly against their becoming pregnant used more effective, consistent contraception. In addition, adolescents who felt more strongly that becoming pregnant within the next year would be bad or unpleasant were more effective in their use of contraceptives.

Despite the success of value x expectancy models in establishing the role of conscious motivation as a predictor of behavior, much of the variation in reproductive behavior has remained unexplained by the variables included in the models. Recently, alternative theoretical models have been developed that suggest processes that may mediate the relationship between cognition and behavior.[20] These newer theories of motivation and behavior invoke varied concepts, but share an assumption that behavior is at least partially guided by processes that involve symbolic representations. Some of the theories focus on self-schemata. Schemata are organizations of beliefs and feelings about a given object. They provide a way of organizing information about the world, and exert an influence on behavior, largely through associated "scripts" about how given situations should unfold. Individuals hold schemata about other people and groups, as well as about themselves.[21] Just as schemata can guide how an individual responds to others, they can influence one's own behavior and choices.

Other theories of motivation have focused on the motivating qualities of goals and the effects of feedback on the fit between goals and current behavior.[22] These theories stress that people's expectations of reaching a goal will influence their motivation to engage in behaviors they believe will help them attain that goal. The study of the relationship of pregnancy to salient goals held by adolescents is likely to shed light on an important source of motivation for pregnancy. Teenage pregnancy is associated with dropping out of school and having fewer years of completed education.[23] There appears to be reciprocal causation. Although pregnancy may precipitate dropping out of school, girls who are frustrated by school and are seeking alternative sources of identity and esteem may consider pregnancy to be a positive alternative.[24] Lack of scholastic achievement and educational aspirations have been associated with the conscious desire to become pregnant,[25] the occurrence of pregnancy,[26] and the decision to continue a pregnancy once it occurs.[27] However, little is known about other goals associated with motivation to seek or avoid pregnancy, or about the role that self-schemata (the adolescent's perception of herself and expectations for what she will be like) may play in such motivation. The research described later in this chapter addresses these questions, among others.

Ethnicity and Social Class

Although research has shown that there are differences in rates of pregnancy in different ethnic groups, little is known at the psychological level about how motivation for pregnancy differs for adolescents according to ethnic group and social class. Different ethnic groups may indeed hold distinct cultural values about pregnancy and children, but it is often difficult to separate the effects of ethnicity from those of socioeconomic status.[28]

The economic opportunities of different social classes have predictable effects on young women's goals and behavior. From a cost-benefit perspective, it appears that for adolescents with lower educational aspirations, the opportunity costs of becoming pregnant may be less than for those who value education more highly. For example, adolescents with economically limiting background factors, including lower socioeconomic status, lower academic ability, and residence with a single parent, are more willing to consider nonmarital childbearing.[29] However, these are not the only factors. For example, when ethnicity and background are held constant, young women who would consider nonmarital childbearing have also been found to engage in more problematic behavior, such as disciplinary problems in school, and to have lower educational aspirations.

Cultural values of various ethnic groups may contribute to differences in motivation for pregnancy, beyond the effects of social class. Several studies have found that proportionately more black teenagers than white report that they would like to become pregnant,[30] and that black adolescents are more willing to consider nonmarital childbearing than are Hispanic or white adolescents;[31] these relationships hold even when educational aspirations and social class are taken into account, although the differences are not as great. One study of pregnant adolescents found that Hispanic teenagers are more likely than either white or black teenagers to desire pregnancy.[32]

Other studies provide suggestions about the ways in which cultural differences could affect young women's motivations to become pregnant. For example, young black women are more likely than young white women to prefer having their first child before the age of 20, and their ideal age for first marriage is older than their ideal age for having their first child.[33] The relationship of marriage and childbearing may differ in other cultural groups; Hispanic and white adolescents who become pregnant are more likely to marry than are black adolescents.[34] Finally, white adolescents who become pregnant are more likely than adolescents from other ethnic groups to have a family history of psychiatric illness, to have lost a parent through death, or to be a runaway, suggesting that among whites pregnancy may more often be a "solution" to psychological problems.[35]

Recent research of our own suggests a possible mediating pathway whereby cultural differences influence motivation for pregnancy. Among a sample of sexually active, unmarried adolescents seeking care from one of several health clinics for adolescents, black adolescents reported that their mothers had their first child at a significantly younger age than did whites or Asians, while the age reported for Hispanic teenagers' mothers fell in between. Similarly, black teenagers wanted to have their first child at a younger age than did whites; Hispanic adolescents, although not significantly different from other groups because of sample size, named a desired age close to that given by blacks, and Asians an age older than that by whites.

Social pressures against pregnancy also vary by ethnicity. All Asian teenagers reported that the people important to them felt strongly that they should not become pregnant within the coming year, while 81 percent of black adolescents reported this; white and Hispanic teenagers registered percentages that fell between these. Fewer Hispanic than Asian, white, or black adolescents felt that getting pregnant in the next year would be bad or unpleasant.

When asked about the acceptability of abortion in the event of their becoming pregnant in the coming year, Hispanic and black adolescents tended to report that most of the people important to them were against their having an abortion, while white teenagers tended to report that most of the people important to them were supportive of their having an abortion; the responses of Asian teenagers fell in the middle on this question. Similarly, Hispanics and blacks thought that they probably would not have an abortion if they became pregnant in the coming year, whereas whites thought that they would; again, Asians' responses fell in the middle.

These findings suggest that black adolescents may value early childbearing relatively more than do other groups and find abortion to be relatively unacceptable. Hispanics also value childbearing, but at a somewhat older age; abortion may not be acceptable to them. White adolescents tend to value later childbearing and favor the alternative of abortion. Asians value delayed childbearing, but the findings are not clear about whether they consider abortion acceptable.

Current Research

As we noted earlier, motivation for pregnancy can derive from many levels, ranging from social and economic structure to individual, psychological variables. Our current research examines two kinds of influence, both at the level of the individual. One kind is conscious motivation for pregnancy: the young woman's views of the consequences of pregnancy, and whether the balance of favorable versus unfavorable aspects provides motivation to become pregnant or to avoid pregnancy. The other kind is preconscious motivation for pregnancy: factors that may create pressures for or against pregnancy of which the young woman herself may not be aware. Both of these are being assessed for their relationship to contraceptive use and the occurrence of pregnancy over an eighteen-month period.

Our sample consists of 290 sexually active, unmarried female adolescents aged 14 to 19, who sought health care at one of several health clinics for adolescents. These clinics serve different populations and include a wide range of patients. About half of the participants were drawn from three university-based clinics that provide care primarily to low-income, high-risk adolescents. The other half were drawn from a clinic based in a large health maintenance organization (HMO) that serves working- and middle-class families. Young women at these clinics who agreed to participate in the research were interviewed for about one hour following their medical visit and are being followed at three six-month intervals by telephone interview over an eighteen-month period. The average age of participants was 17 years at the initial interview. The group is ethnically diverse: 49 percent black, 22 percent white, 14 percent Hispanic, 8 percent Asian, and 7 percent of mixed or other ethnicity.

Conscious motivation for pregnancy is operationalized within an expectancy x value framework, the theory of reasoned action.[36] We are measuring general attitude toward pregnancy, beliefs about the consequences of becoming pregnant, values associated with those consequences, perceptions of general normative expectations regarding their becoming pregnant, perceptions of expectations of specific other people, and conscious intentions regarding pregnancy, as well as attitudes and intentions regarding the use of contraceptives and abortion.

We are assessing preconscious motivation for pregnancy in a number of ways. As a means to identify each adolescent's salient goals, we first use an open-ended format to encourage the participant to talk about her life, her hopes and fears for herself in the future, and issues of concern to her now. Later in the interview, we ask her to determine whether becoming pregnant would help or hinder her efforts to reach desired outcomes, become the self she wants to be, and avoid undesired selves.

The most indirect measure of motivation is the use of a projective technique. Projective techniques involve presentation of an ambiguous stimulus to which an individual is asked to respond. The theory underlying the use of such techniques is that the ways in which a person responds to an ambiguous cue will reflect his or her own concerns, traits, needs, and/or attitudes.[37] One such technique, the thematic apperception test (TAT), asks people to complete a story on the basis of a picture cue. The resulting stories are coded for various themes. The TAT has been used, for example, to measure need for achievement and need for power.[38] In a variant of the TAT pictures, individuals are given in written form the beginning of a story and are asked to complete it, indicating what happens to the major character(s). Responses to a story stem in which a woman succeeds in academic pursuits, for example, have been coded to indicate "fear of success" when women complete the story in ways that show negative themes associated with the character's apparent success (for example, denying the achievement, unhappiness in her social life, subsequent failure).[39]

In the current research, adolescents were asked to complete the following story:

> Kim and Mike have been dating for a while. A few months ago they started having sex. Kim's period is several weeks late. She has a pregnancy test and finds out she is pregnant. Could you tell me what happens after that? How does Kim feel? What does she do? How does everything turn out?[40]

We expected that the stories produced in response to this cue would reflect subjects' positive and negative associations with pregnancy. At the same time, we did not necessarily expect stories to make explicit the content of adolescents' motivations, such as desire to achieve autonomy or demonstrate commitment to a partner, especially because some of these motivations are not available consciously. In addition, stories may reflect more than adolescents' own concerns and interests; they could also reflect awareness of social norms or their imagining of various alternatives.

Since we are only partway through the follow-up interviews, results regarding the relationship of stories to subsequent use of contraceptives and the occurrence of pregnancy are not available. Therefore, it remains to be seen whether the positive or negative valence of stories actually predicts use of contraceptives and pregnancy. However, the stories have been coded and can be compared to conscious motivation for pregnancy. The stories were rated on five dimensions: general positive or negative valence toward pregnancy; how Kim feels about being pregnant; the outcome of the whole episode; how Kim's relationship with her boyfriend is affected; and whether Mike wants Kim to have the baby. Only about a third of the subjects (n = 90) mentioned how Mike felt about Kim having the baby. The remaining four dimensions were highly intercorrelated (Cronbach's *alpha* = .80), so they were combined into a single scale reflecting degree of positive preconscious motivation toward pregnancy. As indicators of conscious desire for pregnancy, we used responses to two questions regarding pregnancy in the next year: how strongly the young woman would like or not like to become pregnant, and how good or bad it would be to become pregnant. Because these were correlated .75, we combined them to form a scale representing conscious motivation for pregnancy.

We expected that conscious and preconscious motivation for pregnancy would be consistent for some adolescents; for others, the desire for pregnancy may occur at only one or the other level. For example, an adolescent may express no conscious motivation, but the story may reveal positive associations about pregnancy. In fact, that was what we found. Conscious and preconscious motivation for pregnancy is significantly but modestly related (r (156) = .33, $p < .001$), indicating that there is some overlap in the two levels of motivation, but also a fair amount of divergence. To explore further the relationship between conscious and preconscious motivation, we categorized adolescents as being either positively or negatively motivated toward pregnancy, for each of the conscious and preconscious levels. Adolescents who had neutral to positive scores for conscious motivation were coded as having positive motivation to become pregnant at the conscious level; the rest were coded as having negative conscious motivation. The same coding was done for preconscious motivation.

As shown in table 7.1, most teenagers were consistent in their conscious and preconscious motivation for pregnancy: 50 percent were negatively motivated both consciously and preconsciously, and 11 percent were positively motivated both consciously and preconsciously. However, 6 percent indicated positive conscious motivation for pregnancy and at the same time showed negative preconscious motivation. Finally, 33 percent of the participants reported negative conscious motivation for pregnancy but told stories reflecting positive preconscious motivation. Thus, knowledge about preconscious motivation for pregnancy yields additional information that is not necessarily consistent with conscious reports about desire for pregnancy.

Examples of some of the stories about Kim are provided below to illustrate how conscious and preconscious motivation for pregnancy may converge or diverge. Most stories also reveal some degree of inner turmoil and indicate that a decision about pregnancy involves the consideration of various contingencies, such as Kim's age, her boyfriend's desires, and whether she can continue her education.

TABLE 7.1. Relationship between Conscious and Preconscious Motivation for Pregnancy among Young Women

	Conscious Motivation		
	Negative	*Positive*	*Totals*
Preconscious			
Motivation	*n* (%)	*n* (%)	*n* (%)
Negative	78 (50%)	10 (6%)	88 (56%)
Positive	51 (33%)	17 (11%)	68 (44%)
Totals	129 (83%)	27 (17%)	156 (100%)

As we mentioned, most participants in the study were consistent in their conscious and preconscious motivation for pregnancy, with 50 percent of the teenagers being negatively motivated both consciously and preconsciously. One such teenager, a Hispanic 19-year-old, told the following story:

> I know that she is feeling really upset because she's really a kid herself. She can't support or raise a child at this age. And I bet her boyfriend is all "see ya later, I don't have to deal with this." 'Cause that's usually how guys take that attitude. And now she's going to have to be by herself dealing with it. I know that she's going through the worst time of her life because nobody really knows how she feels. She probably has an abortion. Never speaks to that guy again. He probably tries to come back to her now that she has had an abortion, and hasn't even helped her through anything. She will say, "Well, forget you anyway," and be a lot more careful next time. It was a really stupid thing to do. And that's what she'll remember, that it was really dumb, also really hard. She'll probably never forget it.

In the stories by those who were negatively motivated toward pregnancy both consciously and preconsciously, Kim sometimes had an abortion, as in the story above. However, some adolescents told a story in which Kim has a baby, with negative results. An example of this is the story told by a black 16-year-old:

> Kim is frightened . . . Mike wants the child. He relishes the fact of being a father, but he's not ready for the responsibility. So Mike makes up some little tiny excuse to leave Kim. Kim is alone. She wants the baby, but she knows she's not ready to have a baby yet. So she decides to have an abortion. But, being young and immature and having everyone say, "Kim, you should have this abortion, you can't go on with your life if you don't have this abortion," she turns around and does the opposite of what everyone else wants her to do. She has the baby. Two years later Kim hasn't finished school yet, she's living in a slum, and Mike's nowhere to be found. Ten years later her son or daughter is already into illegal activities and Kim is just right where she was when Mike left. She hasn't grown emotionally, and she hasn't grown financially, she's just—living.

Among the 11 percent of participants whose stories showed positive preconscious motivation to become pregnant and also reported positive conscious motivation for pregnancy, was a 17-year-old black adolescent who completed the story in the following way:

If she really cared for him, she would have the baby. If he put forth the feeling that he cared for her and told her that he'd like care of the baby, she should have it, cause I wouldn't really believe in abortion, so she should have it. If she felt that she didn't want to have no baby she shoulda took something for it. And most likely she woulda had the baby and the baby healthy and they probably together. . . . I hope he still take care of the baby. . . . She should feel happy that she pregnant—well, not happy that she pregnant—but happy that she bringin' somebody in the world that she could care for if she don't have nobody else to care for and nobody care for her. She could take what she didn't get from her parents on to her baby. She could give them the care.

Only a few (6 percent) of the teenagers expressed conscious motivation to become pregnant but told stories reflecting negative associations about pregnancy. One of these was a black 15-year-old, who said:

She would want to keep it and she wouldn't know how he would feel about it so she asks him. He's surprised and he doesn't want to keep it. So, she feels she wants to keep it but she can't do it on her own. It took them a while to decide and they decide that—Can I say that they decide they're going to keep it? [You can say whatever you want.] Well, theys gonna keep it and all. And then before the baby is born they was together and then after the baby was born they got separated. And they just broke up. And everything is going bad. She gets mad because he has another, you know, seeing other people. That's not what she want and it's like he don't care anymore. [Everything turns out] terrible.

Perhaps the most interesting group is those young women, constituting 33 percent of the sample, who consciously did not want to become pregnant but nevertheless told stories reflecting positive motivation for pregnancy. A few of these (10 percent of the sample) told stories showing neutral or mixed motivation, and most of them (23 percent of the sample) told clearly positive stories. The neutral stories did not convey a positive sense of pregnancy in terms of good things happening because of the pregnancy. Rather, the pregnancy seems not to interfere with future good things happening and may reflect a lack of motivation to avoid pregnancy. For example, a black 17-year-old told this story:

So Kim has the baby. She has to drop out of high school for a year. But then, after she has the baby she went back to school, got her a good education, went to college. She was an A student in college. She was majoring as a computer technician. . . . She was able to choose from any job she wanted to and be a success. . . . She made pretty good money, and she didn't have to worry about too much.

Some young women who were consciously motivated to avoid pregnancy told stories that revealed very clear positive motivation for pregnancy. For example, a black 16-year-old said:

She's probably scared. If her boyfriend was all for it she probably keep it. They probably are all happy, plan on getting married—not for the baby's sake, but just in my story they're gonna get married anyway. And they would have a baby. She would finish school, go on to college. Her boyfriend would help take care of the baby and stuff. So she wouldn't have to like miss out or anything. And they live happily ever after.

As we noted at the beginning of this chapter, most research on adolescents assumes that young women are not motivated to become pregnant. The preliminary results from our research indicate that there is some variation in the extent to which pregnancy is associated in adolescents' minds with positive themes and outcomes. Miller,[41] in a study of the "wantedness" and "unwantedness" of pregnancy, found that there was more wantedness than unwantedness. Translating "wantedness" into the terms of our research, we may well find that there is more motivation for pregnancy at a preconscious level in which pregnancy is seen as desirable but not actively sought, than at a conscious level in which there is an explicit intention to get pregnant. For the greatest understanding of the dynamics of adolescent pregnancy, both levels should be taken into account.

Notes

This research was supported in part by grants from the National Institute of Child Health and Human Development and from the John D. and Catherine T. MacArthur Foundation Research Network on Health-Promoting and Disease-Preventing Behavior.

1. Catherine S. Chilman, *Adolescent Sexuality in a Changing American Society: Social and Psychological Perspectives* (Washington, D.C.: U.S. GPO, 1978); George Cvetkovich and Barbara Grote, "Psychosocial Maturity and Teenage Contraceptive Use: An Investigation of Decision-making and Communication Skills," *Population and Environment* 4, 4 (1981): 211–25; Arthur Elster and Elizabeth McAnarney, "Medical and Psychosocial Risks of Pregnancy and Childbearing during Adolescence," *Pediatric Annals* 9, 3 (1980): 89–94; Sadja Goldsmith, Mary Gabrielson, and Ira Gab-

rielson, "Teenagers, Sex, and Contraception," *Family Planning Perspectives* 4 (1972): 32–38; Luella Klein, "Antecedents of Teenage Pregnancy," *Clinical Obstetrics and Gynecology* 21 (1978): 1151–59; Steven P. Schinke, Betty J. Blythe, Le Wayne D. Gilchrist, and Gloria A. Burt, "Primary Prevention of Adolescent Pregnancy," *Social Work with Groups* 4 (1981): 121–35.

2. Deborah L. Rhode, "Adolescent Pregnancy and Public Policy" (chap. 15).

3. Farida Shah, Melvin Zelnik, and John F. Kantner, "Unprotected Intercourse among Unwed Teenagers," *Family Planning Perspectives* 7 (1975): 39–44.

4. Jerome R. Evans, Georgiana Selstad, and Wayne Welcher, "Teenagers: Fertility Control Behavior and Attitudes before and after Abortion, Childbearing, or Negative Pregnancy Test," *Family Planning Perspectives* 8, 4 (1976): 192–200; Peggy B. Smith, Laurilynn McGill, and Raymond B. Wait, "Hispanic Adolescent Conception and Contraception Profiles," *Journal of Adolescent Health Care* 8 (1987): 352–55.

5. Sherry L. Hatcher, "Understanding Adolescent Pregnancy and Abortion," *Primary Care* 3, 3 (1976): 407–25.

6. Joseph W. Scott, "Sentiments of Love and Aspirations for Marriage and Their Association with Teenage Sexual Activity and Pregnancy," *Adolescence* 28, 72 (1983): 889–98.

7. Dean R. Coddington, "Life Events Associated with Adolescent Pregnancies," *Journal of Clinical Psychiatry* 181 (1979): 39–48.

8. Malkah T. Notman and J. J. Zilbach, "Family Aspects of Nonuse of Contraceptives in Adolescence," *Fourth International Congress of Psychosomatic Obstetrics and Gynecology*, Tel Aviv (1974): 213–17.

9. Harvey Rosenstock, "Recognizing the Teenager Who Needs to Be Pregnant: A Clinical Perspective," *Southern Medical Journal* 73, 2 (1980): 134–36.

10. Therese Benedek, "The Organization of the Reproductive Drive," *International Journal of Psychoanalysis* 41 (1960): 1–15; Burton Lerner, Raymond Raskin, and Elizabeth Davis, "On the Need to Be Pregnant," *International Journal of Psychoanalysis* 48 (1967): 288–97.

11. Kristin Luker, *Taking Chances* (Berkeley: University of California Press, 1975).

12. Julius Kuhl and Jurgen Beckmann, "Introduction and Overview," in Julius Kuhl and Jurgen Beckmann, eds., *Action Control: From Cognition to Behavior* (New York: Springer, 1985), pp. 1–8.

13. Nancy E. Adler, "Decision Models in Population Research," *Journal of Population* 2 (1979): 187–202.

14. Lee Roy Beach, Frederick L. Campbell, and Brenda D. Townes, "Subjective Expected Utility and the Prediction of Birth Planning Decisions," *Organizational Behavior and Human Performance* 24 (1979): 18–28; Lee Roy Beach, Brenda D. Townes, Frederick L. Campbell, and G. W. Keating, "Developing and Testing a Decision Aid for Birth Planning Decisions," *Organizational Behavior and Human Performance* 15 (1979): 99–116; Brenda D. Townes, Lee Roy Beach, Frederick L. Campbell, and Donald C. Martin, "Birth Planning Values and Decisions: The Prediction of Fertility," *Journal of Applied Social Psychology* 7 (1977): 73–88.

15. Icek Ajzen and Martin Fishbein, *Understanding Attitudes and Predicting Social*

Behavior (Englewood Cliffs, N.J.: Prentice-Hall, 1980); Martin Fishbein and Icek Ajzen, *Belief, Attitude, Intentions, and Behaviors: An Introduction to Theory and Research* (Reading, Mass.: Addison-Wesley, 1975).

16. Diane Vinokur-Kaplan, "Family Planning Decision-making: A Comparison and Analysis of Parents' Considerations," *Journal of Comparative Family Studies* 8 (1977): 78–98; Diane Vinokur-Kaplan, "To Have—or Not to Have—Another Child: Family Planning Attitudes, Intentions, and Behavior," *Journal of Applied Social Psychology* 8 (1978): 29–46; Paul D. Werner, Susan E. Middlestadt-Carter, and Thomas J. Crawford, "Having a Third Child: Predicting Behavioral Intentions," *Journal of Marriage and the Family* 37 (1975): 348–58; Andrew R. Davidson and James J. Jaccard, "Population Psychology: A New Look at an Old Problem," *Journal of Personality and Social Psychology* 31 (1975): 1073–82.

17. Judith L. Smetana and Nancy E. Adler, "Decision-making regarding Abortion: A Value X Expectancy Analysis," *Journal of Population* 2 (1979): 348–57.

18. Ajzen and Fishbein, *Understanding Attitudes.*

19. Nancy E. Adler, Susan M. Kegeles, Charles Wibbelsman and Charles E. Irwin, Jr., "A Decision-theory Analysis of Adolescent Contraceptive Behavior," *Journal of Pediatrics* 116, 3 (1990): 463–71.

20. Icek Ajzen, "From Intentions to Actions: A Theory of Planned Behavior," in Kuhl and Beckmann, *Action Control*, pp. 11–39; Julius Kuhl, "The Expectancy-Value Approach within the Theory of Social Motivation: Elaborations, Extensions, Critique," in N. T. Feather, ed., *Expectations and Actions: Expectancy-Value Models in Psychology* (Hillsdale, N.J.: Erlbaum, 1982), pp. 125–60; Arie W. Kruglanski and Yechiel Klar, "Knowing What to Do: On the Epistemology of Actions," in Kuhl and Beckmann, *Action Control*, pp. 41–60.

21. Hazel Markus, "Self-schemata and Processing Information about the Self," *Journal of Personality and Social Psychology* 35, 2 (1977): 63–78.

22. Charles Carver and Michael F. Scheier, "Control Theory: A Useful Conceptual Framework for Personality-Social, Clinical, and Health Psychology," *Psychological Bulletin* 92 (1982): 111–35; Charles Carver and Michael F. Scheier, "A Control-Systems Approach to the Self-regulation of Action, in Kuhl and Beckmann, *Action Control*, pp. 237–65; William T. Powers, *Behavior: The Control of Perception* (Chicago: Aldine, 1973).

23. Frank L. Mott and William Marsiglio, "Early Childbearing and Completion of High School," *Family Planning Perspectives* 17 (1985): 234–37; Linda J. Waite and Kristin A. Moore, "The Impact of an Early First Birth on Young Women's Educational Attainment," *Social Forces* 56 (1978): 845; Dawn M. Upchurch and James McCarthy, "Adolescent Childbearing and High School Completion in the 1980s: Have Things Changed?" *Family Planning Perspectives* 21, 5 (1989): 199–202.

24. Rosenstock, "Recognizing the teenager."

25. Shah, Zelnik, and Kantner, "Unprotected Intercourse."

26. Luella Klein, "Antecedents of Teenage Pregnancy," *Clinical Obstetrics and Gynecology* 21 (1978): 1151–59; Myra Leifer, "Psychological Changes Accompanying Pregnancy and Motherhood," *Genetic Psychology Monographs* 95 (1977): 55–96; Phil-

lip M. Sarrel and Ruth W. Lidz, "Psychosocial Factors: The Unwed," in Mary Calderone, ed., *Manual of Family Planning* (Baltimore: Williams and Wilkins, 1970), pp. 249–64.

27. Elster and McAnarney, "Medical and Psychosocial Risks"; Marvin Eisen, Gail L. Zellman, Arleen Leibowitz, Winston K. Chow, and Jerome R. Evans, "Factors Discriminating Pregnancy Resolution Decisions of Unmarried Adolescents," *Genetic Psychology Monographs* 108 (1983): 69–95.

28. Donna L. Franklin, "Race, Class, and Adolescent Pregnancy: An Ecological Analysis," *American Journal of Orthopsychiatry* 58 (1988): 339–54; Frank F. Furstenberg, Jr., "Race Differences in Teenage Sexuality, Pregnancy, and Adolescent Childbearing," *Milbank Quarterly* 65 (1988): 381–403; Ann Phoenix, "The Social Construction of Teenage Motherhood" (chap. 4); Frank F. Furstenberg, Jr., and Kathleen Mullan Harris, "When Fathers Matter/Why Fathers Matter" (chap. 10).

29. Allan F. Abrahamse, Peter A. Morrison, and Linda J. Waite, "Teenagers Willing to Consider Single Parenthood: Who Is at Greatest Risk?" *Family Planning Perspectives* 20 (1988): 13–18.

30. Shah, Zelnik, and Kantner, "Unprotected Intercourse."

31. Abrahamse, Morrison, and Waite, "Teenagers Willing."

32. Smith, McGill, and Wait, "Hispanic Adolescent."

33. Robert T. Michael and Nancy B. Tuma, "Entry into Marriage and Parenthood by Young Men and Women: The Influence of Family Background," *Demography* 22 (1985): 515; Kristin A. Moore, M. C. Simms, and C. L. Betsey, *Choice and Circumstance: Racial Differences in Adolescent Sexuality and Fertility* (New Brunswick, N.J.: Transaction, 1986).

34. Marianne E. Felice, Paul G. Shragg, Michelle James, and Dorothy R. Hollingsworth, "Psychosocial Aspects of Mexican-American, White, and Black Teenage Pregnancy," *Journal of Adolescent Health Care* 8 (1987): 330–35; Smith, McGill, and Wait, "Hispanic Adolescent."

35. Coddington, "Life Events"; Felice, Shragg, James, and Hollingsworth, "Psychosocial Aspects."

36. Ajzen and Fishbein, *Understanding Attitudes.*

37. Claire Selltiz, Laurence S. Wrightsman, and Stuart Cook, *Research Methods in Social Relations*, 3d ed. (New York: Holt, Rinehart and Winston, 1976).

38. David C. McClelland, *Power: The Inner Experience* (New York: Irvington, 1975); David C. McClelland, *Achievement motivation* (New York: Free Press, 1984).

39. Matina S. Horner, "Toward an Understanding of Achievement-Related Conflicts in Women," *Journal of Social Issues* 28 (1972): 157–75.

40. This story, and the responses to it, are taken from the authors' unpublished research.

41. Warren Miller, "Relationship between Intendedness of Conception and the Wantedness of Pregnancy," *Journal of Nervous and Mental Disease* 59 (1974): 396–406.

GLYNIS M. BREAKWELL

8 PSYCHOLOGICAL AND SOCIAL CHARACTERISTICS OF TEENAGERS WHO HAVE CHILDREN

The purpose of this chapter is to describe some of the social and psychological characteristics of young people who have children before reaching the age of 20, using data from a large-scale cohort sequential study of 16- to 20-year-olds in Britain.[1] Earlier studies contained a number of methodological weaknesses that in many cases served to perpetuate the perception of teenage pregnancy as a problem. But little of that earlier literature comes from Britain; in contrast to social researchers in the United States and Latin American countries, those in Britain have rarely focused upon the correlates of teenage pregnancy. This reflects the fact that teenage pregnancy is not seen as a major social issue in Britain.

The figures on teenage pregnancy show that the rate of live births has been reasonably constant at around 30 per thousand women for a decade. This is a relatively low rate and has not given rise to social concern. Most of the births included in these figures are to women of 18 and 19 and, for that group, there is little evidence of any medical ill effects accruing to either the mother or the child.

The proportion of illegitimate births to women under 20 has doubled in the same period. Unwed teenage women, when they find that they are pregnant, are less likely to get married and twice as likely to have an abortion as they were in the early 1970s.[2] The fact, however, that the same trend is evident for women in all age groups has perhaps deterred any moral outrage, and consequent research interest, which may have been focused specifically upon teenage mothers.[3]

Sociodemographic Characteristics of Teenage Mothers

There is considerable evidence from other parts of the world about the sociodemographic, educational, and psychological characteristics of women who undergo pregnancy as teenagers. Wilson found that compared to a group matched on sociodemographic characteristics, forty-four girls who had become pregnant before the age of 16 were more likely to have been academic underachievers at age 11, to have made an appearance in a juvenile court, and to have been referred to a child guidance or psychiatric clinic at an early age.[4] They were likely to be illegitimate, come from large families, and have mothers who were themselves teenagers at the time of their daughter's birth.[5] Gottschalk and colleagues concluded that their sample of seventy-six women in America who became pregnant before the age of 16 had received less parental supervision and discipline and were less religious than a comparison group from the same schools.[6]

This pattern is supported by data from Chile. Luz Alvarez and colleagues compared the sociocultural characteristics of 129 pregnant and 100 nonpregnant teenagers of low socioeconomic status attending the same outpatient clinic.[7] The pregnant girls proved to have lower IQ levels, less schooling, and lower aspirations, and to be focused on immediate gratification rather than long-term goals. Their norms for behavior were permissive, they did not practice any religion, and members of their peer group supported their liberal attitudes.

When sociodemographic characteristics are not matched in order to allow comparison on other dimensions, it becomes clear that there are substantial differences between those who become pregnant and those who do not. Stiffman's group studied 1,590 U.S. inner-city females aged 13–18 who used health clinics. They were able to compare females who were or had been pregnant with those who were sexually active but not pregnant and those who were sexually inactive.[8] Everyone in the sample came from an economically disadvantaged neighborhood, but the homes of those who had been pregnant were significantly less stable than those of either of the other groups. Either one or both biological parents were absent for 76 percent of those who had been pregnant. They were also more likely to have a seriously mentally ill person or one who had a drug or alcohol problem within the close family. Relationship problems and stressful life events show the same pattern. The group who were or had been pregnant did not differ from the others in physical health, but they, together with the other sexually active group, had higher rates of mental health problems and symptoms of conduct disorders.

Kiernan described the large-scale 1980 study done in Britain.[9] She reported information on 2,020 women born in March 1946 who had been studied longitudinally for twenty-six years at the point when she wrote her article. Of these, 13 percent had become mothers as teenagers and 52 percent were mothers by age 25. Teenage mothers, women who became mothers at ages 20 to 24, and women without children by age 25 were compared. Teenage mothers were more likely to have parents with minimal levels of education who had married younger. They were more likely to come from families of manual workers and to have more siblings than the other mothers. Teenage mothers had lower scores on tests of verbal, reading, mathematical, and general abilities at ages 8, 11, and 15. Predictably, they attained lower educational qualifications and left school earlier (aged 15). They were the least ambitious about their future careers and were the most likely to be in manual occupations and semi-skilled rather than skilled jobs. Their spouses were also more likely to fit this profile. Kiernan's findings are supported by smaller scale but intensive studies that have followed.[10]

Family Relationships

Poor family relationships have been said to be especially influential in contributing to teenage pregnancy:[11] the mother-daughter relationship is generally perceived as strained. Abernethy described the unmarried pregnant girl as likely to become isolated and low in self-esteem, not liking her mother and finding her an inadequate role model.[12] More recently, this finding has been questioned by Townsend and Worobey, who found no significant differences between the pregnant and nonpregnant in the intimacy, attachment, and strength of feeling expressed by mother-daughter pairs.[13] Their findings probably result from better sociodemographic matching of the pregnant and nonpregnant samples. Taking opinions about the relationship from both the mother and daughter probably also affects the accuracy of the estimates provided: daughters may express fewer critical opinions of their mothers when they know their mothers will also be interviewed. This interpretation is supported in the data by the finding that both mothers and daughters were overwhelmingly positive about each other.

The role played by the mother of the pregnant teenager was emphasized by Ortiz and Nuttall.[14] They studied forty-three pregnant Puerto Rican teenagers, of whom twenty-two had their fetus aborted, in order to determine the impact of family support upon decisions to have an abortion. They found that the teenagers who decided against abortion were influenced and supported by family and friends, particularly their mothers. Those who chose to have an abortion, perhaps surprisingly, reported a greater religious faith than those who carried the baby to term.

Self-concept

A large number of studies have claimed that teenage females who become pregnant have lower self-esteem or engage in self-devaluation, despite a diverse array of methods for measuring self-conception and evaluation.[15] Protinsky and colleagues found that pregnancy was associated with feeling estranged and ashamed, never acquiring an adequate understanding of how to defer gratification, distrusting others, and lacking confidence in the work-employment domain.[16] There is also evidence that pregnancy at this age is associated with social isolation[17] and a sense of anomie.[18] These findings are paralleled by studies that have shown teenage mothers to have an external locus of control—they feel that they cannot control their lives and what happens to them.[19] They see themselves propelled by fate, chance, or circumstance but not by their own effort or ability. Studies further hint that this perceived lack of control is tied to an increased willingness to take risks because personal responsibility for actions is never really accepted.[20]

Streetman, however, studied ninety-three 14- to 19-year-old females, seventy of whom had at least one child, and measured self-esteem and levels of normlessness (being unaware of dominant societal rules) and powerlessness.[21] This is one of the few studies to report no differences in self-esteem between mothers and nonmothers.

Teenage Fathers

Studies of teenage fathers are few. In fact, Vinovskis argues that the male partners of teenage mothers have been largely ignored in policy-making and by researchers.[22] Yet in Britain, at least, one fifth of all legitimate births to teenage women involve teenage fathers and three-fifths, fathers aged 20–24.[23] These ages reflect prevalent courtship patterns for teenagers, which indicate that a male is about two years older than his female partner.

Barret and Robinson in an extensive literature review indicate that most information on teenage fathers is available only from indirect sources:[24] potentially biased maternal reports like those found in Furstenberg and Talvite;[25] surveys of teenage males in general; those of teenage males before they become fathers; and studies of older unmarried men that include teenagers in their samples. There are exceptions to this pattern in the late 1980s. In terms of fathers' sociodemographic profile there is now reasonably good evidence. Elster and Panzarine found that in the United States teenage fathers had lower occupational achievements and lower educational attainments than their age peers,[26] and a similar pattern was found in Britain by Simms and Smith.[27] Simms and Smith discovered that teenage men had the same sort of background as the women they made pregnant: they had a poor educational attainment record, were predominantly employed in unskilled or semi-skilled manual jobs, and came from large families. Many had parents who were divorced, and their parents had often had their first children while teenagers.

There is also data concerning the self-concept of teenage fathers. For instance, Robinson and Barret report a study of twenty-four unmarried fathers in the United States (twelve under 21 years old, twelve over).[28] They compared levels of self-esteem and anxiety. The two groups did not differ. Similarly, Rivara's group, comparing one hundred teenage fathers with one hundred nonfathers, found no significant differences in self-image or personality adjustments.[29] In the lower socioeconomic subcultures from which the samples were drawn, teenage fatherhood was seen as a common occurrence. One might expect to see more relation between fatherhood and self-concept if levels of financial, domestic, and emotional responsibility for the child were taken into account as covariates. In fact, in the Simms and Smith study, where about half of the men interviewed had married the mother of their child after the birth, around 60 percent reported that they had changed for the better after the child arrived, becoming more mature and responsible.

The studies I have outlined generally conclude that, as a whole, teenage females who have children are more likely to come from poor socioeconomic backgrounds, have a poor educational attainment and lower IQ, have lower occupational aspirations and find work in semi-skilled manual jobs, come from broken homes, have mothers who had their first child in adolescence, marry men who are poorly educated and work in manual occupations, have more siblings, and be illegitimate than their age peers who do not have children. They are more likely to hold norms which allow sexual permissiveness and are less likely to practice religion. They have poorer supervision and support from parents, especially their mothers. They have a less stable self-concept and lower self-esteem; higher levels of distrust of others; greater estrangement and sense of shame; and an insecurity about their own ability to cope in employment. Many of the studies suggest that such women consider motherhood an acceptable alternative to independence and work. There is little evidence on teenage fathers, but they do not seem to differ in salient ways from their peers who do not have children.

Methodological Problems in Studies of Teenage Pregnancy

There are a number of methodological inadequacies which characterize most of the studies I have just discussed. Some of these center upon design problems in the study itself, others on interpretation difficulties when the study is completed.

In many of these studies, the sampling is opportunistic—all females of a certain age attending a clinic may be studied merely because access is feasible. Generalizations made from the sample are consequently suspect, especially since most samples are very small. Some of the sampling frames would predicate the negative results found in a majority of the studies because they use only populations of low socioeconomic status in poor neighborhoods. There are, of course, exceptions to this problem.[30] But this concern about the validity of the sample means we must treat most evidence with great caution.

Also, the studies do not compare male with female parents. The result is a tendency to problematize the women and ignore their male partners. If such studies are used as a basis for developing policy or strategies of intervention, this imbalance may result in an inappropriate understanding of the processes (social and psychological) that lead a teenage woman to become pregnant. There is a tendency to use such information about teenage mothers to produce highly individualistic explanations of their actions—there is supposed to be something about them as individuals that results in their pregnancy. This approach fails to acknowledge that pregnancy is actually a product of a complex interaction of factors, including the woman's relationship with her partner.

Most studies are not longitudinal, so that variables like self-esteem are measured only once, after the woman is pregnant or has given birth.[31] This is particularly problematic for researchers often imply that attitudinal or self-concept variables predispose teenagers to conception, when in reality variations in these variables may be a product of the experience of becoming pregnant.

There is too little attention paid to the likely psychological differences between people who are expecting a baby and people who already have a baby. In many studies, pregnant teenagers and teenage mothers are treated as a single category. For nonreactive variables (such as prior academic performance or IQ measured at age 11) this may be acceptable. But it is unacceptable for reactive variables like self-concept, which may change as a result of knowledge of the pregnancy itself.

Problems accrue when these flawed studies are interpreted as well. Because most studies use small samples, researchers are deterred from using sophisticated multivariate analyses of data. Typically, researchers examine differences between parent and nonparent groups using a single variable like education or self-concept at a time. This may obscure the fact that such variables are themselves correlated. The direction and power of causal relations between variables are never revealed. Several studies show, for instance, that teenage mothers have lower levels of academic achievement and lower self-esteem than their peers. The task of the interpreter is then to establish how far low self-esteem is associated with teenage motherhood rather than simply with poor educational performance. Multivariate, especially structural, analyses would reveal this, but it is unrealistic to expect them to be used on very small samples.

Some problems of interpretation arise because researchers rarely explore the effects of the research itself upon the participants in their studies. After all, teenagers interviewed expressly because they are either already parents or about to be parents are likely to respond in some way (either positively or negatively) to the research process itself. This is inevitable. But just because such effects are inescapable does not mean researchers should ignore them. It is important to report how participants respond to the researchers and what they infer to be the motives for the study. Without this information, it is difficult to establish what responses to questions really mean. This is a particular problem where participants feel they are studied *only* because they are parents or pregnant. If the study is clearly embedded in other research issues as well, respondents may be more inclined to offer unbiased information about themselves and their views. Certainly, they would find it less easy to guess the hypotheses behind the research and either provide the socially expected answers or generate information designed to obstruct and obfuscate.

It should be recognized that interpretation of evidence on the correlates of teenage pregnancy is culturally and temporally specific. Generalizations from one ethnic group to another or from one decade to another are fraught with potential misinterpretation. The social meaning of motherhood or indeed fatherhood in teenage years varies greatly. To the extent that there are cultural differences in how far it is either expected or accepted there will be cultural differences in its psychological precursors and effects. In a subculture where teenage motherhood within marriage is approved, we can predict that women who show the psychological traits of conformity and compliance would be likely to become mothers early and to maintain high self-esteem in so doing. In a subculture or period when teenage motherhood is not condoned, nonconformists would become mothers early; they might also be expected to show decreasing self-esteem or psychological stability when facing the consequent social stigma. Such distinctions may appear obvious. The problem lies in incorporating them into the interpretation of evidence from samples drawn across subcultures or ethnic groups. If researchers took care to analyze differences across subgroups within their samples the problem could be minimized, but, in the main, this has not happened. Simple analyses merely conflate differences to produce a homogenized picture of teenage parenthood. This inaccurate portrait has been accentuated further by interpreters' failure to explore differences between those who rear their child themselves and those who have minimal or no contact with it.

The 16–19 Initiative

Many of the problems in design and interpretation of studies can be avoided by using a large-scale random sample of teenagers when the prime focus for the study is not parenthood. In Britain, the Economic and Social Research Council has funded such a longitudinal study of young people aged 15–20, which is known as the 16–19 Initiative. For the rest of the chapter, I shall use data from this study to assess the social and psychological correlates of teenage parenthood in Britain in the period 1987 to 1989. The information was generated through three annual postal questionnaires. The initial sample of 4,874 was drawn randomly from education authority lists of all the young people living in particular areas,[32] and there was no reason for the teenagers to believe that they had been singled out because of any special characteristic of their own.

Respondents provided information in all three surveys on a wide range of topics: employment and education histories, family background and homes, value systems, political attitudes, friendships and social activities, and self-concept. They were also asked whether they had any children of their own. At the time of the first survey, 1 percent (forty-nine) had a child;[33] by the second survey, one year later, 2.25 percent of males and 4 percent of females either had or were expecting a child.[34] For females, these figures can be compared with the national figures for teenagers, and they are very close to the percentage that could therefore have been predicted. So the 16–19 Initiative included a reasonably representative proportion of women with children. Unfortunately, there are no corresponding national figures for the male teenage population so it is difficult to know how representative the male sample is.

The longitudinal structure of the study makes it possible to make both standard cross-sectional comparisons of parents with nonparents and longitudinal comparisons of the individual before and after the conception or birth. Perhaps more interesting, it makes it possible to determine whether those who subsequently become teenage parents differ significantly from those who do not before conception ever takes place.

Social Characteristics of Teenage Parents

The data from the 16–19 Initiative support conclusions drawn from other studies in some respects. In terms of an index of educational attainment based upon examination success in the final year of compulsory schooling (16 years of age), it was clear that those without children achieved greater success than either those with a child or those expecting a child.[35] It was notable that, broadly speaking, those who had a child earliest had the poorest educational qualifications. This was not because the child interrupted their education. Their examination failure preceded their parenthood.

It is interesting that both male and female parents showed the same pattern of poor educational attainment. This finding again supports the conclusion that it is not the fact of parenthood which interrupts an educational career. These teenage fathers were rarely involved in the care of their offspring, yet they show the same levels of school failure as the teenage mothers.

The lack of educational attainment is reflected in the occupational histories of those with children. Teenage fathers were more likely than their age peers to leave school at the earliest opportunity and to move straight into unemployment or some form of temporary government training scheme. They did not, however, remain out of work. The majority found full-time paid employment or returned to education at college or went on to further training. It seems that while they may have rebelled and failed at school, they adapted effectively to the adult world of training and work. As one father who was interviewed explained: "I got into a lot of trouble at school. Schoolwork seemed irrelevant, boring. Now, I got responsibilities, with the kid and everything. I got a job and I got to stick to it." Both their poor educational attainment and the low-status work these teenage fathers subsequently tend to get should be seen in the context of their socioeconomic class. If the job of the respondent's father is taken as the criterion of social advantage or status, it is evident that those who become teenage parents come from families with a lower social standing. They are more likely than nonparents to have a father in a partly skilled or unskilled job or one who is unemployed.

The same pattern of family background existed for the teenage mothers. The majority of them were out of work throughout the period of the study, but 15 percent on average did have a job. Clearly, in the case of the women with children, opportunities for employment depended on whether they had retained the responsibility for looking after their child. In just over half of the cases they had. Rearing the child was not related to whether the mothers were married (25 percent were), cohabiting (10 percent were), or engaged to be married (20 percent were). Teenage fathers were significantly less likely to live with their child and to be married or cohabiting. This obviously gives rise to questions about whether they are acting as "fathers" at all. Unfortunately, the 16–19 study does not provide clues as to why fathers were separated from their children. In fact, it is impossible to determine the age or status of the mothers of their children, since this was not included in the battery of issues addressed by the surveys. Other studies have implied that the mother or her family often does not wish the father to be involved.

The social support available to members of the sample was assessed using answers to questions concerning ability to talk to friends about worries or turn to them for financial help. Overall, males report that they have less social support of this sort. However, this trend is reversed for those with a child or expecting one. If they have a child or are expecting one, males reported higher levels of social support; females less, especially when they are expecting. This pattern holds even where only those who have recently had a child are considered.

The finding confirms the stereotype that teenage females can become isolated from friends if they become pregnant. The social support that teenage fathers can call upon seems to go hand-in-hand with their active participation in some types of social activities. Males with a child and those expecting one were more likely than male age peers to frequent public houses, drink alcohol, attend parties and discotheques, and smoke tobacco. While teenage mothers or mothers-to-be tend to be less engaged in such activities, teenage fathers seem to be integrated into a strong, supportive social network of peers.

Self-concept

Two aspects of self-concept were examined: self-efficacy and psychological estrangement. Self-efficacy concerns the sense of competence and control the individual has.[36] It revolves around feeling capable of dealing with problems. Psychological estrangement is allied to the notion of alienation: being disaffected by society and unwilling to accept its rules but feeling powerless to bring about change. Estrangement reflects a sense of normlessness, powerlessness, and meaninglessness in life.[37]

Efficacy and estrangement were measured annually, so it is possible to compare across time those who had children. Efficacy was measured using a six-item scale, which included such statements as "I seem to be capable of dealing with most problems that come up in life." Respondents indicated how far they agreed with each on a five-point scale. Estrangement was indexed on a seven-item scale and included statements like "I sometimes cannot help wondering if anything is worthwhile."

In terms of efficacy, there was a significant difference between those who had children and those who did not. But sex interacted with being a parent to affect efficacy. Basically, males who have a child feel more efficacious than other males but those expecting a child feel least efficacious. Females without children feel most efficacious, followed closely by those with a child, with those who are expecting feeling quite a lot less efficacious. The sex difference is fascinating and not immediately explicable. It is, however, possible to say reasonably categorically that levels of efficacy are unaffected by being a parent per se. No significant differences over time were found. This was true even for those who had already had a child when first contacted for the study and for those who were only expecting one when they replied.

Estrangement, by contrast, revealed no significant differences between those with and without children, no changes over time, and no interaction of sex with parenthood. The absence of differences associated with parenthood or time is important, for it indicates that those who start to have children early are no more psychologically estranged than their peers before they have a child nor do they become so afterward. There is, however, considerable evidence that those with children are likely to hold more fiercely anti-authority attitudes, indicating a tendency to ignore societal constraints or norms. The parent group show greater anti-authority sentiment as much as a year before they become parents. It is interesting that in this case gender seems unimportant: teenage parents of both sexes evince greater anti-authority feeling, despite the fact that males on the whole in the sample tend to be more anti-authority in orientation.

Problems in Profiling Teenage Parents

In interpreting the findings from the 16–19 Initiative, it is important to remember that the differences between parents and nonparents on self-efficacy, school attainment, anti-authority attitudes, and levels of social support are all statistically significant but in absolute terms very small. When these variables are used in a discriminant analysis to guess whether an individual in the sample is a parent, their power is limited, even when they are used in unison. The major single predictor is undoubtedly academic attainment.

The findings from the study echo many of those from smaller-scale studies, but they highlight two salient facts not found in those studies. First, the longitudinal nature of the 16–19 Initiative makes it possible to affirm that the self-efficacy levels of males who have children in adolescence differ from those who do not both before and after they have the child. Efficacy is not altered systematically by having a child. Second, while those who have children express greater anti-authority attitudes, they do not show greater levels of psychological estrangement before, during, or after the child's birth. Negative reaction to authority is not accompanied by a sense of personal alienation despite a, for the most part, socially disadvantaged position (in terms of education, occupational opportunities, and social class). It may be for some that parenthood offers the antidote to psychological estrangement, providing meaningfulness and purpose in a life that gives few other opportunities for self-assertion.

The profiles of teenage mothers and fathers have certain similarities: low levels of educational attainment, working-class backgrounds, poor initial employment histories, and considerable anti-authority feeling. But they differ in significant ways too. Teenage fathers have strong social support networks; they are much involved in such activities as drinking, smoking, partying, and going to bars or pubs; and they are confident of their own ability to cope with problems that might arise. The picture is one of integration in an accepting youth culture that expects wild oats to be sown. Teenage mothers, before ever they become pregnant, are more likely to be isolated and unsupported, lacking the confidence that they can cope, even while they reject the rules imposed by external authorities governing behavior. Those who become teenage fathers seem conformist within a narrowly defined subculture of working-class youth; the women who become teenage mothers are nonconforming and somewhat isolated from social support.

The findings from the 16–19 Initiative emphasize that these profiles predate conception or parenthood—they are substantially unaltered by the transition into parenthood. In showing this within the context of a large representative sample and after multivariate analyses, the 16–19 Initiative offers a move forward in our understanding of the factors which precipitate teenagers, both male and female, into parenthood. But it must be added that the findings are inevitably culturally and temporally specific.

The 16–19 study overcomes many of the methodological problems listed earlier but not this one.

Notes

1. The major object of the study was to explore political and economic socialization in 16- to 20-year-olds. Started in 1987, it lasted four years and was conducted in four geographical areas (Swindon in the southwest of England, Liverpool in the northwest, Sheffield in the northeast, and Kirkcaldy in Scotland) chosen for their diversity in labor market and political structure.

2. Office of Population and Census Studies (OPCS), *Birth Statistics* (London: HMSO, 1985).

3. For statistics, see B. Werner, "Recent Trends in Illegitimate Births and Extramarital Conceptions," *Population Trends* 30 (1982): 9–15.

4. F. Wilson, "Antecedents of Adolescent Pregnancy," *Journal of Biosocial Science* 12 (1980): 141–52.

5. This pattern of teenage mothers being the children of teenage mothers is supported by the longitudinal study of F. Furstenberg, Jr., J. Brooks-Gunn, and S. P. Morgan reported in their book *Adolescent Mothers in Later Life* (Cambridge: Cambridge University Press, 1987).

6. I. Gottschalk, J. Titchner, H. Picker, and S. Stewart, "Psychological Factors Associated with Pregnancy in Adolescent Girls: A Preliminary Report," *Journal of Nervous and Mental Disorders* 138 (1964): 524.

7. M. Luz Alvarez, R. Burrows, A. Zvaighat, and S. Muzzo, "Socio-cultural Characteristics of Pregnant and Non-pregnant Adolescents of Low Socio-economic Status: A Comparative Study," *Adolescence* 85 (1987): 149–56.

8. A. R. Stiffman, F. Earls, L. Robins, K. Jung, and P. Kulbok, "Adolescent Sexual Activity and Pregnancy: Socio-environmental Problems, Physical Health and Mental Health," *Journal of Youth and Adolescence* 16, 5 (1987): 497–509.

9. K. Kiernan, "Teenage Motherhood—Associated Factors and Consequences—The Experiences of a British Birth Cohort," *Journal of Biosocial Science* 12 (1980): 393–405.

10. For example, M. Simms and C. Smith, *Teenage Mothers and Their Partners: A Survey in England and Wales.* Department of Health and Social Security Research Report 15 (London: HMSO, 1986).

11. C. F. Olson and J. Worobey, "Perceived Mother-daughter Relations in a Pregnant and Non-pregnant Adolescent Sample," *Adolescence* 19 (1984): 781–94.

12. V. Abernethy, "Illegitimate Conception among Teenagers," *American Journal of Public Health* 64 (1974): 622–65.

13. J. Townsend and J. Worobey, "Mother and Daughter Perceptions of the Relationship: The Influence of Adolescent Pregnancy Status," *Adolescence* 86 (1987): 487–96.

14. C. G. Ortiz and E. V. Nuttall, "Adolescent Pregnancy: Effects of Family

Support, Education and Religion on the Decision to Carry or Terminate among Puerto Rican Teenagers," *Adolescence* 88 (1987): 897–917.

15. M. Patten, "Self Concept and Self-esteem: Factors in Adolescent Pregnancy," *Adolescence* 64 (1981): 765–78; P. Shiller, "A Sex Attitude Modification Process for Adolescents," *Journal of Clinical Child Psychology* 17 (1974): 50–51; M. E. Horn and L. B. Rudolph, "An Investigation of Verbal Interaction, Knowledge of Sexual Behaviour and Self-concept in Adolescent Mothers," *Adolescence* 87 (1987): 591–98; C. Zongker, "The Self-concept of Pregnant Adolescent Girls," *Adolescence* 12, 48 (1977): 477–88; H. B. Kaplan, P. B. Smith, and A. D. Pokorny, "Psychological Antecedents of Unwed Motherhood among Indigent Adolescents," *Journal of Youth and Adolescence* 8 (1979): 181–207; J. Brooks-Gunn and F. Furstenberg, Jr., "Antecedents and Consequences of Parenting: The Case of Adolescent Motherhood," in A. Fogel and G. Melson, eds., *The Origins of Nurturance* (Hillsdale, N.J.: Erlbaum, 1986), pp. 233–58; F. Furstenberg, Jr., "The Social Consequences of Teenage Parenthood," *Family Planning Perspectives* 8 (1976): 148–64; R. P. Barth, S. P. Schinke, and J. S. Maxwell, "Coping Skills for School Age Mothers," *Journal of Social Service Research* 8 (1985): 75–84.

16. H. Protinsky, M. Sporakowski, and S. Atkins, "Identity Formation: Pregnant and Non-pregnant Adolescents," *Adolescence* 65 (1982): 73–80.

17. R. W. Roberts, *The Unwed Mother* (New York: Harper and Row, 1966).

18. W. J. Goode, "Illegitimacy, Anomie and Cultural Penetration," *American Sociological Review* 26 (1961): 910–25.

19. L. Connolly, "Little Mothers," *Human Behaviour* 11 (1975): 17–23; J. Meyerowitz and J. Maler, "Pubescent Attitudinal Correlates Antecedent to Adolescent Pregnancy," *Journal of Youth and Adolescence* 2 (1973): 251–58.

20. J. D. Osofsky, H. J. Osofsky, and M. O. Diamond, "The Transition to Parenthood: Special Tasks and Risk Factors for Adolescent Parents," in G. Y. Michaels and W. A. Goldberg, eds., *The Transition to Parenthood* (Cambridge: Cambridge University Press, 1988).

21. L. Streetman, "Contrasts in the Self-esteem of Unwed Teenage Mothers," *Adolescence* 86 (1987): 459–64.

22. M. A. Vinovskis, *An "Epidemic" of Adolescent Pregnancy?* (Oxford: Oxford University Press, 1988).

23. OPCS, *Birth Statistics.*

24. R. Barret and B. Robinson, "Adolescent Fathers: The Other Half of Teenage Pregnancy," *Pediatric Nursing* 12 (1986): 278–83.

25. F. Furstenberg, Jr., and K. Talvite, "Children's Names and Parental Claims: Bonds between Unmarried Fathers and Their Children," *Journal of Family Issues* 1 (1980): 31–57.

26. A. B. Elster and S. Panzarine, "The Adolescent Father," *Seminars in Perinatology* 5 (1981): 39–51.

27. Simms and Smith, *Teenage Mothers and Their Partners.*

28. R. Robinson and R. Barret, "Self Concept and Anxiety of Adolescent and Adult Fathers," *Adolescence* 87 (1987): 611–16.

29. F. Rivara, P. Sweeney, and B. Henderson, "A Study of Low Socio-Economic Status, Black Teenage Fathers and Their Non-father Peers," *Pediatrics* 75 (1985): 648–56.

30. For example, the Kiernan study cited in n. 9, Furstenberg's studies, or the work of Simms and Smith.

31. Where follow-up studies have been done, for instance the one by Simms and Smith, it has been evident that there is considerable variability in levels of self-esteem, anxiety, depression, etc., over time, depending on specific life events.

32. I use data from two surveys in this chapter. For the first survey, 6,500 questionnaires were sent out: 4,874 represents a return rate of 74 percent. At the second survey 3,357 replied: a return rate of 69 percent. Two age cohorts were sampled: those who were 15 to 16 and those who were 17 to 18 years old in April 1989. The sample was equally divided by sex.

33. The forty-nine parents break down into the following subgroups: thirty-six females, thirteen males, ten married (six females, four males).

34. In numbers, thirty-two males had a child, sixty-one females; thirteen males and twenty-five females were expecting a child. Of these eighty-three had only one child; seven had two children and three had three. Subsequent analyses revealed no differences between those who had only one child and those who had more than one on any of the variables of interest here.

35. Other studies include A. T. Geronimus, "On Teenage Childbearing and Neonatal Mortality in the US," *Population and Development Review* 13, 2 (1987): 1353–72. In Geronimus's findings, there were no significant differences between those who had a child and those expecting one.

36. A. Bandura, "Perceived Efficacy in the Exercise of Personal Agency," *The Psychologist* 2, 10 (1989): 411–24.

37. S. Hammond, "The Meaning and Measurement of Adolescent Estrangement" (Ph.D. diss., University of Surrey, 1988).

LINDA M. BURTON
CAROL B. STACK

9 CONSCRIPTING KIN: REFLECTIONS ON FAMILY, GENERATION, AND CULTURE

People do not necessarily do what they are supposed to do for kin, but they know what they are supposed to do and when they should do it, and they also know that kin will summon them to do family labor. This chapter presents a framework for examining how families as multigenerational collectives—and individuals embedded within them—work out family responsibilities. We provide a useful lens for viewing how work and responsibility concerning the care of children is delegated, in particular with respect to children born to young mothers. This chapter draws upon a broad variety of examples from diverse family situations as a way of thinking about multigenerational families and childcare across the lifespan. We introduce *kinscripts*, a framework for the interplay of family ideology, norms, and behaviors over the life course. Kinscripts encompasses three culturally defined family domains: kinwork, the labor and tasks that families need to accomplish to survive from generation to generation; kintime, the temporal and sequential ordering of family transitions; and kinscription, the process of assigning kinwork to family members.

The kinscripts framework is derived in part from the perspective of the life course of the families,[1] from studies of kinship,[2] and from literature on family scripts.[3] The principal basis of our concept of kinscripts, however, is the ethnographic research we conducted between 1968 and 1990 with urban and rural low-income multigenerational black extended families in the northeast, southeast, and midwest portions of the United States. Case history data on families involved in these ethnographic studies are used to illuminate components of the kinscripts framework.

This framework was developed to organize and interpret qualitative observations of the temporal and interdependent dimensions of family role transitions, the creation and intergenerational transmission of family norms, and the dynamics of negotiation, exchange, and conflict within families as they construct their life course. It is based on the premise that families have their own agendas, their own interpretation of cultural norms, and their own histories.[4] Families assist individual members in constructing their personal life courses, but in the process families as collectives create a familial life course.[5]

The kinscripts framework can be applied across race, ethnicity, and social class to the range of family forms existing in contemporary American society. Typically, the conceptual frameworks used to interpret the life course of kin are derived from explorations involving white, middle-class families. Kinscripts, in contrast, is an example of a framework that is derived from the study of low-income black families but offers insights for study of mainstream families as well.

The concept of scripts used in the family therapy literature is also an integral part of the kinscripts framework. Family scripts prescribe patterns of family interaction.[6] They are mental representations that guide the role performances of family members within and across contexts. The kinscripts framework extends the notion of scripts to the study of the family life course. Specifically, kinscripts focuses on the tensions that are produced and negotiated between individuals in families in response to scripts. These dynamics are discussed in context of three culturally defined family domains: kinwork, kintime, and kinscription.

Kinwork

Kinwork is the collective labor expected of family-centered networks across households and within them.[7] It defines the work that families need to accomplish to endure over time. The life course of the family is constructed and maintained through kinwork. Kinwork regenerates families, maintains lifetime continuities, sustains intergenerational responsibilities, and reinforces shared values. It encompasses, for example, all of the following: family labor for reproduction; intergenerational care for children or dependents; economic survival, including wage and nonwage labor; family migration and migratory labor designated to send home remittances; and strategic support for networks of kin extending across regions, state lines, and nations.

Kinwork is distributed in families among men, women, and children. Samuel Jenkins, a 76-year-old widower in Gospel Hill, provided his own interpretation of kinwork. After Samuel's oldest daughter died, one of his granddaughters, Elaine, moved in with him along with her three children: a 6-month-old baby, a 2-year-old, and a 3-year-old. Samuel is raising these children. Elaine, he says, is running the streets and not providing care. When asked why he is parenting his grandchildren, he explains: "There ain't no other way. I have to raise these babies else the service people will take 'em away. This is my family. Family has to take care of family else we won't be no more."[8]

Janice Perry, a 13-year-old pregnant woman from Gospel Hill, described her rather unique kinwork assignment. Her contribution to the family, as she understood it, was through reproduction. She states: "I'm not having this baby for myself. The baby's grandmother wants to be a "mama" and my great-grandfather wants to see a grandchild before he goes blind from sugar. I'm just giving them something to make them happy." Janice's mother, Helen, comments further: "I want this baby. I want it bad. I need it. I need to raise a child. That's my job now. My mama did it. It's my turn now."

Samuel Jenkins, Janice Perry, and Helen Perry have clear notions of kinwork within families. While their individual family circumstances are different, kinwork for each one of them is tied to providing care across generations and maintaining family traditions and continuity.

Kinwork is the consequence of culturally constructed family obligations defined by economic, social, physical, and psychological family needs. Henry Evans, a 38-year-old resident of New Town, a northeastern black community studied by Burton, provided a very clear profile of his assigned kinwork.[9] He noted that his kinwork emerged from the physical and psychological needs of his family members. Henry was the only surviving son in his family. His mother had given birth to eleven other sons, all of whom were stillborn or died shortly after birth. At the time of his interview, Henry was providing care for his father, who had recently suffered a heart attack, his 36-year-old sister, who was suffering from a chronic neuromuscular disease, and his 40-year-old sister and her four children. When asked about his family duties, he remarked: "I was designated by my family as a child to provide care for all my family members. My duties read just like a job description. The job description says the following: (1) you will never marry; (2) you will have no children of your own; (3) you will take care of your sisters, their children, your mother and your father in old age; and (4) you will be happy doing it."

Henry went on to discuss how his commitment to the family life course took precedence over his personal goals: "Someone in my family must be at the helm. Someone has to be there to make sure that the next generation has a start. Right now, we are a family of co-dependents. We need each other. As individuals, my sisters and father are too weak to stand alone. I could never bring a wife into this. I don't have time. Maybe when the next generation (his sister's kids) is stronger, no one will have to do my job. We will redefine destiny."

The situation of Henry Evans is not unfamiliar. Hareven, in detailed historical analysis of families who worked for the Amoskeag Company in Manchester, New Hampshire, provides poignant examples of how for many individuals the demands of kinwork supersede personal goals.[10] Comparable evidence is noted in Plath's[11] in-depth interview study of contemporary Japanese families. In each cultural context, across historical time, kinwork was described as self-sacrificing hard work designed to insure the survival of the collective.

Kintime

Kintime concerns the temporal scripts of families. It is the shared understanding among family members of when and in what sequence role transitions and kinwork should occur. Kintime defines family norms for the timing of such transitions as marriage, childbearing, and grandparenthood. It includes temporal guides for the assumption of family leadership and caregiving responsibilities. The temporal and sequencing norms of kintime are constructed in the context of family culture. Consequently, for some families, these norms may not be synchronous with the life schedules of families as identified from patterns assumed to exist in larger society.

Stack's ethnographic study of the migration of black families to and from the rural South provides an example of the relation between kintime and kinwork.[12] She highlights two aspects of kinwork—reproduction and migration. Reproduction is timed in relation to migration, so that young adults have their children first and then migrate to the North to secure jobs and send money back home. Their young children are left in the South to be reared by grandparents or older aunts and uncles. After an extended period of time, the migrating adults return to the South where their children repeat the cycle—they bear children and migrate north.

The temporal sequencing of reproduction and migration in these families reflect a scripted family course of life involving cooperative action among kin. Family members must be willing to assume economic and childcare responsibilities according to schedule. Individuals in families, however, do not always adhere to kintime. A young adult may choose not to migrate, another may leave home but fail to send remittances, and yet others may return home sooner than expected. These individuals are considered insurgent by kin and may create unexpected burdens that challenge family resilience.

Kintime also demarcates rites of passage or milestones within families, including handing down familial power and tasks following the death of family elders. In the Appalachian mountains in the southeastern United States, for example, older women proclaim those few years after the death of their husbands when they alone own the family land to be the time they have the most power in their families. The grown children and nearby community members observe, in a timely fashion, the activities of these elderly rural women. It was still common lore in the 1980s that the year these older widowed women announced plans for planting their last garden would be the last year of their life. In that year, kin vie for their inheritances. Thus, the life course of families involves a scripted cycle of the relegation of power through land ownership, a uniquely crafted kintime.

Kinscription

It is important to understand how power is brought into play within the context of kintime and kinwork. The question this raises is summed up in the tension reflected in kinscription. Rather than accept the attempts of individuals to set their own personal agendas, families are continually rounding up, summoning, or recruiting individuals for kinwork. Some kin, namely women and children, are easily recruited. The importance women place on maintaining kin ties and fostering family continuity has been assiduously documented.[13] Placing preeminent emphasis on kinkeeping—the undertakings necessary to keep connected and transmit family traditions—women often find it difficult to refuse kin demands.

The life course of a young woman, Yvonne Carter, who lives in Gospel Hill, offers an example of the interplay of power, kinscription, and the role of women. When Yvonne's first love died she was 21. Now, at 35, she recounts how the years have unfolded: "When Charlie died, it seemed like everyone said since she's not getting married, we have to keep her busy. Before I knew it, I was raising kids, giving homes to long lost kin, and even helping the friends of my mother. Between doing all of this, I didn't have time to find another man. I bet they wouldn't want me and all my relatives anyway." How relatives collude to keep particular individuals wedded to family needs—a chosen daughter in Japan,[14] a chosen son in rural Ireland[15]—confirms Yvonne Carter's suspicion: she has been recruited for specific kinwork in her family.

Recruitment for kinwork is one dimension of power in kinscription. Exclusion from kinwork is another, as this profile of Paul Thomas, a 36-year-old resident of Gospel Hill, illustrates.

Paul Thomas, down on his luck, out of sorts with his girlfriend, and the oldest of seven children, had just moved back into the home of his mother, Mattie, when he was interviewed. Eleven of Mattie's family members live in her two-bedroom apartment. They include Paul's two younger brothers (one had returned home from the service bringing a wife and child), an unmarried sister, a sister and her child, and a pregnant sister with two children. Paul reported finding his move back home, which was the result of repeated unemployment, particularly difficult under these conditions.

After Paul's return Mattie characterized his history within the family: "Paul left this family when he was thirteen. I don't mean leave, like go away, but leave, like only do the things he wanted to do, but not pay attention to what me or his brothers and sisters wanted or needed. He took and took, and we gave and gave all the time. We never made him give nothing back." In Mattie's view, her son abandoned the family early on, claiming rights but not assuming responsibilities. On a later visit to Mattie's apartment, family members gathered in the living room were asked a general question about doing things for kin. Paul stood up to speak. Addressing this question, with anger and entitlement in his voice, he said: "I come back only for a little while. I am the outsider in the family. The black sheep. I belong, but I don't belong. Do you understand what I mean? I am only important because my mother can say, I have a son, and my sisters can say, I have a brother. But it doesn't mean anything. I can't do anything around here. I don't do anything. No one makes me. My sisters know what they have to do. They always have. They know their place! Now that I'm getting old I've been thinking that someway I'll make my place here. I want Ann [his sister] to name her baby after me. I'm begging you, Ann. Give this family something to remember that I'm part of it too."

Renegade relatives such as Paul attest to subtle dynamics challenging their place within families. These relatives may inadvertently play havoc with family processes while simultaneously attempting to attach themselves to family legacies.

When kin resist family procedures families have been known to use heavy-handed pressure to recruit individuals to do kinwork. However, kin may be well aware that family demands can clash and that it is impossible for the individual summoned to do kinwork to satisfy everyone. In particular, family members assigned to do kinwork cannot be in two places at once. Adults, and even children under such circumstances, may be left to choose between conflicting demands. Stack's study of family responsibilities assumed by children in the rural, southeastern community of New Jericho provides an example of competing demands placed on adolescents as they are recruited for family tasks.

In New Jericho, multiple expectations are transmitted to children whose parents migrated from the rural South to the Northeast. It is not unusual for adolescents, skilled at childcare and other domestic activities, to be pulled in a tug-of-war between family households in the North and South. Kin at both locations actively recruit adolescents to move in with them or join their households. Parents in the North and grandparents in the South are the main contenders. Children find themselves deeply caught in a web of family obligations. At 11 years of age, Jimmy Williams was asked to move to Brooklyn to help his parents with their new baby. But his grandmother needed his help in rural North Carolina. Jimmy responded by saying: "I think I should stay with the one that needs my help the most. My grandmother is unable to do for herself, and I should stay with her and let my mother come to see me."

Jimmy was conscripted by two households within the family network. The decision he made to remain with his grandmother punctuates the leeway given to children to make judgments in the context of personal and family interests. In a similar situation young Sarah Boyce said: "I'll talk to my parents and try to get them to understand that my grandparents cannot get around like they used to. I want to make an agreement to let my brother go to New York and go to school, and I'll go to school down here. In the summer, I will go and be with my parents, and my brother can come down home."

Children are conscripted to perform certain tasks that are tied to the survival of families as a whole. Definitions of these tasks are transmitted through direct and indirect cues from family members. Jimmy and Sarah responded to the needs of kin, taking advantage of the flexibility available to them in negotiating the tasks. That same flexibility is not always available for adults. The situation of Sandra Smith provides an example.

Sandra Smith, married and a mother, found herself pressed between the demands of kin in her family of origin and those of her in-laws in Gospel Hill. She stated: "I'm always the one everybody comes to to take care of children. My mother expects me to raise my sister's three kids. My mother-in-law calls upon me to mind my nieces and nephews while she takes it easy. She expects me to kiss her feet. I won't do it, none of it, everybody can go to hell." Sandra, in fact, did refuse kinwork. When asked what impact her choice would have on her situation in the family, she said: "It means I won't have nobody. But so what, they need me more than I need them."

Pressed between opposing sets of demands and resentments that build up over the years, refusal to do kinwork is a choice some individuals opt for. Refusal, however, may be costly, particularly for those individuals who are dependent on the economic and emotional resources of kin.

The examples of kinwork, kintime, and kinscription provided in this discussion are drawn primarily from our ethnographic studies of low-income, multigenerational black families. These examples illuminate the extraordinary situations of some individuals embedded in families that have scripted life courses. Not all families have such well-defined guidelines. The family guidelines that exist for those who live in Gospel Hill, New Jericho, and New Town emerge out of extreme economic need and an intense commitment by family members to the survival of future generations.

The kinscripts framework is useful for exploring the life course of the families highlighted in this discussion, but it can also be applied to families that construct their life course under different circumstances. Kinscripts is particularly suited to exploring the effects that certain individuals within families have on the lives of kin. In all families, across racial, ethnic, and socioeconomic groups, there are individuals who cannot be counted on to carry out kin tasks; who leave the family fold for reasons of personal survival; who remain as dependent insiders within families making excessive emotional and economic demands on their members; or who return to the bosom of kin because of personal experiences such as unemployment, homelessness, divorce, or widowhood. From each angle and in a diversity of family systems the life course as defined by kinwork, kintime, and kinscription is affected by the personal agendas of family members.

Consider, for example, how the kinscripts framework might be used to explore a kin network in which one member is experiencing divorce. Divorce is fairly common among mainstream American families.[16] During the process, an adult child with dependent children may return to the home of his or her parents. The return may put the scripted life course of kin in disarray, necessitating that collective family notions of kinwork, kintime, and kinscription be restructured. In terms of kinwork, grandparents, who in the past had assumed a less active role in the rearing of their grandchildren, might be expected to take on a more formal surrogate parent role.[17] With respect to kintime, family members might delay certain transitions in response to the divorce—an older parent might put off retirement for a few years to generate enough income to help the adult child reestablish him- or herself financially. Kinscription may also be revised. The adult child experiencing the divorce may have been the family kinkeeper, the person in the family charged with organizing family reunions, documenting family history, and negotiating conflicts between relatives. Given the change in the kin-keeper's life, these duties might have to be reassigned.

Kinscripts can also be applied to explorations of the relations among broad social conditions, unemployment, and the life course of kin. Under ideal conditions, unemployed family members are absorbed by kin as best they can. Given severe socioeconomic conditions, however, tensions among individual needs and kinwork, kintime, and kinscription may emerge. Again, the family life course may have to be redesigned. For example, low-income families attempting to absorb down-and-out members or homeless mothers and children find that sometimes in the face of economic cutbacks and emotional crises they must, however reluctantly, "let go" of family members who cannot pull their weight. When public welfare support decreased in the 1980s, it produced an increasing number of families confronted with this necessity. Stressful economic conditions decrease both individual and family ability to perform effectively. Certain economic and political changes can disrupt kintime, delaying family milestones such as childbearing and adding complexity to family timetables, and inhibit kinwork and kinscription, thereby increasing tensions between the individual and the family life course. The kinscripts framework, drawing on the life-course perspective, is attentive to exploring these issues in the context of social change.

Another application of the kinscript framework is seen in the study of family members who leave the fold of kin. Under certain circumstances, particularly in the case of a dysfunctional family, an individual may temporarily dissociate himself from kin as a means of personal survival and then return to the fold having learned new family skills. Within the context of the kinscripts framework, several questions might be addressed: what implications does the individual's exit from the family have on kinwork, kintime, and kinscription? how does the individual negotiate reentry to the kin network? and what effect does the individual's reentry have on the family's restructuring of the life course?

In summary, our contention is that kinscripts can be a useful framework for research into how families and individuals negotiate, construct, and reconstruct the life course. The utility of this framework is found in observing the interplay of three culturally defined family domains—kinwork, kintime, and kinscription—which offers a different perspective, even though many of the ideas outlined in kinscripts are not new.

As we have defined it, kinscripts represent an attempt to use knowledge generated from the study of black multigenerational families to formulate a framework that can be useful for the study of families in general. Families of color, immigrant families, and working-class families have historically experienced issues that mainstream families have only recently contended with, like juggling work and family roles for women, single parenthood, extended family relationships, and poverty. Important lessons learned from exploring these issues can provide critical insight on the varied life courses of families in contemporary American society.

Notes

The research reported in this chapter was supported by grants from the Rockefeller Foundation and the Guggenheim Foundation to Carol B. Stack and by the National Science Foundation (RII-8613960), the Brookdale Foundation, the Center for the Study of Child and Adolescent Development, the Pennsylvania State University, a FIRST Award from the National Institute of Mental Health (R29MH46057-01), and a William T. Grant Faculty Scholars Award to Linda M. Burton. The chapter was partially prepared while the authors were fellows at the Center for Advanced Study in the Behavioral Sciences at Stanford University. We are grateful for financial support from the John D. & Catherine T. MacArthur Foundation, the Spencer Foundation, and the Guggenheim Foundation. We also wish to thank David Plath, Robert Weiss, Gunhild Hagestad, Ann Crouter, Jean Lave, Blanca Silvestrini, Judy Stacey, Brad Shore, Jane Ifekwunigwe, Cindy Brache, and Caridad Souza for their helpful comments on an earlier draft. We are grateful to the *Journal of Comparative Family Studies* for permission to reprint portions of their article "Kinscripts," volume 24, 1993.

1. See Joan Aldous, "Family Development and the Life Course: Two Perspectives on Family Change," *Journal of Marriage and the Family* 52, 3 (1990): 571–83; Glen H. Elder, Jr., "Families and Lives: Some Developments in Life-Course Studies," *Journal of Family History* 12 (1987): 179–99; Gunhild O. Hagestad, "Social Perspectives on the Life Course," in Robert K. Binstock and Linda K. George, eds., *Handbook of Aging and the Social Sciences*. 3d ed. (New York: Academic Press; 1990), pp. 151–68; Tamara K. Hareven, *Family Time and Industrial Time: The Relationship between the Family and Work in a New England Industrial Community* (New York: Cambridge University Press, 1982); and Tamara K. Hareven, "Historical Changes in the Social Construction of the Life Course," *Human Development* 29, 3 (1986): 171–80.

2. See Joyce Aschenbrenner, *Lifelines: Black Families in Chicago* (New York: Holt,

Rinehart, and Winston, 1975); Micaela Di Leonardo, "The Female World of Cards and Holidays: Women, Families, and the Work of Kinship," *Signs: Journal of Women and Culture in Society* 12 (1986): 440–53; John Hinnant, "Ritualization of the Life Cycle," in C. L. Fry and J. Keith, eds., *New Methods for Old Age Research* (Boston: Bergin and Garvey, 1986); Carol Stack, *All Our Kin* (New York: Harper and Row, 1974).

3. John Byng-Hall, "The Family Script: A Useful Bridge between Theory and Practice," *Journal of Family Therapy* 7 (1985): 301–05; John Byng-Hall, "Scripts and Legends in Families and Family Therapy," *Family Process* 27 (1988): 167–79; and C. M. Steiner, *Scripts People Live: Transactional Analysis of Life Scripts* (New York: Grove Press, 1974).

4. See Gunhild O. Hagestad, "Dimensions of Time and the Family," *American Behavioral Scientist* 29 (1986): 679–94; David Reiss, *The Family's Construction of Reality* (Cambridge: Harvard University Press, 1981); David Reiss and Mary Ellen Oliveri, "The Family's Construction of Social Reality and Its Ties to Its Kin Network: And Explorations of Causal Direction," *Journal of Marriage and the Family* 45 (1983): 81–91; and Charles Tilly, "Family History, Social History, and Social Change," *Journal of Family History* 12 (1987): 320–29.

5. Susan C. Watkins, "On Measuring Transitions and Turning Points," *Historical Methods* 13, 3 (1980): 181–86.

6. Byng-Hall, "Scripts and Legends"; A. J. Ferreira, "Family Myth and Homeostasis," *Archives of General Psychiatry* 9 (1963): 457–63.

7. Di Leonardo, "Female World of Cards and Holidays."

8. All of the voices quoted in this chapter are from the authors' field notes of their research. Names of both people and places have been changed.

9. Linda M. Burton and Robin L. Jarrett, "Studying African-American Family Structure and Process in Underclass Neighborhoods: Conceptual Considerations." Unpublished manuscript, Pennsylvania State University.

10. Hareven, *Family Time and Industrial Time;* Tamara K. Hareven and Randolph Langenbach, *Amoskeag* (New York: Pantheon, 1978).

11. David Plath, *Long Engagements* (Stanford, Calif.: Stanford University Press, 1980).

12. Carol B. Stack, *Call To Home: African Americans Reclaim the Rural South* (New York: Basic Books, 1993).

13. Paula L. Dressel and Ann Clark, "A Critical Look at Family Care," *Journal of Marriage and the Family* 52, 3 (1990): 769–82; Carol Gilligan, *In a Different Voice* (Cambridge: Harvard University Press, 1982); Gunhild O. Hagestad, "The Aging Society as a Context for Family Life," *Daedalus* 115 (1986): 119–39.

14. Plath, *Long Engagements.*

15. Nancy Scheper-Hughes, *Saints, Scholars and Schizophrenics* (Berkeley: University of California Press, 1979).

16. Donald F. Anspach, "Kinship and divorce," *Journal of Marriage and the Family* 38 (1976): 323–35; Gunhild O. Hagestad and Michael S. Smyer, "Dissolving Long-term Relationships: Patterns of Divorce in Middle Age," in S. Duck, ed., *Personal*

Relationships. Vol. 4: *Dissolving Personal Relationships* (London: Academic Press, 1982), pp. 155–88; A. J. Norton and J. E. Moorman, "Current Trends in Marriage and Divorce among American Women," *Journal of Marriage and the Family* 49 (1987): 3–14.

17. Colleen L. Johnson, "Active and Latent Functions of Grandparenting during the Divorce Process," *Gerontologist* 28, 2 (1988): 185–91.

PART THREE   FATHERS

FRANK F. FURSTENBERG, JR.
KATHLEEN MULLAN HARRIS

10 WHEN FATHERS MATTER/WHY FATHERS MATTER: THE IMPACT OF PATERNAL INVOLVEMENT ON THE OFFSPRING OF ADOLESCENT MOTHERS

After a long period of scholarly neglect, social scientists are finally beginning to pay attention to the influence of fathers on children. This new tide of interest in the role of fathers has been so strong that the standard cliché about fathers being slighted in studies of family behavior hardly applies any longer. Recent research on teenage parenthood represents a particularly good example of the growing interest in the extent and consequences of male involvement.

Years ago, Clark Vincent, in a classic study of unmarried mothers, took note of the social invisibility of unmarried fathers. Vincent traced the inattention to the fathers to a number of different sources. The principal one, he claimed, was the patriarchal assumption in American culture that females must be held primarily accountable for sexual transgressions. "The lack of research on unmarried fathers may be very inconsistent with the fact that they represent one-half the illicit-conception equation, but is quite consistent with, and can be understood within the context of, other social practices and attitudes."[1]

For nearly a quarter of a century Vincent's observation was occasionally registered but left unchallenged. Not until the late 1970s did researchers begin to take full cognizance of the missing male partner of teenage mothers. In the past five years a veritable outpouring of studies has appeared on teenage fatherhood. Several recent books have culled from the diverse and scattered literature on this subject,[2] and an excellent review by Parke and Neville,[3] commissioned by the Panel on Adolescent Pregnancy and Childbearing, organized and synthesized the burgeoning research on teenage fatherhood.

Not surprisingly, large gaps remain in our understanding of how males contribute to the process of early family formation and the consequences of paternal involvement for the economic and psychological well-being of their offspring. As Parke and Neville note, almost all research on these critical issues is confined to the transition to parenthood and the period immediately following childbirth. Next to nothing is known about patterns of support and participation by fathers beyond infancy into later childhood and adolescence. This void in our information about the continuing role of fathers means that we are largely ignorant of the long-term consequences of paternal involvement for the development of children and young adults.

There are, however, studies on the effect of fathers' participation after marital disruption has occurred. Many researchers have assumed that greater support from nonresidential fathers would reduce the ill effects of divorce.[4] A few small-scale studies have indeed produced findings that are consistent with that assumption.[5] But results obtained from a nationally representative sample of children in maritally disrupted families found that nonresidential fathers' involvement was unrelated to a variety of child outcomes.[6] Children who had more frequent contact with their fathers and had closer relationships with them were not performing better either socially or emotionally in mid-adolescence.

What might explain the perplexing finding that fathers' involvement does not much matter to the well-being of children? First, the level of paternal involvement by fathers living outside the home could be too low to have much impact on the child. Even children with relatively regular relationships might experience relative deprivation and be sensitive to what is lacking in their relationships with their fathers. Second, the effects of participation might vary widely, depending on the way that male attention was received by the residential parents. If mothers did not welcome or were hostile to high levels of involvement, any positive impact might be negated. More involved fathers could pose a threat to the authority of residential parent surrogates (such as stepparents, boyfriends, uncles, and the like), precipitating conflict and competition. Finally, it is conceivable that fathers generally matter less than we might imagine. If relationships with mothers (or mother surrogates) are positive, the added benefit of a good relationship with a father may not be very significant.

It is difficult to ascertain whether these possibilities apply more broadly to the situation of adolescent parents. We set them forth only as a reminder that the seemingly obvious benefits for children of paternal participation in disrupted (or even intact) families cannot be assumed without stronger evidence than has been produced to date. This chapter examines the consequences of paternal involvement for children's well-being in families formed by adolescent blacks, in an effort to advance our knowledge about the impact of male involvement on children's well-being in a population at great risk of long-term disadvantage. Our study is one of the few to consider the effects of paternal involvement on children in later adolescence and early adulthood. Through the use of a unique longitudinal data set, we have been able to examine the extent and quality of male involvement in the lives of children of teenage mothers for twenty years, and to analyze the effect of that involvement on children's development and well-being as they become young adults. Can we demonstrate that participation by nonresidential fathers (both in and outside the home) affects the well-being of children in later life?

The Baltimore Study

The data are drawn from a study that began in Baltimore during the mid-1960s, as part of an evaluation of this country's first comprehensive care programs for teenage mothers (see appendix A). Some four hundred teenage parents were followed from pregnancy until their children were preschoolers in 1972. The participants were all 18 years old or younger when their first child was born. Most were black, and all came from families that were poor or had only modest means.[7] The first phase of the Baltimore study traced the consequences of early childbearing for the mother and, to a lesser extent, the child. A portion of the analysis dealt with the participation of the males in accounting for the success of the young mother's adaptation to premature parenthood and the early development of their children.

The early findings on male involvement revealed a great deal of diversity. About half of the fathers married the adolescent mother either before or shortly after childbirth. Most of these marriages were short-lived. The continued involvement of formerly married males was only slightly greater than the participation of never-married men at the time of the five-year follow-up.[8] Children sometimes benefited from the involvement of males outside the home, but the payoff for children was modest because so few nonresidential fathers were participating actively in the support and care of their offspring. By contrast, children of fathers living in the home were doing distinctly better. Whether this was because of the greater paternal attention received or because they enjoyed greater economic security, or because the parents were different even before family formation, could not be discerned from the data.

A seventeen-year follow-up was conducted in 1984 to examine the situation of the adolescent mothers and their offspring in later life. Approximately 80 percent of the original sample was re-interviewed, and data were collected on 296 of the children, who were then between the ages of 15 and 17.[9]

Less than a sixth of the fathers were still living in the home at the seventeen-year follow-up, despite the fact that nearly half of the males had resided with their children for some time. Sustained contact with biological fathers living outside the home occurred in a minority of families. About a fifth of the children had seen their nonresidential fathers at least once a week at the five-year follow-up, and a sixth of the children had regular contact at the seventeen-year follow-up. Attrition in contact occurred over time even though more fathers were living outside the home in 1984 than in 1972. Patterns of contact were quite variable. Some fathers increased or resumed contact as their children reached adolescence, while others diminished their involvement.[10]

Three years later, a twenty-year follow-up of the children was undertaken to determine how the next generation was doing as they moved from their teen years into their early twenties. Completed interviews were obtained from 253 youths, 85 percent of the participants seen three years earlier and about two-thirds of all eligible youths from the original sample. Attrition occurred mainly among white families where the mother was apt to marry or move away from Baltimore during the early years of the study. With very few whites remaining in the 1987 sample, our findings are, at most, generalizable only to blacks living in urban areas.

Patterns of Paternal Involvement

The children of the teen mothers were between the ages of 18 and 21 at the 1987 interview. We are therefore able to summarize the experiences of all the children with their fathers during the first eighteen years of their lives—covering the full duration of childhood. Table 10.1 shows that just under half of the children had lived with their biological fathers at some time during their first eighteen years. Only about 9 percent, however,

Table 10.1. Number of Years Spent with Each Type of Father Figure during Childhood

Number of Years	Biological Father		Stepfather		All Father Figures	
	%	Cum. %	%	Cum. %	%	Cum. %
0	53.1	53.1	52.6	52.6	7.5	7.5
1	2.6	55.7	0.9	53.5	0.4	7.9
2	7.9	63.6	6.1	59.6	3.5	11.4
3	6.1	69.7	4.4	64.0	3.9	15.4
4	5.3	75.0	5.7	69.7	2.6	18.0
5	1.8	76.8	4.8	74.6	4.4	22.4
6	0.9	77.6	3.9	78.5	4.8	27.2
7	2.2	79.8	1.8	80.3	5.7	32.9
8	1.8	81.6	1.3	81.6	3.5	36.4
9	0.9	82.5	4.4	86.0	9.6	46.1
10	0.4	82.9	1.8	87.7	5.7	51.8
11	1.8	84.6	3.1	90.8	7.5	59.2
12	—	—	0.9	91.7	3.5	62.7
13	0.9	85.5	3.1	94.7	4.4	67.1
14	—	—	2.2	96.9	5.3	72.4
15	1.8	87.3	0.9	97.8	5.7	78.1
16	2.2	89.5	1.3	99.1	5.7	83.8
17	1.8	91.2	0.9	100.0	4.8	88.6
18	8.8	100.0	—	—	11.4	100.0

resided with them during this entire period. Children who ever lived with their fathers spent a median duration of five years (or less than a third of their childhood) living with them. Typically, these years were early in life, although a small number of children had only recently moved in with their fathers. As we have already reported, the proportion of children living with their fathers declined significantly from early childhood until the seventeen-year follow-up, when they were between the ages of 15 and 17. By mid-adolescence, only 16 percent of the children were still living with their biological fathers. At the final follow-up, this number slipped to 14 percent.

Besides the biological father, however, other males were present in the children's family lives. Three out of five children who never resided with their biological fathers lived with a stepfather or father surrogate before reaching the age of 18. Even among the children who did live with their biological fathers at some point, one-third also lived with a stepfather or surrogate father at another time. Half of these children spent at least six years living with a stepfather—just about the same amount of time that they spent with their biological fathers. As we show in table 10.1, only about 8 percent of the Baltimore youths never resided with any father figure; and at the other extreme, 11 percent lived with a male throughout their entire childhood. On average, the children in this sample spent about half of their early years living with a father of some type.

A quarter of the youths reported at the seventeen-year follow-up that some other male (usually living outside the home) was like a father to them. Often these father figures were kin who had helped raise them. In some cases, they supplemented fathers inside the home, but usually they were mentioned by children who were not living with a father at the time of the interview.

As we mentioned earlier, stepfathers and father surrogates could be viewed as replacements for the biological fathers, as providing complementary relationships, or as competitors. In the analysis that follows, we look at the role of different father figures, contrasting their influence to the influence of biological fathers. Can these other males fill the void created by the disappearance of the biological father?

Contact with the Biological Father

Early in the study, contact and support from biological fathers living outside the home was relatively high. By the time their children had reached mid-adolescence, many of these males had drifted away. Figure 10.1 assembles information from the different waves of the study, showing a pattern of diminishing contact with biological fathers who were not living with their children. We did not collect detailed information on the amount of interaction with these fathers early in the study, but it is likely that almost all children saw their fathers at least occasionally and that most had regular contact with them during infancy. When the children were still preschoolers, nearly half were either living with their fathers or saw them on a weekly basis. By the end of their teens, 14 percent were living with them; only 15 percent were seeing them as often as once a week; 25 percent were not seeing them regularly but had visited them occasionally in the preceding year; and 46 percent had not had any contact with them at all.

Figure 10.1 also traces the patterns of child support provided by nonresidential fathers during the study. A year after delivery, 80 percent of the children were receiving some amount of child support. Four years later, the level of support had plummeted—just one in three received financial assistance from the nonresidential father. By mid-adolescence, the number of children receiving support had dropped to one in six.

Early in the study, never-married fathers were just as likely as previously married males to support their children, but over the long term the

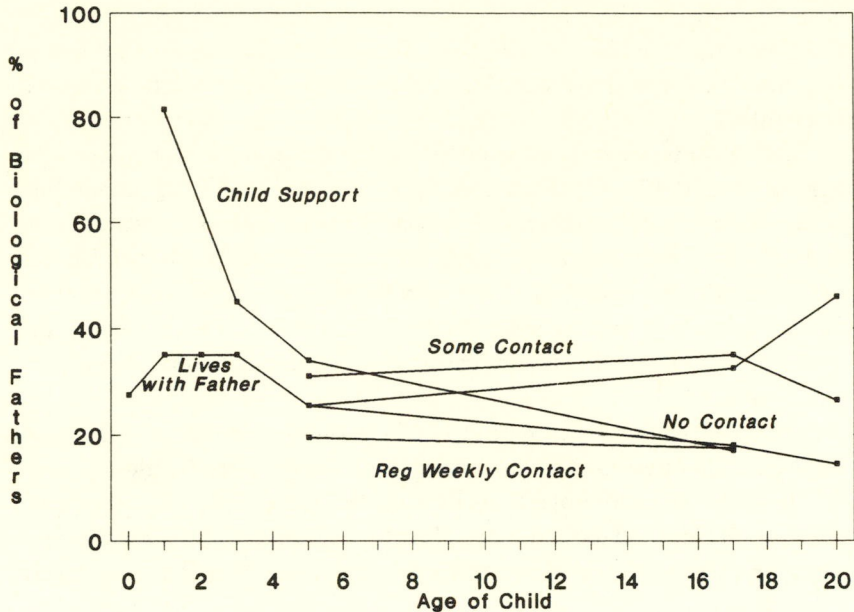

FIGURE 10.1 Percentage of Biological Fathers Providing Child Support Contrasted to Amount of Contact, by Child's Age

fathers who had been married to the child's mother were far more likely to continue to support their children. Of those who were supplying child support in 1972, just one in nine of the never-married men continued to do so in 1984 compared to one in three of the ever-married men. These figures suggest that marriage serves to re-enforce paternal obligations. Fifty-five percent of men who had lived with their children for six or more years were providing child support to their adolescent children, compared to just 17 percent of those who had lived with their children for fewer than three years, and 9 percent of those who never lived with them at all.

Despite some indications early in the Baltimore study that men might take a greater interest in supporting their male than their female offspring, the child's gender was unrelated to the persistence of child support or visitation. However, as we shall see, male children did develop closer bonds with their fathers even though they did not see them more regularly or were not given any greater financial assistance.

The Quality of Father-Child Relations

Unfortunately, little information on the fathers was collected until the five-year follow-up; therefore, we do not know much about the strength of ties between children and their fathers early in life. At the five-year follow-up, we did learn from the mothers that 65 percent of their children who had contact with their fathers "enjoyed" the relationship very much; according to the mothers, 35 percent enjoyed it only somewhat or not at all.

The 1984 interview, conducted when the children were between the ages of 15 and 17, permitted us to measure the quality of father-child relationships more systematically. Children were asked to evaluate *the degree of closeness* and *the extent to which children identified* with their biological fathers (if they had any contact with them) as well as with other father figures living both inside and outside the home. Their responses to the measure of closeness and identification were combined to form an index of attachment.[11]

Figure 10.2 shows the proportion of children who bonded strongly with different father figures. Not surprisingly, children report the highest level of attachment to biological fathers living in the home. Still, only 50 percent are strongly attached to them, according to our measure. By comparison, a similar measure on attachment to mothers revealed that 58 percent were strongly bonded. Both these figures are somewhat below the proportions for all blacks of similar age in the National Survey of Children, which contained an almost identical measure.[12]

The index of attachment nicely captures the decline in the strength of ties with the biological father when he lives outside the home. Overall, just 13 percent (not shown) report strong bonds with nonresidential biological fathers. This figure, however, conceals an important distinction. It includes nearly two-fifths (38 percent) of the adolescents in 1984 who had not seen their fathers in the past year. By contrast, of those who had at least some contact with their biological fathers, 21 percent indicated that they

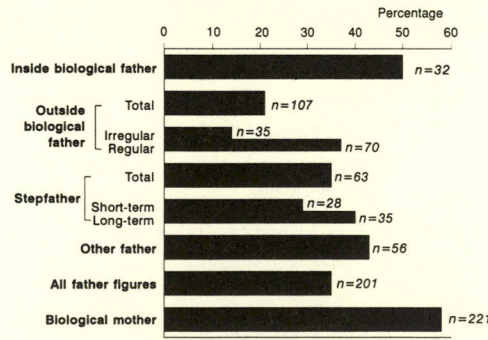

FIGURE 10.2 Percentage Strongly Attached to Father, by Type of Father Figure
Note: Sample size on breakdown of Outside Biological Father is less than total because of missing values on contact.

had a strong bond. This figure rises to 37 percent among those who saw their fathers once a week or more on average. Thus, the gap in bonding narrows substantially when we compare fathers living at home and fathers who have regular contact with their children.

Early contact between fathers and their children has no lasting effect on the level of closeness in their relationship unless it is sustained throughout the study. Although ever-married fathers have invested more in their children than have never-married men, they do not necessarily develop closer relationships with their offspring when they continue to see them. Even those fathers who were in the home for six or more years do not experience a stronger bond with their adolescent children than do fathers who were present for less than six years or were never in the home.

In recent qualitative interviews with a subsample of the children, we learned that many of those most bitterly disappointed with their fathers' efforts had enjoyed a closer relationship earlier in childhood. This may help to explain why so few nonresidential fathers are regarded as important role models by their offspring *even when* the fathers continue to see them on a regular basis and provide child support. These children are experiencing a sense of "relative deprivation" in their relationships with their biological fathers. Here is an account from one of the Baltimore youths, talking about important figures in his life:

Q. But your father has not played a big role in your life?

A. No. He hasn't. My father moved away. . . . Then he moved back here when I was in high school. We are able to talk. I don't respect him. I don't have anything against him, when he first came back, he was pretty much in my life.

A sizable minority (28 percent) of the children were living with a stepfather or a live-in father figure (the mother's boyfriend) in 1984. We refer to all residential fathers other than biological fathers as stepfathers, regardless of whether they were actually married to the child's mother. More than a third of the children living with a stepfather were highly attached to him. To examine only the more stable stepfather relationships, we defined those residential fathers who had lived in the household for six years or longer as long-term stepfathers. Long-term father-child relationships occurred in more than half of the stepfamilies, and 40 percent of the children developed a close bond with the stepfather. In contrast, of the approximately half who had a short-term stepfather in the home (for less than six years), 29 percent were highly attached to him. Evidently, the steady presence of a stepfather is often conducive to developing a strong paternal attachment, just as happens when the biological father resides in the house.

About a fourth of the children mentioned that they had someone other than a biological father or residential stepfather who was "like a father to them." About 43 percent of these children reported having a high-quality relationship with the surrogate father. Overall, 11 percent of the sample had a strong tie to a male who was neither a biological father nor a stepfather.

Taking all these father figures into account, just 1 percent of the children had a strong relationship with two or more fathers; 30 percent reported a strong tie to at least one; and 69 percent had no father figure to whom they were highly attached. Although we did not carry out an extensive analysis of the antecedents of these attachments, we did examine whether children were more likely to form a strong attachment to a father of any type if their mothers had ever married. In fact, adolescents whose mothers ever married were twice as likely to have a close relationship with a father figure as those whose mothers never married. When the mother married the biological father, the probability of a strong father-child bond forming was especially pronounced.

Although boys were not more likely than girls to have contact with a father figure, they did establish closer bonds to their fathers when there was contact. Among those who had contact with any type of father, 44 percent of the boys versus 27 percent of the girls were strongly attached to him. Regardless of the type of father figure, boys consistently report closer relationships than do girls.

In summary, only a small minority of the children of teen mothers form close bonds to their biological father (who may or may not live in the home); a somewhat greater number (but still a small fraction of the total sample) develop strong ties with another father figure, either a stepfather in the home or a relative or former stepfather outside the home. This brings us to the central question of whether relationships with these different father figures affect how well the children do in early adulthood.

In addressing the effect of paternal involvement on children's well-being, we examine the impact of paternal involvement (of both biological fathers and father surrogates) measured in 1984 on various outcomes measured in 1987. The measures in 1984 summarize a history of relationships between children and their fathers. Although a great number of children saw relationships with their biological fathers deteriorate at some point in their childhood, only a handful experienced the opposite situation—a strengthening of ties after early childhood. In consequence, we cannot say a great deal about how changing patterns of paternal involvement affect the development of children. But we can at least be reasonably certain about the direction of causality. We will investigate whether greater involvement of fathers and the establishment of a strong bond with their children before or by mid-adolescence leads to better outcomes in early adulthood.

Measures of Youth Well-Being in Early Adulthood

The twenty-year follow-up provides a wide range of measures of successful adjustment in early adulthood. We have selected four different indicators of well-being: (1) socioeconomic achievement measured by an index of educational and employment attainment; (2) whether the youth had a child before the age of 19; (3) whether the child had spent time in jail; and (4) a subset of items from the Beck Depression Inventory. The construction of these measures is described in greater detail in Appendix B.

A comparison of the Baltimore youths with their counterparts in the National Survey of Children (NSC), a nationally representative study of youths between the ages of 17 and 22, revealed that, at least among blacks, teenage childbearing appears to have only a modest effect in determining the life chances of youths in their late teens (see table 10.2). The patterns of educational attainment and early fertility among children of teen mothers in the Baltimore study and the NSC were almost identical. Imprisonment was far higher in the Baltimore sample, but we are reasonably sure that the disparity is the result of the failure of the NSC (a telephone survey) to get accurate reports and to locate youths who were in jail in their teen years. The NSC did not contain the Depression Scale, but other measures of emotional well-being yielded comparable results. When compared to the children of later childbearers, the offspring of adolescent mothers did not do as well on a wide range of outcomes, but the differential in performance was not very large.

Nonetheless, a number of youths in the Baltimore study were displaying serious problems by their late teens and early 20s. About a third dropped out of high school and did not show any immediate prospect of graduating or obtaining a GED, the test of high school equivalency; almost a quarter (a third of the girls and 15 percent of the boys) had a birth by the age of 19; 16 percent of the youths (2 percent of the girls and 30 percent of the boys) had been or were in jail; and 31 percent showed a strong indication of depressive affect.

The Presence of Fathers and Youth Well-Being

How much of the variability in the four outcomes can be traced to the presence or absence of males in the lives of the youths we studied? We first

TABLE 10.2. Selected Outcome Variables for Baltimore Youths and NSC

Percentage of:	Baltimore Males	Baltimore Females	All Baltimore Youth	NSC Early	NSC Later
Education					
HS Grad or GED	58	68	63	72	81
In School Now	35	39	37	32	51
Ever Dropped Out of HS	40	29	34	23	16
Ever Repeated a Grade	49	36	42	38	29
Marriage and Relation- ships					
Ever Married	2	6	4	—	—
Living with Partner	2	11	6	5	4
Fertility					
Ever Pregnant	42	57	49	—	—
Ever Live Birth	25	38	31	—	—
Had Sex	98	95	96	84	94
Economic					
Currently Employed	58	54	56	54	60
On Welfare in 1986	0	24	12	16	8
1986 Income $1 to 4,999	63	68	66	70	63
$5,000 to 9,999	20	21	20	14	26
$10,000 to 19,999	15	10	12	16	11
Drugs and Delinquency					
Used Alcohol					
Ever	81	74	77	65	65
In Past 12 Months	61	57	58	42	50
Used Pot					
Ever	66	49	57	40	38
In Past 12 Months	36	24	30	15	19
Used Cocaine					
Ever	19	7	13	5	11
In Past 12 Months	9	3	6	2	3
Damaged Another's Property					
Ever	40	15	27	22	17
In Past 12 Months	14	6	10	10	6
Carried Hidden Weapon					
Ever	26	5	15	7	8
In Past 12 Months	14	2	8	4	6
Stole Something Worth $50+					
Ever	18	2	10	2	5
In Past 12 Months	7	2	4	1	2

(continued)

TABLE 10.2. (Continued)

Percentage of:	Baltimore Males	Baltimore Females	All Baltimore Youth	NSC Early	NSC Later
Attacked Person with Intent to Hurt					
Ever	15	9	12	5	11
In Past 12 Months	9	8	8	2	6
Sold Drugs					
Ever	24	5	14	6	2
In Past 12 Months	9	2	5	3	0
Ever Stopped by Police	75	19	47	28	27
Ever Been in Jail	30	2	16	3	3
In Jail Now	17	0	7	—	—
Psychological Well-Being					
Got Help from Mental-Health Professional in Past 3 Years	10	13	12	5	13
How Life Going:					
Very Well	28	35	31	39	44
Number of Participants	125	127	252	103	63

examined a series of bi-variate comparisons that tested the overall effect of the presence of four different types of father figures on each outcome measure: whether a biological father was present in the home; whether the child had contact with the nonresidential biological father; whether a step-father was present in the home; and whether the youth mentioned an adult male (inside or outside the home) who was like a father.

Figure 10.3 displays the results of these bi-variate comparisons in a series of bar graphs. The results compare the magnitude of difference on any of the four outcome measures for the presence (or absence) of different father figures. Take, for example, the initial comparison examining the outcomes for children who were or were not living with a biological father in 1984. The results for the different outcomes three and a half years later are surprising, for they show a relatively modest effect of having a biolog-ical father in the home. While in all cases the relationship was in the predicted direction, it did not reach statistical significance for three out of the four outcome measures, imprisonment being the exception.

Turning to the influence of the biological father outside the home, we found that the overall effect of the child's having contact with him is even less apparent. Children who had contact with nonresidential fathers were

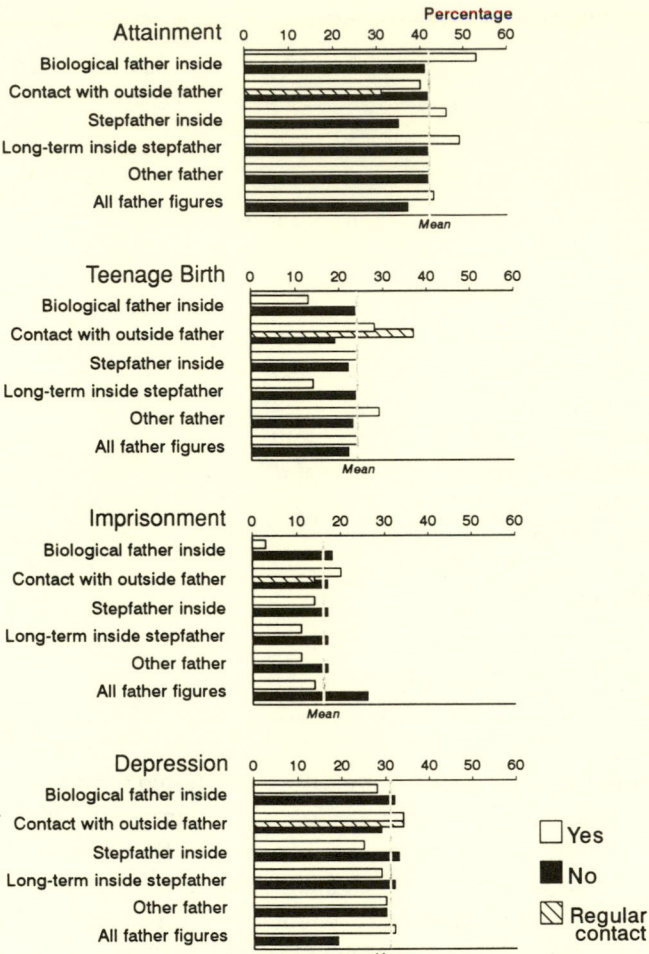

FIGURE 10.3 Youth Outcomes, by Presence of Father Figures

not doing better than youths who had not seen their fathers in the past year in all measures of outcomes. Even when we confined our comparisons to fathers whom children saw regularly, no consistent effects were detected on the outcome measures.

Similar results emerge when we examine the bi-variate effect of other father figures living either inside or outside the home. Children in step-parent households at the time of the 1984 interview were not doing better on the various outcome measures three and a half years later. When we confined our contrasts to children who were in stable stepparent families (where they had resided with the stepfather for at least six years), we detected a modest but not statistically significant effect. Like the children of biological fathers in the home, the youths with long-term stepfathers did not seem to be doing a great deal better in early adulthood than all the other youths in the study.

Finally, we examined the youths living in single-parent households who identified a person who was like a father to them. Compared to their peers who mentioned no such person, these youths fared no better at the twenty-year follow-up, although they were less likely to be high on the depression measure. In sum, the presence of fathers at most appears to have only a weak effect on key outcomes in early adulthood.

There are several possible explanations for the limited impact that a father's presence has on his child's well-being. It may be that the protective benefits of living with the biological (or step-) father is not very conspicuous among the tiny group of children who lived in stably married families because many of these children often do not have very close relations with their fathers. It is also possible that children not living in two-parent families do as well because other father figures assume an important role in their lives, although our bi-variate comparisons seem not to support this explanation. Alternatively, we might find that involvement with fathers of any type may bring only modest advantages to the children in our study. Perhaps, as we pointed out in our introductory remarks, relations with the mother may override the effect of paternal involvement.

These different interpretations can be partially tested with the data at hand. Figure 10.4 examines the same four constellations of paternal involvement, subdivided according to the quality of the relationship between youths and their fathers. Adding the information on the strength of the ties between fathers and their children brings the results into sharp focus. Youths do far better at the twenty-year follow-up if they have a close relationship with any of the different father figures. But close ties count for more when the youths are living with a father than when they are not.

Let us look first at the children who were living with their biological fathers. We recall that these youths were split evenly into those who were close to their fathers and those who were not. Between these two groupings, a huge difference occurs in three out of four outcomes. Among those who had a close bond with their fathers, more than two-thirds were high on the measure of attainment, having entered college or found stable employment after graduating from high school; none had had a child before the age of 19; and only a fifth were high on the depression index. (The incidence of serious problems with the law was also low but not different from the incidence among youths who were not close to their residential biological fathers.) By contrast, the youths living with their

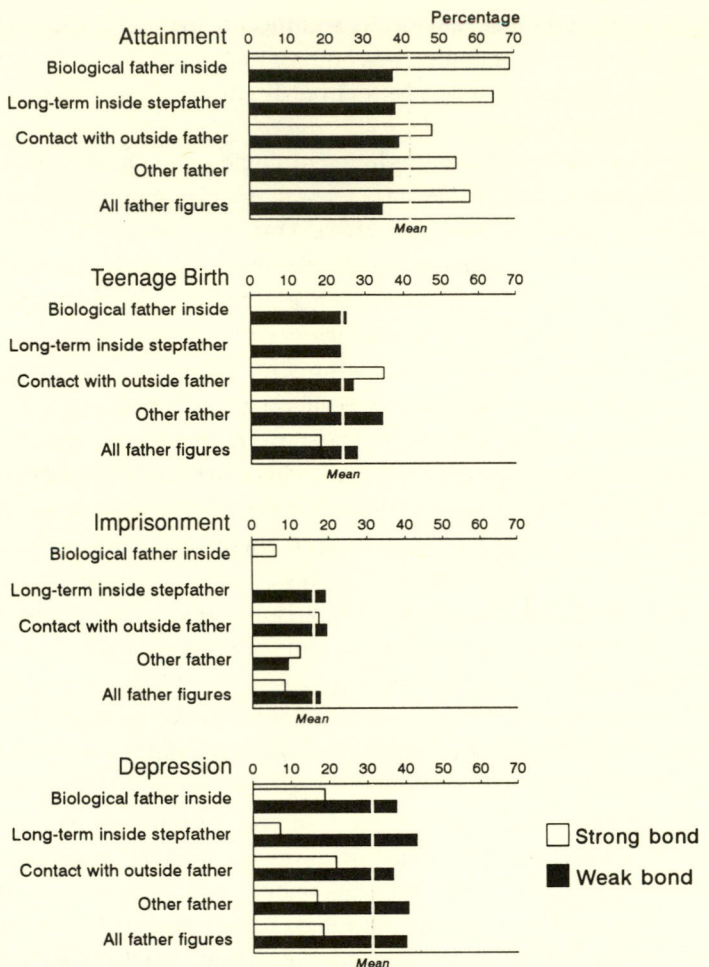

FIGURE 10.4 Youth Outcomes, by Level of Attachment to Father Figures

biological fathers who were not as close were actually doing worse on average than all other youths in the sample.

The identical pattern recurred when we examined the youths who were living in stepfamilies. The third of the youths who had close ties with their stepfathers were performing extremely well in early adulthood, especially if we consider the children who had long-standing and stable relationships with their stepfathers. The offspring in these families were doing as well as the youths who grew up with their biological fathers. It appears that the conjunction of stable *and* close relations with a male figure in the home produces high rates of successful adjustment in early adulthood.

This finding is echoed among the youths who were not living with a father but were strongly attached to him at the time of the seventeen-year follow-up. Although they were not doing as well as the young adults who had had the benefit of growing up with a father in the home throughout early adolescence, they were performing significantly better than youths who had not established a close tie with a father figure in three of the outcome measures. The exception is the measure of teen childbearing where closer ties predict higher rates of teen parenthood. We shall have more to say later about this anomalous result.

Finally, in figure 10.4 we can also see that children who had a close relationship with a male who was like a father to them also did better than average in the three of four outcome measures. Again, anything less than a close tie to a father surrogate does not improve children's chances of doing well in the four outcome measures.

The findings described in figures 10.3 and 10.4 were reproduced in a multi-variate analysis that examined the independent effects of the presence of different father figures and the attachment to each in the outcome measures. We also included the level of attachment to the mother, which may mediate some of the father effects. Finally, we examined the possibility that the effects were different for boys and girls by testing for gender interactions.

Logistic regression was used to estimate the effects that determine each of the four outcomes. Appendix C displays the full set of net effects, while table 10.3 shows the results of our final models of selected effects for each dependent outcome measure. In the multi-variate analysis, we combined stepfathers and residential biological fathers to indicate the presence of an "inside father."

The multi-variate analysis confirmed the bi-variate findings.

The presence of various father figures has relatively little impact on the youth outcomes. And when we enter the degree of attachment to a father figure in our models, the effect of the father's presence all but disappears, while positive outcomes are enhanced when a strong bond exists with the father (shown in appendix C).

Table 10.3 shows the net effects of a strong attachment to an inside father (biological or step), a nonresidential biological father with whom the youth has contact, and an "other" father. Measures of a father's presence were dropped in the final models, since they did not differentiate any of the outcomes. The effects both of attachment to the mother and of the child's gender are also estimated in each model. The first column under each outcome lists the beta coefficients or the additive effects. The second column shows the odds ratio for each effect.

The results indicate that attachment to a father figure has beneficial

TABLE 10.3. Independent Effects of Attachment to Father Figures on Outcomes in 1987

	Attainment		Teenage Birth		Imprisonment		Depression	
	b	odds ratio	b	odds ratio	b	odds ratio	b	odds ratio
Gender of Child	.092	1.10	−1.24**	.29	2.91**	18.4	−.552	.58
Close to Inside Father	.767*	2.15	−1.33*	.26	−1.58*	.21	−.997*	.37
Close to Outside Father	.226	1.25	1.10*	3.00	−.30	.74	−.339	.71
Close to Other Father	.524	1.69	−.08	.92	−.12	.89	−1.116	.33
Close to Mother	−.307	.74	.10	1.11	−.72	.49	−.319	.73
Intercept	−.400	—	−.623	—	−3.165	—	−.169	—
n	221	—	221	—	221	—	221	—

*.05 \ Levels of Significance
**.01 /

effects in all outcome measures as the youths enter adulthood. Again, the only exception is the impact of a close tie with the nonresidential biological father on teenage childbearing. Children who live with their biological fathers or stepfathers in long-term relationships benefit the most from strong bonds with their inside fathers. Youths who were strongly attached to a residential father were twice as likely to have entered college or to have found stable employment after high school; 75 percent less likely to have been a teenage parent, 80 percent less likely to have been in jail, and half as likely to have experienced multiple depression symptoms. The positive effects of a close bond with an inside father are significant for all of the outcomes measuring a successful transition to adulthood.

A strong attachment with another father figure also appears to improve a youth's chances of high attainment and to reduce depression symptoms, although the effects are not statistically significant. The probability of a teenage birth and imprisonment is also reduced if youths have close bonds with other males who are like fathers to them; however, these effects are weak.

A close bond with the outside biological father has the least impact on youth outcomes. Although the children who had contact with and were strongly attached to their nonresidential biological fathers were more likely to have high measures of attainment and more likely to avoid imprisonment and depression, the advantage of the attachments is only marginally beneficial.

In fact, a perverse effect is evident for the teenage-birth outcome. Youths who were strongly attached to their nonresidential fathers were more likely to experience early childbearing than those who were not attached to their outside biological fathers or had no contact with them. Our exploration of gender interactions revealed why this result occurs. Boys who had contact with and were strongly attached to their nonresidential fathers were more likely to report a teen birth than were girls who had close ties with their outside fathers. Since boys are over represented among youths having strong bonds with their outside fathers, this interaction increases the overall chances of teenage childbearing for youths attached to their outside fathers.[13]

Oddly, the level of attachment to the biological mother has very little impact on the well-being of youths as they enter adulthood. A close tie with the mother does not mediate the effects of attachment to a father figure, nor does it improve the chances of educational or economic attainment or lower the probability of teenage childbearing. Closeness to the mother does reduce the likelihood of imprisonment and depression, but not significantly. We were surprised to find that those children who had close bonds with their mothers were not doing significantly better in the measures of well-being in 1987 than were the youths who were not close to their mothers. Perhaps this is because the variability in maternal closeness was low, but it may suggest that this measure takes on different meaning when it is applied to mothers rather than fathers.

These results redefine our understanding of the psychological impact of fathers in the lives of disadvantaged children. They also help to explain the frequently contradictory findings of earlier research that attempted to establish the psychological benefits for children of paternal involvement. Do fathers contribute to the child's psychological well-being, apart from the economic assistance that they provide? The answer appears not to be a straightforward yes or no.

The presence of a father inside the home confers only a modest advantage when we examine four varied measures of children's well-being; contact, even regular contact, with fathers outside the home had little effect on positive youth outcomes. Children benefit only from a close paternal relationship. Unfortunately, more often than not, the ties that they develop with fathers are neither continuous nor close.

Public policy cannot regulate family intimacy, but it may be able to foster conditions that promote stronger bonds between children and their fathers. The Baltimore study furnishes evidence that marriage, especially a marriage that survives, indirectly increases the likelihood of successful adjustment in early adulthood by boosting the odds of a strong paternal bond. Unfortunately, we know little about the conditions that produce stable marriages.

It is believed that economic security, especially for males, may contribute to the desirability of marriage and its durability. While such a belief seems plausible enough, it is not buttressed by a great deal of data. There is no simple correlation between economic cycles and separation statistics, but there is some support for the proposition that unions falter or are never formed when expectations of male contributions are low. We need to look more carefully at ways of increasing the economic benefits of marriage in hopes that it may indirectly lead to a greater sense of children's well-being.

Clearly, marriage is not always in a woman's or a child's best interests. Unstable marriages and conflictual relationships within marriage elevate the chances of a poor relationship with a father outside the home. And our data show that a poor relationship is worse than no relationship at all. It may interfere with the child developing a bond with another father figure, disturb his or her relationship with the mother, or directly undercut the child's ability to function as an adult. In consequence, we walk a thin line when we attempt to promote matrimony as a public good if many or most marriages turn out to be unstable or conflict ridden.

The same logic applies in maintaining ties between fathers and children. Obviously, insisting that fathers maintain economic obligations to their children has economic benefits. The maintenance of contact may also have social and psychological advantages for children. Again, however, our evidence suggests a qualified response. Only a third of the males who had regular contact with their children, and even fewer who were providing child support, had developed strong bonds with their offspring. Unless we can manage a better record than that, the claim of psychological benefits for children is dubious, if our results are any indication. We must remember, however, that our findings, if they can be generalized at all, apply only to African Americans who began families at an early age.

No one knows how to foster stronger and more lasting attachments between children and their fathers, whether the fathers are biological or surrogate. Establishing support groups for prospective fathers represents a constructive step, but these services probably do too little for too few fathers over too brief a time to make much difference in children's later lives. The successful design of more lasting programs remains a high priority. This may involve the location in the child's social network of male support figures who may fill in for absent fathers. Whether we can engineer a strong paternal bond by cultivating such ties is a question open to further exploration.

It is also clear from our data that some children do well without a paternal presence. Can we assume that one parent is sufficient so long as that parent is a skillful and loving figure? Perhaps other figures enter the child's life who may not be father surrogates but who provide additional guidance, support, and material assistance. We need to know more about how and why children manage successfully in solo-parent families.

The general rediscovery of the importance of fathers in children's lives is a salutary development in social science research. The restoration of the father's place in the family undoubtedly has important implications for public policy. Our greatest fear, however, is that we may leap to action before we learn what those implications are.

APPENDIX A. Design of the Baltimore Study, 1966–1987

Schedule of Interviews[1]	Interview		Attempted		
	Dates	Participants	Interviews	Number	Percentage
Time 1: during pregnancy	1966–1968	Adolescent Mothers,	404	404	100
		Grandmothers	379	350	92
Time 2: one year after delivery	1968–1970	Adolescent Mothers	404	382	95
Time 3: three years after delivery	1970	Adolescent Mothers,[2]	404	363	90
		Classmates	361	268	74
Time 4: five years after delivery	1972	Adolescent Mothers,	404	331	82
		Children of Adolescent Mothers,	331	306	92
		Classmates	307	221	72
Time 5: sixteen to seventeen years after delivery	1983–1984	Adolescent Mothers or Surrogates	404 35	289	80
		Children of Adolescent Mothers	392	296	7
		National Survey of Children (Blacks, 15 to 16 years old)	96		
Time 6: 18–21 years after delivery	1987	Children of Adolescent Mothers	377	253	67
		National Survey of Children (Blacks, 18 to 21 years old)	169		

[1]This category includes a small number of interviews that were excluded from the analysis because of a large amount of missing or falsified information.

[2]Interviews were also obtained with about one-third of the fathers at this time.

Appendix B. Description of Outcome Measures of Youth Well-Being

Teen birth. This measure indicates whether the adolescent had mothered or fathered a child before the age of 19. Direct questions about childbearing and fertility histories provided the information. All youths had reached the age of 19 (with the exception of a small number who were a few months from their nineteenth birthday) by the 1987 interview, so that exposure was not an issue. Among the adolescents in the Baltimore study, 24 percent had experienced a teenage birth (33 percent of the girls and 15 percent of the boys).

Attainment. This measure is based on an intricate coding scheme entailing academic achievement and subsequent work history. Briefly, our method first considered the adolescent's educational achievement and then adjusted the score by taking into account the employment record. Youths who had graduated from high school and were attending college or graduate school were coded at the high end of the attainment scale. Also, high school graduates in steady employment were scored high on attainment. The youths coded in the middle range were high school graduates who were unemployed but looking for work or were in a training school, and those adolescents still in high school and at grade level. Adolescents still in high school but who had failed one or more grades fell at the low end of the attainment scale. And finally, high school dropouts were also at the bottom of the attainment scale, unless they had accumulated substantial work experience (which moved them up the index slightly). Represented as a three-category index (collapsed from a five-category index), 42 percent were high on attainment, 24 percent fell in the middle range, and 34 percent scored low on attainment.

Depression. This indicator is an additive scale based on a subset of twelve items from the Beck Depression Inventory measuring emotional well-being. Various statements were read to the adolescent concerning his or her emotional state, to which the adolescent responded that he or she had felt that way most of the time, some of the time, only a little of the time, or none of the time during the previous four weeks. Examples of some of the items are: I felt sad; I was bothered by things that usually don't bother me; I did not feel like eating, my appetite was poor; I felt that I could not shake off the blues, even with help from my family or friends; I had trouble keeping my mind on what I was doing; I felt depressed; I felt fearful; My sleep was restless; I felt lonely.

Responses for each item ranged from 0, indicating no incidence, to 3, indicating frequent occurrence of the adverse emotional state. An additive index was constructed from these twelve items by summing their responses. The index was then dichotomized by selecting the proportion who fell above one-half of a standard deviation above the mean indicating excessive symptoms of depression. For the sample as a whole, 31 percent fell in this tail end of the distribution.

Imprisonment. This outcome indicates whether the adolescent had ever spent any time in jail, prison, or a correctional facility. Delinquent behavior among the Baltimore children displayed the typical gender pattern: 3 percent of the girls and 29 percent of the boys had spent some time in jail, or 16 percent overall who had ever been in jail. These percentages differ from table 10.2 because of missing values.

	Attainment		Teenage Birth		Imprisonment		Depression	
	1	2	1	2	1	2	1	2
Gender = Boys	.12	.08	−.96**	−1.05**	2.54**	2.80**	−.77**	−.59
Inside Father	.40	.17	−.14	.23	−.66	−.13	−.36	.06
Contact with Outside Father	−.13	−.20	.87*	.72	.16	.23	.21	.23
Other Father	.14	−.02	.43	.52	−.39	−.90	−.14	.10
Early Child Support	.19	.26	−.40	−.57	.20	.11	−.004	.02
Close to Inside Father	—	.65	—	−1.37*	—	−1.48	—	−1.04
Close to Outside Father	—	.27	—	1.00	—	−.55	—	−.48
Close to Other Father	—	.51	—	−.33	—	.70	—	−1.24
Close to Mother	—	−.31	—	.02	—	−.68	—	−.19
Intercept	−.59	−.48	−1.09	−1.00	−3.38	−3.10	−.37	−.34
n	219	215	219	215	219	215	219	215

*.05 ⟍
       ⟩ Levels of Significance
**.01 ⟋

Notes

We are grateful for support from the Ford, Hewlett, Robert Wood Johnson, and Rockefeller Foundations. An earlier version of this chapter is being published by Temple University Press.

1. Clark Vincent, *Unmarried Mothers* (New York: Free Press, 1961), p. 5.

2. Arthur Elster and Michael E. Lamb, *Adolescent Fatherhood* (Hillsdale, N.J.: Lawrence Erlbaum, 1986); Bryan Robinson, *Teenage Fathers* (Lexington, Mass.: Lexington Books, 1988).

3. Ross D. Parke and Brian Neville, "Teenage Fatherhood," in Cheryl D. Hayes, ed., *Risking the Future* (Washington, D.C.: National Academy Press, 1987), 2: 145–73.

4. P. Lindsay Chase-Lansdale and E. Mavis Hetherington, "The Impact of Divorce on Life-Span Development: Short and Long-Term Effects," in Paul B. Baltes, David L. Featherman, and Robert Lerner, eds., *Life-Span Development and Behavior* (Hillsdale, N.J.: Lawrence Erlbaum, 1989), 10: 105–50; Robert E. Emery, *Marriage, Divorce, and Children's Adjustments* (Beverly Hills: Sage Publications, 1988); Robert Weiss, *Marital Separation* (New York: Basic Books, 1975).

5. E. Mavis Hetherington, M. Cox, and R. Cox, "The Aftermath of Divorce," in Joseph H. Stevens, Jr., and Marilyn Matthews, eds., *Mother-Child, Father-Child Relations* (Washington, D.C.: National Association for the Education of Young Children, 1978), pp. 149–76; Robert D. Hess and Kathleen A. Camara, "Post-Divorce Family Relationships as Mediating Factors in the Consequences of Divorce for Children," *Journal of Social Issues* 6 (1979): 79–98; Judith S. Wallerstein and Joan B. Kelly, *Surviving the Breakup* (New York: Basic Books, 1980).

6. Frank F. Furstenberg, Jr., S. Philip Morgan, and Paul A. Allison, "Paternal Participation and Children's Well-Being After Marital Dissolution," *American Sociological Review* 52 (1987): 697–701.

7. Frank F. Furstenberg, Jr., *Unplanned Parenthood* (New York: The Free Press, 1976).

8. Frank F. Furstenberg, Jr., and Kathie Talvitie, "Children's Names and Paternal Claims: Bonds between Unmarried Fathers and Their Children," *Journal of Family Issues* 1 (Winter 1979): 31–57; Frank Mott, "When Is a Father Really Gone?: Paternal-Child Contact in Father-Absent Homes," *Demography* 27 (Fall 1990): 499–517.

9. Almost all of the children lost to follow-up had left the study in the first phase. Some, especially the small number of whites in the sample, had moved out of the Baltimore area and were excluded; about 10 percent of the children had been put up for adoption or had died. For further details about the sample, see Frank F. Furstenberg, Jr., Jeanne Brooks-Gunn, and S. Philip Morgan, *Adolescent Mothers in Later Life* (New York: Cambridge University Press, 1987).

10. Frank F. Furstenberg, Jr., and Kathleen M. Harris, "The Disappearing American Father? Divorce and the Waning Significance of Biological Parenthood." Paper

presented at the conference on "Demographic Perspectives on the American Family: Patterns and Prospects," Albany, N.Y., April 1990.

11. The index of attachment was constructed using children's responses from two items measuring closeness and identification in the father-child relation:
How close do you feel to your father?
1. extremely close
2. quite close
3. fairly close, or
4. not very close?
How much do you want to be like the kind of person he is when you're an adult?
1. a lot
2. quite a bit
3. just a little, or
4. not at all?
The response distributions were standardized by categorizing the top two responses as high and the bottom two as low. An additive index was then formed by summing the high response so that a 2 on the index indicated that the father-child bond was very strong ("high" on both measures of attachment). Levels of strong attachment shown in subsequent tables and figures thus refer to this high score on the index, where attachment in the father-child relation is the greatest.

12. Kathleen M. Harris and Frank F. Furstenberg, Jr., "Affective Mobility: The Course of Parent-Child Relations in Adolescence." Paper presented at the annual meeting of the American Sociological Association, Washington, D.C., August 1990.

13. When we explored the possibility that attachment to a father figure may result in different outcomes for boys and girls, no significant interactions were found, with the exception that boys who were highly attached to their nonresidential fathers were more likely to report a teenage birth than girls who had a close bond with their outside fathers. However, the effects of the interactions between gender and attachment revealed an interesting pattern with regard to the outcomes. Girls who were strongly attached to a father figure experienced greater success in the outcome measures than did the boys who were attached to a father. This result explains why we observed no gender differences in the four outcomes. Boys more often enjoy a close relationship with their fathers than do girls, and the steady presence of a father may increase their chances of doing well, if only because it provides the arena for forming a close bond with a father figure. But even though girls are less likely to become strongly attached to a father figure, they apparently derive greater benefits from that attachment. In other words, controlling for all other effects, when a girl forms a close bond with a father, her chances of favorable outcomes are better than when a boy is highly attached to a father. However, because more boys develop close ties with a father figure, the interactive effect balances the compositional effect, resulting in similar probabilities of a successful transition to adulthood by gender.

GINA ADAMS
KAREN PITTMAN
RAYMOND O'BRIEN

11 ADOLESCENT AND YOUNG ADULT FATHERS: PROBLEMS AND SOLUTIONS

In recent years there has been rising interest in the young men who father the children of adolescent mothers, and the clamor has increased for policies, penalties, and programs that are targeted toward this group. The interest is not because more babies are born to teenage mothers, which is in fact not the case. Rather, it is because the babies born to teen mothers are increasingly born to unmarried mothers, the majority of whom end up poor. In 1988 about 489,000 teenagers gave birth, down from 656,000 in 1970. However, fewer than four out of ten babies born to teens in 1988 were born to married teens, down from seven out of ten in 1970.[1] And the poverty rates for young female-headed families are appalling. In 1986, 84 percent of the children under the age of 3 in female-headed families where the mother was younger than 22 were living in families with annual incomes below the federal poverty line ($8,700 for a family of three in 1986).[2]

The poverty of young female-headed families, and the welfare costs associated with this group, have led to a growing belief that young absent fathers must be forced to assume financial responsibility for their children. Declining marriage rates have contributed to a common social perception that young unmarried fathers are irresponsible, careless victimizers of young women, and have little or no interest in their children.

It is, however, becoming increasingly clear that the situation of these men is much more complex than is suggested by the stereotype. While some young fathers fit the stereotype, others do not. This chapter examines the validity of the stereotype, and explores the complexities and pressures facing adolescent and young adult fathers.

An accurate picture of this group is essential to the development of programs and policies for young fathers, their partners, and their children. Data on young fathers are often hard to obtain, but at least partial answers are available to three commonly asked questions: What is the age and socioeconomic status of the partners of adolescent mothers? What is known about young fathers' willingness to accept responsibility for their children? What factors seem to influence the support provided by young absent fathers? The answers to these three questions allow a fourth to be answered: What should be done for young fathers? They also force us to face squarely a fifth: What should be done for young families that, even with the presence or financial support of the father, are unable to bring in an adequate income?

Only by addressing these questions can we develop effective policies that deal with the problems presented by adolescent and young adult fathers.[3]

The Difficulty of Obtaining Data on Young Fathers

As a threshold matter, it is important to recognize the difficulty of obtaining data on young fathers. It is harder to compile statistics on young fathers than on young mothers, for several reasons. Until recently, much of the research on parenthood in general, and adolescent parenthood in particular, has focused on the role of the mother. In consequence, national surveys traditionally have not asked young men about reproductive issues or fertility.

Second, except when he lives with his child, it is almost impossible for national surveys to assess if a young man has fathered a child unless he is aware that he has and chooses to admit the fact to the survey taker. It is not known how many fathers are unaware that they have fathered children, but it is clear that some fathers who do know refuse to admit it. As a result, national survey data only provide information about the characteristics of a select group of young men, and it is not clear how applicable this information is to the population of young absent fathers overall.

Finally, several studies have provided information on a small number of fathers who participated in particular programs or research efforts, but it is difficult to compare behaviors across the various populations analyzed by these studies. Some studies included adolescent fathers, some included young men (many of them not adolescents) who fathered children by adolescent mothers, and some included young men who voluntarily stepped forward to participate in social service programs for young fathers. While providing useful information, many of these studies have not allowed researchers to draw conclusions about all young fathers because they did not involve nationally representative samples of young men.

One consequence of the inadequacy of the data is that it is impossible to determine how many young or adolescent fathers there are. We do know that approximately 111,000 of the women (of all ages) who gave birth in 1988 said that the fathers of their children were younger than 20 years old; however, not all of these mothers were adolescents.[4] We also know that about 7 percent of the young men in their 20s reported in a national survey that they had fathered a child as a teenager, although we do not know how many additional young men did not admit to the fact.[5] A final complicating factor is that it is likely that some unknown number of fathers have children by more than one woman; we cannot assume that there are equal numbers of fathers and mothers.

How Old Are the Fathers?

Although the data on young fathers are far from complete, two things are clear. First, many adolescent mothers do not report the ages of the fathers on their babies' birth certificates. Recent unpublished data show that slightly more than one-third of the adolescent mothers did not report the ages of the fathers. Most of the young mothers who did not were unmarried.[6] Second, the limited research that does exist reveals that the majority of these fathers are in their early 20s (see table 11.1 a–c). Only about 30 percent of the fathers whose ages were reported were younger than 20 years old when their children were born, and another 56 percent were in their early 20s. About 11 percent were between the ages of 25 and 29, and very few were 30 or older.

Fathers married to teenage women who give birth tend to be somewhat older than the partners of unmarried teens. In 1983 less than one-quarter of the married fathers were teens, 60 percent were 20 to 24 years old, and the remaining 15 percent were older than 25. It is far more difficult, however, to get a sense of the ages of the partners of unmarried teen mothers because of the huge gaps in information. In looking only at the partners for whom there is information, it appears that unmarried partners are slightly younger than married partners. Roughly 43 percent of single mothers who reported the age of their child's father said he was younger than 20, about 44 percent said that the father was between the ages of 20 and 24, and 13 percent said that he was older than 25.

These facts are hardly surprising. About two-thirds of all births by teenage women are by young women 18 and 19 years old, while only 2 percent are by teenagers younger than 15.[7] Reflecting the general social trend of the male partner being somewhat older than the female, the data suggest that the male partners of teenage women are, on average, about two years older than them.[8] In a majority of the births by teenage women, therefore, the father is likely to be 20 or older.

These data on the age of the father have a number of implications. First, they suggest that programs trying to reach the fathers of children born to adolescent mothers need to use multiple outreach strategies rather than

Table 11.1a. Mothers Younger than 20 and the Reported Age of the Fathers of Their Children, by Age, Race, and Marital Status of the Mother at the Time of Birth of the Child, 1983[a]

Age of Father	All Mothers Younger Than 20 (in percentages)			All Mothers Younger Than 20 Reporting Age of Father (in percentages)	
	Married	Unmarried	Total	Unmarried	Total
Younger than 18	3	4	4	13	6
18–19	22	10	15	30	24
20–24	60	15	36	44	56
25–29	12	3	7	9	11
30+	4	1	2	4	3
Not reported	1	66	36	—	—
	100	100	100	100	100
Total number of mothers	228,962	270,076	499,038		
Percentage of all mothers in marital status category	46	54	100		

NOTE: Percentages may not total 100, owing to rounding.

[a]Data on the age of the father are collected from information recorded on the birth certificate. This information is not always reported and therefore is not available for a number of births.

SOURCE: Unpublished data from the National Center for Health Statistics. Calculations by the Children's Defense Fund. Reprinted by permission of the Children's Defense Fund.

Table 11.1b

| | All Mothers Younger Than 20 Reporting Age of Father (in percentages) | | | |
Age of Father	Younger Than 15	15–17	18–19	Total
Younger than 18	40	13	2	6
18–19	31	35	19	24
20–24	24	43	61	56
25–29	4	6	13	11
30+	2	2	4	4
	100	100	100	100
Total number of mothers	9,752	172,673	316,613	499,038
Percentage of all unmarried mothers	90	68	46	54
Percentage of all mothers not re-porting age of father	70	46	30	36

limited to school-based approaches. Programs also need to recognize that their clients span a wide age range, and that they may need a correspondingly wide range of services. Moreover, while age is not the sole predictor of employment and earnings potential, the fact that many of these fathers are in their early 20s suggests that they are better able to support the young mothers financially than they would be if they were adolescents.

A young father can take responsibility for his child in many ways. While the most accepted approach is to marry and live with the mother of the child, sharing whatever resources he may have directly with his family, a young man can assume significant obligations in other ways. Correctly gauging the extent to which young men behave in responsible ways toward their children thus requires an examination of marriage patterns among young fathers, as well as other responsible behavior among young men who do not marry the mothers of their children.

Responsibility through Marriage

Given the common stereotype of young unwed fathers, it is important to emphasize that 42 percent of teenage mothers are married to the father when they give birth and an additional 20 to 24 percent marry him within a year after the birth.[9] Therefore, a significant number of the young fathers are behaving in a way traditionally considered responsible. None-

Table 11.1c

	All Mothers Younger Than 20 Reporting Age of Father (in percentages)			
Age of Father	Total White	Total Black	Unmarried White	Unmarried Black
Younger than 18	5	10	12	14
18–19	23	27	29	31
20–24	57	50	45	44
25–29	11	10	10	8
30+	4	3	4	3
	100	100	100	100
Total number of mothers	342,183	142,105	135,716	126,300
Percentage of all unmarried mothers	40	89	100	100
Percentage of all mothers not reporting age of father	25	62	62	70

theless, the proportion of adolescent births that occur within marriage has declined precipitously since 1970.[10] This trend is related to a number of broader demographic patterns.

First, fewer teens and young adults, overall, are married, regardless of whether they are parents. In 1970, for example, about 25 percent of 18- and 19-year-old girls and about 8 percent of 18- and 19-year-old boys had ever been married. By 1986 these percentages had dropped to about 12 percent and 4 percent, respectively.[11]

Second, the proportion of adolescent first births that are conceived premaritally has risen. In the early 1960s, only 46 percent of first-time teen mothers gave birth to babies conceived out of wedlock—a proportion that increased to more than 70 percent by 1980–1981.[12]

Finally, young unmarried men and women are far less likely than in earlier decades to marry if the young woman gets pregnant. In the early 1960s more than half of the teen women who conceived premaritally and continued the pregnancy married before childbirth. By the early 1980s only one-third of these teen mothers married before they gave birth.[13]

While society uses marital status at the time of the birth of a child as a measure of the father's responsibility, a number of factors make this measure somewhat less than adequate.

First, marriages can and do occur after the birth of the child. One study found that almost one-fifth of the women aged 15–17 who were unmarried when their children were born, and about one-quarter of those who were

18 or 19 when they had their children, were married within one year. About 39 percent and 44 percent of these age groups, respectively, were married within three years. It is not possible to determine, however, whether these women married the biological fathers of their children.[14]

Second, it should be stressed that marriage (before or after the birth of the child) is no guarantee of a stable home life and responsible parents. In 1981, for example, the divorce rate for young women who were married between the ages of 15 and 19 was more than twice the divorce rate for the female population as a whole. The divorce rate for male adolescents was also substantially higher than the rate for the overall male population.[15]

Third, many underestimate the extent to which young men behave "responsibly" (as defined by either marrying or living with their children) because they fail to take into account multiple family obligations. A recent study by Robert Lerman of Brandeis University examined young men who admitted to being absent fathers and found that 5 percent of those who were between the ages of 18 and 21, and almost 20 percent of those who were aged 22–25, said that they lived with some, but not all, of their children.[16] A significant portion of these young men were simultaneously absent fathers and resident fathers.

Finally, marriage is not the only way that a young man and woman can live together as a functioning family. Although data on this topic are scarce, one study suggests that, especially among Hispanic adolescents, "informal marriages"—including living together—are not uncommon.[17]

Responsible Fatherhood outside Marriage

Assessing the range of support provided by young absent fathers is complicated because of the different kinds and levels of support, including acknowledging paternity (informally or legally), keeping in contact with the mother and child, providing in-kind support (such as childcare, food, and clothing), and providing financial support (informal or formal child support). No comprehensive data are available on the number of young absent fathers who provide these varying forms of support.

Several studies, however (including the work of Mercer Sullivan, and Joelle Sander and Debra Klinman), have surveyed young men who acknowledge having fathered children about the kinds of support they provide, or have questioned young unmarried mothers about the extent of paternal assistance they have received. These studies, though limited, reflect that a significant number of these young men provide emotional, in-kind, or financial support to the child and the mother, at least in the first years of the child's birth.[18]

Acknowledging Paternity

Acknowledgment of paternity, the first sign of responsibility for a young absent father, comes in different forms and for different reasons. There are two levels of paternity acknowledgment—formal (legal) and informal (community)—and two methods of it—voluntary and involuntary. Unfortunately, there are no good estimates of how many young fathers acknowledge paternity in any of these forms. It is nonetheless important to understand the range of options open to young men: that paternity can be informal as well as legally adjudicated, that establishing paternity can be a successive process as opposed to a single act, and that measures of legal paternity may, in some communities, severely underestimate actual behavior. For example, in his ethnographic study of inner-city black teenage fathers, Sullivan found: "For the males, establishing paternity could involve three successive stages. First, they had to establish to their own satisfaction that they had caused the pregnancy. If they were convinced, they then had to decide whether to acknowledge paternity to the girls, the girls' families, and their own families. Finally, they had to choose whether or not to acknowledge paternity legally."[19]

Informal acknowledgment of paternity. Sullivan's work suggests that informal acknowledgment of paternity is a common occurrence, especially in low-income, minority, and rural communities. His findings also suggest that, to some extent, informal acknowledgment and informal support arrangements may be community-accepted substitutes for legal paternity and court-ordered child support.

Informal acknowledgment can be either voluntary or involuntary. Voluntary acknowledgment typically seems to be accompanied by some effort to provide support, while involuntary acknowledgment appears to involve a general community consensus about the identity of the young father, regardless of whether he provides support. Sullivan's study found that, at least in the inner-city black community he examined, there was little community support for young men who refused to acknowledge their children.

Legal establishment of paternity. The legal establishment of paternity can take place irrespective of whether the father has informally acknowledged his child, and it provides certain legal benefits for the child. The most important is a right to child support, as fathers cannot be ordered to contribute to the support of children born out of wedlock until paternity is legally established. But there are other benefits as well, both financial and nonfinancial. For example, legal paternity makes it far easier to establish a child's eligibility for many rights that come to a child through the father-child relationship, including Social Security payments, veteran's benefits, worker's compensation, and a number of other public and private benefits. Nonfinancial benefits may include access to information about the family's medical history for the child and the establishment of legal rights to custody, adoption, and visitation.

As with informal paternity, legal paternity can be either voluntary or involuntary. In most states, to establish legal paternity voluntarily a father can file a statement either with the court or with the Vital Statistics Bureau. That statement, which is usually signed under oath, becomes a legal document establishing paternity. Unfortunately, in some states the father cannot voluntarily acknowledge paternity in a legally binding way without going to court. Involuntary legal determination of paternity is often instigated by the mother, or by the state on behalf of the child and mother, in order to obtain a court order for child support.

Little information is available about the number of unmarried adolescent mothers who legally establish paternity, voluntarily or involuntarily, although a study by Sandra Danziger of unmarried adolescent mothers in Wisconsin found that about two out of five had legally identified the fathers of their children within three to four years after the birth.[20]

Nonfinancial Support

Some young unmarried couples continue to be involved with each other after the child is born. Although it is difficult to get an accurate account of the extent of such contact, certain studies of small groups of young unmarried mothers found that roughly half of them were still seeing the young fathers in the first year after the children were born. However, the likelihood of the mother maintaining an informal, nonmarital relationship with the father decreased over time. Some of these couples eventually married, but most eventually ceased contact.[21]

Similarly, these studies found that about half of the young unmarried mothers reported that the absent fathers remained in contact with the children, visiting regularly, particularly during the first years after the birth. The extent of this contact appears to be related to the strength of the relationship between the young parents (as well as the father's willingness and ability to provide support).

In addition to seeing their children, some young fathers also provide various types of in-kind assistance. For example, Sullivan's study of inner-city young black fathers in New York City found that many of them assisted with childcare, often with the aid of their families.[22] All of the young fathers who participated in the Teen Father Collaboration (a national research and demonstration project designed to work with teen fathers and prospective teen fathers) reported that they provided some form of in-kind help, such as food, childcare, clothing, and taking the child to appointments.[23]

Financial Support

The popular stereotypical view is that most young absent fathers do not provide any financial assistance to their children. But various studies have shown that a substantial proportion of these young men do provide financial assistance to the child and the child's mother, and that such assistance can take two forms—informal financial contributions or legally mandated child support.

Many of the studies have found patterns of informal financial assistance. One such study found that almost two-thirds of young single teenage mothers received some form of financial assistance from the father of the child in the first year after the birth of the child.[24] Other research indicates that such assistance is usually rather modest in scope, and that it may be irregular because of the unstable employment experiences of many young men. As with other forms of informal assistance, informal financial support appears likely to decrease over time.[25]

Legally Mandated Child Support

Legally mandated child support can be obtained in two ways: a mother can use a private lawyer to seek a support award (through either a contested process or a voluntary agreement that may be entered with the court), or she can go to the state child-support enforcement agency for assistance in establishing or enforcing a child-support order.

The child-support system does not operate identically for women who receive Aid to Families with Dependent Children (AFDC) and for women who do not. If a mother who does not receive AFDC requests assistance from the state child-support enforcement agency, the state can collect a fee and reasonable costs for any services it provides. States have the option to collect and distribute the child-support payments made by the absent parent in non-AFDC cases, even before the payments fall in arrears, if a parent requests that service.

Women who do receive AFDC benefits, however, are required, as a condition of eligibility, to assign their child-support rights to the state. The state then becomes responsible for establishing paternity and obtaining a support order (if the mother has not already done so) as well as for enforcing the order. AFDC recipients must cooperate (except in very limited circumstances) with the state agency in pursuing support from the absent parent. In these cases, the state collects the payment and—with the exception of the first $50, which is allowed to go direct to the family—uses the payment to reimburse the state and federal government for the cost of the AFDC benefit. In general, the family loses eligibility for AFDC if the monthly child-support payments exceed the AFDC payment by more than $50.

While the legal child-support enforcement system is complicated and varies among jurisdictions, the basic steps to receiving child-support payments are the same across the country and involve at least some of the following points: (1) A mother must know who the absent father is and decide that she wishes to obtain formal child support from him. (2) Before paternity can be established or support can be collected, the mother or the child-support agency must know where the father is. (3) Legal paternity must be determined before the child-support obligation can be established. (4) When the father is identified, the mother must establish a child-support obligation; a legally binding document is necessary to set the amount of the child-support obligation and to make the obligation enforceable. (5) Once the award level has been set, the child-support payments become due according to whatever schedule was agreed upon or ordered. If the father fails to pay what he owes, the mother or her representative must initiate enforcement proceedings to collect delinquent payments.

In reality, the child-support system has been less than effective. In 1986, for example, the child-support enforcement system was able to collect payments in only 10 percent of the AFDC cases and in only 31 percent of the non-AFDC cases for which assistance had been requested.[26]

While recent improvements have been made, the structure of the system has given child-support enforcement agencies incentives to pursue only the most cost-effective cases. In most cases, there has been little incentive to pursue the cases for never-married women, both because these cases usually require establishment of paternity and because, on average, the never-married fathers in paternity cases are not as sound financially as other fathers. Since most adolescent mothers have never been married to the father of their child and since their partners are younger, adolescent mothers are at a considerable disadvantage under the current system.

Although good national data on the extent to which adolescent mothers receive child support are not available, there are national data on child support among never-married mothers of all ages. Because adolescent mothers are disproportionately likely never to have married the father of their child, these findings are likely to provide some insights into the child-support patterns of young mothers—especially when combined with general data available on adolescent mothers and young fathers.

Overall, these data suggest that adolescent mothers are at a disadvantage at each point in the child-support process outlined above. Never-married mothers are at least four times more likely to decide not to pursue child support than other mothers; they are three times more likely to be unable to locate the father; and they are as likely as other mothers to receive some payment once a child-support obligation is established, but the average amount they receive is only half that received by women who have previously been married.[27]

Given that 60 percent of babies born to teens are born to unmarried teens (the vast majority of whom have never been married), and that two-thirds of these mothers do not include the father's age on the birth certificate (and therefore are unlikely to have named the father at the time of birth), adolescent mothers appear to be particularly likely to reject their right to pursue child support and, in consequence, to be in special need of outreach, education, and assistance. This suggests that increased efforts should be made to establish paternity at the time of the birth and to locate the absent father.

Also, because the level of the child-support award is based somewhat on the father's ability to pay, adolescent mothers are likely to have lower awards than older mothers. While the partners of teen mothers are likely not to be teens, most are younger than 25, and the earnings of young men are likely to be low. Therefore, increased enforcement efforts alone are unlikely to result in significant increases in child-support payments for adolescent mothers.

The Support Capability of Young Absent Fathers

Because most partners of adolescent mothers are in their early 20s, we might expect that young absent fathers have the financial ability to support their children. The available data, however, suggest that young unmarried fathers—whether teens or adults—are a particularly vulnerable economic group. Teen fathers run an especially high risk of unemployment and disproportionately lack the educational credentials, basic academic skills, and employment experience needed to secure steady, well-paying jobs. Also, young fathers are more likely than older fathers to have had behavior problems involving school suspensions and illegal activities. As a consequence, they tend to be less able to provide significant support to their children, although this disadvantage may lessen over time.[28]

Educational attainment. Young fathers are more likely than older fathers to lack the credentials and the basic academic skills necessary for stable employment. A recent study by William Marsiglio found that young men who acknowledged being teen fathers were, regardless of their marital status, much more likely to have been high school dropouts than were other young men.[29] Lerman found similar results when he looked at the educational attainment of unmarried fathers in their twenties.[30] As is true for young women, young men who were married when they became teenage fathers were the most likely members of their age group to have dropped out of school—about 62 percent of them had not completed high school by the time they were in their mid-20s, compared with between 35 and 41 percent of those who were unmarried and between the ages of 11 and 19 when their children were born (table 11.2). In contrast, only about 14 percent of the young men who had not fathered children as teenagers had failed to complete high school by the time they were in their twenties.

TABLE 11.2. High School Completion Status of Teenage Fathers (Interviewed When 20 to 27 Years Old), by Age and Marital Status at Time of Birth and Type of Diploma (in percentages)

| | High School Completion Status | | | | |
| | | Graduated | | | |
	Dropout	All	*Diplomas before age 20*	*GED before age 20*	*GED or diploma after age 20*
All young men	6.0	84.1	75.8	4.3	4.0
Men aged 11–17, unmarried at birth of child	40.7	59.4	39.6	11.3	8.5
Men aged 18–19, unmarried at birth of child	35.1	65.0	52.6	3.7	8.7
Men aged 11–19, married at birth of child	61.5	38.6	21.0	10.4	7.2
Young men who had fathered no children or waited until they were 20 or older	14.1	86.0	78.2	4.1	3.7

SOURCE: William Marsiglio, "Adolescent Fathers in the United States: Their Initial Living Arrangements. Marital Experience and Educational Outcomes," *Family Planning Perspectives* 19, 6 (Nov./Dec. 1987): 247.

Note: Reprinted by permission of the Children's Defense Fund.

Young fathers also appear to have lower levels of basic academic skills than do young men who have delayed parenthood. For example, Lerman found that young fathers scored significantly lower on a number of tests of academic skills than did other young men.[31]

Employment experience. Although less information is available on the employment experience of adolescent or young fathers, existing research suggests that many adolescent fathers and young unmarried fathers are unemployed, or are employed irregularly or in part-time jobs. For example, almost two-thirds of the adolescent fathers in the Teen Father Collaboration, most of whom were 17 and 18 years old, indicated that they were unemployed, and half of those who were employed worked only part-time.[32]

Living arrangements. Many young fathers, even those in their 20s, live with their parents or extended families; this fact, although by no means a precise indicator, may suggest that they may have difficulty in supporting a family. For example, a total of about two-thirds of the teenage fathers in the Teen Father Collaboration lived with their parents (30 percent) or extended families (37 percent), while 18 percent lived with their partners or wives, and only 4 percent lived alone.[33] Similarly, Lerman found that almost two-thirds of the unmarried fathers aged 19 to 26 lived with at least one parent or with extended family members, while 16 percent lived alone, 12 percent lived with a partner of the opposite sex, and 8 percent lived with a nonrelative.[34]

The Father's Resources and "Responsible" Behavior

There seems to be little correlation between a young father's ability to provide support and his involuntary acknowledgment of paternity. Some evidence, however, indicates that the ability to provide support affects whether a young father voluntarily acknowledges paternity. And, not surprisingly, it affects the level and kind of support provided if he has established paternity, whether legally or informally.

Recent research on adolescent fatherhood generally suggests that adolescent males may be reluctant to take on the responsibilities of fatherhood because of either perceived or actual inability to support a family adequately.[35] For example, one representative study by Sullivan found that "stepping off"—a term used to describe abandoning one's baby—was "precipitated as much by un- and underemployment and related involvement in crime as by callousness."[36] Sullivan also found that the young father's assumption of the father role depended not only on his own personal resources but also on whether he could count on assistance from his family. A number of these young fathers had relatives who provided child care or made other contributions to the child's well-being.

The decision to "step off" may not always be a matter of choice. A young father's inability to provide financial support may also affect his relationship with the young mother and her family and their willingness to allow him to participate actively as a parent. Sullivan found that in order for the young father to continue to be able to see their children or to maintain relationships with the mothers, they had to be willing to help support financially and care for the child.[37] Some young fathers in Sullivan's study, however, reported that their girlfriends' families recognized the lack of employment opportunities available in the community and would allow the father access to the child so long as they saw that he was trying to behave responsibly.

The limited data that examine differences across communities in the response to early parenthood suggests a related point. Although substantial cultural differences exist among black, Hispanic, and white low-income communities, employment opportunities available to these groups appear to play a key role in fathering behavior. Thus, some cultural variances in responsible behavior may be at least partially due to differences in economic resources.[38]

What Should Be Done?

There is widespread agreement that a young man who fathers a child should behave responsibly toward the child, and that policies and programs should help or, if necessary, force young men to be responsible parents. There is far less agreement, however, as to what constitutes responsible behavior and how we can encourage it. The difficulty faced by policymakers is how to devise a set of policies that deal appropriately with the wide range of responses by young fathers, and with the socioeconomic realities that confront them. The question is, What can be done that will simultaneously help the young men who do have a sense of personal responsibility toward their children to fulfill their responsibility and encourage young men who lack that responsibility to fulfill theirs?

First, for young men who are not married to the mothers of their children, the legal link between childbearing and childrearing must be strengthened. Second, support systems and comprehensive service programs must be developed to help meet the complex problems faced by some young fathers, particularly poor and minority fathers, regardless of their marital status.[39] Third, public policies must reflect the understanding that child-support enforcement and service programs can have only limited effects without broader changes in the economic opportunities available to young parents.

The Legal Tie between Biological and "Responsible" Fatherhood

The legal connection between fathering a child and exercising parental responsibility must be strengthened. Despite the value of informal paternity establishment and support systems, legal paternity identification and effective child-support enforcement have additional benefits: an increased likelihood that absent fathers who are not willing to provide support will be legally required to do so, and an increased likelihood that the support provided will extend beyond the first few years of the child's life.

At the same time, however, a strengthened legal enforcement system must enhance, rather than damage, the existing informal support system that is built on a sense of personal responsibility.

There are two areas in which we must target efforts to strengthen the legal link between biological fatherhood and "responsible" fatherhood, both of which involve the child-support enforcement system. The first step is to increase the likelihood of establishing paternity. The second is to improve the likelihood that the absent father will support the child.

Legal establishment of paternity. The likelihood that paternity will be legally established when a child is born to unmarried parents can be increased in a number of ways. Each of these approaches should emphasize the benefits of establishing paternity as close to the time of the child's birth as possible, since young parents' relationships tend to lessen over time, making it more difficult to find the father.

Some specific ways to improve the establishment of paternity include: (1) simplifying the process of establishing paternity, perhaps by increasing the number of states that have adopted the Uniform Parentage Act; (2) developing extensive outreach and public education campaigns—targeted to both male and female teens—about the legal rights and responsibilities of parenthood; (3) encourage child-support agencies to pursue paternity determination cases more aggressively; (4) encouraging service agencies, in addition to child-support agencies, that work with young parents (mothers and fathers) to establish paternity and the legal rights of parenthood for their clients.

Improving the likelihood of support from the absent parent. As we noted earlier, younger mothers who have a child-support order appear to receive less child-support income that do older mothers. Three possible explanations for these findings are differences in the fathers' willingness to pay, differences in the fathers' ability to pay, and less intensive enforcement efforts for young absent fathers by courts and child-support enforcement agencies.

To the extent that the problem lies in the young fathers' unwillingness to pay or in inadequate enforcement, increased enforcement efforts—such as a more active pursuit of delinquent payments by young fathers—should benefit young mothers. It is fairly clear, however, that a number of young fathers—particularly those who are very young or poor—do not pay because they lack the resources, suggesting that strategies focusing only on strengthening enforcement efforts are unlikely to succeed with these groups.

A number of studies have suggested that child-support enforcement and collection efforts should be more flexible when working with younger fathers and that they should take into account the constraints on the fathers' immediate ability to pay. Suggestions include broadening the definition of child support from financial contributions to include in-kind contributions as well, and changing the focus of child-support collection from maximizing short-term support to maximizing long-term support—for example, encouraging the father in appropriate cases to forgo immediate income in order to make educational or job-training investments that will enhance his long-term earning potential.

Helping All Young Fathers to Be Good Parents

Our society accepts that young mothers face many difficulties in trying to meet the demands of adulthood and parenthood, and it recognizes that comprehensive social-service programs can be effective in helping them cope with early parenthood. Many young fathers, regardless of their marital status, have similar difficulties. They have needs that, if left unmet, can hamper their efforts to be good and responsible parents.

In particular, studies have found that adolescent fathers, regardless of their race or ethnic background, are likely to be concerned about the following issues: (1) their ability to support a child—some of the specific worries that they face include: whether to complete school or to drop out to get a job, whether they will be able to find a job, how they are going to be able to support a family, and where they are going to live; (2) the health of the young mother and the baby; (3) parenting issues, such as whether they will be good fathers or will be able to spend as much time with their child as they hope to; (4) interpersonal relationships, including their relationships with the child's mother, with their family, and the young mother's family, and the effects that parenthood would have on their relationships with their peers; (5) other issues, such as legal representation in the child-support process and general and reproductive health problems.[40]

Given the success of comprehensive service programs in working with young mothers, similar programs have recently been developed for young fathers as well. In general, these programs either provide a range of services directly or assist young fathers in receiving services offered by other agencies.

These services, most of which are included in many general youth programs, can be provided to young fathers in a number of ways, and usually involve some combination of the following: (1) educational services, including dropout prevention, remedial education, and Graduate Equivalency Degree courses; (2) employment and vocational services, including job placement, good training, and job counseling; (3) counseling, either for the young father as an individual or for the young couple together; (4) establishment of paternity; (5) legal representation for paternity and child-support issues; (6) parenting training and education; and (7) health education, including general health as well as reproductive health and family-planning education.

Improving the Plight of Young Families

Policies and programs to increase young fathers' responsibility toward their children must be developed in tandem with larger policies and programs that increase society's responsibility toward teenagers and young families.

Data from the late 1980s indicate that two-thirds of the infants and toddlers in families headed by young adults (younger than 22 years of age) lived below the federal poverty level. Of the 531,000 young children in families headed by young adults, 333,000 (63 percent) lived only with their mothers. More than four out of five (84 percent) of the young children in these families headed by young females lived below the poverty line.[41]

It is very tempting to blame this situation on the absent fathers, to argue that if they were in the homes or, at least, contributing to the families, these rates would be significantly lower. But there are strong economic and sociological reasons why they have not married the mothers, why child support is not pursued by many teen mothers, and why, if pursued and awarded, child-support payments are not sufficient to lift these families out of poverty. The three major reasons are:

Rising unemployment. Today, less than half of the high school graduates younger than 20 years of age and not enrolled in college hold full-time jobs, compared with more than two-thirds in the late 1960s. Only one in three male high school dropouts works full time.[42]

Rising underemployment. The proportion of all workers younger than 25 years of age involuntarily working part time because full-time employment was not available increased by nearly one-half between 1979 and 1985.[43]

Declining earnings. Average annual earnings for 20- to 24-year-old males fell by more than 25 percent between the early 1970s and the mid-1980s, and the decline in earnings for male high school dropouts exceeded 40 percent. In the early 1970s, 60 percent of all men aged 20 to 24 were able to earn enough to lift a family of three above the official federal poverty line, but by the mid-1980s only 42 percent could do so.[44]

This growing inability of young men to earn adequate wages has taken its toll on young families in two ways. First, it has discouraged family formation: regardless of race or education, 20- to 24-year-old men with earnings above the poverty threshold for a family of three are three to four times more likely to be married than are young men with below-poverty earnings.[45] Second, it has reduced the chances that young families, whether headed by a single mother or by a married couple, will escape poverty. Because young absent fathers are among the young men who have suffered the sharpest declines in their earning ability, they are unlikely to be able to provide substantial support. In consequence, more than four out of five young single mothers are poor. Furthermore, many young married couples are also poor. The most recent data reflect that more than one-third of the children living in households headed by young married couples are poor.[46]

Complex and profound changes in the American economy since the early 1970s have made it more difficult for young men and women to achieve economic self-sufficiency. For example, dramatic shifts in employment from manufacturing industries to the service sector have contributed to a steady erosion in inflation-adjusted wages for young workers. Relatively weak employment growth during the current economic recovery also has failed to reverse declines in full-time employment rates among young Americans, particularly young men.

These sweeping macroeconomic trends are neither easily nor quickly reversed. Yet building a stronger economic base for America's next generation of young families will not be possible unless a national commitment is made to address these issues. Essential first steps include: (1) halting the erosion of the wage base by raising the minimum wage; (2) stemming the decline in employment rates among disadvantaged youths by mounting effective job-creation efforts in low-income communities; (3) providing basic support systems for all families that are unable to earn enough to provide for their families, by increasing levels of AFDC payments and by providing adequate AFDC to two-parent families that are in need because of unemployment or underemployment, in accordance with the Federal Family Support Act of 1988.

With unmarried teenagers forming a higher proportion of all teenage parents each year, we have had a commensurate tendency to chastise young men for their personal irresponsibility—for impregnating partners they do not marry and for fathering children they do not support. But the problem is complicated. While society should continue to insist that young men accept personal responsibility for the children they father, it should also help them to fulfill that responsibility and recognize its own obligations toward young families. Stiffening child-support enforcement and increasing comprehensive service programs for young fathers are essential, but they alone will not lift the majority of young families with young children out of poverty. The erosion of the minimum wage, the increasing number of families with working parents living below the federal poverty level, the shrinking number of poor families offered support through AFDC, and declining levels of assistance are all signs of our nation's neglect of teenagers and young adults. Our society's irresponsible behavior toward teenage parents and their children is no less critical than the irresponsibility of the fathers we are so quick to condemn.

Notes

1. National Center for Health Statistics, *Monthly Vital Statistics Report* 39, 4, supplement (15 August 1990): 32.

2. U.S. Bureau of the Census, Office of Economic Opportunity, unpublished data. Calculations by the Children's Defense Fund.

3. This chapter was adapted from Gina Adams and Karen Pittman, "Adolescent and Young Adult Fathers: Problems and Solutions" (Washington, D.C.: Children's Defense Fund's Adolescent Pregnancy Prevention Clearinghouse, May 1988). Our chapter draws heavily from a meeting held at the Children's Defense Fund in the fall of 1987 with six researchers and program experts on adolescent males and young fathers.

4. National Center for Health Statistics, *Monthly Vital Statistics Report* 39:26.

5. Robert Lerman, "A National Profile of Young Unwed Fathers: Who Are They and How Are They Parenting?" Commissioned paper for the Forum on Child Support Services for Young Families, Center for the Support of Children, Washington, D.C., September 1987.

6. National Center for Health Statistics, unpublished data. Calculations by the Children's Defense Fund.

7. National Center for Health Statistics, *Monthly Vital Statistics Report* 39:16.

8. National Center for Health Statistics, "Teenage Marriage and Divorce, United States, 1970–81," *Vital and Health Statistics* 21, 43. Publication No. (PHS) 85–1921 (September 1985): 19.

9. National Center for Health Statistics, *Monthly Vital Statistics Report* 39:32.

10. *Ibid.*, 39:33.

11. U.S. Bureau of the Census, "Marital Status and Living Arrangements: March 1986." Current Population Reports Series P-20, no. 418 (Washington, D.C.: Department of Commerce, January 1987).

12. Martin O'Connell and Carolyn C. Rogers, "Out-of-Wedlock Births, Premarital Pregnancies, and Their Effect on Family Formation and Dissolution," *Family Planning Perspectives* 16, 4 (July/August 1984): 159.

13. *Ibid.*

14. *Ibid.*, 16:160.

15. National Center for Health Statistics, "Teenage Marriage and Divorce," 43:19.

16. Lerman, "National Profile of Young Unwed Fathers."

17. Mercer Sullivan, *Teen Fathers in the Inner City: An Exploratory Ethnographic Study* (New York: Vera Institute of Justice, April 1985).

18. Sullivan, *Teen Fathers in the Inner City;* Joelle Sander and Debra Klinman, *The Final Report of the Teen Father Collaboration* (New York: Bank Street College of Education, 1986).

19. Sullivan, *Teen Fathers in the Inner City*, p. 34.

20. Sandra Danziger, "Adolescent Welfare Mothers and the Fathers of Their Children: Legal Ties, Family Relationships, and Economic Prospects." Unpublished paper (University of Michigan, School of Social Work, August 1987.)

21. Ross D. Parke and Brian Neville, "Teenage Fatherhood," in Cheryl Hayes, ed., *Risking the Future: Adolescent Sexuality, Pregnancy, and Childbearing*, (Washington, D.C.: National Academy Press, 1987), 2:154.

22. Sullivan, *Teen Fathers in the Inner City*, p. 60.

23. Sander and Klinman, *Final Report of Teen Father Collaboration.*

24. Parke and Neville, "Teenage Fatherhood," 2:162.

25. Parke and Neville, "Teenage Fatherhood," 2:162.

26. U.S. Department of Health and Human Services, Office of Child Support Enforcement, *Eleventh Annual Report to Congress*, vol. 2, Fiscal Year 1986 Statistics.

27. U.S. Bureau of the Census, "Child Support and Alimony: 1985 (Advance Data from March–April 1986)," Current Population Surveys, Series P-23, no. 152 (Washington, D.C.: Department of Commerce, August 1987).

28. Lerman, "National Profile of Young Unwed Fathers"; William Marsiglio, "Adolescent Fathers in the United States: Their Initial Living Arrangements, Marital Experiences and Educational Outcomes," *Family Planning Perspectives* 19, 6 (November/December 1987): 247–50.

29. Marsiglio, "Adolescent Fathers in the United States," p. 247.

30. Lerman, "National Profile of Young Unwed Fathers."

31. *Ibid.*

32. Sander and Klinman, *Final Report of Teen Father Collaboration.*

33. Sander and Klinman, *Final Report of Teen Father Collaboration.*

34. Lerman, "A National Profile of Young Unwed Fathers," p. 27.

35. Parke and Neville, "Teenage Fatherhood."

36. Sullivan, *Teen Fathers in the Inner City,* p. 57.

37. Sullivan, *Teen Fathers in the Inner City.*

38. Mercer Sullivan, *The Male Role in Teenage Pregnancy and Parenting: New Directions for Public Policy* (New York: Vera Institute of Justice, 1990), pp. 32–33.

39. Sullivan, *The Male Role,* pp. 46–48.

40. These are recurring themes in most of the research on adolescent and young adult fathers, as compiled by the Children's Defense Fund.

41. U.S. Bureau of the Census, Office of Economic Opportunity, unpublished data. Calculations by the Children's Defense Fund.

42. Cliff Johnson and Andrew Sum, *Declining Earnings of Young Men: Their Relation to Poverty, Teen Pregnancy, and Family Formation* (Washington, D.C.: Children's Defense Fund's Adolescent Pregnancy Prevention Clearinghouse, May 1987), p. 9.

43. *Ibid.,* p. 7.

44. *Ibid.,* pp. 6–7.

45. *Ibid.,* p. 11.

46. U.S. Bureau of the Census, Office of Economic Opportunity, unpublished data. Calculations by the Children's Defense Fund.

PART FOUR SOCIAL POLICY

MARGARET C. SIMMS

12 ADOLESCENT PREGNANCY AMONG BLACKS IN THE UNITED STATES: WHY IS IT A POLICY ISSUE?

In this book, a number of different perspectives on the issue of teenage pregnancy are presented. There is the perspective of the United Kingdom versus the United States, the perspective of whites versus minorities, and the perspective of the individual versus the community. What becomes clear from a review of this volume is that there is no one "correct" perspective, but rather a complex set of issues that require careful sorting before conclusions are reached. This is especially important when trying to frame policy solutions for "the problem." This chapter attempts to do some of that sorting with respect to teenage pregnancy and childbearing among black Americans.

Determining the Parameters of the Problem

Sally Macintyre and Sarah Cunningham-Burley ask the right questions in chapter 3 when they suggest that the major issue in teenage childbearing is "for whom [births to teenagers] are problematic and in what ways."[1] From this question they delineate several reasons for the perception of teenage pregnancy as a problem, including: poverty, single parenting, premature sexual activity, failure to complete education or training, and inadequate parenting skills.

Macintyre and Cunningham-Burley then discuss the extent to which these problems are peculiar to teenage mothers. From the British perspective, many of the problems do not seem unique to teenagers; they are typical of mothers in their 20s as well. Moreover, their analysis suggests that inadequate education and skills training are not a major problem, because British teenagers typically have completed their education before becoming parents. This type of analysis calls into question a focus on teenage childbearing, and even suggests that parenthood among never-married women is not a serious problem.[2]

Several chapters in this book suggest that the major issue for many who condemn early parenthood is a moralistic one. From their perspective the idea of young women (or girls) engaging in sexual activity and confronting others with the consequences of their actions is a key factor in the outcry against teenage motherhood.[3] Some even worry that policy initiatives might be directed more toward returning women to "paternalistic rule" than toward helping them achieve economic independence.[4] As a black woman working in an organization that is particularly concerned with the impact of public policy on black Americans, I find myself viewing the debate with amazement. While I am not naive enough to think that all who are attempting to call attention to the issue have the mothers' and their children's best interests at heart, I think that any attempt to minimize both the problem and the importance of returning adult males to families reflects a failure to understand fully the impact that early and single parenthood has had on the black community in the past two decades.

In the 1960s, Senator Daniel Patrick Moynihan incurred the wrath of the black community by suggesting that black families were deteriorating and that the future did not bode well so long as the trend toward female-headed families proceeded without intervention.[5] In the wake of the controversial debate that followed, few were brave enough to point out that things were getting a lot worse a lot faster than Moynihan had predicted. The fact that white families were also increasingly headed by women, suggesting that broader socioeconomic changes were at work than those cited by Moynihan, did little to make public discussion of the issue more palatable, even (or especially) for blacks. Finally, in the early 1980s, leaders within the black community decided that changing family structure could no longer be ignored. The black community's economic and social well-being was in danger unless individuals within the community were willing to admit that there was a serious problem, one that required the coordinated efforts of both the private and the public sectors.

A representative statement on the issue can be found in a publication of the Committee on Policy for Racial Justice, a group of twenty-nine black scholars who meet periodically to deliberate issues of importance to the black community. In their statement, entitled *A Policy Framework for Racial Justice*, they note: "Accumulated social and economic pressures, feeding upon the long-standing effects of American racism, have produced a special crisis for the black family today. This crisis underlies many problems facing the black community, especially entrenched poverty, which is closely correlated to the pronounced vulnerability of the large and growing number of black families headed by single mothers. No strategy designed to improve the status of black Americans can ignore the central position of the black family as the natural transmitter of the care, values, and opportunities necessary for black men, women, and children to reach their full potential as individuals."[6] They then elaborate on the problem of adolescent pregnancy: "Female-headed households arise from a number of different circumstances. A rising number emerge from teenage pregnancies, and a permanent male partner to contribute to the economic and other responsibilities of family life is absent from the start. The consequences are predictable. Children grow up with few consistent male role models. In many cases, the young mothers of these children are themselves hardly removed from childhood—their education is incomplete, their preparation for parenthood underdeveloped, and their own personal potential unfulfilled."[7]

With statements similar to these by a number of black leaders, the dam was broken, and the issue was addressed head on.

Acknowledging that a major problem exists does not lead directly to a policy solution without further analysis of the issue. In my opinion, the main concern should not be early *sexual activity* or teenage *pregnancy*. The main problem is early *childbearing*, which of course relates to the first two events. Early sexual activity all too often entails a lack of responsible use of contraceptives. Pregnancies can be terminated by abortions, but avoiding pregnancy is an easier and less painful course of action, both emotionally and psychologically. However, the main social (and individual) problem is the incidence of early childbearing among black women, because of its association with single parenting and a life of poverty.

What, then, is the primary cause of the current situation? How is it related to changing patterns of marriage and childbearing? Is this a problem across all age groups? Will the children (and their mothers) "grow out of it"?

Once the problem has been properly defined, who determines the solution? Who is to carry it out? Clearly, if the problem is one of "morals," few would call for a governmental solution, although some have suggested that many current government policies make it harder for the family and the community to keep the young on the "correct" path.[8] If the problem is one of resources, any number of policies (or perhaps several in concert) might be appropriate.

Determining the Magnitude of the Problem

Since 1960, the prevalence of female-headed families within the black community has increased sharply. Today the majority of black children live in single-parent families, most with their mothers. Three-fifths of black children are born out of wedlock. For these children, the future can be fairly bleak. They are likely to live their entire lives in single-parent families, and approximately two-thirds of them will live in poverty.[9] In addition, some recent research suggests that these conditions, in combination, will mean that black children are increasingly likely to be at risk of low educational attainment, involvement in crime, early parenthood, unstable marital relations in later life, and other unfavorable outcomes.[10]

Such risks for black children are of special importance for the black community. In the period since the Second World War, the black community has made significant strides toward achieving equality within American society. Enhanced economic opportunity brought about by overall economic growth and increased occupational diversification contributed to both absolute and relative income gains for black households. However, since the mid-1970s, those advances have been captured by an ever smaller proportion of the black community. In consequence, the income gap *within* the black community has grown.

In 1969 the top 20 percent of families received 42.7 percent, while the bottom 20 percent received only 4.8 percent of total income within the black community. By 1988 the proportion of income received by blacks in the top 20 percent had increased to 47.9 percent, while that of the bottom 20 percent had shrunk to 3.3 percent.[11] Family structure changes that have paralleled the growing inequity have been both a cause and a consequence of economic change.

It is difficult to quantify the extent to which changes in the structure of economic opportunity have affected marriage within the black community, but some evidence indicates that economic and industrial change have played a role in family formation and stability within the black community. Between the mid-1970s and the mid-1980s the employment and real earnings levels of young black males declined.

In 1989 testimony before the House Select Committee on Children, Youth, and Families, policy analysts Andrew Sum and Neal Fogg reported on their recent analysis based on Current Population Survey data.[12] Sum and Fogg found that young black males experienced a fall in real annual earnings of nearly 28 percent between 1973 and 1987, with black male dropouts and those with no postsecondary education suffering declines of 44 percent and 36 percent, respectively. While all groups of males except college graduates showed significant declines, black males were the most adversely affected. The decline is attributable to increases in the numbers who did not work at all, increases in the difficulty of obtaining full-time, year-round employment, and decreases in real hourly wages. The decline in manufacturing employment opportunities seems to be partially responsible for some of these adverse trends.[13]

The decline in economic opportunity parallels the decline in marriage among young blacks. Other studies suggest that the stress of unemployment also places excessive strain on existing marriages and helps account for some of the increase in divorce and separation among blacks.[14] Some analysts have suggested that economic change has contributed to a decline in marriage not so much because of a decline in the position of black males but because the advances in employment made by black women have made them more financially independent. Reynolds Farley, for example, points out that the ratio of black women's median income to black men's median income increased from 46 percent in 1969 to 80 percent in 1984. While this is true, it hardly suggests that the majority of black women have adequate resources to cope with the demands of single parenting.[15]

If, in fact, single parenting is a major contributor to the worsening economic conditions of black children, what proportion of it can be attributed to teenage pregnancy? As has been pointed out elsewhere, the rate of teenage childbearing among blacks declined significantly between 1970 and 1985.[16] Moreover, the rate of out-of-wedlock childbearing also declined, from 96.9 births per thousand unmarried females between the ages of 15 and 19 in 1970 to 88.8 per thousand in 1985. The apparent rise in childbearing among never-married black women stems not from increased fertility among single women but from a sharp decline in marriage among black women under the age of 25. While nearly three-fifths of black women had married by the age of 25 in 1970, less than one-fourth had married before their 25th birthday in 1985. So even though young single black women are having fewer babies, they are much more likely to be unmarried when the babies are born. In addition, the birth rate among married black women has declined much more than that among unmarried women, making the births to unmarried women a larger proportion of all births to blacks.

Although only 34 percent of the births to unmarried black women in 1985 were to teenagers, those who have their first child as an unmarried teenager represent a disproportionate share of economic deprivation within the black community. These mothers constitute the majority of long-term welfare recipients and may be increasingly less likely to get off public assistance in the absence of outside intervention. Never-married black mothers under the age of 25 are much less likely to be working than their peers. In 1986 only 44 percent of those between the ages of 18 and 24 were in the labor force, and nearly one-half of them were unemployed. Given their low rates of employment and the low skill levels of many who are employed, more than three-quarters of young black mothers who head households are raising their families in poverty.[17]

Some commentators have argued that drawing conclusions about long-term prospects on the basis of current data about the condition of teenage mothers is premature. They cite data indicating that teenage mothers do not constitute the bulk of welfare dependents at any point in time and that most of these mothers are rarely reliant on welfare for extended periods. Others point out that many teenagers have little incentive for postponing childbearing and that their prospects are unlikely to be better if they wait until they are in their 20s to have children.[18]

Some individuals with this point of view cite recent work by Frank Furstenberg and others, which indicates that women who were teenage mothers in the 1950s and 1960s did not suffer significant long-term adverse consequences as a result of early parenthood.[19] However, even Furstenberg stated at a Stanford conference on adolescent pregnancy that the current generation of young mothers may not fare as well as those of a generation ago, since the changes in the economy I mentioned earlier may provide them with fewer options for economic advancement than were available to their mothers (either through marriage or through employment). This opinion is supported by data from a recently completed study by the Joint Center for Political and Economic Studies.[20]

Cynthia Rexroat's analysis of census data indicates that never-married female family heads are more likely to be poor now than in prior years (even after several years of economic expansion in the post-1982 period) and that their degree of poverty may be greater. This is especially true for never-married mothers in their 20s. They are less likely to be employed than at earlier periods, more likely to be in economically depressed areas, and more likely to be dependent on public assistance. The deterioration in the employment opportunities for never-married mothers is a significant contributor to the continued high incidence of poverty among black children. If these families had been able to "hold their own" relative to other types of black families—that is, if their economic situation had remained the same relative to that of other types of black families over time—poverty rates for black children would have dropped from 42.4 percent in 1969 to 30.2 percent in 1984, even with the increased incidence of never-married mothers among black families.

Rexroat states that this trend suggests serious consequences for the growing number of black children in families headed by a never-married woman. She estimates that black children remaining in such families can expect to spend fifteen of their eighteen childhood years in poverty. Such prospects confront a growing number of families; approximately one-fourth of the black children born since 1980 are living in families headed by never-married women, up from one-sixth of young children in the late 1970s and one-tenth a decade earlier.

The risks to these children cannot be measured in economic terms alone. The absence of a male parent has other adverse consequences. Recent research suggests that the presence of two adults can contribute to improved outcomes for children in several spheres. For example, Furstenberg's work indicates that a stable and close relationship with a male figure in the home can be beneficial to both young males and young females. It seems that adult males may serve not only as role models for young males but also as examples of positive male-female relationships for young women. And young women with high self-esteem (resulting in part from good father-daughter relationships) would be likely to have higher personal aspirations as well.[21]

Extended family households and inter-household support networks can offset some of the economic and psychological stress of single parenting. Here again, evidence would suggest that these systems are least likely to be available to those who need them. Less than one-tenth of black families headed by a single woman had two earners in 1984, as compared to three-fourths of black families headed by a married couple. In fact, single-mother households are less likely to have related adults, with or without jobs, now than in earlier periods. While about 70 percent of black married couple families have included related adults since 1960, the proportion of single-mother households with related adults dropped from 44 percent in 1960 to 15 percent in 1985.[22] Even when it comes to inter-household support systems, these families may be disadvantaged relative to other black households. In a series of studies using the National Survey of Black Americans, Robert Taylor and others found the size and likelihood of support networks to be positively related to income and to living in the

South (although this was only significant for elderly blacks), suggesting that black single mothers who have low incomes and live in the North and Midwest may have fewer or smaller support systems to draw on.[23]

What Is the Appropriate Policy Intervention?

A determination that teenage childbearing is a major contributing factor to the declining economic status of children does not lead automatically to an appropriate solution. First, some policies that spring to mind have little impact on economic conditions. Promoting marriage among young blacks, for example, is not only problematic on normative grounds but is also unlikely to be an effective solution. As an economist once said, many black women would have to marry *two* black men to lift their families out of poverty.[24] Proposals aimed at delaying childbearing are also inadequate in the absence of other initiatives that make delay advantageous. Moreover, strategies to prevent teenage childbearing, although necessary, are not sufficient; it is equally critical to improve the economic and social conditions in which single-parent families live, in order to enhance the prospects for stable black families in the future. If there are no economic gains to postponing childbearing, there is little purpose to the effort.

Most important, when viewing the problem of teenage childbearing within the black community, it is necessary to propose solutions that address the needs of men as well as women. Most black males face obstacles that are similar to (if slightly less severe than) those that black women face. So long as these men cannot obtain jobs providing them with incomes that enable them to make a substantial contribution to family well-being, it is unlikely that the full range of choices concerning family formation will be available to black women.

For both black males and black females, a three-pronged strategy is necessary to provide adequate options for the next generation. One set of policies should be targeted toward the population that is currently at risk; a second set would provide a "second chance" to those who become parents at a young age; and a third would focus on young children.

To the extent that teenage parenting is a significant contributor to the economic and social problems within the black community, what are appropriate strategies for delaying childbearing among young black women? In a recent book on racial differences in teenage sexuality, Kristin Moore, Margaret Simms, and Charles Betsey explore several explanations for high rates of out-of-wedlock childbearing among black teenagers.[25] Among the possible reasons for such behavior, the authors examine early sexual activity, knowledge and availability of contraception, educational and occupational aspirations, and views about marriage.

Delaying early childbearing may require a delay in sexual activity, at least among young teenagers, since there is a direct association between age and responsible use of contraceptives. Although most young teenagers know where babies come from, it is not clear that a large proportion of them have the maturity to practice contraception diligently. Available data show that older teenagers are more likely to practice contraception consistently. Even among those teenagers who understand the importance and proper use of contraception, a significant proportion do not always use contraception. While inconsistent use of contraceptives is not limited to those with poor skills and low aspirations, teenagers with higher aspirations do seem to be better contraceptors and are more likely to terminate pregnancies when they occur.[26]

There would seem to be a role for both the public and private sectors in delaying childbearing. I agree with Diana Pearce that a "just say no" approach or one that attempts to return to the 1950s philosophy that only "bad girls" have sex before marriage is not a positive step. However, there are certainly programs that can be undertaken or expanded, both within the schools and within the community, that encourage young people to engage in responsible behavior.[27] And such policies should be gender neutral. Clearly, a policy that focuses just on females is dealing with only one-half of the problem and only one-half of the potential solution. We also need programs that promote self-esteem and empower women to resist the pressure to have sex before they feel they are ready for it. Some programs are in fact already in existence. The major task is to promote replication of these successful programs.

A major incentive for delaying childbearing is having an alternative goal. Although postponing childbearing until after marriage used to be an important objective for many young women, it is less important today, certainly for young black women. This is not necessarily a result of a low value attached to marriage, but rather a fairly accurate assessment of its likelihood. Given the decline in marriage among black women under the age of 25, waiting for the wedding before having the baby would be synonymous with childlessness in the eyes of many young women.

Improving the economic opportunities for black women and black men will require a greater commitment by the government and the private sector. Education and training are important for obtaining a high-wage job, and this will increasingly be the case. Individuals who pursue education beyond high school fare better in the job market and receive higher returns on investment in a college education. This is particularly true for members of minority groups. And individuals with less than a high school education fare much worse than their peers who have high school diplomas. Data from the Survey of Income and Program Participation show that monthly earnings double with the completion of high school and nearly double again with the completion of college.[28]

Projections of job opportunities over the next decade indicate that a smaller proportion of jobs will require only a high school diploma, while a larger proportion will require some postsecondary education. But education alone will not be enough, since employment and earnings data show that blacks (and other minorities) continue to suffer from discriminatory treatment in employment and education.[29] To ensure significant progress, the public and private sectors will have to make a concerted commitment to counteracting racial bias in the labor market and in access to educational opportunities. If young men and women see few future rewards (or unequal rewards) for continued schooling, they have very few incentives to persist in the acquisition of skills or to resist the immediate rewards that might be obtained from early childbearing, low-wage employment, or illegal activities.

Reversing the trends in family structure within the black community will require close attention to today's children. Everything that we know about the relationship between educational achievement and behavior suggests that the point of intervention that is least costly and most effective is before children reach adolescence. Therefore, the problem of teenage parenthood will not be solved until we improve children's educational experiences and the links between these experiences and economic opportunity.

The importance of a good primary education shows up in a number of areas. Children who fall behind in school find it difficult to catch up, and if they fail to measure up to expectations, they frequently fall into an attitude of waiting for the time when they can drop out. Whether they use pregnancy as an excuse for dropping out or leave school prior to pregnancy, the link between poor school performance and early parenthood is quite clear. An analysis of data from the National Longitudinal Survey of Youth by the Children's Defense Fund reveals that 18- and 19-year-olds with poor basic skills were three times as likely to have children as those with moderate or high skills. Among younger women (14- and 15-year-olds), those with poor skills were four to five times as likely to become mothers.[30] Moreover, these young mothers were more likely to have subsequent births as well.

Young mothers in families with incomes below the poverty level were four times as likely to have poor basic skills. Blacks and Hispanics, who are overrepresented among the poverty population, were much more likely to be in the bottom skills groups. Within the sample there were few differences in teenage pregnancy rates across racial and ethnic groups when the researchers made adjustments for the large differences in levels of income and skills among the various groups. Therefore, it would appear that a substantial proportion of the racial differences in teenage pregnancy might be eliminated if basic skills could be improved among the disadvantaged population, even if income disparities remained.

However, reducing income disparities is also crucial to providing an environment for increased educational attainment and deferred parenthood. Children who live in households with adults earning decent wages can see the value of hard work and can observe the characteristics necessary for stable earnings. Moreover, an increase in family income will decrease the pressure (perceived or real) for the adolescent to drop out of school to contribute to the household income, either through the legitimate labor market or through the underground economy.

Who Should Initiate Action?

While there is considerable agreement on the importance of improving the income of black families, both through increased employment and through delayed parenthood, there are strong competing views on the appropriate policy action. Whether blacks should rely exclusively or even heavily on the government for action is one important division. A second issue among those who see a major role for the public sector is who should design and implement the policies that are used to change the situation of blacks at the low end of the income distribution.

Some members of the black community assert that blacks should not look to the federal government to solve their problems, as the necessary assistance is unlikely to be forthcoming.[31] Furthermore, some argue that the managerial class has no right to impose policies on the working-class or underclass population. They suggest that the affected groups should determine the appropriate government strategy. What then is the proper environment for policy formulation, and how can initiatives be developed that maintain individual choice and cultural identity?

The Committee on Policy for Racial Justice suggests that the appropriate strategy involves both private action and government commitment. It emphasizes, in particular, the need for the emerging black middle class to "give back to the community" in a number of ways:

Today, for example, one of the most urgent needs for black organizational life is to develop more effective bridges between the urban poor and the new black middle class outside the ghettos. Organizations at all levels, particularly locally based community organizations, need to address more vigorously the appropriate role and implementation of collaboration across class lines between blacks who enjoy some of the advantages of the society and those who do not.

This challenge does not underestimate the indisputable necessity of government action in addressing both the new and lingering social and economic needs of the black community. To maximize—indeed, often to make community efforts bear fruit at all—government must play a principal role in the process. The complexity and magnitude of the task requires a judicious combination of public and private efforts and resources. At the same time, some of the problems that blacks face cannot effectively be handled by government alone, as blacks know best of all.[32]

William Darity and Samuel Myers, however, take issue with the collaborative approach suggested above. In "Public Policy and the Condition of Black Family Life" they suggest that the collaboration of the black elite with the managerial elite that runs the government bureaucracy will not result in policies that benefit the blacks at whom their policies are directed. They stop short of proposing alternative solutions for the black family "crisis." As their justification of this approach, they state:

> If authentic change is to come about, it must be generated by the initiative of those who directly face the pressures of a world of flux. The black women who must raise families alone and the black men who are being left out of the new age must define their own agenda. They may find it advantageous to seek out new alliances, perhaps to the disquietude of their often paternalistic public and private protectors. For this very reason the ambitious efforts of the black leadership to resolve the black family problem by "stressing the traditional strengths as well as values and resources that have been used to improve the lives of black people" should be approached with caution. The crisis of the black family cannot be resolved for the better by those forces that have contributed to the development of the crisis. The victims, joined by those who are also beginning to experience the same stress and are beginning to diagnose the source in the same fashion, must not be denied the potential to influence the very policies that will affect their lives.[33]

During the first half of the 1980s, blacks found themselves in a policy environment that was not conducive to public action on family issues. During that period they developed new initiatives, many of which have involved community-based, volunteer efforts to assist other blacks in need. The majority have focused on children and youths. An assessment of the extent of these efforts and their relative success has not been completed.[34] However, an honest appraisal of the resources within the black community leads most blacks to admit that substantial public resources are needed to make a significant impact on some of our problems.

In the past three years, a slight change in the political environment has made it possible to develop more targeted government policies for disadvantaged Americans, especially single heads of household and minority youths. A return to employment and training initiatives that focus on those most in need, especially among teenagers, has been a positive step, although we still have a long way to go in terms of commitment of adequate resources.

One may debate the appropriateness of some aspects of the Family Support Act and the revisions in the Job Training Partnership Act, but a focus on teenage mothers by the FSA and an interest in ensuring opportunities for young black males shown by the Department of Labor and recently by the Department of Health and Human Services (under Secretary Louis Sullivan) have brought much-needed attention to the unfinished social agenda in American society. However, failure to understand the importance and complexities of the issue for the black community in the United States can only lead us in the wrong direction.

Notes

The views expressed here do not necessarily reflect those of the Joint Center for Political and Economic Studies, its Board of Governors, or any of its sponsors.

1. Sally Macintyre and Sarah Cunningham-Burley, "Teenage Pregnancy as a Social Problem: A Perspective from the United Kingdom" (chap. 3).

2. Also see Ann Phoenix, "The Social Construction of Teenage Motherhood: A Black and White Issue?" (chap. 4).

3. See Phoenix, "Social Construction of Teenage Motherhood."

4. Diana M. Pearce, "'Children Having Children': Teenage Pregnancy and Public Policy from the Woman's Perspective" (chap. 2).

5. Daniel Patrick Moynihan, *The Negro Family: The Case for National Action* (Washington, D.C.: U.S. Department of Labor, Office of Policy Planning and Research, 1965).

6. Committee on Policy for Racial Justice, *A Policy Framework for Racial Justice* (Washington, D.C.: Joint Center for Political Studies, 1983), p. 9.

7. *Ibid.*, p. 10.

8. See, for example, Charles Murray, *Losing Ground: American Social Policy, 1950–1980* (New York: Basic Books, 1984).

9. Cynthia Rexroat, *The Declining Economic Status of Black Children: Examining the Change?* (Washington, D.C.: Joint Center for Political Studies, 1993).

10. Sara McLanahan, "Family Structure and the Reproduction of Poverty," *American Journal of Sociology* 90 (January 1985): 873–901; Irwin Garfinkel and Sara S. McLanahan, *Single Mothers and Their Children: A New American Dilemma* (Washington, D.C.: Urban Institute, 1986), pp. 26–37; and Gerald David Jaynes and Robin M. Williams, Jr., *A Common Destiny: Blacks and American Society* (Washington, D.C.: National Academy Press, 1989), chap. 10, pp. 509–48.

11. Andrew F. Brimmer, *Trends, Prospects, and Strategies for Black Economic Progress* (Washington, D.C.: Joint Center for Political Studies, 1985), pp. 11–14; U.S. Bureau of the Census, *Money Income and Poverty Status in the United States: 1988*, P-60, no. 166 (Washington, D.C.: U.S. GPO, 1989), p. 37.

12. Andrew Sum and Neal Fogg, "The Changing Economic Fortunes of Young Black Men in the New American Economy of the 1980s." Testimony before the House Select Committee on Children, Youth, and Families, Washington, D.C., 25 July 1989.

13. See Daniel R. Fusfeld and Timothy Bates, *The Political Economy of the Urban Ghetto* (Carbondale: Southern Illinois University Press, 1985), for some analysis of the availability of manufacturing jobs and employment of black males.

14. See discussion in Kristin A. Moore, Margaret C. Simms, and Charles L. Betsey, *Choice and Circumstance: Racial Differences in Adolescent Sexuality and Fertility* (New Brunswick, N.J.: Transaction Books, 1986), chap. 7, pp. 103–25.

15. Reynolds Farley, "After the Starting Line: Blacks and Women in an Uphill Race," *Demography* 25 (1988): 477–96, and Jaynes and Williams, *Common Destiny*, pp. 535–37. For a contrasting view on the effect of black women's employment and an analysis of the role of male employment on marriage, see Mark Testa et al., "Employment and Marriage among Inner-City Fathers," *Annals of the American Academy of Political and Social Science*, 501 (1989): 79–91, and Mark Testa and Marilyn Krogh, "Marriage, Premarital Parenthood, and Joblessness among Black Americans in Inner-City Chicago." Paper prepared for the Joint Center for Political Studies/ Department of Health and Human Services forum on Models of Underclass Behavior, Washington, D.C., March 1990.

16. Margaret C. Simms, "The Choices that Young Black Women Make: Education, Employment, and Family Formation," in *The Changing Economic Status of Black Women*, Bette Woody, Carolyne Arnold, and Jacqueline P. Fields, eds. (Detroit: Wayne State University Press, 1990). In the latter half of the 1980s, the rates moved up slightly.

17. See U.S. Bureau of the Census, *Money Income: 1988*, Simms, "Choices That Young Black Women Make," and Margaret C. Simms, "Education and Early Child-

bearing: The Economic Implications for Women." Paper presented at a NOW LDEF/PEER research seminar, Washington, D.C., 30–31 March 1988.

18. See Phoenix "Social Construction of Teenage Motherhood." Also, a panel at the 1990 American Association for the Advancement of Science conference included papers on this issue by Arline T. Geronimus of the University of Michigan School of Public Health, Dawn Upchurch of Johns Hopkins University, and John McCarthy of Columbia University. See William Booth, "Teenage Pregnancy's Risks Reevaluated," *Washington Post*, 18 February 1990, p. A-8.

19. Frank Furstenberg, Jr., Jeanne Brooks-Gunn, and S. Philip Morgan, "Adolescent Mothers and Their Children in Later Life," *Family Planning Perspectives* 19, 4 (July/August 1987): 142–51; Frank F. Furstenberg, Jr., Jeanne Brooks-Gunn, and S. Philip Morgan, *Adolescent Mothers in Later Life* (Cambridge: Cambridge University Press, 1987).

20. See Rexroat, *Declining Economic Status of Black Children*.

21. For a review of studies of the father's presence on the academic performance of girls, see Carole Morning, "Factors Affecting the Participation and Performance of Minorities in Mathematics," a report to the Ford Foundation, March 1980. Also, research on women managers indicates that father-daughter relationships influence women's entry into nontraditional careers, at least among whites. See discussion in Karen Fulbright, "The Myth of the Double Advantage: Black Female Managers," in Margaret C. Simms and Julianne Malveaux, eds., *Slipping Through the Cracks: the Status of Black Women* (New Brunswick, N.J.: Transaction 1986), pp. 33–45.

22. Rexroat, *Declining Economic Status of Black Children*.

23. Robert Joseph Taylor et al., "Developments in Research on Black Families: A Decade Review," *Journal of Marriage and the Family* 52 (November 1990): 993–1014; Linda M. Chatters et al., "Size of Informal Helper Network Mobilized during a Serious Personal Problem among Black Americans," *Journal of Marriage and the Family* 51 (August 1989): 667–76; and Robert J. Taylor, "Receipt of Support from Family among Black Americans: Demographic and Familial Differences," *Journal of Marriage and the Family* 48 (1986): 67–77.

24. Comments of Heidi Hartmann at the Institute for Research on Poverty conference on the Condition of Minorities, Airlie House, Virginia, November 1986.

25. Moore et al., *Choice and Circumstance*.

26. *Ibid.*, chaps. 3 and 5, pp. 31–45 and 67–86, for a discussion of studies on differences in contraceptive use and differences in pregnancy outcomes.

27. For an analysis of the factors that are important in teenage childbearing, see Allan Abrahamse, Peter A. Morrison, and Linda J. Waite, *Beyond Stereotypes: Who Becomes a Single Teenage Mother?* (Santa Monica, Calif.: Rand Corporation, 1988). Their research suggests that the influences and social restraints that affect the likelihood of early, single parenthood varies by race and ethnicity.

28. U.S. Bureau of the Census, *What's It Worth?: Educational Background and Economic Status, Spring 1984*, P-70, no. 7 (Washington, D.C.: U.S. GPO, 1987).

29. See Margaret C. Simms, *Black Economic Progress: An Agenda for the 1990s* (Washington, D.C.: Joint Center for Political Studies, 1988), and George Silvestri

and John Lukasiewicz, "Projections of Occupational Employment, 1988–2000," *Monthly Labor Review* 112, 11 (November 1989): 42.

30. Children's Defense Fund, "Preventing Adolescent Pregnancy—What Schools Can Do," Washington, D.C., September 1986.

31. See, for example, Glenn C. Loury, "Internally Directed Action for Black Community Development: The Next Frontier for 'The Movement,'" *Review of Black Political Economy* 13, 1–2 (Summer/Fall, 1984): 31–46.

32. Committee on Policy for Racial Justice, *Black Initiative and Governmental Responsibility* (Washington, D.C.: Joint Center for Political Studies, 1987), p. 9.

33. William A. Darity, Jr., and Samuel L. Myers, Jr., "Public Policy and the Condition of Black Family Life," *Review of Black Political Economy* 13, 1–2 (Summer/Fall 1984): 165–87.

34. The Joint Center for Political Studies has conducted several studies of black philanthropic activity and is undertaking an inventory of community-based activities for black male youth. Efforts to date show blacks heavily engaged in donating money and time to community activities of benefit to other blacks.

13 ANTECEDENTS AND CONSEQUENCES: THE NEED FOR DIVERSE STRATEGIES IN ADOLESCENT PREGNANCY PREVENTION

During the past decade there has been a surge of creative effort and constructive rethinking around the issues surrounding adolescent pregnancy in the United States. Researchers, providers, and advocates are recognizing the interrelationships between the incidence of adolescent pregnancy and the prevalence of school failure, unemployment, poverty, and the clustering of adolescent risk-taking behaviors. These complex interrelationships require multipronged interventions that extend beyond more traditional approaches, which consist primarily of providing sex education and access to family planning services. Although progress has been made in improving even these basic approaches, there remain tremendous inconsistencies and a qualitative unevenness. Further, many adolescents continue to face intimidating psychological, physical, and social barriers that interfere with responsible contraceptive behavior.

It is also increasingly apparent that adolescent pregnancy may have as much to do with such factors as dropping out of school, isolation, poverty, unemployment, low self-esteem, and lack of hope for the future as it does with adolescent sexuality. Ironically, many of these factors have long been perceived as only the *consequences* of early childbearing. New evidence demonstrates, however, that they may in fact be the *antecedents* of preg-

257

nancy, which then intensifies their long-term impact. Based on the results of long-term tracking of pregnant adolescents into adulthood, as well as comparisons to other family members, a number of researchers have begun to argue that teenage pregnancy may not in itself have long-term adverse consequences. Rather than focusing on pregnancy, these researchers argue that attention needs to be paid to women's social *circumstances,* and to the poverty that is in fact the major predictor of adverse life outcomes. Simply stated, their conclusion is that adolescent pregnancy and childbearing alone may not be the negative experiences most previous research has purported them to be. Yet whether adolescent pregnancy or poverty is the crucial factor, it is vital that policymakers recognize that many of the problem areas associated with adolescent pregnancy are intimately interrelated, and that their negative and compounding impacts most certainly shape the overall issue of adolescent pregnancy, as well as any effort to develop and implement viable solutions to the problem.[1]

Academic Failure and Adolescent Pregnancy

School failure is a crucial factor along the pathway that results in early childbearing. Although it has long been thought that girls drop out of school because they are pregnant, recent studies show that many girls who become mothers drop out *before* pregnancy. Data from the national High School and Beyond Study showed that, of all those who both dropped out of school and gave birth to a child, 28 percent had left school before conception. A survey of never-married women in their twenties showed that among those who both became pregnant and dropped out of school, 61 percent of pregnancies occurred *after* they had left school; a survey of very young welfare mothers showed that 20 percent were already out of school before conception.

Level of education is a more significant predictor of future prospects than either ethnic or class background, and to a great extent determines whether that future will be one of jobs or unemployment, welfare or independence, early or planned parenthood, and lawful or unlawful behavior. In a study comparing the impact of childbearing on school continuation, researchers examined school graduation rates of teenagers who gave birth while still enrolled in school and graduation rates for those who gave birth after dropping out of school. The research demonstrated that early childbearing significantly reduces the school completion rates of young women who had already dropped out of school before pregnancy or childbirth. In contrast, among adolescents still in school at the time of childbirth, the study found that childbearing appeared to have little direct impact on the chance of completing school. The strongest determinant of a teenage mother's eventual educational attainment was found to be whether she was in school at the time that she gave birth, rather than her age at the time of the birth.

It is important to note, however, that young women who remain in school while they are pregnant (especially those who stay in school throughout the pregnancy and birth) are a self-selected and motivated group. Although the researchers examined eventual educational attainment (high school diploma or GED), they did not examine the timeliness of high school completion. It is likely that childbearing, while not preventing the woman from completing high school, did cause delays in school completion and most likely changed the nature and variety of available life choices, including the option to continue with postsecondary education.[2]

A principal reason given by both sexes for dropping out of school is school itself: its perceived irrelevance to their needs, and their own poor academic achievement. School-related reasons were primary for 29 percent of blacks, 21 percent of Hispanics, and 36 percent of whites. Two national surveys have also produced substantial evidence about the association between school achievement and childbearing. The High School and Beyond Study, looking at each ethnic group separately, found that white, black, and Hispanic sophomores with low academic ability (the lowest third of their class) were twice as likely to become unwed parents by their senior year as those students with greater academic ability. The National Longitudinal Survey of Youth found that females in the bottom 20 percent of basic reading and math skills were five times more likely to become mothers over a two-year period than those in the top 20 percent.[3]

Several researchers suggest that the poor academic achievement of many girls and their sense that school is irrelevant to their needs are, at least partially, attributable to the treatment they receive in the educational system. Recent studies show that both male and female teachers have different expectations of their students according to sex. Teachers are likely to give girls less attention than boys; to direct rote memorization questions at girls but to encourage independent thinking in boys by asking them complex, open-ended questions; to reprimand girls for speaking out of turn but to tolerate this behavior in boys; and to offer girls less substantive evaluation of their work than is offered to boys (for example, neatness of handwriting versus quality of content). In addition, educational materials such as books, films, and displays continue to emphasize male achievement throughout history and ignore the accomplishments of women. Many materials reinforce traditional gender-role stereotypes of women as homemakers and men as professionals, giving girls the impression that they have fewer opportunities than their male peers. When such experiences are combined with poverty, racial discrimination, and low parental education level, many young women may be inclined to see parenthood as one of the few meaningful or attractive future options available to them.[4]

The High School and Beyond Study documents the relationships among dropping out of school, adolescent pregnancy, and lack of economic opportunity in a national study that followed young people during and after their high school years. Among the study's findings are that the nongraduate females, married or not, are six times as likely as graduate females to have children; nongraduate females are nine times as likely as high school graduate females to receive welfare assistance; and nongraduates are at least four times as likely as graduates to engage in unlawful behavior.

A major implication of this study is that the lack of at least a high school diploma is frequently associated with severely negative impacts, including incidence of early childbearing, welfare dependence, and unemployment. However, it is important to note that the sample in this cross-sectional study was limited only to those students who had been enrolled in high school for some time and does not provide any data about results on those students who had already dropped out of school even before entering high school. In addition, the study did not include information on variables of interest apart from school completion that may also have differentiated graduates from nongraduates, and that may have played a role in the outcomes measured. Nevertheless, the data in the study suggest that education, in conjunction with other factors (like poverty status), may be a key to explaining negative outcomes associated with early childbearing.

Recently, several researchers have argued that the negative impact of adolescent childbearing on educational outcomes and subsequent employment may not be as serious as previously thought. Arline T. Geronimus and Sanders Korenman's research compares pairs of sisters who came from comparable backgrounds and began childbearing at different stages. Based on results that documented only negligible differences in the sisters' education and family income level, these researchers argue that delaying pregnancy will not help poor women escape poverty. A parallel study argues that circumstances associated with poverty, including poor education and an increased likelihood of secondary sector employment, contribute to an increased likelihood of adolescent childbearing, particularly among black teenagers. Regardless of their age when they first give birth, black women experience fewer employment opportunities. The anticipated payoffs of education are thought by these women to be so limited that early motherhood appears a viable alternative. However, such arguments fail to address the issue of long-term and costly impacts upon the life of the mother, her infant, family, and society in general. Whether or not a young woman bears a child early in life, society remains responsible to provide its youth—particularly its most vulnerable youth—with the educational and life opportunities that would make early childbearing a genuine option.

Such research suggests that teenage efforts to prevent pregnancy may have limited value; unless there are additional and effective educational or employment interventions, adolescents will continue to exhibit limited motivation to avoid early childbearing. Without these additional supports it becomes highly unlikely that a young woman, whether in her adolescent years or in her early adult years, will experience positive educational, health, and employment outcomes.

Adolescent Pregnancy as a Risk-Taking Behavior

Sexual activity and factors affecting it may be considered in isolation or may be viewed as part of a constellation of risk-taking behaviors that jeopardize physical or psychological health. Many adolescents face health problems that have a social origin. Rates of sexually transmitted diseases have increased dramatically in the past two decades among adolescents. Substance abuse is relatively common: by the time U.S. adolescents are high school seniors, 70 percent of them use alcohol, 30 percent smoke marijuana, and 11 percent use stimulants, such as cocaine, on a regular basis. Moreover, the average age at which risk-taking behavior begins is steadily decreasing. Researchers are beginning to see increasingly clear patterns emerge from this cluster of risk-taking behaviors among some adolescents, behaviors involving early sexuality, substance use, criminal activity, and low academic achievement.

If unprotected sexual activity is part of a behavior pattern, then an understanding of its initiation and continuation may be enhanced by knowledge about co-existing behaviors. For example, much adolescent sexual intercourse is unplanned, and it often occurs when one or both partners are using drugs and/or alcohol. The sequential relationships between risk behaviors (for example, the smoking of cigarettes leading to experimentation with alcohol and/or other drugs) has been well documented. However, there have been no national studies that have specifically focused on youth who engage in multiple-risk behaviors, and no efforts to link certain risk-taking behaviors in terms of both motivation and outcome. The reckless use of alcohol or drugs may culminate in unprotected sex, and both behaviors are symptomatic of the same attitudinal

factors, such as the inability or unwillingness to forego short-term gratification in order to minimize the chances of long-term problems.[5]

Existing research on adolescents was recently reviewed to calculate the
overlap among problem behaviors among American youth. Using simu-
lated estimates, Joy Dryfoos projects the number of adolescents considered to be at moderate, high, and extremely high risk of risk-taking behaviors, including unprotected sexual intercourse, drug use, and juvenile
delinquency. Based on these calculations, approximately three of America's 33.8 million youths are in the highest risk category, four million are at
high risk, and seven million are at moderate risk. Such estimates point to
the need for multiple interventions. Certain strategies, such as improving
schools, would be appropriate across the board, while special case-
management services may be particularly important for students at high
risk. Ignoring the interrelation of risk-taking behaviors when designing
policy limits the effectiveness of any societal response. Interdisciplinary
efforts are needed to plan comprehensive and integrated health, social,
educational, and community strategies. For example, family life and health
educators must be prepared to deal with appropriate methods of contraception in addition to helping adolescents grapple with the issues of drug
and alcohol use that will most likely interfere with the effective use of
contraceptive methods. In order to implement this multidisciplinary approach successfully, policymakers need access to multiple funding streams
that can be combined to sustain integrated service interventions.

Barriers to Adolescent Health Care

A number of service barriers prevent many adolescents from reducing risk-taking behaviors, including unprotected sexual activity. While
family planning clinics and private providers served nearly three million
sexually active adolescents under the age of 20 in 1983, more than an
estimated two million were underserved. Even among teenagers who utilize these services, consistent use of them remains low. At many family
planning clinics, 40 to 60 percent of the teenage clients never return for the
periodic checkups that are crucial to ensure effective use of contraceptives.[6]

Adolescents face many barriers to seeking and obtaining health care.
Some barriers, like poverty, affect all age groups, but teenagers often encounter additional obstacles. Parental-consent requirements and perceived or actual lack of confidentiality can be barriers to obtaining sensitive
counseling services, including family planning care. In addition, health-
care services are seldom available in locations convenient for teenagers,

and service hours frequently coincide with school and work schedules. While these latter barriers exist for adults as well, they can assume a magnified dimension for adolescents, who often regard health care as a low priority. Even when teenagers circumvent these barriers and do manage to obtain health care, they regularly fail to follow the provider's instructions, or to follow through on referrals or return visits.

Delivering quality care to adolescents requires an integrated approach. The provision of multiple services at one site can be accomplished through the co-location of care providers and/or agencies, or through the use of case-management or linkage programs that both facilitate cross-referrals and stress effective follow-up. For example, if a teenage girl goes to a traditional family planning clinic for birth control or to a doctor for a sports physical and it appears that she has a drug problem, she will probably be referred elsewhere for drug treatment, which will often prove ineffective. What is needed is an integrated approach that responds to the adolescent's multiple psychological, environmental, and physical needs. Despite the efforts of some traditional clinics to stay in touch with their teenage patients and encourage them to follow through on referrals, the reality is that a fragmented, episodic approach to health services (including adolescent pregnancy prevention efforts) allows many adolescents to fall through the cracks.[7]

Studies have shown, however, that teenagers will use health care services if they are conveniently located, free or low-cost, confidential, comprehensive, and staffed by those with expertise in caring for adolescents. One study compared the use of integrated services designed for adolescents to the segmented services of traditional clinics and found that the comprehensive clinics served a higher percentage of the teenagers in their geographic areas. In 1980 Johns Hopkins University conducted a study to learn why teenagers selected a particular family planning clinic. The most important reasons given were confidentiality, a belief that staff cared about teenagers, close proximity to home, and favorable recommendations from friends.[8]

A priority target for program interventions must be those adolescents whose social, economic, educational, and personal risk-taking behaviors place them at the greatest risk of premature parenthood. To be effective, strategies should reflect diverse value systems and cultural differences, and respond to the economic and educational disparities among youth. A growing awareness of this diversity—and the need for interventions that reflect it—is apparent at the local community, city, county, state, and national levels. By bringing together an array of agencies, organizations, and programs that provide a variety of resources, we can target more appropriate interventions at teenagers' specific and changing needs. Interventions are needed along the full continuum of services—from adolescents who are not sexually active, to adolescents who need assistance in obtaining contraceptive services, to adolescents who are pregnant and parenting and require programs to assist them with health, education, and social services.[9]

Strategies to Assist Pregnant and Parenting Adolescents

Policymakers have generally felt much more comfortable about supporting programs that help pregnant teenagers and their infants than about supporting programs aimed at postponing a first pregnancy. Of primary concern have been whether the mother and infant are healthy, whether the first birth is followed by another within too short a time, and whether the teenage parent is able to graduate from high school and presumably attain financial self-sufficiency. Attention to these areas has been shown to mitigate significantly the negative impact of early parenthood.[10]

Even though only a subset of eligible pregnant and parenting adolescents receive the services they need, a number of comprehensive programs have been developed and tested. These programs offer education, counseling, and social and medical assistance either throughout the pregnancy or through the first year or two of parenthood. The programs can be based in schools or other community settings. Although one organization usually serves as the lead agency, the programs are characterized by effective partnerships. This interaction model was first promoted at the federal level by the Adolescent Health Services and Pregnancy Prevention Act of 1978, implemented by the Office of Adolescent Pregnancy Programs (OAPP).

The goals of many programs are successful completion of school, a decrease in the incidence of births in rapid succession, and economic self-sufficiency for the adolescent and her baby. Some programs offer case-management services, while others provide a special child-development lab where infants and toddlers receive quality childcare while parenting adolescents and pregnant teenagers develop nurturing skills, self-esteem, and confidence in their parenting abilities. Some programs have prenatal education that covers human sexuality and family planning, risks of teenage pregnancy, adoption, prevention of birth defects and low birth weights, fetal development, physical and psychological aspects of pregnancy, and childbirth education and preparation, including Lamaze instruction.

A number of successful interventions have been developed and evaluated in the field of adolescent pregnancy and parenting. Several recent follow-up studies also demonstrate that program intervention during the pregnancy and subsequent to the birth appear to have played an important role in ameliorating the potentially negative effects of early childbirth. In a twenty-year follow-up study of a group of women who were pregnant in the late 1960s, long-term success (defined as current employment or support by a spouse and attainment of a high school education or its equivalent) was associated with several factors: having completed more school prior to becoming pregnant; participating more actively in a program intervention offered to this group twenty years previously; being at school with no subsequent pregnancy twenty-six months after the birth; feeling in control of one's life with little social isolation, and feeling little isolation twenty-six months after the birth; and life-long fertility control (defined as having one or two children after the index child). Among this group most former teenage mothers completed a reasonable amount of education and became economically self-sufficient.[11]

To counteract the impact of adolescent pregnancy on the lives of the young women and their families, more strategies are necessary to reach larger numbers of young people in need of services. When developing comprehensive approaches, it is important that interdisciplinary services (health, educational, and social support) be available during the crucial period from pregnancy through the early years of childbearing.

Health Services

Access to comprehensive perinatal health care is imperative to mitigate the well-documented health problems pregnant adolescents often encounter. Health outcomes for adolescents have been shown to be successful if adequate prenatal care is available early enough in pregnancy. Community-based prenatal care is cost effective and essential, either through the establishment of perinatal clinics or by expanding existing services so that every pregnant teenager has early access to care. Outreach efforts, including the creative use of public media, are needed to inform pregnant teenagers of the advantages of seeking early prenatal care, the availability of services in their own communities, and ways to access care.

Prevention of repeat unplanned pregnancy during the adolescent years is also an important goal. Substantive counseling regarding current plans and future goals should be provided along with access to affordable and acceptable contraceptives. Participation in appropriate educational or vocational programs is also an important strategy to increase the adolescent's motivation to delay repeat pregnancy.

Social, Economic, and Educational Support

With the birth of a child, teenagers face the important responsibility of providing financial support. Many adolescents are still too young to establish their own households, and even older teenagers typically lack the financial resources for independent living. The teenager's parents may themselves have limited resources that cannot stretch to include the new grandchild. Although teenagers generally cannot support their children, they can receive help in identifying social agencies that might assist them. Case-management services are necessary to connect pregnant and parenting teenagers with programs and agencies that provide financial support and services, such as Aid to Families with Dependent Children and food stamps.

Increased job opportunities, particularly for fathers who are typically past adolescence and often lack employment skills, are also essential to support the formation of young families. The role of schools and businesses in meeting the special needs of pregnant and parenting adolescents requires further development. Parenting adolescents must be given the training and educational opportunities necessary for self-sufficiency and career advancement. Schools and businesses should develop additional work programs with wages, childcare, and transportation, all of which would be conditional on remaining in school. Schools should help pregnant and parenting teenagers (and other teenagers) develop educational and employment goals beyond the training phase, and encourage career advancement through education.

Childcare

Lack of affordable, accessible, quality childcare services for adolescent parents is a major barrier to youth self-sufficiency and adequate child development. There is a need for community-based—preferably school-based—services to care for the infants and preschool children of adolescents. If school sites are not feasible for daycare services, adolescent parents need adequate transportation between home, childcare site, and school to ensure the continuation of their education. It is imperative too that this support continue from secondary school through vocational training, junior college, and other college programs. Childcare services should also be available for young people not enrolled in school.

Providing comprehensive service delivery by linking several providers is an effective means for meeting the multiple needs of pregnant and parenting adolescents. Strong case management is needed to ensure that young clients participate in all services. A thorough case-management plan would include continuous individual counseling and ongoing assessment of client needs, social service program brokerage, referral and follow-up, and system advocacy. The system mix may need to vary according to the adolescent's age and developmental level, and it is important to emphasize the *duration* of the program; intervention cannot be too brief, or initial gains will in many cases be lost.

Approaches to Preventing Adolescent Pregnancy

Despite mounting public interest and the existence of thousands of local programs and special projects, no single, comprehensive, transferable model that any community could adopt and build upon has yet emerged. Much remains to be learned about which prevention programs are the most effective; the key ingredients, however, for any major effort are beginning to become evident. Early intervention, sustained contact, and follow-up seem to be common factors in successful strategies. However, there are few evaluative studies that verify this, and there is uncertainty as to whether multifaceted approaches are more effective than single-faceted ones.

Comprehensive approaches, in which the health, social, and educational needs of teenagers are all addressed within a coordinated system of care, are considered effective and promising. Some believe that comprehensive programs respond best to teenagers' multiple and simultaneous needs; others favor specially targeted or focused approaches, such as family planning services directed at teenagers. To be successful, both comprehensive and single-focus programs require long-term community commitment, adequate funding, and significant, sustained outreach. A common theme is the need for multi-pronged approaches to solve this extremely complicated, multifaceted, and sometimes socially ingrained problem.

In the past, many pregnancy prevention programs met with unexpectedly limited success, because they focused on a single aspect of sexuality or pregnancy. Past prevention efforts (which continue to shape most current programs) typically combined medical and public-health models that made contraceptives and birth-control information more accessible to teenagers. The theory was that, armed with adequate information and services, adolescents would be motivated to take precautions. Although the importance of high-quality health-education efforts and access to family planning services cannot be overemphasized, the traditional public-health approach seems to reach only a portion of those at risk of an unintended pregnancy. Comprehensive approaches are increasingly being tried in a variety of settings, but there still is a tendency for programs to seek and promote a single strategy as the "answer" to teenage sexuality when, in fact, no single intervention reaches all the various segments of the adolescent population. The following summary reflects a continuum of efforts, from categorical approaches that emphasize one type of program (for example, effective family life education), to comprehensive programs that integrate family planning services within a full array of health and mental-health services, to ecological models that attempt to incorporate efforts to prevent adolescent pregnancy within a larger attempt to expand the life options of young people, thereby increasing their motivation to delay the initial pregnancy.

Current interventions in the field of adolescent pregnancy postponement fall into three major categories: (1) programs that support deferring sexual activity and delaying childbearing; (2) programs that maximize adolescents' abilities to make responsible decisions about sexual activity in the context of their lives; and (3) programs that facilitate sexually active adolescents' access to contraceptive services. The following models are highlighted because they employ different strategies and different resources in their successful attempts to keep adolescents in school, and because they go beyond traditional approaches in order to build students' competence in basic skills and address their needs realistically. Common features of these programs include relevance to the needs of youth and the coordination of resources. Several of them include extensive evaluation components as well.

Deferring sexual activity. With the dramatic increase in the number of sexually active young people, parents, religious leaders, health and social service professionals, and others have raised questions about the sexual pressures that young people encounter. Across the United States, numerous efforts are underway to encourage young people to delay initiating sexual intercourse until they are older. The goals of these programs are to reach adolescents early with information on how and why to defer sexual activity, to increase their awareness of pressures to become sexually active, to reinforce their ability to say no, and to build positive assertive skills. Most of these models utilize a curriculum to achieve their goals and target very young teenagers (aged 12 to 15) in an attempt to reach students before they become sexually active. Most of the programs also involve parents through special information sessions and shortened versions of the curriculum so that they can reinforce the teenagers' learning experiences at home.

One of the best known programs is Postponing Sexual Involvement, developed by Grady Memorial Hospital and Emory University in Atlanta. This "How to Say No" Program helps adolescents learn to identify the pressures that make it difficult to say no. Two of the four sessions deal with the social pressures teenagers face and encourage them to consider how they can meet these needs without becoming sexually active. Participants also discuss advertisements that use sex to sell products, sexual messages in music and on television, and direct peer pressure. Assertiveness techniques are taught and demonstrated in the third session and practiced in the fourth. A follow-up session held several months after the initial meetings reinforces these skills. Specially trained peers who work with younger teenagers are considered key to the process, because the very young teenagers tend to listen more to them than to adults. The program has also been adapted for use in schools, community settings, and churches. Recent evaluation results have documented that both males and females who had not yet had sex and who participated in the program were subsequently much less likely to engage in sex than were similar students who did not participate in the program. When participants engaged in sex after the course, they did so less frequently than did nonparticipants. The program did not have a measurable impact on students who had engaged in sex before the beginning of the course.

Beginning in 1988, Education, Training, and Research Associates (ETR), conducted an in-depth evaluation of the life-skills counseling model. In this study, two tenth-grade classes in each of twenty-four schools were randomly selected to receive either a twelve-session life-skills treatment or the standard (control) curriculum. Outcome measures included knowledge and behavioral intentions and emphasized behaviors such as past and current sexual activity, contraceptive use, and pregnancy planning. For the trained group, knowledge about reproduction and birth control, the intention of practicing appropriate skills to avoid pregnancy, and communication with parents about pregnancy prevention were significantly greater after the test and at the six-month follow-up. The trained group also had a greater tendency to use birth control—especially those who began sexual activity after the program. No differences in the frequency of sex, numbers of pregnancy scares, or actual pregnancies were found. Although skill-training programs alone should probably not be expected significantly to prevent the number of pregnancies, this program offers some promise of adding to the pregnancy-prevention effects of allied school, home, and community activities.[12]

Other programs have been developed based on research showing a definite relation between parental involvement and delayed sexual activity. These programs are geared to encourage stronger family participation in the teaching of values. For example, mother-daughter and father-son workshops, such as those sponsored by Planned Parenthood of Central California in Fresno, are designed to increase communication within the context of learning more about adolescence and sexuality. Five weekly workshops provide families with opportunities to open channels of communication. Sessions for female adolescents cover the topics of body image, self-esteem, puberty, menstruation and women's health issues, human reproduction, peer pressure, decision making, sexually transmitted diseases, and adolescent pregnancy. Each week participants receive a homework assignment that requires families to set aside twenty minutes to discuss family values and the topics covered in class.

Developing life options. Emerging themes in the postponement of adolescent pregnancy cluster around two concepts: increasing the life options available to a young person and increasing the capacity to make decisions. *Capacity* refers to knowledge and skills required to prevent unintended childbearing, including sex and family life education, access to birth-control services, and availability of abortion as a backup to contraceptive failure. Life-option interventions are needed to provide the rationale for postponing pregnancy, the skills necessary for completing an education and entering the labor force, and alternatives to early motherhood. Strategies include dropout prevention, individual counseling and support, job training, and job placement.[13]

Pregnancy postponement programs should be connected with other aspects of the adolescent's life, because the motivation to prevent an unintended or early birth is linked to an individual's perception of other possible life alternatives. Teenagers with strong achievement orientations and clear goals for the future are likely, if sexually active, to be regular and effective users of contraceptives. A teenager who is doing well in school and in the family and community is more likely to delay pregnancy than one who is not. In contrast, young people facing limited life options—poor teenagers and teenagers with few academic skills—are at greatest risk of early parenthood, whether or not sexually specific services are available to them. This ready access to family planning services is necessary but not sufficient for both groups of young people.[14]

Although life-option interventions may not specifically focus on postponement of pregnancy, their contribution to the adolescent's self-esteem and aspirations may have an indirect effect on it. It is important to note that these life-option interventions are useful in providing enhanced services to young people regardless of whether they have a direct effect on the incidence of teenage pregnancy. They may be even more valuable for the adolescent who is raising her baby.

Life-option programs may be further extended by incorporating family life education and access to birth control. In a number of schools, family life education is now being joined with vocational education and emerging as "life planning," with a strong message that if teenagers want to achieve their career goals, they must delay childbearing. Parental involvement programs, peer counseling programs, formal referral mechanisms to community clinics and services, and school-linked services are among current efforts to help communities develop meaningful interventions. Many youth agencies, such as Girls Clubs, Boys Clubs, YWCA, 4-H, Girl Scouts, and Boy Scouts, have committed themselves to developing pregnancy prevention programs at the local level and to working within a broad national coalition to advocate legislation in this area.

Family life education. Adolescents need a great deal of background information in order to make informed reproductive choices. Although family life education has not been shown to affect behavior consistently, it has been shown to affect positively (1) knowledge (particularly for young adolescents) about birth control, sexually transmitted diseases, and the probability of becoming pregnant; (2) communication and decision-making skills; and (3) parent-child communication, resulting in better discussion of sexual issues within the family. Research has documented that family life education does not significantly affect the amount of sexual activity among students. Advocates of family life education programs in public school curricula argue that children and adolescents must receive accurate information in order to develop a sense of personal responsibility for their sexual behavior.[15]

Educational interventions vary considerably in scope and timing. New Jersey was the first state to implement a mandatory family life education program from kindergarten through high school in all public school districts. Students in grades K to 6 have two class periods per week, and students in grades 7 to 12 take the class daily for one eight-week period. Programs are developed locally in four broad areas defined by the state commissioners for education and health and human services: interpersonal relationships, human sexual development, responsible personal behavior, and the creation of strong families. Few other states, however, have formally adopted this type of program. In most cases, family life education is not offered to adolescents until the ninth or tenth grade, and more often than not it is presented in a brief and fragmented manner as part of other curricula, rather than as a separate course.[16]

One community in South Carolina made a successful effort to extend family life education beyond the confines of the schools. It adopted a multi-pronged public-health information intervention project that simultaneously targeted parents, teachers, church representatives, community leaders, and children enrolled in the public school system with messages designed to reduce adolescent pregnancies. These messages sought to promote decision-making and communication skills, self-esteem, and understanding of human reproduction and contraception. In 1984 the pregnancy rate and the number of live births dropped 50 percent in the county in which the program operated, a significantly greater reduction than in three nearby sociodemographically similar counties that offered no targeted intervention programs.[17]

Many efforts to postpone adolescent pregnancy do not include a component that focuses on young men. This often reflects a lack of male staff involved directly in educational and service programs for family planning. One promising effort called "Project Alpha—A Man-to-Man Talk about Teenage Pregnancy" attempts to change that pattern. This national initiative is sponsored by the Alpha Phi Alpha Fraternity and the March of Dimes Birth Defects Foundation and has been replicated in a number of communities. The program focuses on helping young men learn about their role in responsible childbearing and incorporates three major components: (1) knowledge about human reproduction and development, as well as the psychosocial and legal consequences of teenage pregnancy; (2) motivation to clarify values, set goals, and make decisions that are consistent with these goals; and (3) motivation to share information on responsible parenting with their peers, family, and communities. Young men are selected to attend this seminar series based on their leadership skills and are then encouraged to share the information with their peers. Sessions are led by volunteers working with community doctors, lawyers, clergymen, and other leaders. Although the program has not been formally evaluated, it appears to have some success, attributable to solid volunteer support and the opportunities it presents to work with strong male role models.

Another example of partnerships between community-based organizations and adolescents is reflected in the Teen Outreach Program (TOP) originated by the Missouri Junior League and local schools. This program provides students with volunteer community-service placements as well as weekly support groups that include discussions about adolescent pregnancy and sexuality. The effort to integrate youth into community settings contributes to creating a greater sense of self-esteem for many of these youngsters. In the third year of evaluation of this program, the TOP students began the year at somewhat higher risk of school failure and school suspension, and the proportion of them from nonintact families was greater than the proportion among the comparison students. In spite of these differences, at the end of the school year the TOP students had far lower rates of school suspension and dropout, differences that persisted after controlling for background variables. Participation in the program was significantly related to lower pregnancy rates. Although further evaluation is continuing, one-year partial follow-up data show that, while the school enrollment advantage of the TOP students persists over time, the lower pregnancy rates do not. This latter finding suggests that the program's primary result is to delay some pregnancies and births.[18]

School-related model programs. As we have seen, school dropout and pregnancy are closely intertwined, and implementing effective efforts to keep adolescents in school is crucial. The Summer Training and Education Program (STEP), begun by Public/Private Ventures, a Philadelphia-based research and demonstration agency, is an innovative model that addresses adolescent pregnancy within the context of career, academic, and personal goals. It aims to improve the basic skills of disadvantaged youth, keep students in school, and prevent teenage pregnancy by providing academic assistance, summer employment, life-skills instruction, and counseling to academically at risk 14- and 15-year-olds. The program follows students for two consecutive summers and provides support.

Although it will be several years before data will be available to evaluate the long-term objective of stemming the school dropout rate, the program has already been shown to be successful in reducing summer learning loss. This learning loss, which poor youth experience to a far greater degree than their more advantaged peers, has been shown to be a contributing factor in school dropout. Students participating in STEP were also shown to have more knowledge of contraception and sexually related behavior than the control groups. A further sign of promise is that participants who were already sexually active were more likely to use contraceptives after the program than were sexually active students in the control group. The program has also demonstrated that academic assistance and work experience for youth can be successfully combined, that coordination of services and collaboration among service providers is essential for systems to succeed, and that the relative amenability of younger adolescents to behavioral change makes the middle-grade years an essential and optimal point for intervention. The original model program was tested in five communities throughout the United States and was in the process of being replicated in more than fifty additional sites during the 1989 academic year.[19]

Throughout the United States there is a variety of dropout prevention efforts, including alternative educational degree programs and vocational training programs. Thus far, no systematic evaluation has been conducted of how successful these various programs have been in providing the alternative life options considered necessary to the postponement of child-birth by adolescents.[20]

Increasing access to family planning services. There is a renewed focus on the role of family planning clinics in overcoming young people's psychological barriers to seeking reproductive health care. However, reduced program funding and a lack of public consensus on the acceptability of family planning services for adolescents have hampered the development of a full-fledged campaign to widen public acceptance of adolescents' use of contraceptives. Many family planning programs do conduct outreach in schools and other community settings to inform young people about the availability of services, which are often free or offered on a sliding fee scale. Some clinics are also taking a look at the type of counseling they provide. For example, additional support provided to adolescents for choosing contraceptives through guided counseling and contingency counseling has been tested at several sites.

Only a handful of subsidized family planning clinics are especially geared to serve males. The Young Men's Clinic at Presbyterian Hospital in New York is a hospital-based model program offering a comprehensive array of health services, including family planning and condom distribution. Sessions are held once a week exclusively for 13- to 21-year-old men in need of medical services and counseling. The staff is comprised of young men, often medical students from Columbia University, who guide discussions on health-related issues, including sexual decision making and family planning methods.

School-based health services are now operating in more than 340 communities across the United States. They provide primary health-care services on school campuses, including treatment for minor injuries and illness, sports physicals, immunizations, first aid and acute care, laboratory and diagnostic screenings, health education, counseling, and drug and alcohol education and counseling, as well as services pertaining to sexual decision making and referrals for family planning care. Most clinics require a signed consent form from students' parents before any treatment or counseling can take place. Many clinics open after a thorough needs assessment and community planning process in which students, parents, school staff, and community-agency representatives determine the services the clinic will provide. Some clinics choose not to provide any contraceptive care on site; others provide only education, counseling, and referral for such services; and a few dispense contraceptives at the clinic. Preliminary studies show that services related to family planning account for 10 to 20 percent of all clinic visits.

A three-year demonstration project that linked a junior and senior high school with a storefront clinic in Baltimore reported that pregnancy rates dropped by 30 percent in program schools, compared to an increase of 58 percent in control schools. Researchers also found a seven-month average postponement of first intercourse among program participants. Despite the claims by some critics that school-based clinics encourage or condone sexual activity, findings from other clinic programs show that sexual activity does not increase following establishment of a clinic in a school. School-based clinics that dispense birth-control information, provide referrals for contraceptive services, or provide birth-control prescriptions affect neither the initiation nor the frequency of sex. Although it is premature to assess the impact of school-based clinics on the problem of adolescent pregnancy, the range and multiplicity of health services they provide are clear indicators of the serious unmet medical needs of young people.[21]

New Jersey recently implemented comprehensive multiservice programs at twenty-nine sites. These programs can be considered "next generation" in terms of their level of comprehensiveness. To reduce the adverse results of service fragmentation, most school-based health programs have developed a comprehensive health approach that de-emphasizes the "one-at-a-time" delivery of services by category. The New Jersey approach goes beyond this to integrate health approaches with a variety of other service needs, such as employment development and recreation.

New Jersey's School-Based Youth Services Program was developed by the state's Department of Human Services, with grants available only to communities that showed broad-based community support. Twenty-four sites are located in or near high schools (ten of which also serve junior high schools), and five are located at or near vocational schools. The state does not mandate a single statewide model, to ensure that programs at each site may be adapted to local needs. The state does stipulate, however, that all services must be available at a single site, and that all sites must offer mental-health and family counseling as well as health and employment services. Parental consent is required for adolescents to participate. Managing agencies include schools, medical schools and hospitals, nonprofit agencies, mental-health agencies, a county health department, a city human resources department, a private-industry council, the Urban League, and a community development organization. All twenty-nine sites offer services in health, employment, family counseling, mental health, substance abuse, information and referral, and recreation; nineteen sites also offer family planning; and others offer transportation, daycare services, and 24-hour hotlines.

Ecological approaches. An evolution in the development of innovative pregnancy prevention program models has begun to take place during the past several years. Recognition of the limitations inherent in categorical health-care programs that address only one specific area (for example, family planning, mental health, physical health, and drug and alcohol prevention) has led to the development of more comprehensive health-care models like those found in school-based health centers, adolescent clinics, and other community-based approaches that combine a variety of these categorical services. Staff in these programs soon became aware of a wide variety of problems unrelated to health, such as social, educational, economic, and motivational issues, that deeply affect the youthful client. New approaches take into account the need to provide health services in concert with a number of educational, employment training, and social services in order to change the overall environment and open up opportunities for youth.

Recognizing that single, isolated interventions will not always work in postponing adolescent pregnancy, because they do not necessarily address the underlying causes of the problem, the Children's Aid Society's Community Center in Central Harlem has developed an innovative multidimensional approach. The program operates during the late afternoon and early evening, and students and their parents can choose from a variety of activities and programs. There are five components to the program: (1) an extensive family life education program (two to three hours a week for fifteen weeks) that covers gender roles, relationships, and contraception; (2) individual sports (squash, golf, tennis, and swimming); (3) enhancement of self-esteem through the performing arts; (4) career awareness and employment, including summer jobs; and (5) health and human services, including family planning information and provision of contraceptives. Sexually active adolescents who are practicing birth control are monitored weekly to ensure consistent use of contraceptives. In addition, adolescents and their parents are given academic assistance, including tutoring and help with homework. Students graduating from high school are guaranteed a free college scholarship through the program, as are their parents.

The program operates at three sites, and in its initial three years only three participants became pregnant. These results are particularly dramatic and encouraging when compared to the extremely high adolescent pregnancy and school dropout rates of other youngsters who live in the same area. Because the program is established on a voluntary basis and systematic random assignment to an "intervention group" and a "nonintervention group" is not feasible, these results may reflect motivational factors, academic potential, and family support of the adolescent's involvement in the program, which in turn affect the success rate of the program. While this program (like many other intervention strategies) cannot preclude the possibility of a strong self-selection bias on the part of adolescents and their families, the intensive community planning process, the location of the program in some of the highest-risk communities, and a strong outreach component help to ensure that the program will reach those adolescents most at risk of repeating the patterns of early childbearing common to the surrounding community.

The costs incurred for each participant in this program and other interventions programs may be considered relatively high (ranging from $1,200 to $1,400 per participant per year for the program described above, and from $250 to $400 per student per year for school-based health services). But these costs are much lower than those incurred by families and other taxpayers when a young woman needs societal support to raise her infant. For example, an analysis of public costs incurred in California for families begun by teenage mothers shows that in 1985 alone taxpayers spent $3.09 billion, primarily in major public expenditures on Aid to Families with Dependent Children (welfare), Medicaid for health care, and food stamps. Had all these births been delayed until the mother was 20 years old, 40 percent, or $1.23 billion, of public funds would have been saved in that year alone.

Although not all adolescents who give birth are dependent on public support, and those who are may be in receipt of support only some of the time, a family begun by a first birth to a teenager in California in 1985 will on average cost the public $17,942 over the next twenty years. Were this birth delayed until the mother is 20 years old, taxpayers would save $7,177 per family over the next twenty years. Additional costs and savings accrue if a pregnancy is prevented among teenagers aged 15 or younger. While a specific cost-benefit analysis has not been conducted comparing investments in early prevention and intervention programs with treatment programs for adolescent pregnancy, such an analysis might be influential in arguing for additional funding in the area of youth development. Currently many of the pilot and demonstration programs are reaching only small segments of the population in need of services. Even federally funded programs, such as the network of family planning programs, estimate that their efforts are reaching no more than one-third to one-half of all their potential clients.[22]

Initiating adolescent pregnancy prevention interventions at an earlier point in the child's development was a basic premise of the Urban Middle School Adolescent Pregnancy Prevention program. Sponsored by the Ford Foundation and the Carnegie Corporation of New York, the program sought to strengthen school and community agency collaborations in an effort to prevent adolescent pregnancy and school dropout. In eight sites across the country, middle schools (fifth to eighth grades, 10- to 14-year-olds) developed a variety of programs, ranging from after-school enrichment programs to the development of comprehensive health services and extensive family life education and life-options curricula integrated into the classroom. Underlying themes in each program stressed improving academic skills and self-esteem, strengthening career orientations, and preventing school dropout. An evaluation study has been completed on the project, documenting the large numbers of young adolescents who have been reached by the program and the positive collaborative relationships that have been established by schools and outside community agencies at most of the sites. However, collecting long-term impact data on both the incidence of adolescent pregnancy and school dropout rates was not a feasible component of the study.

The New Futures program, sponsored by the Annie E. Casey Foundation, is one of the most innovative and ambitious current initiatives. Its overall goal is to strengthen the capacity of diverse institutions to work together to integrate services and improve the "service climate" for youth. The program aims to reduce adolescent pregnancy, school dropout, and youth unemployment by incorporating case-management services for at-risk youth through a restructuring of local youth-serving institutions. The five-year program requires that sites develop and maintain an inter-disciplinary, multi-agency collaborative system to plan, advise, and oversee each project, including the development of performance standards and indicators of successful outcomes. Each of the five cities in which the program operates is provided with $10 million in funding, which must be matched dollar-for-dollar by the community. While each city will most likely develop its own policies, programs, and procedures and produce its own set of outcomes, there is great interest in studying whether the concept of integrated services for youth is a workable strategy in the prevention of adolescent pregnancy.

Full-fledged comprehensive programs in which social service and community agencies co-locate at school or alternative community sites (such as recreation and community centers) are an important means to improving adolescent health care in general, but not all communities will select this option. As an alternative approach, outreach social workers and other service providers could be placed in community settings to provide triage for various services that adolescents often fail to find or utilize. Emerging from the comprehensive health-care models are several features that have implications for the development of other interventions. These include continuity of care; coordination and comprehensiveness of services; targeting of at-risk adolescents; collaboration among students, parents, schools, and service agencies; flexibility in delivering care; and integration of health education, preventive health services, and counseling within the student's educational world.

Future efforts to prevent adolescent pregnancy must respond to a dual need: (1) to support efforts to replicate, disseminate, and institutionalize successful program models in order to reach many more young people across the country, as part of a national initiative on youth; and (2) to expand currently available family planning services, including community outreach and case-management services, to help adolescents increase their overall use of contraceptives. These efforts should target both male and female adolescents and young adults. It is important, however, to recognize that even if the best programs were to be widely instituted and funded at an appropriate level, they would continue to be stop-gap measures. Changes need to occur within a broader framework of youth development, including the need to resolve the underlying societal issues, like poverty and racism, that have contributed so significantly to the problem of adolescent pregnancy. Without a commitment to fundamental social change in the society at large, we shall continue to bear both the private and the public costs of unintended adolescent pregnancy.

Public Policy and Federal Funding

There is a great deal of ambivalence at the federal level about adolescent pregnancy prevention policies. The widespread discomfort with adolescent sexual behavior (and its consequences) is reflected in the types of programs that currently receive federal funding. The primary source of public funding for pregnancy prevention is the Family Planning Services and Population Research Act of 1970 (Title X), which helps support some forty-five hundred family planning clinics nationwide. Official ambivalence about the problems and realities of adolescent sexual activity is also demonstrated in the lack of federal funding for family life education. With the exception of OAPP-funded "say no to sex" programs, no categorical federal funds have ever been earmarked for education about family life or sex.[23]

An argument can be made that almost every federal and state intervention directed at families and children falls into a category that can be broadly defined as life-options programs. Federal health dollars are used either to reimburse health-care providers for services to eligible individuals in various entitlement programs or to provide grants to states or community-based organizations for a variety of health-related activities. However, the extent and type of services paid for by or offered to youths through federal programs depend considerably on the degree to which states give priority to this population group. In consequence, it is for the most part not possible to document how many adolescents are served by public programs or how much federal and state money is spent on these adolescents.[24]

A coordinated public policy requires: (1) a fundamental commitment by communities, agencies, and public policymakers; (2) the most effective use of available funding through coordination of service providers and funding agencies; and (3) the development of viable private and public partnerships that support the funding of programs aimed at postponing pregnancy. Chief among these activities should be the commitment to increase the level and availability of funding for family planning services, as well as their variety and location. Such a policy requires the development of a strong political base that will place adolescent pregnancy prevention (and youth development and opportunities in general) on the agenda. Extensive efforts must be undertaken to expand existing family planning programs, which will entail overcoming the image of controversy that has enveloped the subject of family planning in recent years, largely as a result of the strident public argument over abortion policies. Federal and statewide policies that include prevention of adolescent pregnancy and access to family planning services are needed to provide an overall sense of direction to private and public institutions. These policies should also take cognizance of the adolescent social, health, education, and employment needs that surround the issue of adolescent pregnancy prevention.

An expanded family planning constituency that will support ongoing family planning programs should be a national priority. Family planning providers and agencies must play an active role in creating partnerships with families, schools, churches, clients, other service programs, business, and the media to implement strategies for reducing adolescent pregnancy. Many of these partnerships can, in turn, become the basis for establishing coalitions to lobby on behalf of adolescents and their right to receive confidential contraceptive services, and to nurture other community development efforts that affect youth. Communities must be well informed about the problem and consequences of unintended pregnancy; education helps build community consensus about strategies that should be implemented at the local level, including increased access to contraceptive services.[25]

Because teenage pregnancy is not a single, isolated phenomenon but a complex problem that results from many interrelated factors, intervention strategies must be multifaceted to be effective. Different groups of teenagers may require different outreach and program approaches. Racial, cultural, gender, age, and economic differences must be taken into account when designing these approaches. An ideal strategy would combine several of the models and elements I have described and implement them in combination with the use of a case manager, a continuous counselor, or an advocate providing counseling and brokerage of services to those adolescents at the highest risk of pregnancy.

In addition, community-based prevention, pregnancy, and early parenthood programs need to involve several organizations willing to coalesce around this issue. Such combined efforts produce greater efficiency in the use of available community resources and create links among a variety of concerned groups, resulting in greater coordination of service delivery to clients, the creation of a stronger sense of identity, a broader funding base, and the benefits of shared management and evaluation systems.

At a time when state and federal funding is increasingly limited to the most basic government services, programs in social services, health, and education will need to target adolescents whose social, economic, and educational profiles place them at the greatest risk of premature parenthood. Such special targeting may be especially necessary for programs that adopt intensive case-management approaches; their caseloads must be limited to ensure program effectiveness. Finally, it is important to recognize that efforts directed at reducing unintended adolescent pregnancy will be successful only if we also involve the political, economic, medical, educational, and religious institutions that exert a critical influence on any effort to reduce or prevent teenage pregnancy and childbearing.

Notes

1. D. M. Upchurch and J. McCarthy, "Adolescent Childbearing and High School Completion in the 1980s: Have Things Changed?" *Family Planning Perspectives* 21 (1989): 199; A. Geronimus and S. Korenman, "The Socioeconomic Consequences of Teen Childbearing Reconsidered." Research Report nos. 90–190 (Ann Arbor: University of Michigan Population Studies Center, 1990), p. 5.

2. Karen Pittman, "Preventing Adolescent Pregnancy: What School Can Do." Adolescent Pregnancy Clearinghouse publication (Washington, D.C.: Children's Defense Fund, September 1986), p. 4; Joy Dryfoos, "Youth at Risk: One in Four in Jeopardy." Unpublished report (New York: Carnegie Corporation, 1987), pp. 1–15; Hispanic Policy Development Project, "1980 High School Sophomores: Whites, Blacks, Hispanics—Where Are They Now?" *Research Bulletin* 1, 1 (Fall 1986): 3;

D. M. Upchurch and J. McCarthy, "The Timing of a First Birth and High School Completion," *American Sociological Review* 55, 2 (April 1990): 224–34.

3. Pittman, "Preventing Adolescent Pregnancy."

4. Melanie de Nys and Laura Wolfe, "Learning Her Place—Sex Bias in the Elementary School Classroom." Peer Report 5 (Washington, D.C.: National Organization for Women Legal Defense and Education Fund, 1985), p. 5.

5. Claire Brindis and Rita Jeremy, *Adolescent Pregnancy and Parenting in California: A Strategic Plan for Action* (San Francisco: Center for Reproductive Health Policy Research, Institute for Health Policy Studies, University of California, 1988), p. 46; A. Eugene Washington, "Pelvic Inflammatory Disease in Adolescents," *Research Highlights* 2, 6 (July/August 1986): 2 (available from the Institute for Health Policy Studies, University of California, San Francisco); Victor C. Strasburger, "Sex, Drugs, Rock 'n' Roll," *Pediatrics* 76, 4 (October 1985): 659–63; Joy Dryfoos, *Adolescents-at-Risk: Prevalence and Prevention* (New York: Oxford University Press, 1990), pp. 13–18.

6. Alan Guttmacher Institute, *Organized Family Planning Services in the United States, 1981–1983* (New York: Alan Guttmacher Institute, 1984), p. 12.

7. Lillian Tereszkiewicz and Claire Brindis, "School-Based Clinics Offer Health Care to Teens," *Youth Law News* 8, 5 (September/October 1986): 1–5.

8. Children's Defense Fund, "Building Health Programs for Teenagers." Adolescent Pregnancy Clearinghouse publication (Washington, D.C.: Children's Defense Fund, May 1986), p. 11; Laurie Zabin and Sam Clark, Jr., "Institutional Factors Affecting Teenagers' Choice and Reasons for Delay in Attending a Family Planning Clinic," *Family Planning Perspectives* 15, 1 (January/February 1983): 205–17.

9. Brindis and Jeremy, *Adolescent Pregnancy and Parenting in California*, p. 5.

10. S. M. Horwitz, L. V. Klerman, H. S. Kuo, and J. F. Jekel, "School-age Mothers: Predictors of Long-Term Educational and Economic Outcomes," *Pediatrics* 87, 6 (June 1991): 862–68.

11. Horwitz et al., "School-Age Mothers," 862–68; F. F. Furstenberg, J. Brooks-Gunn, and S. P. Morgan, *Adolescent Mothers in Later Life* (New York: Cambridge University Press, 1987), p. 232; D. F. Polit, "Effects of a Comprehensive Program for Teenage Parents: Five Years after Project Redirection," *Family Planning Perspectives* 21 (1989): 164–87.

12. Marion Howard and Judith McCabe, "Helping Teenagers Postpone Sexual Involvement," *Family Planning Perspectives* 22, 1 (1990): 21–26. Other recently developed curricula and projects that emphasize the strong advantages of abstinence and/or delaying adolescent pregnancy include the Life and Family National Demonstration Project operated by Search Institute in Minneapolis; the Family Life Model Demonstration Project operated by the Roman Catholic Diocese of Rochester, New York; the Fertility Appreciation for Families Project sponsored by Family of the Americas Foundation; "Will Power/Won't Power" and "Choices and Challenges" sponsored by the Girls Club of America; the Sex Respect Curriculum published by Respect for Sexuality; the Life Planning Education Curriculum created by the Center for Population Options; and the Prevention Education Curriculum available through ETR. Several of these programs feature curricula that seek to build the

assertiveness skills needed to say no to sex while teaching young people the potential economic, social, and emotional costs of early childbearing. Initial evaluations show that some of these programs have only a short-term effect, while others appear to have a longer-range impact. See Richard Barth, Joy Fetro, and Nancy Leland, *Preventing Teenage Pregnancy with Social and Cognitive Skills* (Santa Cruz, Calif.: ETR Associates, 1990). See Brindis and Jeremy, *Adolescent Pregnancy and Parenting in California*, for a discussion of these and other programs.

13. Joy Dryfoos, "Preventing Teen Pregnancy: What Works," *Planned Parenthood Review* 6 (1986): 6–8.

14. Karen Pittman, Sharon Adams-Taylor, and Ray O'Brien, "The Lessons of Multi-Site Initiatives Serving High Risk Youths." Adolescent Pregnancy Prevention Clearinghouse report (Washington, D.C.: Children's Defense Fund, 1989), p. 5; Claire Brindis, *Adolescent Pregnancy Prevention: A Guidebook for Communities* (Palo Alto, Calif.: Health Promotion Resource Center, Stanford Center for Research in Disease Prevention, 1991), pp. 8–14.

15. William Marsiglio and Frank Mott, "The Impact of Sex Education on Sexual Activity, Contraceptive Use and Premarital Pregnancy among American Teenagers," *Family Planning Perspectives* 18, 2 (1986): 151–61; Darlene Dawson, "The Effects of Sex Education on Adolescent Behavior," *Family Planning Perspectives* 18, 4 (1986): 162–70.

16. Murray Vincent, A. Clarie, and M. Schluchter, "Reducing Adolescent Pregnancy through School and Community-Based Education," *Journal of the American Medical Association* 257, 24 (1987): 3382–86.

17. *Ibid.*

18. Brindis and Jeremy, *Adolescent Pregnancy and Parenting in California*, pp. 115–16.

19. Laurie Zabin, Marilyn Hirsch, and Edward Smith, "Evaluation of a Pregnancy Prevention Program for Urban Teenagers," *Family Planning Perspectives* 18 (1986): 119–26.

20. Brindis and Jeremy, *Adolescent Pregnancy and Parenting in California*, pp. 47–48.

21. Marsiglio and Mott, "The Impact of Sex Education," 151–61.

22. Dawson, "The Effects of Sex Education," 162–70.

23. See Susan E. Harari and Maris A. Vinovskis, "Adolescent Sexuality, Pregnancy, and Childbearing in the Past" (chap. 1).

24. T. Ooms and S. Herendeen, "The Unique Health Needs of Adolescents: Implications for Health Care Insurance and Financing." A background briefing report and summary of meeting highlights developed for the Family Impact Seminar (Washington, D.C.: American Association for Marriage and Family Therapy, Research, and Education Foundation, 1988), pp. 4–6; Claire Brindis, "Reducing Adolescent Pregnancy—The Next Steps for Programs, Research, and Policy," *Family Life Educator* 9, 1 (Fall 1990): 15–20 (available from Network Publications, Santa Cruz, Calif.).

25. Vincent et al., "Reducing Adolescent Pregnancy," 3382–86.

CAROLE JOFFE

14 SEXUAL POLITICS AND THE TEENAGE PREGNANCY PREVENTION WORKER IN THE UNITED STATES

The present state of sexual politics in the United States—in which a highly visible and re-energized right wing is using sexuality-related issues as a chief means of mobilizing its supporters—has significant consequences for those who work in the field of teenage pregnancy prevention. This field, once regarded largely as the province of those in public health and social services, has now become a key battleground in the New Right's political offensive. The issue of teenage pregnancy, similar to those of AIDS, sex education, and above all abortion, has shown a significant capacity to draw once apolitical people into the political process.

The considerable politicization of sexual issues means that, even at the local level, matters that were once fairly straightforward—such as who can be hired, what they can say, and where they can say it—are now highly problematic, occasionally explosive. (On the day a new Planned Parenthood clinic opened in the Philadelphia suburbs, offering birth control but not abortions, gunshots were fired into its windows.)

In this chapter, I shall describe briefly the development of this phenomenon of the politicization of sexual issues in American society over the past twenty years, and I shall then discuss how this larger political climate informs the activities of a group of pregnancy prevention workers operating at the local level in the Philadelphia area. My argument will be that the activities of this group are indeed constrained very significantly by organized sexual conservatives; I shall also argue, however, that the agendas of prevention workers are complicated, in less evident ways, by the differential responses to teenage sexuality that exist among the providers themselves, and within their constituent communities.

The Rise of Sexual Politics, 1971–1992

The specific attacks on teenage pregnancy prevention programs discussed here must be understood in the context of the rise of the New Right, particularly its "pro-family" wing, which began to develop in this country during the 1970s. As a number of commentators have noted, a key distinguishing feature between the Old Right and the New Right is the emphasis put by the New on so-called social issues in contrast to the Old's concentration on foreign policy issues, especially the threat of international communism.[1] While it is true that such issues as school text books and sex education programs were of concern to Old Right groups like the John Birch Society, the decision to mobilize around "family" issues at the grass-roots level, especially among the previously nonpolitical, is distinctly New Right. The first successful campaign of this movement—"the opening shot in the battle over the family," in the words of one participant[2]—was the childcare bill passed by Congress in 1971. The bill was subsequently vetoed by President Richard Nixon, who, together with legislators, felt intense pressure from newly mobilized grass-roots activists, many of them housewives in church-based groups.

The pro-family movement continued to build momentum throughout the decade, with the Equal Rights Amendment campaign and the passage of the Supreme Court decision legalizing abortion in 1973, Roe v. Wade, serving as particularly important stimuli to conservatives. As Rosalind Petchesky has put it, the antiabortion movement that developed after *Roe* served as a "battering ram" for a host of additional New Right concerns, such as opposition to feminism, the welfare state, other issues of sexuality like homosexuality and birth control, and so on.[3] The White House Conferences on the Family, at the tail end of the Carter administration,[4] and especially the Reagan presidential campaign in 1980 further energized the pro-family movement, and abortion in particular became firmly implanted as a feature of American politics.

While abortion may occupy center stage as the pre-eminent issue of the pro-family movement, it is crucial to realize how closely linked, for anti-abortionists, are the issue of abortion and seemingly less charged matters like birth control and sex education. This connection is a historical development, which can be tied to the dramatic successes of the New Right in the 1970s and 1980s. Previously, the conventional rule of thumb in American politics—at least in electoral politics—was that it was considered legitimate, even among conservatives, for legislators who opposed abortion to support birth control "so as to make abortion unnecessary."[5] This historic compromise began to break down after the election of Ronald Reagan in 1980, primarily because the Reagan campaign payoffs to New Rightists occurred exactly in those branches of government most directly concerned with family issues, including sexuality. Although conservatives throughout the first Reagan administration complained bitterly about their exclusion from such centers of power as the State Department, Treasury Department, and so on, they *were* rewarded handsomely with key appointments in the Department of Health and Human Services and the Department of Education. For example, such crucial appointments as head of the Office of Population Affairs—that branch of government most directly concerned with the distribution of birth-control services—were offered to a succession of political appointees, whose major qualifications appeared to be long service in the Right-to-Life movement and other conservative causes.[6]

The Planned Parenthood Federation of America bears mention as a particuliar object of right-wing wrath. The federation's central involvement in the political defense of abortion nationally, as well as its provision of abortion and birth-control services through affiliates, meant enormous visibility for the organization during the 1970s and 1980s. To its opponents, Planned Parenthood has become, in the words of one antiabortion leader, "the most demonic force in American society today."[7]

Thus, ever since the election of Reagan, antiabortion activity in the federal government, and in many state governments, has become virtually inseparable from opposition to birth control and sex education. In the first months of the Reagan administration, New Right congressmen made repeated attempts to abolish Title X of the Public Health Act, the program that makes family planning services available at little or no cost to low-income women. Although Title X survives, it continues to be attacked and restricted in various ways by conservative legislators.[8] Title X is a particularly enraging program to many sexual conservatives because it provides free, confidential services to teenagers. The enormous usefulness of Title X as a negative symbol to the Right is that it combines two major features long opposed by conservatives, above and beyond the movement's opposition to birth control. First, it is a "social program," involving a federal bureaucracy, that makes services available free to the poor. Second, Title X represents the quintessential example of "big government's" willingness to override parental authority, because of the stipulation that teenagers may receive confidential services.

The major national initiatives against teenage sexuality by sexual conservatives in government have been through legislation passed in the late 1970s during the Carter administration, the Adolescent Family Life Act.[9] This legislation, one of the first acts intended to confront directly the newly acknowledged issue of teenage pregnancy, was forced by political pressure to redirect its mission from pregnancy prevention—that is, a focus on birth-control education and services—to services for already pregnant teenagers. A further redefinition of the program took place in the Reagan era when the promotion of sexual abstinence among teenagers became the centerpiece of the Office of Adolescent Pregnancy. Among the most visible, and in certain circles most ridiculed, programs associated with this agency have been the so-called Chastity Centers, a network of counseling centers established with the specific purpose of urging sexual abstinence among teenage females.

While the "Chastity Center" program itself has been continually embroiled in the courts, because of alleged violations of church-state separation in the use of federal funds (since many grants were made to religious institutions),[10] the significance of this program is nonetheless considerable. It squarely established sexual abstinence as an official "policy" response by sexual conservatives to the problems of teenage sexuality and childbearing. Connaught Marshner, a leading New Right spokeswoman, has summarized well the divide between the pro-family movement and others on the matter of teenage pregnancy: "They [liberals] begin with the premise that teenagers should not have babies. We begin with the premise that single teenagers should not have sex."[11]

As I shall make clear later in this chapter, it is in fact not only pro-family adherents who believe in sexual abstinence for teenagers. Many, if not most, "liberals" who work directly in the field of pregnancy prevention also deeply believe in the desirability of the choice of abstinence for teenagers, and they actively promote this option. The key difference of course is that, historically, most prevention programs presented abstinence as one of several options for teenagers, in a context that also included information on birth control. The control of federal and state programs by pro-family appointees means that agencies in need of funds will increasingly be pressured to make proposals that focus *only* on abstinence; similarly, we can expect that educational materials—on both disease and pregnancy prevention—prepared by government bureaucracies will increasingly cite only abstinence, and that the media, which already have a long-standing aversion to the advertising of contraceptives, will quite likely emphasize abstinence in editorials and public service spots, with perhaps some exceptions made in response to the AIDS crisis.[12]

And what of sexual politics in the George Bush era? As of this writing, near the end of Bush's fourth year, it is clear that although the far-right wing may have less influence overall than during the Reagan presidency, sexual conservatives remain tightly in control of reproductive matters. Or, put somewhat differently, George Bush—whose claims to the Reagan legacy have always been distrusted by New Right leaders—has chosen abortion as the issue that will demonstrate his conservative credentials.

Thus the Bush presidency has been marked by events very similar to those of the Reagan years: the intense scrutiny (and veto power) by New Right loyalists of important presidential appointees like Louis Sullivan to head the Department of Health and Human Services, ensuring that such nominees pass the abortion "litmus test"[13]; the scandals created by conservative legislators and bureaucrats over two large-scale surveys on sexual behavior—proposed by social scientists to a government agency as a means to better information on how to combat AIDS—which ultimately resulted in the surveys' demise[14]; the continued wrangling over Title X; the continuing freeze on policies that would allow research on fetal tissue obtained from abortions[15]; and the Bush administration's promotion of an "import ban" on RU-486, which has prevented research on this drug's abortifacient and other medical uses, such as treatment for breast cancer.[16]

But it has been the Supreme Court that has raised abortion politics to a feverish pitch in the early 1990s, through the antiabortion sentiments that were a factor in the selection of the justices Bush appointed and the Court's abortion-related decisions under Bush. The 1989 *Webster* decision upheld states' abilities severely to regulate abortion services, and two decisions the following year upheld requirements that parents be notified when teenagers receive abortions.[17] The Rust v. Sullivan decision, handed down in May 1991, will have the most impact on family planning—as well as abortion—services. In this decision, the Court upheld a ruling that prohibited employees in federally funded family planning clinics from counseling patients about the option of abortion. *Rust* stimulated enormous public reaction—as much for its perceived assault on free speech as for its antiabortion character—and Congress passed legislation to overturn the so-called gag-rule provisions of this decision. President Bush promptly vetoed this legislation, and an attempt to override the veto failed by twelve votes.[18] A number of Title X clinics, at which many teenagers receive family planning services, have announced their unwillingness to comply with the provisions of the gag rule, and at this writing it is not clear to what extent family planning services will be curtailed because of the loss of federal funding. Finally, a number of abortion cases making their way toward the Supreme Court will offer the Court the opportunity to overturn Roe v. Wade outright.[19]

In short, the heightened tensions around the abortion issue will doubtless have enormous impact on the larger climate of sexual politics in the country in the foreseeable future—although in ways not entirely clear. On the one hand, it seems indisputable that the politicization of sexuality will continue and intensify as a force in American society. Especially if *Roe* is overturned, the abortion struggle will become even more visible and bitter than it has been in the past, with battlegrounds ranging from the 1992 presidential elections to local sites such as hospitals, clinics, and private doctor's offices (and homes).[20] Predictably, sexual conservatives in charge of governmental programs will renew their arguments against birth-control programs as a *cause* of unwanted pregnancy and will, in some cases, make the argument that some forms of birth control should themselves be considered abortifacients. Family planning workers will argue, along with other pro-choice adherents, that it is the young and the poor who will most likely be the first to suffer under abortion restrictions, and thus will be the most vulnerable to illegal and dangerous abortionists.

On the other hand, it may be that the increasing precariousness of legal abortion will lead to a renewed legitimacy of birth control among the American public (and hence among elected officials). The dramatic changes in access to abortion that would inevitably follow from an overturning of *Roe* might serve, therefore, to begin to uncouple politically the issues of abortion and contraception that were so successfully linked by the Right in the 1980s.[21] Perhaps the one certainty of which we can speak is that the immediate future will not see any "resolution" of the issues under discussion here.

"Project Working Together" in Philadelphia

The national climate of sexual conservatism is best illustrated by examining its impact in practice; the activities of a group of teenage pregnancy prevention workers in the Philadelphia area provide a useful case study. In this region, a number of factors converge to make the atmosphere for teenage pregnancy prevention work particularly inhospitable. There is a large Catholic population with a very visible and, in comparison with other cities, conservative archdiocese. The influence of the archdiocese extends in matters beyond the church, especially those involving disputes over sexual morality. For example, there are periodic flare-ups in the city of Philadelphia over the disposition of United Way funds, with the church arguing against any provision of support to institutions that perform or facilitate abortions. Similarly, the church exerts some informal influence on such measures as sex education in the public schools and the establishment of school-based clinics that provide contraceptive services.

The city also has a loosely connected network of quite conservative clergymen, black, white, and Hispanic, who take similarly negative stands against sex education and, especially, the notion of dispensing contraception in the schools.[22] Finally, in the Philadelphia area, as in the state as a whole, there is a particularly strong antiabortion movement, with virtually all freestanding abortion clinics in the area under chronic siege. In the immediate aftermath of the *Webster* decision, Pennsylvania was the first state successfully to implement restrictions on abortion services, and Planned Parenthood v. Casey, a Pennsylvania case that reached the Supreme Court in 1992, while not achieving its intended goal of overturning *Roe*, did succeed in establishing further massive restrictions on abortion services.

In this decidedly challenging climate, a local foundation committed a substantial amount of money to eleven agencies in the city of Philadelphia and the surrounding counties for "innovative" programs in teenage pregnancy prevention. Funding began in 1988 for a period of three years. Collectively, these funded programs are known as Project Working Together. Although each agency is charged with developing its own unique program, providers from each agency meet together periodically, and a strong sense of colleagueship has emerged. Generally speaking, the major emphases of the Working Together programs are these: to develop new outreach strategies (with local schools as a prime, although not sole, target); to develop a regionwide media campaign that is both effective and acceptable in a politically conservative environment; to target younger (that is, aged 14 and below) adolescents for programming, and to encourage them to delay sexual activity; and to develop new clinic procedures that will make visiting a clinic a less fearful and more positive experience. Such procedures include walk-in clinics specifically for teenagers and an ambitious experiment entitled "Smart Start," which involves offering teenagers the option to delay pelvic examinations and blood tests when they first receive contraceptive services.

The school district in Philadelphia, although a prime target of this project's efforts, has been extremely resistant to family planning and sex education activities for about the past ten years. Whereas previously there had been a fair amount of contraceptive and sexual information allowed in the

Philadelphia schools, since about 1980—because of the factors I outlined above—there have been very strict controls on outside speakers coming into the schools. Speakers and materials connected with Planned Parenthood, for example, have been absolutely banned from school grounds. A sex education curriculum that included contraceptive information was held up for several years thanks to conservative opposition, and once in place, according to numerous observers, it has been only selectively implemented.

In spite of this forbidding context, recent experiences of some of the Working Together staff suggest a changing atmosphere in the schools. Undeniably, these changes are driven by concern about AIDS and drug use. These two issues, with the obvious threats they pose to a low-income population, appear to be taken quite seriously by the Philadelphia and regional school districts,[23] and they have led to a new openness toward outsiders, which the pregnancy prevention workers are skillfully exploiting. For example, several of the outreach workers associated with the Working Together programs manage to enter the schools on "AIDS Awareness Days" and then proceed to talk about condom use as a measure against AIDS, rather than solely as a measure to prevent pregnancy. Although the drug issue may seem to be one step removed from pregnancy prevention, here too outreach workers have skillfully capitalized on drug concerns to maneuver their way into the schools—arguing the link between drug use and AIDS, and then between AIDS transmission and unprotected intercourse.

One reason, of course, why these workers are managing to enter the schools through these routes is that despite the politics of central school administrators, many individual principals and teachers desperately want their students to have information on pregnancy prevention and sexual behavior. There seems to be considerable variation, both within city and regional schools, as to how much autonomy individual principals and teachers feel they have vis-à-vis their superiors. Similarly, there are variations among top-level central administrators as to their commitment to pregnancy prevention activities and, correspondingly, their willingness to take political heat on this issue.

Although many of the Working Together staff speak with frustration of an inability even to get into the schools, or of plans that are cancelled at the last minute because of a principal who gets cold feet, others tell of teachers and principals who do not seem to share their colleagues' sense of caution and intimidation. Perhaps the most extreme case of this was a teacher in a suburban county who first invited one of the project workers to speak in her classroom about sexual responsibility, including birth-control options, and shortly thereafter personally brought one of her female students to the clinic for family planning services. As the worker said, "'We couldn't believe it!' But she [the teacher] said, 'This is on my own time, after school hours, and I really feel this kid is at risk for a pregnancy—which she certainly would not be able to handle.'"

In some schools, moreover, outreach workers are being "officially" allowed access to students without the pretense of being there as drug or AIDS prevention workers. (Technically, of course, one can argue that these days in fact all pregnancy prevention workers are also AIDS workers as well, since information on this and other sexually transmitted diseases is now a standard part of each family planning worker's "rap.") Even in this changing climate, however, the negotiations surrounding the circumstances of outreach worker involvement in the schools are highly circumscribed. Here, for example, are portions of a directive sent by a school official to various clinics to offer various programs within certain schools: "Any pamphlets or instructional aids identified as being associated with Planned Parenthood, CHOICE [a health referral hotline in Philadelphia], Center for Population Options [a national organization that distributes family planning information] and the Family Planning Council [the organization that serves as the conduit for Title X funds in the Philadelphia area] *may not* be distributed to students" (emphasis in original—presumably this ban reflects the fact that all these groups are associated in one way or another with a pro-choice stand on the abortion issue). "Any class discussion on abortion must be confined to a definition and may not include counseling." And, "Dispersal and information re: procurement of condoms to students is prohibited."

As these quotations indicate, the abortion issue is particularly heavy baggage for the teenage pregnancy prevention worker. And this is true not only in school-related efforts but in other community outreach efforts as well. Although the Working Together projects are not, strictly speaking, involved with abortions, they are all located in facilities that either provide abortions or offer abortion counseling and referrals. The abortion taint is particularly evident when it comes to the several Planned Parenthood affiliates funded by the program. One success story in particular illustrates both the special burden the name Planned Parenthood carries and the chilling effect of the abortion controversy on its workers' perceptions of what constitutes feasible programming. Two outreach workers from a suburban county Planned Parenthood affiliate put considerable effort into organizing a "community forum" on teenage pregnancy. This was not a simple task, because the community has a number of extremely active Right-to-Life groups and other church-based pro-family groups that regularly picket the clinics of this affiliate, even though no abortions are performed there. In short, in this community, as in many others, Planned Parenthood has been successfully portrayed as "controversial," and even community groups with no official position on abortion find it simplest to avoid association with the organization. The workers nonetheless succeeded in getting several churches and other community groups, such as Big Brothers and Big Sisters, to co-sponsor the event and to help ensure an audience drawn from their memberships. The secret of their success, according to the organizers, was always to place Planned Parenthood last on the list of sponsors, even though it did virtually all the work.

The forum itself consisted of five speakers, all of them teenage parents (four female and one male).[24] Although the message from each was "Don't make the same mistake I did" (given in a particularly poignant fashion by the male, who spoke of having had to give up a college athletic scholarship in order to support his daughter), what was striking was the absence of any speaker who had chosen an abortion as a response to an unwanted pregnancy. The organizers concluded (quite correctly, in my view) that to have had such a speaker would have jeopardized the event and made any future collaborative community events impossible.

Another instance of a Working Together project's self-imposed taboo on public discussion of abortion occurred when a young indigent woman, known to a worker through outreach efforts, became pregnant for the second time. The worker learned (quite late in the pregnancy) through a third party that this teenager had wanted an abortion but did not know how to obtain one free of charge. The outreach worker felt enormously frustrated ("This is a person living in squalor in one room with five other people, who can't take care of the one kid she has") because, had the worker been informed of the pregnancy in time, she could have arranged a subsidized abortion. She acknowledged that because of her policy of never mentioning the abortion issue in our outreach efforts—to avoid controversy—it was reasonable that this pregnant teenager had not thought to ask her for help.

Such incidents give some flavor of the uncertain terrain in which pregnancy prevention workers must currently operate. Some settings are absolutely closed to them—this is especially true for those who work at Planned Parenthood affiliates. More often, however, some settings are open to them *sometimes*, depending on the predisposition of a particular administrator, principal, or agency director. Even when entrée is gained, however, negotiations typically take place as to what can and cannot be mentioned (for example, birth control but not abortion, or abstinence but not birth-control methods). Faced with their perception of the enormity of the problems with which they are attempting to deal—too many premature pregnancies and skyrocketing rates of sexually transmitted diseases— pregnancy prevention workers obviously find the climate of hostility (or, at best, uncertainty) tremendously frustrating.

Internal Differences among Working Together Staff

It would be a mistake, however, to understand the situation facing these workers as simply that of a cohesive group being constrained by powerful right-wing forces. To understand the politics of pregnancy prevention efforts we must also consider the interesting internal differences among the workers themselves as to the appropriate messages to give teenagers. These differences appear to exist, in complex ways, along generational and racial lines.

In generational terms, most of these workers can be divided into two groups, "idealists" and "realists." The idealists (typically older than 40) primarily counsel sexual abstinence (more specifically, abstinence from intercourse), while the realists (usually younger than 40) are more likely to view teenage sexual activity as inevitable and hence focus on responsible use of contraceptives. The generational differences also have a racial cast, in that the strongest idealists tend to be middle-aged black women, while the strongest realists tend to be younger white women. The younger black women and the handful of younger black men in Project Working Together also tend to present themselves as realists, although these younger blacks are mindful of the sensibilities of the idealists. The lack of any white frontline staff older than 40 in these projects makes it difficult to say how completely racial and generational differences converge here, but the differences between younger and older blacks makes one suspect that the division is primarily generational.

In the real world, of course, both idealist and realist workers juggle both messages—for example, lauding the virtues of delaying intercourse but also explaining how to get and use contraceptives. Nevertheless, a worker's choice of camp does affect in powerful, if subtle, ways the worker's relationship with teenage clients. An illustration of the differences in approach between realist and idealist workers occurred at an informal meeting of staff from a number of Working Together projects. Susan, a young white woman in her twenties, was demonstrating a video tape she had made for discussion with teenagers. The video contained snippets from various MTV videos and scenes from Spike Lee's film *School Daze*. Susan's rationale for preparing this kind of video, which contained many quite sexually explicit scenes, was that her video drew on films, songs, and existing videos with which teenagers were already most engaged, enabling her to give a "guided discussion" of such issues as the objectification of females, the use of sex in exchange for material objects, and so forth.

Reactions to Susan's video among other workers present varied greatly. While some—especially staff in their twenties—were quite enthusiastic and wished to use her tape in their own programs, others were decidedly less enthusiastic. Sylvia, a black woman in her fifties, who led teenage discussion groups at a community health center in a working-class black neighborhood, shook her head throughout the tape. When I asked the group if they would feel comfortable showing this tape at their agencies, her answer was an emphatic "NO! . . . I don't want to show them *more* MTV . . . I want to get those kids out of heat!"

This incident is revealing for several reasons. Besides making clear the workers' differing responses to teenage sexual activity—which seemed to fall quite strongly along generational lines—the video incident suggests the extent to which racial questions were also a powerful, if largely unspoken, issue influencing reactions to this particular tape and, indeed, to most of the project's materials. Virtually all the singers and actors in the tape are black, and, for a complex of reasons,[25] nearly all the participants in Working Together programming are either black or Hispanic. Thus, when the members of Working Together's multiracial staff talk among themselves about "the problem of teenage pregnancy" or, more pointedly, the problem of "irresponsible sexual behavior among teens," they are usually talking about minority youth. Inevitably, there is a certain amount of awkwardness, especially for minority staff, in such conversations with colleagues (although, in general, the interracial relations among them seem quite strong).

But the significance of the staff's racial differences goes beyond occasional awkwardness and must be understood in terms of the different agendas that white and nonwhite members of staff bring to this work. The white members see pregnancy prevention among youth (especially females) as their primary function. They have a primarily individualistic bias, in the sense that they are focused on helping individual teenagers have a chance for the "better" life (that is, finishing school and establishing a career), which is arguably dependent on delayed childbearing. The black and Hispanic workers, of course, do not disagree with this agenda. But they go beyond it and see as another appropriate focus of Project Working Together the reconstruction of minority families and minority communities.

According to these workers' beliefs, many individual families—indeed, whole communities—have been tremendously weakened by rampant premature pregnancy (as well as by drugs and economic catastrophe). Among minority workers, far more than among their white colleagues, one hears concerns about the impact of premature childbearing on the teenager's family of origin (especially the new grandmother, who very likely will be called upon to raise the teenager's child) as well as on the teenage mother herself; similarly, minority staff members are far more likely to worry about the consequences of inadequate parenting for the children of teenagers. Put another way, whereas whites primarily worry about what premature childbearing does to the teenager's life chances, minority workers worry about what it does to the minority community as a whole.

Therefore, minority workers see as a crucial aspect of their work the building of stronger ties between teenagers and their parents, and the building of bases of support between the households of the families with which they deal. In this family-based context, the strong advocacy of sexual abstinence that occurs in many programs is intended not only as a means of birth control but also as a route to re-establish parental and community authority over teenagers.

The use of pregnancy prevention programs as a means to "community reconstitution" can be seen very strongly in those projects tied to neighborhood-based institutions (as opposed to hospital or Planned Parenthood affiliates). One particularly striking incident occurred in a parent-child discussion series held in a community health center.[26] Although ostensibly oriented toward "sexual communication" between parent and child, with the express purpose of helping family members in their efforts to delay sexual activity among younger adolescents, the series in fact turned into a generalized support group for the mostly single-parent families who attended. One evening, after a mother had told a particularly harrowing story of being terrorized in her own home by her daughter's boyfriend, a drug user, the leader commented that the mother should have telephoned group members to come to her aid: "*You* are each other's families now."

The greater emphasis put by minority workers on family and community creates its own set of dilemmas. The courting by staff of parents and influential community leaders, especially local ministers, to become involved in Working Together programming often means pressures to adopt a strong "antisex" line, which workers know will jeopardize their credibility among many teenagers. Sylvia, the black worker I mentioned earlier, summarized the problem well: "We have to figure out programs that don't scare the parents and don't bore the kids."

While the staff may share the parents' goal of "restoring parental authority," this too creates problems, because the staff typically advocate a more democratic relationship between parent and child than some parents would like. This is particularly true in cases where parents' strategies for preventing unwanted pregnancy have been to impose what are seen (by staff as well as teenagers) as excessively strict limits, like not allowing daughters out of the house after school.

In sum, a powerful and vigilant political movement of sexual conservatism, internal differences among workers, and further differences between the workers and their constituencies all complicate the activities of those who seek to prevent pregnancy among teenagers. By focusing on the various constraints inherent in this work, however, it is decidedly not my intention to suggest that pregnancy prevention workers are not doing an effective job. On the contrary, it is noteworthy that, given such constraints, they remain as dedicated and effective as they are.

Notes

I thank Jane Balin, Lisa Ratmansky, and Saskia Subramanian for their field assistance and for many helpful discussions. I am also grateful for the research assistance of Eve Hershkopf and the editorial advice of Deborah Rhode.

1. Alan Crawford, *Thunder on the Right: The "New Right" and the Politics of Resentment* (New York: Pantheon, 1988); Rosalind Petchesky, *Abortion and Women's Choice: The State, Sexuality and Reproductive Freedom* (Boston: Northeastern University Press, 1990), chap. 2: "The Antiabortion Movement and the Rise of the New Right," pp. 241–85.

2. Onalee McGraw, *The Family, Feminism and the Therapeutic State* (Washington, D.C.: Heritage Foundation, 1980), p. 2.

3. Petchesky, *Abortion*, p. 242.

4. Gilbert Steiner, *The Futility of Family Policy* (Washington, D.C.: Brookings Institute, 1981), chap. 2.

5. Carole Joffe, "The Abortion Struggle in American Politics," *Dissent* (Summer 1981): 268–71.

6. Carole Joffe, *The Regulation of Sexuality: Experiences of Family Planning Workers* (Philadelphia: Temple University Press, 1986), pp. 42–43. A famous example of this kind of appointment that "backfired" is the case of C. Everett Koop, the Philadelphia physician who was appointed by Reagan to be surgeon general; Koop had virtually no public-health background but did have excellent credentials as an antiabortion crusader. He proved to be extremely controversial, though—and an unexpected hero of liberals—when, in response to the AIDS crisis, he advocated very straightforward education about condom use to schoolchildren. He further enraged conservatives, and delighted liberals, when he refused to issue a report, requested by the Reagan administration, that "proved" longlasting negative effects on the

physical and mental health of abortion recipients. An illuminating account of the repeated attempts at control of the surgeon general's office by Reagan staffers—and Koop's determined resistance—is found in Koop's book, *Koop: The Memoirs of America's Family Doctor* (New York: Random House, 1991).

7. *Moral Majority Report*, 25 June 1985.

8. For further discussion of the ongoing attempt to modify Title X, especially as it pertains to teenagers, see Deborah L. Rhode, "Adolescent Pregnancy and Public Policy" (chap. 15).

9. Steiner, *Family Policy*, chap. 3; Maris Vinovskis, *An "Epidemic" of Adolescent Pregnancy? Some Historical and Policy Perspectives* (New York: Oxford University Press, 1988), chaps. 1 and 2; and Constance Nathanson, *Dangerous Passage: The Social Control of Sexuality in Women's Adolescence* (Philadelphia: Temple University Press, 1991).

10. Bowen v. Kendrick, 487 U.S. 589 (1988).

11. Connaught Marshner, *The New Traditional Woman* (Washington, D.C.: Free Congress Research and Education Foundation, 1982), p. 9.

12. Cheryl Hayes, ed., *Risking the Future: Adolescent Sexuality, Pregnancy, and Childbearing* (Washington, D.C.: National Academy of Sciences, 1987), pp. 91–92: "Advertising of nonprescription contraceptives is essentially banned by broadcasters [and] advertising of prescription methods is prohibited by the federal government." In the aftermath of the stunning announcement, in November 1991, by basketball star Magic Johnson of his infection with the AIDS virus, hopes were raised anew that the television networks would change their advertising policy. However, in the period immediately following this incident, only the Fox network announced its willingness to advertise condoms—but "only if condoms are promoted as a method of disease prevention; those [ads] that refer to contraception will not be used." *Washington Memo*, 22 November 1991, p. 6.

13. On the Sullivan nomination, which was marked by the nominee making several conflicting statements about his abortion position, see "Cabinet Choice Fielding Hard Questions in Drills," *New York Times*, 5 February 1989, p. 26. On the continued use of the abortion "litmus test" in Bush appointments, see "President Picks Hispanic Woman to Become U.S. Surgeon General," *New York Times*, 18 October 1989, p. 20.

14. "Sex Study of Students Cancelled Because Conservatives Object," *New York Times*, 21 July 1991, p. A-11; "Apprehensive NIH Defers Sex Survey: Political Concerns Cited for Decision," *Washington Post*, 25 September 1991, p. A-1.

15. Rachel Gold and Dorothy Lehrman, "Fetal Research under Fire: The Influence of Abortion Politics," *Family Planning Perspectives* 21, 1 (January/February 1989): 10–12.

16. Michael Klitsch, "Antiprogestins and the Abortion Controversy: A Progress Report," *Family Planning Perspectives* 23, 6 (November/December 1991): 275–82.

17. Webster v. Reproductive Health Services, 492 U.S. 490 (1989); Hodgson v. Minnesota, 110 S. Ct. 2926 (1990); and Ohio v. Akron Center for Reproductive Health, 110 S. Ct. 2972 (1990).

18. Rust v. Sullivan, 111 S. Ct. 1759 (1991). On the origins of the gag rule as an

administrative coup by New Right operatives within the Reagan administration, see Walter Dellinger, "Gag Me With a Rule," *New Republic* (6 and 13 January 1992): 14–16.

19. In June 1992 the Supreme Court handed down its decision on a Pennsylvania case, Planned Parenthood v. Casey, a decision which many had anticipated would involve a flat overturning of Roe v. Wade. The Court, although upholding most of the restrictions contained in *Casey*, nonetheless reaffirmed, by a 5–4 majority, the basic legitimacy of *Roe*. Though in some respects this reaffirmation can be seen as a pro-choice victory, it was nonetheless made clear, at the time of the *Casey* decision, that four of the current Justices stand ready to overturn *Roe*—which ties the immediate fate of *Roe* to the presidential elections of 1992. Had George Bush won reelection, he would have had the capacity—and almost certainly the opportunity—to appoint the deciding fifth, anti-*Roe* Justice. Other abortion cases from Guam, Louisiana, and Utah now making their way toward the Supreme Court will offer it further opportunities in the near future to reconsider the fate of *Roe*.

20. According to Stanley Henshaw, "85% of nonhospital facilities that served 400 or more abortion patients a year reported some form of antiabortion harassment in 1988." See "The Accessibility of Abortion Services in the United States," *Family Planning Perspectives* 23, 6 (November/December 1991): 246.

21. Shortly after the observations for this chapter were completed, and coinciding with the introduction of Norplant, the contraceptive implant, into the United States at the end of 1990, a new willingness arose among certain conservative politicians to advocate coercive contraception, with Norplant, in particular, being touted by some as an "answer" to the "welfare crisis." In some respects, of course, this should be seen not as a "new development but rather as a return to older forms of eugenic discourse, which are always a possibility in any discussion of the dissemination of birth-control technology. It remains to be seen how this older "population control" motif, long a staple of conservative thought, will coexist with the more recent anti-birth-control sentiments of New Right conservatives. See Matthew Rees, "Shot in the Arm: The Use and Abuse of Norplant," *New Republic*, 9 December 1991): 16–17.

22. In spring 1991, in response to a proposal (eventually passed) to distribute condoms in Philadelphia high schools, an influential organization of black clergy strongly opposed the proposal, citing the "biblical principle of sexual abstinence before marriage." "Black Ministers Oppose Condoms for City Schools," *Philadelphia Inquirer*, 9 May 1991, p. B-1.

23. This apparent openness to AIDS education by Philadelphia-area administrators is matched by nationwide data suggesting that of all teachers currently providing sex education, "90–96% cover AIDS . . . and only 52% provide information about sources of birth control." Jacqueline D. Forrest and Jane Silverman, "What Public School Teachers Teach about Preventing Pregnancy, AIDS, and Sexually Transmitted Diseases," *Family Planning Perspectives* 21, 2 (March/April 1989): 65–72.

24. In this section, I am particularly indebted to field observations done by Saskia Subramanian.

25. In part, this racial breakdown in program use reflects the extreme segrega-

tion of Philadelphia housing patterns; a number of the Project Working Together programs are located in virtually all-black or Hispanic neighborhoods. In other agencies, with more mixed populations, whites may make use of clinic services, but, with few exceptions, they do not take part in Working Together *programming* (e.g., discussion groups and peer education projects). Although I do not have any direct data bearing on this question, it is reasonable to assume, as some Working Together staff have suggested to me, that this is another manifestation of the racial separateness characteristic of other similar social services in the area: a program perceived as "black" will be shunned by whites.

26. In this section I draw on field observations done by Jane Balin.

DEBORAH L. RHODE

15 ADOLESCENT PREGNANCY AND PUBLIC POLICY

Although teenage pregnancy has recently emerged as a major social "problem," its frequency is by no means a recent social phenomenon. The appropriate age for sexual relations and parenthood has always been a matter of cultural definition, and in the United States it has varied considerably across time, region, class, race, ethnicity, and gender. Over the past two centuries, the age at which childbirth is biologically possible has declined, while the period of adolescents' economic dependence has increased. One result of these changes has been a growing cultural conflict over reproductive choices during the transition to adulthood. During the past two decades, the rising birth rate among unmarried teenagers has prompted increasing national concern but no coherent policy. Much of the problem stems from disputes over the nature of the problem. Is the primary issue morality, fertility, or poverty? What choices should adolescents make in sexual relationships, what role should the state play in shaping the choices available, and who should decide those questions?

This chapter explores public policies on adolescent pregnancy against their broader historical, legal, and socioeconomic backgrounds. Its central premise is that such policies have frequently misdescribed the problem and misled as to the solution. Too often, decision makers have located the problem at the individual level and faulted teens who want "too much too soon" in sexual relationships. Insufficient attention has focused on the societal level, on structures that offer female adolescents "too little too late": too little reason to stay in school, too little assistance in birth control, too little opportunity for childcare, health services, vocational training or decent jobs, and too little understanding of the responsibilities of single parenthood. Both legislative and judicial decision making has proceeded without adequate information on the experience of women or the consequences of various public policies.[1]

To understand the limitations of current frameworks, some historical background is useful. Since specific policies toward adolescent pregnancy are a recent development, their evolution must be understood in terms of broader reproductive, family, and regulatory patterns. An overview of those patterns suggests certain dynamics that are particularly relevant to contemporary debates: the variation in cultural norms concerning teenage sexuality and the class and racial biases in public policy responses.

Historical material on adolescent sexual activity is limited, in part because only in the last century has adolescence been recognized as a distinct developmental phase. However, research on premarital intercourse, premarital pregnancy, and out-of-wedlock births provides some indirect evidence of cultural norms.[2]

Until the nineteenth century, American attitudes toward early childbearing were relatively permissive. Pregnancy among very young adolescents was rare, since the average age of menstruation was 15 or older. Available evidence reveals no strong prejudice against teenage fertility when the couple was willing to marry and could become economically independent. Nor was premarital sexual intercourse among adolescents seen as especially problematic. Although many colonial communities made efforts to punish fornicators of all ages, intimacy during courtship met with somewhat greater tolerance, as the practice of bundling in New England and Middle Atlantic regions suggests. Because courting couples often lived at considerable distance from each other, in housing that had little heat, privacy, or extra space, they were often permitted to share the same bed as long as they remained fully clothed or kept a bundling board between them. Sexual intercourse was not expected to occur, but if it did the parties were expected to marry. The assumption was that a woman would go from her father's to her husband's household without any intervening period of independence. Bastardy was a serious offense in a culture that made families the central social and economic unit. The mother—and father if he could be identified—was subject to criminal penalties and social opprobrium, while the child experienced similar stigmas and various legal disabilities. Until the mid-eighteenth century rates of illegitimacy remained low, around 3 percent of all births, although rates of premarital pregnancy varied over time and region; an estimated one in three brides was pregnant among seventeenth-century Chesapeake immigrants and one in ten among New England residents.[3]

During the latter part of the eighteenth century, premarital pregnancies and out-of-wedlock births began to rise. The increase in part reflected greater geographical mobility and the breakdown of stable communities during the war and post-war periods. Formal enforcement of bastardy and fornication laws ceased, and informal sanctions weakened. For some young women, pregnancy also became a means of insuring that they rather than their parents controlled the choice of husband. By the late eighteenth century, an estimated 30 percent of brides were pregnant. Most premarital intercourse took place as part of courtship, but if pregnancy occurred and marriage did not, the costs were borne disproportionately by women. Paternity could be difficult to prove and fathers difficult to locate. Special hardships fell on indentured servants who were impregnated by already married masters.[4]

For women of color, sexual norms evolved out of different cultural traditions and, for blacks, out of different sociolegal constraints imposed by slavery. Many Native American tribes condoned premarital intercourse and among some a first birth usually preceded marriage. Under bondage, blacks had no formal right to marry and their African heritage often provided no sanctions against premarital sexual activity. In a plantation culture, early fertility increased women's value. Accordingly, many slave communities did not stigmatize premarital intercourse or childbirth, although couples typically preferred stable unions when possible.[5]

In the mid-nineteenth century, the growth of religious revival movements and moral reform societies, together with the cultural idealization of domesticity, more actively discouraged adolescent sexual relations. Conventional medical wisdom, which assumed that early intercourse drained "vital life forces," also contributed to that trend. Rates of premarital pregnancy declined to 10 percent and in white middle-class communities a strong double standard prevailed. The increasing importance of education, particularly for males, counseled against early marriage, while for most young women pregnancy without marriage was disastrous; the inadequacy of work and welfare options for mothers made single parenthood difficult, if not impossible. Gender discrimination in employment was widespread, and until the Depression, public assistance programs provided meager subsidies, while frequently excluding unmarried or otherwise "unfit" mothers from coverage. The social stigma against "fallen" women added to these difficulties and the law did little to cushion their impact. Judicial determination of paternity and enforcement of child support was available in theory but often inaccessible in practice, given the financial, procedural, and psychological burdens of litigation. For most female adolescents, marriage was the only respectable solution to an early pregnancy. However, at least from an economic standpoint, that solution generally did not represent a major sacrifice, since few women expected to develop the educational and employment skills that would permit financial independence.[6]

Among some groups of women, the sanctions against premarital sexual activity were less pronounced. Young urban working-class women were less subject to community or family oversight and accounted for most of the rise of premarital pregnancy rates, to around 23 percent at the close of the nineteenth century. Although relatively well-to-do blacks assimilated white middle-class norms of chastity, many lower-class and rural black communities condoned premarital intercourse and out-of-wedlock births. Particularly among tenant farming families, child labor was a crucial economic asset, and early fertility often enhanced rather than diminished a woman's standing. Such attitudes frequently persisted among migrants. Within these communities, young single mothers received support from kinship networks that mitigated the costs of nonmarital childbearing.[7]

In the culture generally, rates of premarital sexual intercourse jumped sharply during the 1920s and then remained stable until the 1960s. A variety of forces contributed to the liberalization of sexual mores: urbanization, wartime experiences, media images, and rising opportunities for unchaperoned activities in college, automobiles, and recreation centers such as dance halls. Kinsey's 1948 study reported that about half of all women and 90 percent of men had engaged in premarital sexual intercourse. But until the late 1960s, most women, particularly white middle-class women, viewed such intimacy as a prelude to marriage, and the dominant culture retained strong sanctions against out-of-wedlock births. Adolescents received mixed messages; the popularization of Freudian psychology and the sexual imagery flooding the media made intimate relations seem more acceptable, while teen advice manuals, parental pressures, and socioeconomic constraints gave the opposite signal. Polls during the 1950s and early 1960s revealed that only a quarter of all Americans approved of premarital intercourse. Most adults were equally opposed to sex education programs, which were commonly accused of "teaching vice to little children." The dominant message was the one popularized by a leading guide, *Facts of Life and Love for Teens:* "anything beyond a good night kiss could lead to trouble."[8]

That trouble was experienced disproportionately by women. Outside of certain black communities, young women who became pregnant often faced grim alternatives: undesired marriages, illegal and unsafe abortions, social ostracism, and exclusion from educational programs. Some temporary support and vocational assistance were available through homes for unwed mothers. Adoption agencies also offered placement alternatives for their infants, an option that about 90 percent of all single mothers accepted, generally under varying degrees of pressure. However, services for unwed parents were highly inadequate and could not mitigate the public stigma, psychological trauma, and educational and economic disadvantages that often accompanied nonmarital births. Such costs were exacerbated by a legal system that treated "promiscuous" female (but not male) adolescents as delinquent, and visited additional penalties on illegitimate children, such as exclusion from insurance and governmental entitlement programs.[9]

As this overview suggests, American norms for adolescent sexual expression and childbearing reveal strong variations but certain common themes. During some eras and within some subgroups, early premarital intercourse has not been viewed as especially problematic, provided that any resulting childbirth remained within marital unions or, in many black communities, within a kinship network. Yet for much of American history, the dominant white, middle-class culture has also imposed substantial costs on premarital sexual activity. Those costs have been paid largely by women.

Legal doctrine reflected and reinforced these broader cultural patterns. Until the nineteenth century, there was little formal regulation of birth-control practices. Folk wisdom regarding contraceptive techniques was passed down across generations and, during the antebellum period, some devices began to be advertised publicly. Relatively few married couples, however, appear to have practiced birth control. Effective contraception often required male cooperation or technical knowledge not yet available, and social norms encouraged high birth rates. For unmarried women, the only reliable means of limiting fertility was abortion. Under early common-law provisions, it was permissible until "quickening," the point at which a fetus moved in the woman's body and, according to ecclesiastical doctrine, acquired a soul.[10]

During the nineteenth century, the same ideological forces that made premarital sexual activity less acceptable made birth control less accessible. In 1873, Congress passed the Comstock Law, which prohibited dissemination of information about abortion or contraception. Over the next several decades, all but one state made abortion a felony, and many raised the age at which females could legally consent to sexual activity. Such restrictions responded to various concerns. Moral reformers worried that any separation of sex from procreation would result in increased venereal disease, "psychological derangement," and social instability. In addition, the decline in fertility rates among the "better classes" during the late nineteenth and early twentieth centuries sparked fears of "race suicide." Many physicians shared these concerns, and also found restrictions on abortion and contraceptive services to be an effective means of undercutting their competitors—midwives and other lay practitioners who provided such services. Although the organized medical profession generally presented its campaign against birth control in moral and spiritual terms, nineteenth-century religious leaders were relatively uninterested in the effort.[11]

Yet neither did the newly emerging feminist movement actively oppose the physicians' campaign, despite the significance of reproductive issues for women's independence. To some movement leaders, these issues seemed "too narrow . . . and too sordid." For others, they were too threatening. Contraception appeared to reduce the risks of extramarital sex and thus to jeopardize traditional domestic relationships. For the vast majority of late nineteenth- and early twentieth-century women, marriage and motherhood were the best sources of economic security and social status. To most white middle-class wives, any threat to the family was a threat not worth provoking, particularly if the major gain was to license sexual activity, which many had experienced as a duty rather than a pleasure. Although most leaders of the women's rights movement were committed to "voluntary motherhood," they wished to ensure that it remained within marital relationships and that birth control occurred through abstinence rather than through other, "degrading," methods. Feminists recognized unwanted pregnancies as a "problem," but assumed that the solution was to eliminate unwanted sex.[12]

As a result, the initial campaign for reproductive freedom remained largely independent of the organized women's movement. Moreover, that campaign often lost sight of egalitarian principles and concrete concerns of many groups, including young, low-income, and minority women, who most needed assistance. In attempting to broaden their movement's appeal, most early family planning activists emphasized eugenics and supported policies giving physicians control over the distribution of birth control materials. Since few doctors were willing to provide such materials to unmarried minors, and low-income and minority women often lacked access to physicians' services, this approach left many sexually active couples without protection. Yet most leaders, including Margaret Sanger, disavowed any support for abortion and presented their preventive approach as a sufficient alternative.[13]

Appeals to eugenics helped fuel the campaign for sterilization practices that resulted in involuntary fertility control for thousands of slightly retarded or impoverished women, particularly among minority groups. During the 1890s, the development of reasonably safe surgical techniques laid the foundations for a wave of compulsory sterilization laws, which received Supreme Court blessing in 1927. In Buck v. Bell, the Court permitted the sterilization of Carrie Buck, an institutionalized and assertedly "feeble-minded" daughter of a feeble-minded mother, after she had given birth to an illegitimate feeble-minded child. Writing for the majority, Justice Holmes concluded that "three generations of imbeciles are enough." Subsequent evidence exposed the risks of such decision making. Carrie Buck does not appear to have been mentally deficient; she was institutionalized to hide a pregnancy resulting from rape by one of her foster relatives.[14]

In the late 1930s and 1940s, the eugenic sterilization movement began to decline, partly in response to scientific evidence undermining its premises and to the lessons of Nazi Germany. Without overruling *Buck*, the Supreme Court cast doubt on its reasoning and limited its application in a subsequent decision that invalidated mandatory sterilization laws for habitual criminals. However, family planners, public hospital administrators, and welfare officials continued to condition assistance on "consent" to sterilization by poor and minority women, who were assumed to lack competence or motivation for other birth-control techniques. Coercive and uninformed sterilization remained a major problem until the 1980s, when well-publicized litigation and the promulgation of federal regulations finally began to curb abuses. Yet proposals to coerce certain groups of women to allow implants of a long term contraceptive, Norplant, have rekindled earlier concerns. In light of this legacy, birth-control strategies have often provoked suspicion or resistance within minority communities, and the issue continues to raise broader questions of nationalism, separatism, and cultural survival.[15]

Throughout most of the twentieth century, the reproductive rights movement has reflected class and racial biases. The movement's earliest legal victories involved reinterpretations of federal statutes to permit prescription and distribution of birth-control materials where permissible under state law (for example, in order to prevent disease). The result was that women who could afford a sympathetic private physician could usually obtain contraceptives. Those with sufficient resources were also sometimes able to establish a physical or psychological justification for a legal abortion; alternatively, they could afford a relatively safe illegal one, or travel to a more permissive jurisdiction. For the young, poor, uneducated, or unsophisticated, the options were far more limited. Despite efforts by some community organizations to provide assistance for low-income and minority groups, misconceptions about conception as well as deaths from self-induced abortions were common.[16]

Legal restraints on birth control gradually weakened in response to various cultural forces: liberalization of sexual mores, efforts to prevent venereal disease, women's rising educational opportunities and workforce participation, and increasing economic pressures to curtail fertility. After 1960, the availability of an oral contraceptive helped liberalize public attitudes and practices, and concerns about global overpopulation had similar effects.

Beginning in the mid-1960s, the Supreme Court issued a series of decisions that both responded and contributed to these trends. In 1965, a majority of Justices interpreted the due process clause to protect private use of contraceptives by married couples. Decisions in 1972 and 1977 extended that right to unmarried minors. Although the Justices' reasoning differed, a majority found constitutional grounding for a limited right of privacy in matters related to procreation. According to the Court's opinion in Eisenstadt v. Baird, the state's interest in discouraging promiscuity could not justify bans on contraceptive sales to minors since it would be "unreasonable" to infer "pregnancy and the birth of an unwanted child [as an appropriate] punishment for fornication." Due process and equal protection concerns also convinced lower courts to begin striking down public school policies that excluded unwed mothers but not unwed fathers.[17]

During the 1960s, many of the same forces underlying liberalized contraception policy also encouraged abortion-law reform. As improvements in medical technology reduced the circumstances in which abortion was necessary to preserve a mother's life, the rigidity of existing statutes became more apparent. Women's increased employment and sexual activity also increased the number of unwanted pregnancies. Physicians faced growing pressure to evade both the letter and spirit of the law, and that pressure was reflected in abortion rates. By the 1960s, most estimates indicated that about a million abortions were performed annually, few of them legally; approximately one abortion occurred for every three to four live births. Abortion was the most frequent form of criminal activity after gambling and narcotics violations, and its perpetrators were also its victims. Procedures could be painful and dangerous if performed hastily or by unskilled practitioners. Somewhere between one and ten thousand women died each year as a result of botched abortions, and more suffered permanent physical or psychological injuries. Predictably, those most at risk were young, poor, and minority women. These human costs prompted increasing reform activity.[18]

Changes in public sentiment were apparent in state legislative initiatives, in national opinion surveys, and ultimately in Supreme Court rulings. In 1973, the Supreme Court issued its landmark decision Roe v. Wade. There, a majority of Justices concluded that an adult woman had fundamental privacy interests entitling her to terminate a pregnancy without restriction during its first trimester. That ruling set off some of the most strident and sustained criticism in the Court's history. In its aftermath, the Justices remained enmeshed in controversies over maternal health and funding regulations designed to restrict abortions.[19]

Beginning in the late 1970s, the Supreme Court issued a number of decisions upholding some of the most substantial restrictions. In Maher v. Roe and Harris v. McRae, a majority of Justices sustained denial of public funds for abortion even for women entitled to childbirth subsidies. Subsequent decisions in Webster v. Reproductive Health Services (1989) and Planned Parenthood of Southeastern Pennsylvania v. Casey permitted further constraints on reproductive choice. *Webster* upheld bans on abortion in public facilities and permitted requirements of costly tests to determine fetal viability in the second and third trimesters of pregnancy. Planned Parenthood v. Casey struck down spousal notification provisions as an undue burden on reproductive choice but sustained other requirements, including pre-abortion waiting periods, provision of information concerning fetal development, reporting procedures for abortion facilities, and parental consent for minors. Although the Court declined invitations to overrule *Roe* and return abortion issues to state legislatures, it clearly signaled greater tolerance for state restrictions on reproductive rights. Since adolescents are disproportionately likely to lack private funds for abortions and to delay the decision to abort until after the first trimester, they are particularly vulnerable to such restrictions.[20]

In upholding limitations on reproductive choice, the Court has been strikingly insensitive to the needs of young and poor women. Underlying the majority's analysis is a revived form of the much-discredited distinction between benefits and burdens. According to the court in Harris v. McRae, the government has

> place[d] no obstacles—absolute or otherwise—in the pregnant woman's path to an abortion. . . . By making childbirth a more attractive alternative, the state may have influenced a woman's deci-

> sion but it has imposed no restriction on access to abortion that was not already there. . . . The financial constraints that restrict an indigent woman's ability to enjoy the full range of constitutionally protected freedom of choice are the product not of governmental restrictions on access to abortions, but rather of her indigency.[21]

This reasoning is problematic on several levels. The notion that the state has played no role in creating economic constraints on choice suggests an extraordinary degree of myopia: welfare, education, employment, housing, tax, and innumerable other public policies always affect income distribution. It is of course true that indigency limits the exercise of many fundamental rights. Yet it is also the case that the right at stake was as significant as others for which the Court has required state assistance, such as court costs in divorce proceedings or free transcripts for defendants in criminal cases. Moreover, the usual justification for the government's failure to provide such assistance—conserving scarce resources—has been unavailable in abortion-funding cases. When these cases arose, the average cost of subsidizing childbirth was close to ten times that of underwriting abortions. Since many indigents' children would also require continuing welfare support, the statutes in question have been inexplicable as revenue-saving measures. Rather, the government has sought to accomplish indirectly what it cannot do directly: to coerce women into completing unwanted pregnancies.[22]

Federal regulations have sought to impose further restrictions on reproductive choice by barring provision of information about abortion in government-funded health programs. In 1991, in Rust v. Sullivan, the Supreme Court sustained those regulations on reasoning similar to that in *Harris*. Under the *Rust* majority's analysis, it was irrelevant that indigent women would be unable to obtain abortion-related services; those individuals were in no worse position than if the government chose not to provide any assistance at all. Yet as dissenting Justices noted, such a decision ran counter to well-established precedents holding that federal funds could not be conditioned on content-based restrictions of speech.[23]

The targets of these abortion-related restrictions are the women least able to protect themselves through conventional political channels and least able to support an additional child. Although most indigent women have continued to receive subsidies after federal cutbacks through state or private sources, limitations on funding and lack of information about its availability impose significant barriers. Young, unsophisticated teenagers have been among those most at risk. States with adolescent pregnancy initiatives generally prohibit the use of public funds for abortion and impose other limitations on access. The result, as subsequent discussion suggests, is to constrain reproductive choices and increase their physical risks and psychological trauma.[24]

When questioned about the justice of the government's selective attempt to coerce childbirth, President Jimmy Carter replied that "there are many things in life that are not fair." Why the state should amplify that unfairness remains unanswered. Moreover, the political conflicts that have constrained abortion decision making have been equally apparent in policies specifically directed toward adolescent pregnancy. And the costs have been equally substantial.[25]

The late 1960s and early 1970s witnessed the first perception of teenage pregnancy as a major social problem. The increase in public concern was not a function of increases in adolescent fertility. In fact, rates of childbirth among females ages 15–19 dropped 45 percent between 1957 and 1983, largely because of liberalization of contraceptive and abortion policy. Although the birth rate began to rise again in the late 1980s, it still remained substantially lower than in the decade before the *Roe* decision. When teenage childbearing became a focus of attention, the reasons had less to do with its frequency than with a cluster of volatile issues involving sexuality, abortion, family values, and welfare policy.[26]

During the past quarter-century, although fewer teens were having children, more were having sex, more were becoming pregnant, and more were becoming single mothers. By the late 1980s, the United States had the highest teen pregnancy rate in the developed world. Approximately 45 percent of adolescent females were sexually active before marriage, an increase of over 15 percent since 1971, and substantial numbers used contraceptives intermittently or ineffectively. The result was a million teen pregnancies each year, and about four-fifths of these were unintentional. An estimated four out of every ten American women were becoming pregnant at least once before age 20, a rate that has doubled since 1950. About half of that group were carrying their pregnancy to term (20 percent of all adolescents), and half of those who did so were unmarried. By the late 1980s, estimates indicated that less than 5 percent of all unmarried teens and less than 1 percent of blacks were placing their children for adoption, a dramatic shift from earlier eras. The rate of teenage childbirth among blacks has become almost two and one-half times greater than among whites; among Hispanics, the rates have become almost twice as great. Over a quarter of single black women have had at least one child by the age of 18. Although teens under age 15 have accounted for only 2 percent of all adolescent mothers their rate of pregnancy has been increasing.[27]

Although such patterns are widely assumed to constitute a social problem, there is no consensus on its cause or cure. At the risk of some oversimplification, it makes sense to distinguish two dominant positions in public debate. Most liberals "begin with the premise that teenagers should not have babies [while most] conservatives begin with the premise that single teenagers should not have sex." For conservatives, the problem involves primarily moral and fiscal concerns: premarital sexuality is not only objectionable in itself, it promotes other objectionable practices, such as abortion and the destruction of fetal "life," or nonmarital childbearing and the erosion of traditional values and financial self-sufficiency. For liberals, the problem involves primarily health and socioeconomic status: single parenthood is linked with disrupted education, reduced employment opportunities, and an increased likelihood of poverty for mothers, as well as heightened medical risks and developmental difficulties for their children.[28]

Each of these definitions of the problem is itself problematic on both descriptive and prescriptive levels. Most conservative and liberal accounts distort the dynamic they seek to counteract. Both constituencies have overstated the adverse consequences of adolescent pregnancy and understated the barriers to addressing it. Such distortions are in some sense endemic to the American political process. The most effective way of getting an issue onto the policy agenda is usually to paint it as a crisis that can be addressed without major political conflict or financial expenditure. Yet the construction of the issue best suited to attracting public notice and building coalitions for reform is often ill-suited to generating adequate policy responses. This is clearly the case with adolescent pregnancy. Conflicting definitions of the problem have resulted in political compromises that are inadequate to serve societal needs.[29]

From conservatives' perspective, recent increases in teenage sexuality, pregnancy, and nonmarital childbirth are both a cause and consequence of deeper social difficulties. As growing numbers of adolescents reject conventional family patterns, more adults have viewed the situation with subdued "moral panic." In their view, the problem is immorality, not poverty, and stems from cultural permissiveness, a decline in parental authority, and a weakening of community sanctions against illegitimacy.[30]

That position gained increasing public attention during the 1992 presidential campaign. Vice President Dan Quayle attracted substantial media coverage, first by calling for social sanctions against unmarried women (including a leading television-series character) who bear children and call it "just another lifestyle choice." He subsequently faced questions about how he would reconcile his absolutist antiabortion commitments with family values if his own daughter told him that she had decided to have an abortion. Initially he responded that he would "counsel her and talk to her, and support her whatever decision she made," although he hoped she would not choose an abortion. After widespread outcry from all points on the political spectrum, he backpedaled slightly. Both he and his wife, Marilyn Quayle, made it clear that if their daughter were to become pregnant now, at age 13, "she'll take the child to term." However, he reaffirmed his willingness to support whatever decision an adult daughter made. This compromise hardly mollified many commentators, who noted the hypocrisy of his support for a choice by his own family member that he would deny to women generally. Others noted the irony of his double standards, which are reflected in current abortion law. In the "Quayle world, an 18-year-old gets to be supported whatever her decision. A 13-year-old gets to have a baby. This is no joke. It's the foolishness that passes now for public policy." [31]

From conservatives' perspective, however, these policies are still too permissive. Public subsidies for birth-control programs are held accountable for legitimating conduct they should seek to prevent. According to New Right legislators such as former Senator Jeremiah Denton, author of the federal Adolescent and Family Life Act, "the most effective oral contraceptive yet devised is the word 'no.'" Under conservatives' analyses, any outreach program designed to prevent pregnancy rather than sex appears counterproductive; it encourages the activity that creates the problem. [32]

Most available research, however, fails to support such claims. Studies of contraceptive and abortion services generally find no evidence that their availability has increased sexual activity. The vast majority of adolescents seek assistance only after they have engaged in sexual intercourse. Comparative data underscore the point. Many European countries have rates of adolescent sexual activity equivalent to those in the United States, but substantially higher rates of contraceptive use and lower rates of adolescent pregnancy and abortion. [33]

Although liberals tend to be more permissive toward teenage sexual activity, they are typically no less judgmental than conservatives about teenage childbirth. Both groups share assumptions about the experience of adolescent pregnancy that rest on dubious factual premises. Most public debate conflates unintended with unwanted pregnancy and ignores data indicating that adolescent attitudes fall across a spectrum. As earlier discussion and other chapters in this volume make clear, the frequent caricature of children having children is highly distorted: two thirds of all births to teenagers are to 18- and 19-year-olds, and only a tiny percentage are to mothers under 16. The equally common assumption that early pregnancy constitutes a direct path to poverty is equally exaggerated. The leading longitudinal study by Furstenberg, Brooks-Gunn, and Morgan, involving predominantly black adolescent mothers in Baltimore, found that the majority was eventually able to obtain a high school education, secure full-time employment, and avoid welfare dependency. About two thirds of the children have completed or are close to completing comparable levels of schooling and only a quarter have become teenage parents themselves.[34]

So, too, many factors commonly assumed to be consequences of early pregnancy—educational difficulties, low self-esteem, poverty, and unemployment—appear to be partial causes as well. For example, although adolescent mothers are more likely to drop out of school than peers of similar socioeconomic backgrounds, it is unclear how much of this difference is due to childbearing and how much to lower academic commitment and competence. Recent studies suggest that most young mothers leave school before becoming pregnant rather than the converse and that mothers who give birth while in school are as likely to graduate as their peers. If such findings are confirmed, then labeling early parenthood the paramount problem will misrepresent the appropriate solution.[35]

A growing number of scholars has also suggested that early pregnancies are more adaptive for economically and racially subordinate groups than is commonly acknowledged. According to researchers such as Arline Geronimus, Mary Edwards, and Mark Testa, teenagers who are no longer in school may find advantages to having their most intensive parenting demands during a period when they have fewest employment opportunities and greatest access to free childcare assistance from their relatives. Since young black mothers are likely to live in an extended family, they often have better access to networks of kin support and childcare than older mothers. From a physiological standpoint, early motherhood is far less problematic than conventional accounts imply. Most health risks currently associated with teenage childbirth are attributable to socioeconomic status and the failure to obtain adequate prenatal care. If such care were available, some analysts believe that childbearing by poor women between ages 16 and 19 would pose fewer risks to mothers or newborns than later childbearing because many medical problems associated with poverty increase with age.[36]

Such claims have become matters of considerable dispute. Some commentators challenge the conclusions regarding health difficulties and claim that if risks to infants after the first few months of birth are considered, early childrearing carries significant disadvantages. Recent research also suggests that a substantial number of young mothers remain outside of support networks and find family childcare inadequate. Even if, as the

Baltimore study suggests, most adolescent mothers are eventually able to achieve financial independence, a significant number experiences enduring poverty and many face prolonged periods of severe hardships. So, too, children of teenage mothers have disproportionate difficulties, such as high rates of delinquency and low rates of educational attainment. Although it is unclear how much of their problem is attributable to socioeconomic variables and how much to parental age and capacity, at least some evidence suggests that young adolescents are less well equipped for certain childbearing demands. In any event, the existence of such controversies points up the need for qualifications largely missing in current policy debates.[37]

Similar qualifications are necessary to assess conventional solutions for the adolescent pregnancy "problem." Recent data call into question the widespread assumption that economically and racially subordinate groups gain significant benefits from deferring parenthood until marriage or the completion of education. Divorce rates for such young couples are substantial, and various factors, including relatively high rates of unemployment, violence, suicide, and substance abuse, have reduced the pool of eligible male partners. Although the extent to which such factors explain current racial differences in family formation remains subject to debate, it is clear that marriage is not an adequate solution for many pregnant adolescents.[38]

Moreover, because women of color remain concentrated in occupations that offer low pay and little return for completing secondary education, they often have relatively little to lose from early childbearing. Thus, some longitudinal studies have found little difference in the labor market position of black women who gave birth in their teens and those who did not. Similar findings have emerged from research comparing adolescents who became mothers with their sisters who delayed childbearing: deferral of parenthood and additional schooling did not significantly increase income or reduce welfare dependency. By contrast, a recent study of largely black Baltimore teenagers found that those who obtained abortions did better economically and educationally than adolescents who gave birth, even after controlling for various demographic and motivational factors.[39]

Although such conflicting data underscore the need for further research, one general point attracts widespread consensus. Childbirth patterns are responsive to socioeconomic and cultural forces that vary considerably across class, race, and ethnicity. As research summarized in Part II of this volume makes clear, expectations about future opportunities play an important role in shaping collective norms and individual choices at both conscious and preconscious levels.

The point of this discussion is not, as Arline Geronimus emphasizes, that "in the best of all possible worlds, teen childbearing would be personally or socially optimal." It is, however, to suggest that "we are very far from the best of all possible worlds, and that there are serious flaws in the logic of current policy approaches intended to get us there." As the following discussion makes clear, conflict and confusion over the nature of the adolescent pregnancy "crisis" has seriously compromised societal responses.[40]

The central problem in formulating public policies on adolescent pregnancy lies in too narrow a definition of what the problem is. According to the most comprehensive cross-cultural data from Western industrialized nations, two key factors accounting for the high teenage fertility rate in the United States are the culture's "ambivalent, sometimes puritanical attitudes regarding sex," and the existence of a large population subgroup that is economically deprived. At the ideological level, the problem in formulating policy lies in cultural conflict about sexual expression, family authority, and reproductive choice. At the material level, the problem reflects an unwillingness to translate societal concerns into financial commitments and to invest in the necessary research and support structures for populations at risk.[41]

Much of the difficulty in designing adolescent pregnancy policy reflects deeper cultural ambivalence. Few if any societies exhibit a more perverse combination of permissiveness and prudishness in their treatment of sexual issues. A majority of Americans no longer view premarital intercourse as wrong, and the media bombards teens with scenes of sexual involvement and innuendo. Sex is often presented as a goal in and of itself, with little discussion of its risks or of responsible contraceptive behavior. Female adolescents remain subject to double standards that make spontaneous intercourse seem acceptable but suggest that adequate preparation is evidence of promiscuity. Conventional norms present casual sex as unacceptable but declare teenagers too young for serious relationships. On major television networks, sex sells everything from automobiles to laundry detergent but advertisements for birth control remain almost taboo. Our cultural imagery links masculinity with sexual prowess and femininity with sexual attractiveness. Yet we expect decision makers to pay homage to traditional values and accept policies that preach abstinence and restrict adolescent access to birth control.[42]

This cultural ambivalence over teenage sexual activity has been apparent in the increasing federal, state, and local policies that address the issue. In 1978 Congress passed the first national legislation specifically focusing on teenage pregnancy, the Adolescent Health, Services, and Pregnancy Prevention Act. In essence, the act amended a prior statute to make federally funded contraceptive services (excluding abortion) available to adolescents. As reviews of that legislation make clear, congressional debate was ahistorical, uninformed, and more attentive to political pressures than to adolescent needs. By supporting contraception as an alternative to abortion, the act was able to unite pro-choice and pro-life constituencies. However, it provided such limited services for such a limited percentage of teens that its impact remained minimal. In addition, the statute's inadequate provision for evaluation prevented informed judgments about which subsidized services were most cost-effective.[43]

Three years later, Congress passed the Adolescent Family Life Act (AFLA), which reflected a similar political compromise. The legislation secured support for pilot demonstration projects and their evaluation, but funding limitations again prevented adequate analysis of program impact. Moreover, the act focused on encouraging "chastity" and "sexual self-discipline" rather than on providing contraceptive services, and banned any use of federal funds for abortion counseling. Many programs receiving AFLA funds have been religious. Their instruction has included distribution of pamphlets on "Reasons to Wait," which remind readers that "God wants us to be pure," and advises them to "pretend Jesus was on [their] date." Despite evidence of widespread church-state entanglement, a 1988 Supreme Court decision sustained the act. Funding for AFLA programs has remained at low levels, and its limited availability reflects an uneasy political truce. Federal policy remains caught in the cross fire between liberals, who favor government-subsidized birth-control services for adolescents, and conservatives, who argue that providing such assistance undermines parental authority and legitimates sexual promiscuity.[44]

Similar political controversies have occurred at state and local levels and have resulted in similar policy constraints. During the 1980s, over two-thirds of the states developed initiatives regarding adolescent pregnancy, but only a few targeted contraception for significant efforts. Although about three-fourths of all high schools and junior high schools offered some form of sex education, only about a fifth identified adolescent pregnancy as one of their concerns. To avoid antagonizing vocal conservative minorities, many local decision makers have vetoed both contraceptive counseling and school-based clinic services. By the early 1990s, only about one hundred clinics were operating nationwide, and only about two dozen schools had condom distribution programs: over half of all sexually active teens lacked adequate reproductive health services. The cost, inaccessible locations, and nonconfidentiality of existing programs have imposed substantial barriers to contraceptive choice.[45]

A related limitation in existing policies involves federal inattention to male attitudes and behavior. Program design has often proceeded as if pregnancy occurs via the stork. Too little focus has centered on men who pressure their partners to have sex or to have a baby that will demonstrate their own virility but who are unable or unwilling to support a child. Particularly in low-income communities, rising rates of unemployment, school failure, drug use, and criminal activity have compromised opportunities for responsible parenting. Although federal policy has begun to give more attention to fathers, its scope has been severely constrained, and only a few states with adolescent pregnancy initiatives address such needs.[46]

The cost of these policy limitations is considerable. As earlier discussion made clear, restrictions on contraceptive services discourage contraception, not sex. Many teens grossly underestimate the risk of unprotected sexual activity and overestimate the risks of various forms of contraception. Given the increasing rates of unintended pregnancies, AIDS, and drug-addicted offspring among teenage populations, federal refusal to provide adequate outreach services carries enormous personal and social costs.[47]

Parental consent requirements in birth-control programs have reflected similar political compromises, and adolescents have paid the price. A 1981 regulation by the Department of Health and Human Services would have required parental notification for teens seeking contraceptives in all federally funded clinics. Although lower federal courts enjoined enforcement of that "squeal rule," subsequent surveys indicated that about a fifth of hospitals and well over a third of private physicians voluntarily have required parental consent before prescribing contraception. Many states and localities have similarly mandated parental involvement for minors seeking abortions, while over a third of hospitals and about a fifth of surveyed clinics have voluntarily adopted comparable rules. Such restrictions reflect another attempt to mediate between conservatives, who oppose any abortion or provision of birth control to adolescents, and liberals, who favor such assistance.[48]

Litigation challenging parental notification and consent policies has also resulted in compromises, and they make little long-term sense. In a series of cases during the late 1970s and early 1980s, the Supreme Court held that states could require parental consent or notification for abortion services to minors as long as adjudicative procedures were available to bypass such requirements under specified circumstances. To a majority of Justices, parental involvement rules were justified by the "peculiar vulnerability" of adolescence and the importance of preserving family ties. However, a minor should be able to avoid consent and notice requirements by establishing in court either that she is sufficiently mature and well-informed to make an independent decision concerning abortion or that, even if she is immature, the abortion would be in her best interest.[49]

In 1990, a sharply divided Court sustained further restrictions on adolescents' abortion rights. A majority of Justices in Hodgson v. Minnesota upheld a requirement that both parents be notified before an adolescent's abortion if a judicial procedure is available to bypass that requirement under the circumstances previously identified. In Ohio v. Akron Reproductive Services, the Court sustained a legislative scheme that required physicians personally to notify one parent, placed heightened burdens of proof on minors seeking judicial bypass of the notice requirement, imposed delays of up to twenty-two days for bypass applicants, and failed to insure confidentiality. In upholding the reasonableness of these regulations, the majority concluded: "It is both rational and fair for the State to conclude that, in most instances, the family will strive to give a lonely or even terrified minor advice that is both compassionate and mature. . . . It would deny all dignity to the family to say that the State cannot take this reasonable step in regulating its health professions to ensure that, in most cases, a young woman will receive guidance and understanding from a parent.[50]

On a symbolic level, this resolution is understandable. As one Californa legislator noted, most decision makers "are parents too." And most parents feel that they should be involved in matters that call for mature guidance. A notice-plus-bypass procedure affirms the value of parental involvement but also recognizes that in some instances such involvement may result in punitive or otherwise counterproductive measures. Yet on a practical level, this compromise carries significant costs, and the law has offered a poor forum for assessing them. Legislative and judicial decision making generally has proceeded without demanding or assembling adequate data on the effects of mandatory parental involvement. Do such requirements result in greater communication on matters involving sexuality and birth control? What are the consequences for teenagers? How many experience better parental relations, how many suffer increased physical risks from self-help or delayed decisions to abort, how many decide not to abort, and what are the effects of that decision? Finally, how well are legal procedures likely to function? How many minors evade consent requirements by seeking abortions out of state? Do petitions to bypass parental involvement result in thoughtful exercise of judicial discretion? Or should the resources consumed by courts and counsel in bypass cases be directed to more productive approaches, such as pregnancy prevention?[51]

Although initial legislative and judicial decision making proceeded without systematic evidence on these points, subsequent research has provided partial answers. Yet the data available have had disturbingly little policy impact. For example, parental knowledge does not correlate with more effective contraceptive practices on the part of adolescents. About half of all adolescents seek birth control services without informing their parents, and about half that group (a quarter of all teens) will not seek such assistance if parents must consent or receive notification. Only 2 percent of surveyed adolescents indicate that policies requiring parental involvement would cause them to restrict their sexual activity. Statutory notice requirements do not significantly increase the likelihood that teenagers will consult their parents on birth control matters.[52]

Nor have judicial bypass procedures usefully contributed to adolescent decision making. Of some 1,300 Massachusetts abortion cases involving petitions to bypass parental consent, courts found the adolescent to be mature in 90 percent of these cases and in all but five of the remainder held that abortion was in her best interest. Four of those cases were either overturned on appeal or resulted in abortions authorized by another judge. In the single case where the court refused to permit termination of the pregnancy, the petitioner accomplished that objective in another state. Although the frequency of adolescent abortion has declined in Massachusetts since the implementation of consent requirements, almost all the decline appears attributable to an increase in out-of-state abortions.[53]

Studies of other state notification procedures similarly find that all but a tiny percentage of bypass petitions are granted, but that the procedure itself imposes substantial barriers, particularly for poor, minority, and very young teenagers. As is true with other abortion restrictions, the individuals most adversely affected by parental involvement rules are those least able to bear the costs of early childbirth. Adolescents have often been deterred by the lack of information about legal assistance, the risks of public exposure, the costs of multiple trips to distant locations, and the fear of courtroom interrogations. That fear is understandable given the judicial questions some minors encounter, such as: How will you feel about having a dead child? Are you aware that abortion can jeopardize your future fertility? Would your parents be willing and able to raise your baby? Notice and consent requirements increase the risk of physical abuse, psychological trauma, medically threatening delays, and unwanted childbirths. In effect, such rules compound the "peculiar vulnerability" they are designed to address.[54]

Those involved in administering consent regulations express little support for their requirements. Criteria for assessing teenagers' maturity and best interests are arbitrary and inconsistent, while judicial cross-examination often increases the guilt and misery that accompanies unwanted pregnancies. As the dissent in *Hodgson* recognized, and the results in bypass cases reflect, it is almost impossible to identify circumstances in which a minor is too immature to make an abortion decision for herself but in which her best interest lies in having a child she does not want. Given the increased medical and socioeconomic risks associated with carrying a fetus to term, on what basis could courts legitimately seek to compel childbirth? In case studies of Massachusetts and Minnesota regulations, participants in the legal process overwhelmingly agreed that resources now spent on obtaining judicial rubber stamps of bypass petitions should be allocated to more productive strategies.[55]

This is not to understate the value of fostering better communication between parents and children concerning responsible sexual behavior. It is rather to suggest that involuntary notification is an ineffective means of fostering such communication. Virtually every major professional study has concluded that compulsory parental involvement ill serves adolescent needs and family relationships. A preferable strategy would be voluntary parental outreach programs. Such programs seek to improve family communication and adolescent decision making skills while avoiding the notice or consent requirements that deter teenagers from seeking assistance. Yet all too often legislative, judicial, and administrative analyses have proceeded without consideration of alternative strategies for parental involvement. As with other teenage pregnancy initiatives, policymakers have offered compromises more responsive to symbolic politics than to practical needs.[56]

In formulating more effective public policies, a critical first step is to convince decision makers and their constituents to rethink the problem that teenage pregnancy presents. No significant progress can occur as long as Americans view the issue in terms of individual rather than societal responsibilities and insist on policies that reflect traditional family values rather than contemporary adolescent needs. The alternative framework proposed here begins from different premises and demands different resource priorities. Its objectives are to enhance adolescents' capacity for informed and uncoerced choices and to expand the choices available. These objectives in turn require policy initiatives that not only increase birth-control information and assistance, but also respond more effectively to education, employment, health, and welfare needs.

A more promising policy approach will depend on more systematic research. Despite the recent attention to the adolescent pregnancy "crisis," we know surprisingly little about certain key issues. What factors predict effective use of contraceptives among sexually active teens? What strategies are most successful in promoting responsible sexual behavior and how do they differ across gender, class, age, race, and ethnicity? How much of the disadvantage for young mothers and their children is attributable to age and how much to other demographic and socioeconomic factors? What individual coping strategies and social programs are most effective in reducing that disadvantage?[57]

Yet despite these gaps in current understanding, we know more than enough about the inadequacies of current frameworks to identify more promising alternatives. The most obvious inadequacy involves birth-control information and assistance. Widespread ignorance among teenagers concerning the substantial risks of unprotected sexual activity and the relatively low risks of contraceptive use demonstrates the need for fuller information. Increasing rates of AIDS among adolescents further underscore the urgency of that need. Yet since existing educational programs have had little measurable impact on contraceptive behavior, more innovative campaigns are necessary from multiple sources, including schools, community organizations, and the media.[58]

Such campaigns should include greater attention to decision making skills for both sexes. Encouraging men to exercise greater responsibility in sexual relationships from an early age is a crucial part of reproductive freedom for women. More emphasis should also center on empowering female adolescents to resist pressures for unwanted sexual intercourse or parenthood. Many teenage women report engaging in sexual activity that they do not find pleasurable, and deciding to have a baby more because of peer and family influence than because of affirmative desires to rear a child. All too often, single motherhood becomes an ill-considered means to other ends: a way to assert independence, to punish parents, to gain prestige, or to win approval from their child's father. Better education, mentoring, peer counseling, and community outreach strategies should be available to help young women assess and assert their own best interests. Especially for young teenagers, abstinence can be a feminist strategy, but not on the terms conservatives usually offer. Rather, the objective should be a revived but reformulated understanding of what the nineteenth-century women's movement labeled "voluntary motherhood."[59]

To make reproductive choices truly voluntary will also require more accessible birth control. As noted earlier, a majority of sexually active teens lack adequate reproductive health services, and many are deterred by the cost, distance, nonconfidentiality, and stigma associated with existing clinics. To reduce unplanned pregnancies, we need to reduce the barriers to reproductive planning, such as parental notification and consent requirements, harassment of clinic users, and shortages of free or low-cost services. Comprehensive health programs located in or near schools are among the most promising outreach strategies, for they can avoid singling out participants who request contraceptive assistance and can offer accessible follow-up services. Development and distribution of alternative birth-control technologies, such as RU 486, should become higher public priorities.[60]

Yet if we are serious about not just removing the obstacles to choice but expanding the choices available, further initiatives are necessary. First and most fundamental, we must find ways to improve school programs and reduce dropout rates. Particularly in low-income communities, the current educational structure seems irrelevant to immediate needs and promises little economic security. Female adolescents who lack confidence in their own abilities and future prospects often see little to lose from early pregnancy and childbearing. Low expectations about educational and vocational opportunities readily become self-fulfilling prophecies. Young women who leave school are disproportionately likely to become pregnant, to have multiple pregnancies, and to experience poverty and welfare dependency.[61]

Breaking this cycle will require changing adolescents' aspirations and experience. More programs are needed to expand life-planning options, build self-confidence, improve school performance, increase literacy, and strengthen vocational skills. Additional support is necessary for scholarships and bilingual assistance. These initiatives must be coordinated with other opportunities for vocational training, job placement, and higher education, so that participants can see ways to achieve status and self-worth apart from early parenthood. We cannot respond effectively to teenage motherhood without responding also to the broader range of social problems that make motherhood seem to be a teenager's best option. Nor can we address the inadequacy of paternal support without also addressing the inadequacy of unemployment, education, and drug treatment opportunities.[62]

The importance of some of these initiatives has attracted growing attention. Recent changes in federal welfare regulations require adolescent AFDC recipients to obtain job training and skills instruction if childcare is available, and to participate in continuing education if they lack a high school degree. Although the effectiveness of these requirements has yet to be assessed, past experience with similar vocational programs suggests grounds for caution. Participants typically register minor income gains in comparison with program cost. So, too, recent efforts to increase paternal child support for AFDC families are likely to be of limited effectiveness, given most fathers' inadequate financial resources. Significant progress for adolescent parents is likely to require broader macroeconomic interventions and antipoverty initiatives, such as increases in minimum wage, job-creation strategies, and expanded health, housing, childcare, family counseling, and income-transfer policies.[63]

More emphasis must also center on expanding prenatal services and coordinating responses to various risk-taking behaviors, including drug and alcohol abuse, as well as unprotected sexual activity. The necessity of such initiatives is underscored by the increasing number of infants who are deformed or disabled as a result of maternal addictions. Recent efforts to prosecute addicted mothers rather than provide adequate treatment programs again points up the risks in placing blame at the individual rather than societal level. It is neither just nor effective to condemn teenage mothers who make tragic choices while ignoring the constraints on choices that are available.[64]

All these policy initiatives must be formulated with greater community involvement and more responsiveness to variations within and among ethnic groups. Third-generation Puerto Rican women have different concerns from those of recent emigrees from Mexico, and blacks from urban ghettos face different constraints from those of teenagers from middle-class suburbs or impoverished rural communities. Public policies need to take fuller account of culturally specific attitudes and kinship support structures affecting early childbirth. No single set of interventions will be equally effective with all subgroups; rather, we need multiple strategies that directly enlist families at risk.[65]

The policy alternatives identified here do not constitute a modest agenda. But neither can we expect major progress until we translate our rhetorical concerns into resource commitments. Coherent policies on teenage pregnancy require a redirection of adult priorities.

Notes

The comments of Annette Lawson and Michael Wald and the research assistance of Joan Krause and Wendy Olsen are gratefully appreciated.

1. Sharon Thompson, "Search for Tomorrow: On Feminism and the Reconstruction of Teen Romance," in Carole S. Vance, ed., *Pleasure and Danger* (Boston: Routledge and Kegan Paul, 1984), p. 350.

2. Susan E. Harari and Maris A. Vinovskis, "Adolescent Sexuality, Pregnancy, and Childbearing in the Past" (chap. 1); John Demos and Virgilio Demos, "Adolescence in Historical Perspective," *Journal of Marriage and the Family* 31 (1969): 632.

3. Maris A. Vinovskis, *An "Epidemic" of Adolescent Pregnancy?* (New York: Oxford University Press, 1988), pp. 3–21, 32; John D'Emilio and Estelle B. Freedman, *Intimate Matters: A History of Sexuality in America* (New York: Harper and Row, 1987), pp. 10–28, 32–33, 43–46. For sanctions against fornication, see *ibid.*, p. 13; Michael D. Freeman and Christina M. Lyon, *Cohabitation without Marriage: An Essay in Law and Social Policy* (Aldershot, Eng.: Gower, 1983); Edmund S. Morgan, "The Puritans and Sex," in Michael Gordon, ed., *The American Family in Social-Historical Perspective.* 3rd ed. (New York: St. Martin's Press, 1983), p. 311.

4. Henry B. Parkes, "Morals and Law Enforcement in Colonial New England," *New England Quarterly* 5 (1932): 431, 442–43; Vinovskis, *"Epidemic,"* p. 13; D'Emilio and Freedman, *Intimate Matters,* pp. 32–33, 43, 73. For a discussion of sexual images of women, see *ibid.*, pp. 43–46; Laurel Thatcher Ulrich, *Good Wives: Image and Reality in the Lives of Women in Northern New England, 1650–1750* (New York: Knopf, 1982).

5. D'Emilio and Freedman, *Intimate Matters,* pp. 8, 13, 65, 87, 97–100; James Axtell, *The Indian Peoples of Eastern America: A Documentary History of the Sexes* (New York: Oxford University Press, 1989), pp. 71–72; John Upton Terrell and Donna M. Terrell, *Indian Women of the Western Morning: Their Life in Early America* (New York: Dial Press, 1974), pp. 116–17, 121; Herbert G. Gutman, *The Black Family in Slavery and Freedom, 1750–1925* (New York: Pantheon, 1976), pp. 295–96; Eugene D. Genovese, *Roll, Jordan, Roll: The World the Slaves Made* (New York: Pantheon, 1974), pp. 461, 465–66; Daniel Scott Smith, "The Long Cycle in American Illegitimacy and Prenuptial Pregnancy," in Peter Laslett, Karla Oosterveen, and Richard M. Smith, eds., *Bastardy and Its Comparative History* (Cambridge: Harvard University Press, 1980), p. 37; Dorothy Sterling, ed., *We Are Your Sisters: Black Women in the Nineteenth Century* (New York: W. W. Norton, 1984), pp. 32–33. See also sources cited in n. 7, below.

6. The nineteenth-century cult of domesticity is reviewed in Barbara Welter, "The Cult of True Womanhood, 1820–1860," *American Quarterly,* 18 (1966): 151. For religious revivalism and the growth of moral reform societies, see, e.g., Carroll Smith-Rosenberg, *Disorderly Conduct: Visions of Gender in Victorian America* (New York: Knopf, 1985), pp. 109–28. For medical wisdom, see Edward Clarke, *Sex in Education: Or a Fair Chance for Girls* (Boston: Houghton, Mifflin, and Company, 1873), pp. 104, 137; Barbara Ehrenreich and Deidre English, *For Her Own Good: 150 Years of the Experts' Advice to Women* (Garden City, N.Y.: Anchor, 1978), pp. 113–18; Vinovskis, *"Epidemic,"* p. 10; D'Emilio and Freedman, *Intimate Matters,* pp. 178–84; Harari and Vinovskis, "Adolescent Sexuality." For social welfare policies, see Michael B. Katz, *In the Shadow of the Poor House: A Social History of Welfare in America* (New York: Basic Books, 1986); Mimi Abramovitz, *Regulating the Lives of Women: Social Welfare Policy from Colonial Times to the Present* (Boston: South End Press, 1988), p. 145; Jacqueline Jones, *Labor of Love, Labor of Sorrow: Black Women, Work, and the Family from Slavery to the Present* (New York: Basic Books, 1985), pp. 266–67, 307–08. Discrimination in employment is reviewed in Alice Kessler-Harris, *Out to Work* (New York: Oxford University Press, 1982); Deborah L. Rhode, *Justice and Gender:*

Sex Discrimination and the Law (Cambridge: Harvard University Press, 1989), pp. 38–48. As Constance Nathanson notes, the sanctions for illegitimacy varied somewhat, depending on whether the circumstances suggested "innocence betrayed," mental deficiency, hereditary weaknesses, or original sin. Despite these variations, however, there was "scarcely any other way [in which] a woman [could] lose status so completely," as Constance A. Nathanson, quoting Kingsley Davis, writes in *Dangerous Passage: The Social Control Sexuality in Women's Adolescence* (Philadelphia: Temple University Press, 1991), p. 104.

7. Kathy Lee Peiss, *Cheap Amusements: Working Women and Leisure in Turn-of-the-Century New York* (Philadelphia: Temple University Press, 1986), pp. 62, 70–71, 108–10; Christine Stansell, *City of Women: Sex and Class in New York* (New York: Knopf, 1986), pp. 1789–1860; D'Emilio and Freedman, *Intimate Matters*, pp. 199–200, 272–73, 299–300; Charles S. Johnson, *Shadow of the Plantation* (Chicago: University of Chicago Press, 1934), pp. 49–63. For contemporary discussion of these patterns, see Carol B. Stack, *All Our Kin: Strategies for Survival in a Black Community* (New York: Harper and Row, 1974), pp. 108–15; Leon Dash, *When Children Want Children: The Urban Crisis of Teenage Childbearing* (New York: William Morrow, 1989), pp. 238–62.

8. D'Emilio and Freedman, *Intimate Matters*, pp. 256, 262–65, 333; Joseph F. Kett, *Rites of Passage: Adolescence in America, 1790 to the Present* (New York: Basic Books, 1977), pp. 258–60; Alfred C. Kinsey, Wardell B. Pomeroy, Clyde E. Martin and Paul H. Gebhard, *Sexual Behavior in the Human Female* (Philadelphia: W. B. Saunders, 1948), pp. 321–26; B. K. Singh, "Trends in Attitudes Toward Premarital Sexual Relations," *Journal of Marriage and the Family* 42 (1980): 387; David B. Tyack and Elisabeth Hansot, *Learning Together: A History of Coeducation in American Schools* (New Haven: Yale University Press, 1990), p. 223 (discussing instruction in "vice"); Patricia J. Campbell, *Sex Education Books for Young Adults, 1892–1979* (New York: R. R. Bowker, 1979), p. 93 (discussing conduct beyond a kiss).

9. Karen DeCrow, *Sexist Justice* (New York: Random House, 1974), pp. 268–79; Herma Hill Kay, *Text, Cases and Materials on Sex-Based Discrimination* (St. Paul, Minn.: West, 1988), pp. 375–81. Maris Vinovskis, "An 'Epidemic' of Adolescent Pregnancy? Some Historical Considerations," *Journal of Family History* 6 (1981): 205 (discussing adoption rates); Jane Gross, "Anti-Abortion Revival: Homes for the Unwed," *New York Times*, 23 July 1989, pp. A-1, A-25; Harry Krause, *Illegitimacy: Law and Social Policy* (Indianapolis: Bobbs-Merrill, 1971); Edward Vincent, "Illegitimacy," *International Encyclopedia of Social Science* (1988), pp. 7, 85, 88; Rickie Solinger, *Wake Up Little Susie: Single Pregnancy and Race before Roe v. Wade* (New York: Routledge, 1992), pp. 168–86. See also sources cited in n. 8.

10. Linda Gordon, *Woman's Body, Woman's Right: A Social History of Birth Control in America* (New York: Grossman, 1976), pp. 45–53, 69–71. Plantation economies benefited from high fertility rates, but some slaves nonetheless resorted to folk methods of birth control, especially when they were subjected to coerced intercourse with white owners or overseers. See Jessie M. Rodrique, "The Black Community and the Birth Control Movement," in Kathy Peiss and Christine Simmons, with Robert A. Padgug, eds., *Passion and Power: Sexuality in History* (Philadelphia: Temple Univer-

sity Press, 1989), p. 138. See also Rosalind Pollack Petchesky, *Abortion and Woman's Choice: The State, Sexuality, and Reproductive Freedom* (New York: Longman, 1990), pp. 45–50; James C. Mohr, *Abortion in America: The Origins and Evolution of National Policy, 1800–1900* (New York: Oxford University Press, 1978), pp. 18–43.

11. John P. Harper, "Be Fruitful and Multiply: Origins of Legal Restrictions on Planned Parenthood in Nineteenth-Century America," in Carol Berkin and Mary Beth Norton, eds., *Women of America: A History* (Boston: Houghton Mifflin, 1979), pp. 246–65; James Reed, *The Birth Control Movement and American Society: From Private Vice to Public Virtue* (New York: Basic Books, 1978), pp. 40–41, 188 (quoting Alexander Skene); William Henry Chafe, *The American Woman: Her Changing Social, Economic, and Political Roles, 1920–1970* (New York: Oxford University Press, 1972), p. 100; Sheila M. Rothman, *Woman's Proper Place: A History of Changing Ideals and Practices, 1870 to the Present* (New York: Basic Books, 1978), p. 46; Nancy Woloch, *Women and the American Experience* (New York: Knopf, 1984), p. 394; Kristin Luker, *Abortion and the Politics of Motherhood* (Berkeley: University of California Press, 1984), pp. 27–28; Gordon, *Woman's Body*, pp. 59–60; Reva Siegel, "Reasoning from the Body: A Historical Perspective on Abortion Regulation and Questions of Equal Protection," *Stanford Law Review* 44 (1992): 261.

12. Carrie Chapman Catt, quoted in Gordon, *Woman's Body*, pp. 109–11, 238; D'Emilio and Freedman, *Intimate Matters*, pp. 57–73, 80–81; Reed, *Birth Control Movement*, p. 132.

13. Ellen Chesler, *Woman of Valor: Margaret Sanger and the Birth Control Movement in America* (New York: Simon and Schuster, 1992); David M. Kennedy, *Birth Control in America: The Career of Margaret Sanger* (New Haven: Yale University Press, 1970), pp. 115–21; Angela Y. Davis, *Women, Race & Class* (New York: Vintage Books, 1981), pp. 210–19; Petchesky, *Abortion*, pp. 87–93.

14. See Thomas M. Shapiro, *Population Control Politics: Women, Sterilization, and Reproductive Choice* (Philadelphia: Temple University Press, 1985); Petchesky, *Abortion*, pp. 130, 180; Buck v. Bell, 274 U.S. 200, 205, 207 (1927); J. Ralph Lindgren and Nadine Taub, *The Law of Sex Discrimination* (St. Paul, Minn.: West, 1988), p. 413 (discussing Stephen Jay Gould's analysis of Buck v. Bell).

15. Petchesky, *Abortion*, pp. 130, 159, 179–80; Lindgren and Taub, *Law of Sex Discrimination*, pp. 413–18; Skinner v. Oklahoma, 316 U.S. 535 (1942); Hyman Rodman, Betty Sarvis, and Joy Walker Bonar, *The Abortion Question* (New York: Columbia University Press, 1987), p. 74 (describing medical services conditioned on agreement to sterilization); Robert G. Weisbord, *Genocide? Birth Control and the Black American* (Westport, Conn.: Greenwood Press, 1975); Patricia J. Williams, *The Alchemy of Race and Rights* (Cambridge: Harvard University Press, 1991), p. 218; Philip Reilly, *The Surgical Solution: A History of Involuntary Sterilization in the United States* (Baltimore: Johns Hopkins University Press, 1991); Rodrique, "Black Community"; People v. Johnson (Tulare Supr. Ct. No. 29290, 2 Jan. 1991) imposes the implant of Norplant as a condition of probation for black woman convicted of child abuse; Faye Wattleton, "Perspective on Race and Poverty: Using Birth Control as Coercion," *Los Angeles Times*, 13 January 1991, p. M-7 (describing the proposal to use Norplant to

reduce the underclass); Tamar Lewin, "A Plan to Pay Welfare Mothers for Birth Control," *New York Times*, 9 February 1991, p. A-1 (describing Kansas state legislator's proposal to condition welfare benefits on agreement to use Norplant).

16. Rodman, Sarvis, and Boner, *Abortion Question*, p. 154; Davis, *Class*, p. 210; Luker, *Abortion*, pp. 36–39; Petchesky, *Abortion*, pp. 45–50; Solinger, *Wake Up Little Susie*, pp. 4–5. See discussion in the text accompanying nn. 34–38.

17. Griswold v. Connecticut, 381 U.S. 479 (1965); Eisenstadt v. Baird, 405 U.S. 438, 448 (1972); Carey v. Population Services International, 431 U.S. 678 (1977); Ordway v. Hargraves, 323 F. Supp. 1155 (D. Mass. 1971); Shull v. The Columbus Municipal Separate School District, 338 F. Supp. 1376 (N.D. Miss. 1972); Farley v. Reinhard (No. 15569, N.D. Ga., 22 Sept. 1971) in *Clearinghouse Review* 5 (1972): 620; Barbara A. Babcock, Ann E. Freedman, Eleanor Holmes Norton, and Susan E. Ross, *Sex Discrimination and the Law: Cases and Remedies* (Boston: Little, Brown, 1975), p. 1033.

18. Luker, *Abortion*, pp. 55–76; Frederick S. Jaffe, Barbara L. Lindheim, and Philip R. Lee, *Abortion Politics: Private Morality and Public Policy* (New York: McGraw-Hill, 1981), pp. 22–24.

19. Roe v. Wade, 410 U.S. 113 (1973).

20. Maher v. Roe, 432 U.S. 464 (1977); Harris v. McRae, 448 U.S. 297 (1980); Webster v. Reproductive Health Services, 492 U.S. 490 (1989); Planned Parenthood of Southeastern Pennsylvania v. Casey 112 Sup. Ct. 2791 (1992); Jaffe et al., *Abortion Politics*, pp. 143–45.

21. Harris v. McRae, 448 U.S. at 316. See also Maher v. Roe, 432 U.S. at 474.

22. Jaffe et al., *Abortion Politics*, pp. 143–45. See also dissenting opinions in Harris v. McRae and Maher v. Roe.

23. The regulations affect Title X-funded facilities, which serve some five million low-income women. Rust v. Sullivan, 111 S. Ct. 1759 (1991).

24. Jaffe et al., *Abortion Politics*, pp. 143–46; Stanley K. Henshaw, Asta N. Kenney, Debra Somberg, and Jennifer Van Vort, *Teenage Pregnancy in the United States: The Scope of the Problem and State Responses* (New York: Alan Guttmacher Institute, 1989) p. 56; Brief for the National Abortion Rights Action League et al., in Thornburgh v. American College of Obstetricians and Gynecologists (1985), p. 14 (and sources cited therein); Laura Nsiah-Jefferson, "Reproductive Laws, Women of Color, and Low-Income Women," in Sherrill Cohen and Nadine Taub, eds., *Reproductive Laws for the 1990s* (Clifton, N.J.: Humana Press, 1988) p. 23; Dorothy L. Roberts, "The Future of Reproductive Choice for Poor Women and Women of Color," *Women's Rights Law Reporter* 12 (1990): 59, 63n35.

25. Jimmy Carter, quoted in Sylvia Law, "Rethinking Sex and the Constitution," *University of Pennsylvania Law Review*, 132 (1984): 1016n219.

26. Vinovskis, *"Epidemic,"* p. 25; Elise F. Jones et al., *Teenage Pregnancy in Industrialized Countries* (New Haven: Yale University Press, 1986), p. 37; National Center for Health Statistics, *Advanced Report of Final Natality* (1985) (in 1985 there were 51 births per thousand teens; in 1970, there were 68.3); National Center for Health

Statistics, *Advanced Report on Final Natality Statistics, 1988* (1990) (from 1986 to 1988, the birthrate climbed 10 percent among 15-, 16-, and 17-year-olds).

27. Jones et al., "Teenage Pregnancy in Developed Countries: Determinants and Policy Implications," *Family Planning Perspectives* 17 (1985): 53, 56–57; Janet Benshoff and Harriet Pilpel, "Minors' Rights to Confidential Abortions: The Evolving Legal Scene," in J. Douglas Butler and David F. Walbert, eds., *Abortion, Medicine and the Law* (New York: Facts on File, 1986), pp. 137–44; Cheryl D. Hayes, ed., *Risking the Future: Adolescent Sexuality, Pregnancy and Childbearing* (Washington, D.C.: National Academy Press, 1987), pp. 1, 15, 50, 52–67; Claire Brindis and Rita J. Jeremy, *Adolescent Pregnancy and Parenting in California: A Strategic Plan for Action* (San Francisco: Center for Population and Reproductive Health Policy, University of California, 1988), pp. 32–41 (discussing increase in sexually active teens and divergence in estimated adoption rates of .4 percent for black teens and 12.2 percent of whites); Gross, "Anti-Abortion Revival " (quoting the president of The National Committee for Adoption) p. A-25; Children's Defense Fund, *Teenage Pregnancy: An Advocate's Guide to the Numbers* (Washington, D.C.: Children's Defense Fund, 1988), pp. 11, 22; "Young Teen-Agers Have More Babies," *New York Times*, 31 August 1991, p. A-10.

28. For conservative objections, see Carole E. Joffe, *The Regulation of Sexuality: Experiences of Family Planning Workers* (Philadelphia: Temple University Press, 1986), p. 45 (quoting Cunnaught Marshner); and sources cited in n. 30. For liberal perspectives see Dorothy I. Height, "What Must Be Done about Children Having Children," *Ebony*, March 1985, p. 78; Joycellyn Elders, Jennifer Hui, and Steff Padilla, "Adolescent Pregnancy: Does the Nation Really Care?," *Berkeley Women's Law Journal* (1989–1990): 170; Children's Defense Fund, *Teenage Pregnancy*. For discussion of the disadvantages connected with teenage pregnancy see *ibid.* and Hayes, *Risking the Future*, pp. 123–39.

29. Evelyn L. Brodkin, "Teen Pregnancy and the Dilemmas of Social Policy Making," in Margaret K. Rosenheim and Mark F. Testa, ed., *Early Parenthood and the Transition to Adulthood* (New Brunswick, N.J.: Rutgers University Press, forthcoming).

30. See Nathanson, *Dangerous Passage*, p. 16 (arguing that moral panic is particularly likely when normative violations are compounded by normative conflict over the legitimacy of traditional roles); Sonia L. Nazario, "Abortion Foes Pose Threat to the Funding of Family Planning," *Wall Street Journal*, 8 March 1990, p. A-1 (quoting Tom Phillips, president of Catholics Serving the Lord: "Whenever you increase accessibility, you increase use . . . [and] the problems that go along with use," and Joe Scheidler, founder of the Chicago Pro-Life Action League, claiming that clinics promote a "contraceptive mentality" in which "people are just having sex for fun").

31. Kevin Sack, "Quayle Insists Abortion Remarks Don't Signal Change in His View," *New York Times*, 24 July 1992, p. A-1; Ellen Goodman, "Abortion Double Standard," *San Francisco Chronicle*, 30 July 1992, p. A-25. Then presidential candidate Bill Clinton, who supports both choice and parental consent provisions, more deftly avoided confrontation with that double standard. When asked a similar

question about what he would do if his 12-year-old daughter were pregnant, Clinton responded, "I wouldn't talk to the press about it." Sack, above (quoting Clinton).

32. Petchesky, *Abortion*, p. 270 (quoting Orrin Hatch and Jeremiah Denton); Allan C. Carlson, *Family Questions: Reflections on the American Social Crises* (New Brunswick, N.J.: Transaction, 1988), pp. 102–03 (blaming family planning clinics for increased sexual activity); Bob Gould, "Fear of Feminism: The Right Wing and Family Values," *Social Justice* 17 (1990); 141, 143.

33. Melody G. Embree and Tracy A. Dobson, "Parental Involvement in Adolescent Abortion Decisions: A Legal and Psychological Critique," *Law and Inequality* 10 (1991): 53, 58; Brigid Rentoul, "Cognitus Interruptus: The Courts and Minors' Access to Contraceptives," *Yale Law and Policy Review* 5 (1986): 212, 231–32nn99–100; Eve Paul and Dana Klassa, "Minors' Right to Confidential Contraceptive Services: The Limits of State Action," *Women's Rights Law Reporter* 10 (1987): 45, 46n11; Harrell R. Rodgers, Jr., *Poor Women, Poor Families: The Economic Plight of America's Female-Headed Households* (Armonk, N.Y.: M. E. Sharpe, 1986), pp. 92–93; Ann Harper, "Teenage Sexuality and Public Policy: An Agenda for Gender Education," in Irene Diamond, ed., *Families, Politics, and Public Policy: A Feminist Dialogue on Women and the State* (New York: Longman, 1983), p. 220; Hayes, *Risking the Future*, pp. 153, 208; Jones et al., "Teenage Pregnancy," pp. 57–58.

34. See n. 28 and Diana M. Pearce, " 'Children Having Children': Teenage Pregnancy and Public Policy from the Woman's Perspective" (chap. 2). Compare Elders, Hui, and Padilla, "Adolescent Pregnancy," pp. 170–71 (arguing that adolescent pregnancy eliminates "any glimmer of hope for [teenagers'] future," and that a "poor teenager with a baby is captive to a slavery the 13th Amendment did not anticipate"); with Frank F. Furstenberg, Jr., Jeanne Brooks-Gunn, and S. Philip Morgan, *Adolescent Mothers in Later Life* (Cambridge: Cambridge University Press, 1987), and Frank Furstenberg, Jr., Mary Elizabeth Hughes, and Jeanne Brooks-Gunn, "The Next Generation: Children of Teenage Mothers Grow Up," in Rosenheim and Testa, *Early Parenthood*. See also Sarah McCue Horwitz, Lorraine V. Klerman, H. Sung Kuo, and James F. Jekel, "Intergenerational Transmission of School Age Parenthood," *Family Planning Perspectives* (1991): 168 (reporting the longitudinal study finding that most children of teenage parents had not become teenage parents themselves and noting that studies finding correlations of early parenthood between mothers and offspring failed to control for relevant demographic variables); Sarah McCue Horwitz, Lorraine V. Klerman, H. Sung Kuo, and James F. Jekel, "School-age Mothers: Predictors of Long-Term Educational and Economic Outcomes," *Pediatrics* 87 (1991): 862.

35. For discussion of interrelationships and causal ambiguities, see Frank Furstenberg, Jr., and Jeanne Brooks-Gunn, "Teenage Childbearing: Causes, Consequences, and Remedies," in Linda N. Aiken and David H. Mechanic, eds., *Applications of Social Science to Clinical Medicine and Health Policy* (New Brunswick, N.J.: Rutgers University Press, 1986), pp. 307, 316–17. See also Claire Brindis, "Antecedents and Consequences: The Need for Diverse Strategies in Adolescent Pregnancy

Prevention" (chap. 13). For school drop-out findings, see Dawn Upchurch and James McCarthy, "The Timing of First Birth and High School Completion," *American Sociological Review* 55 (1990): 224; Randall J. Olsen and George Farkas, "Endogenous Covariates in Duration Models and the Effect of Adolescent Childbirth on Schooling," *Journal of Human Resources* 19 (1989): 39.

36. Arline T. Geronimus, "On Teenage Childbearing and Neonatal Mortality in the United States," *Population and Development Review* 13 (1987): 245, 253, 260–62; Mary G. Edwards, "Teenage Childbearing: Redefining the Problem for Public Policy." Paper presented to the American Political Science Association, 30 August 1990; Mark Testa, "Racial Variation in the Early Life Course of Adolescent Welfare Mothers," in Rosenheim and Testa, *Early Parenthood;* Catherine Riessman and Constance Nathanson, "The Management of Reproduction: Social Construction of Risk and Responsibility," in Aiken and Mechanic, *Applications of Social Science:* 251, 262–63.

37. Karen Pittman, *Special Report: A Rebuttal of Two Controversial Teen Pregnancy Studies* (Washington, D.C.: Children's Defense Fund, May 1990) (criticizing Geronimus' study for considering only neonatal morality while excluding risks to older infants and for relying on dated studies of caregiving networks); Cathy Trost, "Census Survey on Child Care Increases Concern about How Much Poor Can Pay," *Wall Street Journal,* 15 August 1990, p. A-10 (noting studies documenting many low-income women's preference for nonfamily childcare); Furstenberg, Brooks-Gunn, and Morgan, *Adolescent Mothers;* Furstenberg et al., "The Next Generation"; Anne C. Peterson and Lisa J. Crockett, "Adolescent Sexuality, Pregnancy and Childrearing: Developmental Perspectives," in Rosenheim and Testa, *Early Parenthood* (noting ambiguities concerning parental competence); Irwin Garfinkel and Sara McLanahan, *Single Mothers and Their Children: A New American Dilemma* (Washington, D.C.: Urban Institute, 1986) (discussing parental competence).

38. See n. 39, below; William J. Wilson, *The Truly Disadvantaged* (Chicago: University of Chicago Press, 1987); Margaret C. Simms, "Adolescent Pregnancy among Blacks in the United States: Why Is It a Policy Issue?" (chap. 12); Maris Vinovskis, "Teenage Pregnancy and the Underclass," *Public Interest* 93 (1988): 87.

39. Compare Elaine McCrate, "Labor Market Segmentation and Relative Black/White Teenage Birth Rates," *Review of Black Political Economy* (1990): 37, Shelly Lundberg and Robert D. Plotneck, "Teenage Childbearing and Adult Wages." Discussion Paper 90-24 (Washington D.C.: Institute for Economic Resources, 1989) (finding that premarital birth reduces wages for white but not black women); Arline T. Geronimus and Sanders Korenman, "The Socioeconomic Consequences of Teen Childbearing Reconsidered." Research Report 90-190 (Ann Arbor: University of Michigan Population Studies Center, Sept. 1990), and A. Steven Holmes, "Teenage Study Hints Gain for Those Having Abortion," *New York Times,* 25 January 1990, p. A-12.

40. Geronimus, "On Teenage Childbearing," p. 273n14.

41. Jones et al., *Teenage Pregnancy in Industrialized Countries,* p. 230.

42. *Ibid.*, pp. 58–62, 240; Brindis and Jeremy, *Adolescent Pregnancy and Parenting in California*, pp. 45–48; Patricia Voydanoff and Brenda W. Donnelly, *Adolescent Sexuality and Pregnancy* (Newbury Park, Ca.: Sage, 1990), pp. 22–27; see n. 48–50, below.

43. Pub. L. No. 95-626, Tit. VI, 92 Stat. 3595–3601; Vinovskis, *"Epidemic,"* pp. 32–39.

44. Pub. L. No. 97-35, 95 Stat. 578, 42 U.S.C. paras. 300z ff.; Maris Vinovskis, "The Use and Misuse of Social Science Analysis in Federal Adolescent Pregnancy Policy," *Social Science Research Institute* (De Kalb: Northern Illinois University Distinguished Lecture Series, November 1989); *Congressional Quarterly Weekly Report,* 27 June 1981, p. 1153; Hayes, *Risking the Future,* pp. 22–25; Appellee's Document No. 73, Docket No. 87-253, Bowen v. Kendrick, 487 U.S. 589 (1988). See also nn. 28, 30, above; Vinovskis, *"Epidemic,"* pp. 198–294.

45. Vinovskis, *"Epidemic,"* pp. 194–203; Hayes, *Risking the Future,* pp. 143–45; Elders, Hui, and Padilla, "Adolescent Pregnancy," p. 177; Henshaw, Kenney, Somberg, and Van Vort, *Teenage Pregnancy,* pp. 46, 65; Theodora Downs and Susan Solonka, *Background Briefing Report, Evolving State Policies on Teen Pregnancy and Parenthood: What More Can the Feds Do to Help* (Washington, D.C.: Family Impact Seminar: American Association for Marriage and Family Therapy, 1990); Jacqueline Darroch Forrest and Jane Silverman, "What Public School Teachers Teach about Preventing Pregnancy, AIDS and Sexually Transmitted Diseases, *Family Planning Perspectives* 21 (1989): 65 (noting that on the average, schools devote less than two hours a year to contraceptive instruction, and many withhold all information concerning birth control); Carole Joffe, "Sexual Politics and the Teenage Pregnancy Prevention Worker in the United States" (chap. 14); Tamar Lewin, "Studies on Teenage Sex Cloud Condom Debate," *New York Times,* 8 February 1991, p. A-14. See also nn. 43–44, above, and nn. 46–51, below.

46. Children's Defense Fund, *Adolescent and Young-Adult Fathers: Problems and Solutions* (Washington, D.C.: Children's Defense Fund, 1988); pp. 2–6, 16–18; Children's Defense Fund, *What about the Boys: Teenage Pregnancy Prevention Strategies* (Washington, D.C.: Children's Defense Fund, 1988); Catherine Chilman, "Feminist Issues in Teenage Parenting," *Child Welfare* 64 (1985): 225; Brindis and Jeremy, *Adolescent Pregnancy and Parenting in California,* pp. 133–34; Vinovskis, *"Epidemic,"* pp. 166–68. For discussion of the disjuncture between norms supporting parental responsibility and the capacity of low-income fathers to provide assistance, see Mercer Sullivan, *The Male Role in Teenage Pregnancy and Parenting: New Directions for Public Policy* (New York: Vera Institute for Justice, 1990); Mercer Sullivan and the Study Group on the Male Role in Teenage Pregnancy and Parenting, "Absent Fathers in the Inner City," *Annals of the American Academy of Political and Social Science* 501 (1989): 48; Henshaw, Kenney, Somberg, and Van Vort, *Teenage Pregnancy,* p. 51.

47. See text accompanying n. 33; Embree and Dobson, "Parental Involvement," p. 58; Catharine Chilman, *Adolescent Sexuality in a Changing American Society: Social and Psychological Perspectives* (Washington, D.C.: Dept. & Publications No. (NIH) 79-1426, 1979; 2nd ed. 1983); Kristin Luker, *Taking Chances: Abortion and the Decision*

Not to Contracept (Berkeley: University of California Press, 1975); Kristin A. Moore, Margaret C. Simms, and Charles L. Betsey, *Choice and Circumstance: Racial Differences in Adolescent Sexuality and Fertility* (New Brunswick, N.J.: Transaction, 1986), pp. 31–37; Dash, *When Children Want Children*, pp. 68, 115, 127, 136. Also see n. 58, below.

48. 48 Fed. Reg. 3600, 3614 (1983); Rentoul, "Cognitus Interruptus"; Planned Parenthood Federation of America v. Schweiker, 559 F. Supp. 658 (D.D.C.), aff'd, 712 F.2d 650 (D.C. Cir. 1983); State of New York v. Heckler, 719 F.2d 1191 (2d Cir. 1983); American Civil Liberties Union of Northern California, *Minor's Rights to Abortion: The Challenge to California's Parental Consent Laws* (San Francisco: American Civil Liberties Union of Northern California, 1991). See also n. 52, below; American Civil Liberties Union, Reproductive Freedom Project, *Parental Notice Laws: Their Catastrophic Impact on Teenagers' Right to Abortion* (New York: American Civil Liberties Union Foundation, 1986); Benshoof and Pilpel, "Minors Rights," p. 152n60; Hayes, *Risking the Future*, p. 155. By the late 1980s, about twenty states had parental involvement mandates, but over half were not in force because of judicial or administrative determinations of unconstitutionality. See ACLU *Parental Notice Laws*.

49. Planned Parenthood Association of Kansas City v. Ashcroft, 462 U.S. 476 (1983); H. L. v. Matheson, 450 U.S. 398 (1981); Bellotti v. Baird, 443 U.S. 622, 634–35, 637–39, 643–44 (1979); Planned Parenthood of Central Missouri v. Danforth, 428 U.S. 52 (1976).

50. Hodgson v. Minnesota, 497 U.S. 417 (1990); Ohio v. Akron Reproductive Services, 497 U.S. 502 (1990).

51. Mark E. Rust, "Old Enough to Conceive, Old Enough to Abort?" *California Lawyer* 49 (March 1988): 30, 35 (quoting Maxine Waters); Robert M. Mnookin, *"Bellotti v. Baird:* A Hard Case," in Robert H. Mnookin, ed., *In the Interests of Children* (New York: W. H. Freeman, 1985), p. 149. For a critique of the Supreme Court's approach to adolescent pregnancy issues, see Ruth Colker, "An Equal Protection Analysis of United States Reproductive Health Policy: Gender, Race, Age, and Class," *Duke Law Journal* (1991): 324.

52. Mnookin, *"Bellotti v. Baird,"* p. 149; Asta M. Kennedy, Jacqueline D. Forrest, and Aida Torres, "Storm over Washington: The Parental Notification Proposal," *Family Planning Perspectives* 14 (1982): 185, 190; Susan F. Newcomer and J. Richard Udry, "Parent-Child Communication and Adolescent Sexual Behavior," *Family Planning Perspectives* 17 (1985): 169, 189; Blum et al., "The Impact of a Parental Notification Law on Adolescent Abortion Decision-Making," *American Journal of Public Health* 77 (1987): 619–20 (showing that in Minnesota, which has a notification law, 65 percent of parents were informed; in Wisconsin, which does not, 62 percent were informed). See studies cited in Benshoof and Pilpel, "Minor's Rights," pp. 144–45; Nanette Dembitz, "The Supreme Court and a Minor's Abortion Decision," *Columbia Law Review* 80 (1980): 1251, 1255–58; Theresa M. Walker, "California's Parental Consent Statute: A Constitutional Challenge," *Hastings Law Journal* 40 (1988): 169, 200. See also Embree and Dobson, "Parental Involvement," pp. 69–70 (noting few differences between adult and adolescent decision making on birth control).

53. Mnookin, *"Bellotti v. Baird,"* pp. 239–40; Virginia G. Cartoof and Lorraine V. Klerman, "Parental Consent for Abortion: Impact of the Massachusetts Law," *American Journal of Public Health* 76 (1986): 397.

54. In Minnesota, only nine bypass petitions were denied between 1981 and 1986. See Hodgson v. Minnesota, 497 U.S. 497, n21 (1990). See ACLU, *Parental Notice Laws*, pp. 9–15; Patricia Donovan, "Judging Teenagers: How Minors Fare When They Seek Court-Authorized Abortions," *Family Planning Perspectives* 15 (1983): 259–60, 265, and "Your Parents or the Judge: Massachusetts' New Abortion Consent Law," *Family Planning Perspectives* 13 (1981): 224; Hodgson v. Minnesota, 648 F. Supp. 756, 763–64 (D.C. 1988), *rev'd*, 110 S. Ct. 2926 (1990); American Academy of Pediatrics v. Van de Kamp, (Cal D. Ct. 1990), trial transcript, pp. 273–74, 282–84, Brief for Respondents, pp. 19–21; Bellotti v. Baird, 443 U.S. 634–35; Embree and Dobson, "Parental Involvement," p. 76 (noting that the small number of abortion providers and judicial decision makers in some communities multiplies barriers).

55. For experts' views see Mnookin, *"Bellotti v. Baird,"* p. 258; ACLU, *Parental Notice Laws*, pp. 1, 13, 17; Donovan, "Judging Teenagers," pp. 265–66; Hodgson v. Minnesota, 110 S. Ct. 2957–58 (Marshall, J., dissenting in part). For comparisons of the increased medical, psychological, and socioeconomic costs associated with childbirth in comparison with abortion, see sources cited in Walker, "California's Parental Consent Statute," pp. 196–97; Gary B. Melton and Anita J. Pliner, "Adolescent Abortion: A Psycholegal Analysis," in Gary B. Melton, ed., *Adolescent Abortion: Psychological and Legal Issues* (Lincoln: University of Nebraska Press, 1986). For discussion of inconsistency and trauma resulting from judicial decision making, see sources cited in nn. 53–54.

56. Kennedy, Forrest, and Torres, "Storm over Washington," p. 195; ACLU, *Parental Notice Laws*, pp. 1, 8, 17.

57. Riessman and Nathanson, "Management of Reproduction," p. 259; Furstenberg and Brooks-Gunn, "Teenage Childbearing," p. 319; Hayes, *Risking the Future*, pp. 231–59; Furstenberg, Hughes, and Brooks-Gunn, "The Next Generation."

58. See sources cited in n. 47; Andrew W. Boxer, "Adolescent Pregnancy and Parenthood in the Transition to Adulthood," in Rosenheim and Testa, *Early Parenthood*; Furstenberg and Brooks-Gunn, "Teenage Childbearing," pp. 321–22; Voydanoff and Donnelly, *Adolescent Sexuality*, p. 96; Douglas Kirby, *Sexuality Education: An Evaluation of Programs and Their Effects* (Santa Cruz: Network Publications, 1984), pp. 95–100.

59. Joffe, *Regulation of Sexuality*, pp. 157–58; Dash, *When Children Want Children*, pp. 121–25, 216, 220, 265; see Sara Ruddick, "Procreative Choice for Adolescent Women" (chap. 6); Elijah Anderson, "Sex Codes and Family Life Among Poor Inner-City Youths," *Annals of the American Academy of Political and Social Science* 501 (1989): 59.

60. Brindis and Jeremy, *Adolescent Pregnancy*, pp. 104–05; Jones et al., *Teenage Pregnancy in Industrialized Countries*, pp. 236–38. See, generally, Hayes, *Risking the Future*. For discussion of the inadequacy of contraceptive alternatives, see Cohen and Taub, *Reproductive Laws for the 1990s*.

61. Jewell Taylor Gibbs, "The Social Costs of Teenage Pregnancy and Parenting

in the Black Community: Implications for Public Policy," in Rosenheim and Testa, *Early Parenthood;* Wilson, *Truly Disadvantaged;* n. 35, above, and accompanying text; Brindis and Jeremy, *Adolescent Pregnancy,* pp. 48–49; Hayes, *Risking the Future,* pp. 125–28; Denise F. Polit and Janet R. Kahn, "Early Subsequent Pregnancy among Economically Disadvantaged Teenage Mothers," *American Journal of Public Health* 76 (1986): 167.

62. Gibbs, "Social Costs"; Brindis and Jeremy, *Adolescent Pregnancy,* pp. 85, 88–89; Marion Wright Edelman, *Families in Peril: An Agenda for Social Change* (Cambridge: Harvard University Press, 1987), pp. 58–60; Wilson, *Truly Disadvantaged;* William Wilson and Kathryn M. Neckerman, "Poverty and Family Structure: The Widening Gap between Evidence and Public Policy Issues," in Sheldon H. Danzig and Daniel H. Weinberg, eds., *Fighting Poverty: What Works and What Doesn't* (Cambridge: Harvard University Press, 1986), pp. 232, 252–59; Tom Joe, "The Other Side of Black Female-Headed Families: The Status of Adult Black Men," *Family Planning Perspectives* 19 (1984): 74; Sullivan, *The Male Role;* Sullivan and Study Group, "Absent Fathers"; Hortensia Amaro and Barry Zuckerman, "Psychoactive Substance Use and Adolescent Pregnancy Compounded Risk among Inner City Adolescent Mothers," in Mary Ellen Colten and Susan Gore, *Adolescent Stress: Causes and Consequences* (New York: Aldine de Gruyter, 1991); Center for Population Options, *Teenage Pregnancy and Too-Early Childbirth: Public Costs and Personal Consequences* (Washington, D.C.: Center for Population Options, 1991).

63. David Ellwood, "Conclusion," in David T. Ellwood and Phoebe H. Cottingham, eds., *Welfare Policy for the 1990s* (Cambridge: Harvard University Press, 1989), pp. 269, 272 (noting that supported work programs that cost over $13,000 per participant produced earnings gains of only $1,500); Gary Walker, "Comment," in Ellwood and Cottingham, *Welfare Policy,* p. 141; Gina Adams, Karen Pittman, and Raymond O'Brien, "Adolescent and Young Adult Fathers: Problems and Solutions" (chap. 11); Michael B. Katz, *The Undeserving Poor: From the War on Poverty to the War on Welfare* (New York: Pantheon Press, 1989); Wilson, *Truly Disadvantaged;* Diana M. Pearce, "The Feminization of Poverty: A Second Look" (Washington, D.C.: Institute for Women's Policy Research, 1989); Erik Eckholm, "Forcing Welfare Fathers to Pay Up Hits Stumbling Block: Lack of Jobs," *New York Times,* 20 July 1992, p. A-10.

64. Roberts, "Future of Reproductive Choice," p. 64n39 (describing gross inadequacy of treatment facilities and the growing trend toward prosecution of addicted mothers). See Lisa Maher, "Criminalizing Pregnancy: The Downside of a Kinder, Gentler Nation?" *Social Justice* 17 (Fall 1990): 111; Amaro and Zuckerman, "Psychoactive Substance Use"; Dorothy Roberts, "Punishing Drug Addicts Who Have Babies: Women of Color, Equality, and the Right of Privacy," *Harvard Law Review* 104 (1991): 1419.

65. Children's Defense Fund, *Teenage Pregnancy;* Linda M. Burton and Carol B. Stack, "Conscripting Kin: Reflections on Family, Generation, and Culture" (chap. 9); Nsiah-Jefferson, "Reproductive Laws," p. 23; Brindis, "Antecedents and Consequences"; Edelman, *Families in Peril;* Francis Ianni, *The Search for Structure: A Report on American Youth Today* (New York: Free Press, 1989).

CONTRIBUTORS

GINA ADAMS is senior program associate at the Children's Defense Fund, Washington, D.C.

NANCY E. ADLER is professor of psychology at the University of California, San Francisco, where she is director of the Health Psychology Program.

GLYNIS M. BREAKWELL is professor of psychology and head of the Department of Psychology at the University of Surrey, Guildford, England.

CLAIRE BRINDIS is assistant adjunct professor in the Department of Pediatrics, Division of Adolescent Medicine, University of California, San Francisco, and co-director of the university's Center for Reproductive Health Policy Research.

LINDA M. BURTON is associate professor of human development in the Department of Human Development and Family Studies at Pennsylvania State University.

SARAH CUNNINGHAM-BURLEY is lecturer in medical sociology, Department of Public Health Services, Medical School, University of Edinburgh.

FRANK F. FURSTENBERG, JR., is the Zellerbach Family Professor of Sociology and research associate in the Population Studies Center at the University of Pennsylvania.

SUSAN E. HARARI is a doctoral candidate in history at the University of Michigan and a past fellow with the Bush Program in Child Development and Public Policy.

KATHLEEN MULLAN HARRIS is assistant professor in the Department of Sociology and Carolina Population Center, University of North Carolina, Chapel Hill.

CAROLE JOFFE is professor of sociology and women's studies at the University of California, Davis.

ANNETTE LAWSON is a British sociologist working as an independent feminist scholar. She has been affiliated most recently with the Institute of Human Development at the University of California, Berkeley, and with the Institute for Research on Women and Gender at Stanford University.

SALLY MACINTYRE is director of the Medical Research Council's Medical Sociology Unit in Glasgow, Scotland.

RAYMOND O'BRIEN is program officer for the Center for Youth Development and Policy Research at the Academy for Educational Development, Washington, D.C.

DIANA M. PEARCE is a visiting scholar at Stanford University and director of the Women and Poverty Project in Washington, D.C.

ANN PHOENIX teaches psychology in the Department of Human Studies at Brunel University.

KAREN PITTMAN is vice-president of the Academy for Educational Development and director of the Center for Youth Development and Policy Research, Washington, D.C.

DEBORAH L. RHODE is professor of law and former director of the Institute for Research on Women and Gender at Stanford University.

SARA RUDDICK teaches philosophy and feminist theory at the New School for Social Research.

MARGARET C. SIMMS is director of research programs at the Joint Center for Political and Economic Studies in Washington, D.C.

CAROL B. STACK is an anthropologist at the University of California, Berkeley, and holds joint appointments in the Department of Women's Studies and the Graduate School of Education.

JEANNE M. TSCHANN is assistant adjunct professor in the departments of Psychiatry and Pediatrics at the University of California, San Francisco.

MARIS A. VINOVSKIS is professor of history and a research scientist at the Institute for Social Research at the University of Michigan. Currently he is serving as the research advisor to the assistant secretary of education, Office of Educational Research and Improvement, United States Department of Education.

INDEX

Abernethy, V., 161

Abortion: access to, 3, 56, 82, 306, 308–10; attitudes on, 37, 48, 102, 113, 118, 249, 307, 312–13; attitudes on (cross-cultural), 3, 4, 92, 115, 149, 162; consent/ notification, 12, 48, 288, 309, 318–21; in eighteenth to nineteenth centuries, 305–06; funding, 309, 310, 317; gag rule, 288–89; illegal, 36–37, 306, 308–09; legal decisions, 39, 82, 285, 288, 289, 290, 306, 308–09, 310, 311, 318–19; opposition to, 39, 280, 285, 286, 288–89, 290, 292, 293, 309, 312, 317, 318; politics, 284, 285–86, 288–89, 292–93; rate (U.K.), 60, 62, 75, 82, 160; rate (U.S.), 39, 69, 75, 82, 308; Roe v. Wade, 285, 289, 290, 309, 311; Rust v. Sullivan, 288, 310; Webster

v. Reproductive Health Services, 288, 290, 309

Abstinence, 322; for males, 9; promotion of, 7, 40, 279, 287–88, 293, 294, 296, 306, 316, 317

Adler, Nancy, 114

Adolescence, 23, 103; concept of, 2, 24, 28, 29, 31, 82, 83, 117, 130, 302; process, 83, 127, 128

Adolescent Family Life Act (AFLA), 287, 313, 317

Adolescent Family Life Program, 39

Adolescent Health Services and Pregnancy Prevention Act (1978), 63, 264, 317

Adoption, 102, 118, 305; rates, 2, 305, 311

Aid to Families with Dependent Children (AFDC), 38, 51, 266; child support, 225–26, 235, 324; costs,